GEORGE ROGERS CLARK.
From a portrait by Jarvis, said to be from life.

A HISTORY *of the* MISSISSIPPI VALLEY

FROM ITS DISCOVERY TO THE END OF FOREIGN DOMINATION

The Narrative of the Founding of an Empire, Shorn of Current Myth, and Enlivened by the Thrilling Adventures of Discoverers, Pioneers, Frontiersmen, Indian Fighters, and Home Makers

John R. Spears & A. H. Clark

HERITAGE BOOKS
2016

HERITAGE BOOKS
AN IMPRINT OF HERITAGE BOOKS, INC.

Books, CDs, and more—Worldwide

For our listing of thousands of titles see our website at
www.HeritageBooks.com

A Facsimile Reprint
Published 2016 by
HERITAGE BOOKS, INC.
Publishing Division
5810 Ruatan Street
Berwyn Heights, Md. 20740

Copyright © 1903 A. S. Clark
Brooklyn, N.Y.

— Publisher's Notice —
In reprints such as this, it is often not possible to remove blemishes from the original. We feel the contents of this book warrant its reissue despite these blemishes and hope you will agree and read it with pleasure.

International Standard Book Numbers
Paperbound: 978-0-7884-2106-8
Clothbound: 978-0-7884-5988-7

THIS VOLUME IS RESPECTFULLY DEDICATED
TO THE

Hon. Theodore Roosevelt,

AS A REPRESENTATIVE AMERICAN
AND HISTORIAN.

INTRODUCTION.

This work is to give an account of the things done in the Mississippi Valley during the period of foreign control. It is intended to be a narrative, not a critical, history. The writer has tried to tell about the achievements of the men who traversed the Great Lakes in birch bark canoes, or walked through the passes of the Alleghanies, to reach the Mississippi Valley, and, when there, turned the mighty wilderness into the Garden of the World.

Naturally the story begins with the heroic Frenchmen who first learned the way to the Great Basin. In the days when the people of Massachusetts were establishing a trading post on the Piscataqua River, New Hampshire, and the Virginians were sending an exploring expedition to learn whether a river flowed into Delaware Bay, Jean Nicolet was making peace with the Indians on the shores of Green Bay, Wisconsin. While the Dutch of New Amsterdam were trading with the Indians at Albany, Grosseilliers and Radisson, paddled up the Ottawa River, (though the region was the haunt of the Iroquois), and carried trade goods to the Sioux on the banks of the Mississippi. When the British were taking New York from the Dutch, La Salle was stretching a line of forts from the St. Lawrence River toward the mouth of the Mississippi.

Yet the nation from which the intrepid *coureurs de*

bois and explorers sprang produced also other pioneers whose manner of life was so far removed from that of the woods rangers as to furnish the most striking contrast known to American history. For those were the days of Louis XIV. and XV., when women who were not queens ruled the Court of France. It was not "the brief season of the Canadian summer, the weary winter, the hazards of the crop," that brought failure to the French settlements. The settlements in Louisiana were in a kindly climate and they stood on the richest soil of the earth. The French failed at the south as well as the north because of the fungi spread by the shadow of the French Court. The beginning of the French Revolution was seen in America when the man with the axe drove the lace-bedecked vagabond carrying a sword from the lands west of the Alleghanies.

In the meantime, both the French and the British had supplanted, more or less, another race of people— a race of red men known as Indians. In modern times, while the people of the United States have difficult race problems still in hand, it seems worth while remembering that because those red men were less developed than the white, they were the wards of the whites. The Indians were children, (they were often called so by the men who knew them best), and the white men were rightfully their guardians. It was a responsibility that was ignored and rudely thrust aside, but with such infinitely distressful results as we shall see.

The white men found the Indian passing rapidly from the life of a hunter to that of the agriculturist; but instead of aiding in the transition, the whites, by offering to buy furs, turned the red agriculturists back to the hunter life. They did worse; they created a market for human scalps. For one hundred and fifty years the red men were, by every means incited to shed the blood of animals and men; and then the white man looked upon them with horror and disgust because they were ready to fight for their hunting grounds.

But while the white race as a whole were cultivating the red thirst for blood, a few white men, known as Quakers and Moravians, were dealing with the red men on an entirely different basis. The Quakers and Moravians were subjected to many indignities and even outrages for their peculiarity of regard for the less developed red men. Historians have not failed to denounce them, and frontiersmen have ever groped for words with which to express their disgust when thinking of "Quaker sentiment."

But the story of Gnadenhutten, written in blood that will not "out," proves beyond doubt or question that *the tepees and huts of every red village in the land might have been turned into "Tents of Grace."*

It is a frightful fact that for every red man slain by by the whites, in the frontier wars, at least three whites were slain by the red. That fact is sufficient to damn the white policy, but it is not all; for because of the policy that was pursued by those who despised "Quaker sentiment," we are even now paying more than ten million dollars a year for the expenses of the Indian Bureau. Yet the fact remains that the cost of converting the Delaware Indians of Gnadenhutten from the red savages, which they had been, to the stump-grubbing farmers, which they became, was less than the waste of any one of hundreds of Indian raids.

While the people of the United States have the vestige of a race problem yet unsolved the story of Gnadenhutten is the most instructive of all that are known to the annals of America. Let those who, with bobbing heads, mumble some sort of a creed on Sundays, and live the devil knows how the rest of the week, consider it with care, for to them it has a special significance.

But this is by no means to withhold sympathy from the frontier Americans. Their migration was instinctive; it was due to the innate characteristics of a dominant race. It was inevitable, and in every way desirable. No one has a right to complain because they took the *hunting* grounds of the red man. The Indian should have been deprived of his hunting grounds to the last acre, with the utmost possible speed, and supplied with farms and play grounds instead. It was the manner of taking that cursed the frontiersmen, and they are to be pitied with an infinite pity. The effect of the evil policy on the frontiersmen is the important matter. They were the advance guard of the hosts of civilization and were sent forth to be slaughtered for the salvation and benefit of those who came after. Of 250 men in Robertson's Settlement at Nashville, 229 died by violence inside of twelve years.

In connection with the slaughter of the frontiersmen in the Mississippi Valley it is impossible to ignore the fact that the red men were, during the War of the Revolution and for twelve years after it, sicked on by British officers. That is a story to rouse the indignation of every patriot, and, at first thought, one might say it should be glossed over in this era of growing good feeling between nations. On the other hand, however, one should not forget that to gloss over is to lie. Moreover, the story is worth telling to show the tremendous contrast between that era and the present—a contrast that has been made possible by the development of Christian civilization, and the construction of an American fleet of unequalled war ships.

And that is to say, indirectly, that nations have always been, and are, bullies. They treat the powerful, and no others, with the kindliest consideration. Near the end of the Eighteenth Century we would not create a navy, but we built a ship of war, ballasted it with silver dollars, and sent it to a Mediterranean pirate to purchase his favor. We permitted ourselves to be blackmailed by African corsairs. And in consequence of our craven spirit, the British held a firm grasp on the territory northwest of the Ohio River; the Spanish held Natchez and our southwest territory; the French with their privateers and naval ships, swept our commerce from the West Indies, and all three powers bullied and browbeat our Government officials at almost every interchange of communications. The American State Papers are instructive if unpleasant reading. At the beginning of the Twentieth Century we have in hand battleships with broadside guns of seven-inch and eight-inch caliber—battleships that are far and away superior to anything conceived elsewhere—and we have unruffled peace, with unopposed progress in the development of our civilization.

If we were led by foolish policies in other days, it was because we were foolish, and not because of any lack of examples in right policies. The story of the work of George Rogers Clark in the Illinois country is one of the most instructive in the war annals of the world. There were two methods of repelling the raids of the enemy in those days. The common way was to build a log fort, and when protected by its walls, to shoot every enemy that came in sight. It was a method that became national. We built forts at the Atlantic ports, and, as late as 1890, we built "coast defence" ships. The forts and coast defence ships were not wholly useless. Like the quills of the porcupine, they could prove very useful, under some circumstances. The porcupine method of repelling an enemy was held in high regard for many years by our people.

But George Rogers Clark (an American born a hundred years ahead of his time, he), would have none of the porcupine policy. He saw that the way to protect the frontier was to carry the war to the strongholds of the enemy. He took Kaskaskia and Vincennes. He gave the United States the Northwest Territory. He was urgent for men and means with which to take Detroit. Had his requests been heeded the raids on Kentucky would have ceased, and there would have been no trouble over the Northwest posts in after years.

But because Clark's work was ignored, the broad territory which he had won had to be rewon, and "Mad" Anthony Wayne was the man for the day. Of all the brigadiers of the Revolution, he is best worth memory, but it is not on his "mad" charges in the face of the enemy that his fame is grounded. Those, indeed, were splendid, but that parade of his men with their hair neatly powdered before the attack on Stony Point is significant; so is the further fact that every dog within three miles of the Point was killed before the attack.

Introduction. vii

But of all that this man did, nothing will be remembered longer than the fact that when he came to reconquer the region Clark had won, he trained more than a thousand men of his legion until they could load and fire their rifles with precision while *charging at full speed on the enemy.* Anthony Wayne was the best drill master the American army ever had.

As said, this work is to give an account of the things done in the Great Valley, but necessarily a record had to be made of those proceedings elsewhere by which the destinies of the Valley were influenced. The Spanish, who were really the first to see the Valley, and who at the end of the Seven Years War, obtained New Orleans and the region between the Rockies and the Mississippi, took possession of Natchez and a large section of American soil during the War of the Revolution. They were determined, after the war was ended, not only to hold it, but to grasp all the unsettled part of the Great Valley, regardless of American claims. In this matter the French Government earnestly supported them, and the diplomatic complications that grew out of this condition of affairs, are interesting. In their efforts to "cinch" the territory the Spanish amuse or exasperate the student of history according to his mental attitude toward their peculiar characteristics. But the settlers of the Great Valley, in the days of the Spanish complications, never found the situation amusing, and the fact that the Spanish were not swept out of the Mississippi Valley by a flood tide of indignant backwoodsmen must ever remain a matter of wonder and pride to the American patriot.

By unwavering persistence the Americans foiled

the Spanish shufflings, evasions and obstinacy, so that a time came when Spain traded the great Louisiana territory back to France. The day of its salvation was then close at hand. Napoleon ruled France, and for a brief period, he thought to regain for her all the splendid region on which La Salle had filed the French claim. He bought the Louisiana territory; he thought to take the land east of the Mississippi with an army of 10,000 men. But when the eagle alighted before him with one naked claw representing 30,000 "Prime Riflemen," and the other offering him a purse, his vision was cleared. The transfer of Louisiana to the United States was made through the hatred of the British and the fear of America. He prophesied that the valley of the Mississippi would make the United States a "maritime rival" of the British, and a century after his prophesy was made, the greatest transatlantic lines of steamships are controlled by capitalists whose wealth has been drawn from traffic originating in the Great Basin. But, curiously enough, the development which Napoleon hoped for has only served to draw the English-speaking rivals closer together, instead of driving them apart.

It is a long story, this of the Mississippi Valley, but from the year when Grosseiliers and Radisson first traded for beaver skin on the bank of the upper river, until the day when the Gridiron Flag, hoisted at New Orleans, covered the whole Great Basin, it is a story that can be summed up in one word—*Work*. From the first to the last, the men whose names are memorable in the history of the Valley, whether they were traders like the *coureurs de bois* looking for profit; or empire founders, like La Salle, looking for power; or migrators, like the hosts that followed the Ohio and the Wilderness Road, looking for home sites; or statesmen like Monroe and Livingston, looking for the good of the Nation, all have been men who could and who would work. Work is the one word emblazoned on the escutcheon of the people of the Great Basin.

To show a part of what work has accomplished in the affairs of a mighty region is the chief object of this book, and it is therefore offered to the growing host of good Americans who see clearly that

"The All of Things is an infinite conjugation of the verb *To Do.*"

CONTENTS.

CHAPTER		PAGE
I.	On the Brim of the Great Basin	1
II.	First Exploration of the Mississippi River	13
III.	La Salle and Louisiana	25
IV.	From La Salle to New Orleans	51
V.	Indians of the Mississippi Valley	75
VI.	Work of the French in the Valley	103
VII.	The French Expelled from the Valley, Part 1	119
VIII.	The French Expelled from the Valley, Part 2	133
IX.	The Spanish in the Great Valley	157
X.	Pontiac's War as Seen in the Valley	171
XI.	Crossing the Range	183
XII.	Lord Dunmore's War	209
XIII.	The Home Makers in Kentucky	223
XIV.	On the Frontier during the Revolution	247
XV.	The Work of Geo. Rogers Clark	267
XVI.	As the War Dragged On	287
XVII.	Gnadenhutten	293
XVIII.	Fighting that Followed Gnadenhutten	303
XIX.	The Frontiersmen at King's Mountain	313
XX.	Frontier Home and Civil Life in War Time	319
XXI.	Fighting to Possess Land Already Won	331
XXII.	In the Southwest after the Revolution	355
XXIII.	The Nation Gets Its Own	369
XXIV.	The Garden of America for Americans Only	379

LIST OF ILLUSTRATIONS.

Pen and ink sketches, head and tail pieces, chapter headings, both original and reproductions, by Miss E. S. Clark.

GEORGE ROGERS CLARK . . . . *Frontispiece*
    From a portrait by Jarvis.

	PAGE
INDIAN BRAVES IN COSTUME	ix

    From Catlin's Indians.

JOHN JAY (facing) 1
    From a portrait by Wilkinson, London, 1783.

HEADING OF CHAP. I., INDIAN THROWING TOMAHAWK . . . 1

VIEW OF THE THREE GREAT DIVISIONS OF THE UNITED STATES 8

RIVER ST. LAWRENCE 10
    River St. Lawrence, showing "La Chine" Rapids, early French settlements, etc.

JEAN BAPTISTE TALON 12
    From portrait by Hamel.

HEADING OF CHAP. II., WINTER COSTUME OF INDIAN . . 13

EASTERN PORTION OF JOLIET'S MAP, 1674 15

CENTRAL PORTION OF JOLIET'S MAP, 1674 21

MARQUETTE'S MAP, 1681 23

BLOCK HOUSE AT LEXINGTON, KY. 24

ROBERT CAVALIER, SIEUR DE LA SALLE (facing) 25

HEADING OF CHAP. III. 25
    The building of the "Griffin."

List of Illustrations.

	PAGE
SKETCH OF NIAGARA RIVER, SHOWING ANCIENT PORTAGES	30

    From "Bouchette British Dominions in North America."

FORT NIAGARA 32
    From the "Portfolio," 1813.

MAP OF FRANQUELIN 1684 44

INDIAN CHIEF'S HEADDRESS 50
    From Catlin's Indians.

JEAN BAPTISTE LE MOYNE, SIEUR DE BIENVILLE (facing) . . 51
    From an original portrait.

HEADING OF CHAP. IV. 51
    Indian on horseback from Catlin.

DE LISLE, MAP OF THE COURSE OF THE MISSISSIPPI 1703 . . 52

JEANNE-ANTOINETTE POISSON, MARQUISE DE POMPADOUR . 56
    From a portrait by Harding.

MOLL'S MAP, 1710 58

JOUTEL'S MAP, 1713 65

LOUIS XV., KING OF FRANCE 70
    From a contemporary print.

NEW ORLEANS, 1728 73

LOUIS XIV., KING OF FRANCE (facing) 75
    From a contemporary portrait.

HEADING OF CHAP. V. 75
    Death of Vincennes, from Bancroft's United States.

LOCATION OF INDIAN TRIBES EAST OF THE MISSISSIPPI . . . 82
    From Bancroft's United States.

INDIAN MOUNDS IN OHIO 84
    From Atwater's Antiquities of Ohio.

List of Illustrations.

	PAGE
Ancient Indian Fortifications at Newark, Ohio . . .	90
From The Family Magazine, 1843.	
A Typical Indian Village	96
From a painting by Bierstadt.	
John Law, Projector of the Mississippi Scheme (facing)	103
From a Contemporary print.	
Heading of Chapter VI.	103
A frontier greeting.	
A Portion of Labat's Map, 1722	105
Tail-Piece, an Indian Visit	118
King Philip (facing)	119
From an Original by Paul Revere.	
Heading of Chap. VII.	119
Example of a Log House of the Better Class.	
Map of Celoron's Expedition	128
Fac-Simile of one of Celoron's Lead Plates	129
George Washington at Twenty-five Years of Age (facing)	133
From Irving's Washington, 1st edition.	
Heading of Chap. VIII., Fort Du Quesne 1755	133
Frederick the Great	142
From the Encylopedia Londinensis.	
The Braddock Campaign	144
From Bancroft's United States.	
Fall of Braddock	146
From "Battles of the United States."	
Scene of Braddock's Defeat	148
From Irving's Life of Washington, 1st edition.	

xvi *List of Illustrations.*

	PAGE
TAIL-PIECE, BRADDOCK'S DEFEAT.	156

    From a contemporary copper plate, the legend of which describes Braddock as being in the cart, and Washington the figure to the right.

HERNANDO DE SOTO (facing) 157

    From an early portrait.

HEADING OF CHAP. IX., FORT PITT, 1759 157

DON ANTONIO DE ULLOA, GOV. OF LA., 1764 163

    From an engraving by Scriven.

SIR WILLIAM JOHNSON (facing) 171

    From the London Magazine, 1756.

HEADING OF CHAP. X. 171

    Modern remains of Fort Pitt.

MAJOR ROBERT ROGERS, INDIAN SCOUT, ETC. 173

    From a London portrait of 1770.

DANIEL BOONE (facing) 183

    From an original portrait by Harding.

HEADING OF CHAP. XI. 183

    Signatures to "Walpole's Grant," afterwards included in the "Ohio Company."

MAP OF OHIO LAND GRANTS 190

    From the map of Lewis, 1796.

GEORGE III., KING OF ENGLAND 193

    From a portrait painted in 1760.

AN INDIAN SURPRISE 204

    From a painting by F. O. C. Darley.

TAIL-PIECE, ANCIENT MANNER OF LOADING A RIFLE . . . 208

SIMON KENTON, THE COMPANION OF BOONE (facing) . . . 209

    From a portrait by L. W. Morgan.

List of Illustrations.

	PAGE
HEADING OF CHAP. XII., CORNSTALK'S TOMAHAWK	209

Which is still preserved.

GEN. WM. HENRY HARRISON'S RESIDENCE 220

From an early lithograph.

MAJ. GEN. WILLIAM HENRY HARRISON 220

From an original portrait by J. R. Lambdin.

BENJAMIN FRANKLIN (facing) 223

From a portrait in the Portfolio, 1818.

HEADING OF CHAP. XIII., A CALL TO ARMS 223

A PORTION OF FILSON'S MAP 1785, SHOWING VICINITY OF HARRODSBURG 229

ANOTHER PORTION OF FILSON'S MAP, INCLUDING LEXINGTON 231

MORE OF FILSON'S MAP, WITH LOUISVILLE AS THE CENTRE . 233

ANDREW JACKSON 235

From a portrait by Jarvis.

MRS. ANDREW JACKSON 236

Taken from a portrait, made shortly after ball given in honor of her husband.

A HUNTER ARMED WITH A "DECKHARD" RIFLE 238

From an engraving by Sartain.

TAIL-PIECE PEACE AND WAR 246

OUTACITE, A CHEROKEE CHIEF (facing) 247

From Church's Indian Wars.

HEADING OF CHAP. XIV., BLOCK HOUSE AT FORT STANWIX 247

THE MASSACRE OF THE FAMILY OF JOHANAS DIETZ (1775?) . 252

From a contemporary broadside.

GEORGE ROGERS CLARK (facing) 267

From a portrait from life in possession of Vincennes University, Ind.

List of Illustrations.

	PAGE
HEADING OF CHAP. XV., FORT WAYNE IN 1794	267

    From a contemporary sketch.

COL. GEORGE CROGHAN 274

    From the Portfolio.

INDIAN SCALP DANCE 282

    From The Family Magazine, 1844.

COL. FRANCIS VIGO 284

    From the Magazine of Western History.

GEORGE WASHINGTON AT FIFTY-SIX YEARS OF AGE (facing) 287

    From a portrait by Geoffroy, Paris.

HEADING OF CHAP. XVI., FRONTIER BLOCK HOUSE 287

WILLIAM PENN 292

HEADING OF CHAP. XVII., FROM WEST'S PAINTING OF THE PENN TREATY 293

INDIAN MONUMENT AT GNADENHUTTEN 300

COL. AARON OGDEN (facing) 303

    From a portrait by A. B. Durand.

HEADING OF CHAP. XVIII., FORT LEXINGTON IN 1782 . . . 303

    Now Lexington, Ky.

YORK ON LAKE ONTARIO IN 1812 308

    From a plate in The Portfolio.

MARQUIS CORNWALLIS (facing) 312

    From a portrait by Copley.

HEADING OF CHAP. XIX., STONE MARKING GRAVE OF COL. FERGUSON AT KINGS MOUNTAIN 313

PLAN OF THE ACTION AT KINGS MOUNTAIN 316

    From Ramsey's Annals of Tennessee.

BURIAL PLACE OF COL. FERGUSON 318

    From American Historical Record.

List of Illustrations.

	PAGE
GEN. ISAAC SHELBY (facing)	319
From an engraving by Durand.	
HEADING OF CHAP. XX., PIONEERS EN ROUTE	319
BRIG. GEN. ANTHONY WAYNE (facing)	331
From a pencil sketch by Col. John Trumbull.	
HEADING OF CHAPTER XXI., WAYNE DRILLING HIS MEN	331
A PORTION OF THE MAP OF LEWIS, SHOWING FORT WAYNE AND VICINITY 1796	334
MARIE ANTOINETTE, QUEEN OF FRANCE	337
From a contemporary print.	
MAJ. GEN. ARTHUR ST. CLAIR	338
From a drawing by Col. John Trumbull.	
MAP OF OHIO, MADE BY GEN. RUFUS PUTNAM IN 1804	340
ANOTHER PORTION OF THE MAP OF LEWIS 1796, SHOWING POSITION OF VARIOUS FORTS	348
BATTLE OF FALLEN TIMBER	350
From "Battles of America."	
PLAN OF THE BATTLE OF FALLEN TIMBER	353
JAMES MADISON (facing)	355
From original portrait by Stuart.	
HEADING OF CHAP. XXII., FORT WASHINGTON (NOW CINCINNATI) IN 1790	355
TAIL-PIECE, NIAGARA FALLS FROM THE EARLIEST KNOWN PRINT	368
WILLIAM CHARLES COLE CLAIBORNE (facing)	369
HEADING OF CHAP. XXIII., CAMPUS MARTIUS, AT THE PRESENT SITE OF MARIETTA, OHIO	369
EDMUND CHARLES GENET	370
From a painting by Fouquet.	

List of Illustrations.

	PAGE
THOMAS PINCKNEY	373
From The Portfolio.	
A SCHOOL BOY'S MAP OF THE UNITED STATES IN 1796	374
From Morse's Elements of Geography.	
JAMES EDWARD OGLETHORPE	376
From a contemporary engraving.	
TAIL-PIECE, A POSSIBLE PICTURE OF REV. SAMUEL DOAK	378
ROBERT R. LIVINGSTON (facing)	379
From Irving's Life of Washington.	
HEADING OF CHAP. XXIV., THE FLAG COVERS THE ENTIRE VALLEY	379
THOMAS JEFFERSON	385
From a plate contemporary with Miss. affairs.	
JAMES MONROE	390
From a portrait by Vanderlyn.	
THOMAS B. ROBERTSON	396
From a portrait by St. Memim.	
TAIL-PIECE, "A NEW HOME, WHO'LL FOLLOW?"	401

"And when recording history displays,
  Feats of renown, though wrought in ancient days;
  Tells of a few stout hearts, that fought and died
  Where duty placed them, at their country's side;
  The man that is not moved by what he reads,
  That takes not fire at their heroic deeds,
  Unworthy of the blessings of the brave,
  Is base in kind, and born to be a slave."

JOHN JAY.

Daniel Webster said of him: "When the spotless ermine of the judicial robe fell on John Jay, it touched nothing less spotless than itself."
This portrait was engraved by Wilkinson, London, 1783.

I

ON THE BRIM OF THE GREAT BASIN.

The First Coureur-de-Bois and His Fate—Adventures of Jean Nicolet—An Ambassador with two Pistols—The Courageous Traders Who First Reached the Mississippi—A Trading Station that Was a "First Chance" for Warriors as Well as Peaceful Indians—The Notable Manner in Which the La Chine Rapids Were Named.

The connected historical story of the Mississippi valley begins with the training of the first *coureur de bois,* Etienne Brule, for it was through the enterprising, adventure-loving spirit of this notable class of Frenchmen, the *coureurs de bois,* that civilized people were first led to make permanent settlements within the Great Basin. The Spanish under De Soto had discovered, it is true, the Mississippi in 1541 (as shall be told further on), but nothing came of that expedition save only as the story of it served to inspire one of the greatest of French explorers, more than a hundred years later, the Sieur de la Salle.

It was Samuel de Champlain who made a *coureur de bois* of Etienne Brule—who, in fact, originated the *coureur de bois* system of exploration. Champlain founded the city of Quebec in 1608, making of it, at first, a fur-trading station, but hoping that in the end it would become the capital of a new great French empire. In the year 1609 he discovered Lake Champlain, while on the war path with an Algonquin party, and there, in 1610, not far from the St. Lawrence, he captured an Iroquois brush fort, and killed all but one of the garrison that numbered 100.

In celebrating this victory, of 1610, Iroquet, the Indian chief, gave a young savage named Savignon to the French as a pledge of future friendship and Champlain in return gave Etienne Brule to Iroquet.

So far as the records show Etienne Brule was the first Frenchman to join the *Sauvages*—the wild men of America, and fully to adopt their manner of life. He became one of, as well as one with, them, but he was nevertheless a Frenchman still, and kept his eyes open for his own advantage, and for that of his country. He became a woods ranger and trader on his own account, and an interpreter and ambassador among the Indians for the benefit of his countrymen.

Save only as he showed to Champlain the advantage of having men trained in that fashion among the Indians, Etienne Brule did but little to lead his countrymen toward the Mississippi Valley. There is no record of his having so much as heard of the great stream, though he did, very likely, wander as far west as Lake Superior, for he said he was on the shores of a great lake where native copper was found in nuggets, and he brought a nugget to Quebec to prove the story. He might have accomplished more, for his enterprise was praiseworthy, but he got in trouble with some Hurons, east of Lake Huron, presumably over some red sweetheart, and they killed and ate him. And that was the fate of not a few woods rangers who came after him.

In the meantime another French youth, Jean Nicolet, had come to join Champlain. He arrived in 1618. Because Brule had been serviceable while living among the Indians, Champlain determined to give Nicolet a similar training, and for nine years he lived with the Indians to the eastward of Lake Huron, "undergoing such fatigues as none but eye witnesses can conceive; he often passed seven or eight days without food, and once, full seven weeks with no other nourishment than a little bark from the trees," as an old Jesuit "Relation" says. He had there "his own separate cabin and household, and fishing and trading for himself."

In 1633 Nicolet returned to the St. Lawrence settlements, and in 1634 was sent to explore the region beyond Lake Michigan. The Indians had been telling of the wonders of that country ever since Champlain arrived among them, and Nicolet had returned with a fixed belief that either the Chinese or the Japanese came to that country every year to trade. At any rate it was a people, the Indians said, that used huge wooden canoes instead of little portable canoes of birch bark, and the French thought the huge wooden canoes must be ships.

Nicolet started on July 7, 1634, with a party of Indians and priests who were bound for Georgian Bay (p. 99, vol. viii., Thwaite's edition of Jesuit "Relations"), and the party was thirty days on the road.

With seven Huron Indians for company, Nicolet went first to the Sault Sainte Marie, a noted gathering place for western tribes, but finding no Asiatics there, nor any one that looked like them, he paddled around to Green Bay, on the northwest corner of Lake Michigan, where a still more populous region was found, because of the wild rice growing in the lakes, and in the still waters beyond.

Here a real test of Nicolet's ability as an ambassador was to be made. For the Indians were utter strangers to him and his Hurons, and their language was wholly different.

First of all he landed and "fastened two sticks in the earth, and hung gifts thereon, so as to relieve these tribes from the notion of mistaking them for enemies." When the presents had been discovered and carried away, a lone Huron went in search of the tribe to say by the sign language that a man of the people who manufactured the presents wished to come and deliver many more things of the same kind. This message was kindly received and "they dispatched several young men to meet the manitouriniou—that is to say, 'the wonderful man.'"

"The news of Nicolet's coming quickly spread to the villages round about, and there assembled four or five thousand men." Nicolet dressed himself in "a grand robe of China damask, all strewn with flowers and birds of many colors." Then with a pistol in each hand, he approached the great throng, fired off blank cartridges in his weapons, and finally gravely seated himself in the place left vacant for him.

The "squaws and children fled screaming," but the warriors were so highly pleased that they gave him a feast in which, as he was careful to report, no less than 120 beavers were eaten.

From Green Bay Nicolet went up Fox River to the Mascoutin Indians, whose language he understood. Of them he learned that no Asiatics came to the region. The "strange people" of whom he had heard were Naduesiu (Sioux) Indians, and their large wooden canoes were dugouts—big logs cut to canoe shape. They lived on a great river, not a great sea, and the Indians said Nicolet could reach this great river by a journey of three days from where he was then encamped. It is not unreasonable to suppose that Nicolet went on to visit this Sioux tribe, for in the Jesuit "Relation" for 1640, the writer gives a list of the Indian nations around the upper lakes, which includes the Sioux, and says of the list:

"Sieur Nicolet has given me the names of these nations, *which he himself has visited,* for the most part in their own country."

The next to explore the region south and west of Lake Superior were Menard Chouart des Grosseilliers and Pierre Esprit Radisson. Grosseilliers, as a servant of the Jesuit missionaries, was in **1645**, employed among the Hurons near Georgian Bay, Lake Huron. He returned to the St. Lawrence settlements in 1646, and remained there until 1654, when the call of the wilds—the memory of unrestrained freedom and the beckoning smiles of the Indian maidens—could be no longer resisted. In company with Sieur Radisson, a close personal friend (he had married Radisson's sister), Grosseilliers started for the region where Nicolet had seen 120 beavers served at an impromptu feast.

This journey was one of the most daring known to the history of exploration in any country. For the Iroquois, since the days of their defeats by Champlain, had procured (of the Dutch), and learned to use fire arms. With these new weapons they had crossed the lakes and literally swept the Huron and Algonquin villages from the face of the earth. Even the Esquimo on the shores of Hudson's Bay had felt the power of the Iroquois warriors, while the French themselves had been slaughtered beneath the walls built to guard Montreal, Three Rivers and Quebec. The whole region between the St. Lawrence and the Laurentian Mountains, the Saguenay River and Lake Huron, was, in 1654, left to the undisturbed possession of the furry and feathered animals, save only as Iroquois bands continually prowled to and fro along the streams.

So complete had been the disaster wrought by the Iroquois—so terrified were the Indians of all other tribes—that during the year 1653 not a single skin was brought to Montreal, and "in the Quebec warehouse there is nothing but poverty."

Nevertheless on August 6, 1654, Grosseilliers and Radisson paddled away from Montreal and disappeared up the Ottawa. The daring of the Yankee pioneers who, like Boone and Robertson, plunged alone into the wilds has been praised in the highest terms, and with good reason. But the dangers of one man travelling alone through the forest were far less than those of these two men paddling with trade goods up an open waterway that was the regular highway of the enemy.

On leaving Montreal, Grosseillier and Radisson promised to return in a year. They failed to do so and, naturally, they were mourned as dead. But at the end of August, 1656, they returned accompanied by fifty canoes laden with furs. "Their arrival," says the Jesuit Relation, "caused the country universal joy," and they "landed amid the stunning noise of cannon."

In 1659 these two woods rangers went again to the wilds of Lake Superior and they came back safe on August 21, 1660. They had "wintered with the Nation of the Ox" (i. e., the Sioux), and had visited a remnant of the Hurons whom they found living on "a beautiful river, large, wide, deep, and worthy of comparison with our great river St. Lawrence." (vol. xlv., pp. 163, 235; Thwaite's edition, Jesuit "Relations").

Radisson, in an account which was printed afterwards, says: "We *went to the great river * * * which we believe runs towards Mexico.*" The "Relations" just quoted adds that "our Frenchmen *visited the forty villages of which this (Sioux) nation is composed.*"

Any unprejudiced reading of these "Relations," and of Radisson's account, shows conclusively that these two intrepid woods rangers were on the Mississippi river.

From the Jesuit "Relation" of 1656-7 it appears that a Jesuit priest may have passed over the brim of the Mississippi Valley still earlier. This "Relation" records "some peculiarities of the Iroquois country" as observed by Jesuit missionaries sent to the Onondaga region under the lead of Father Francois le Mercier. One of them saw a spring from which flowed a substance that "ignites like brandy, and boils up in bubbles of flame when fire is applied to it. * * * Our savages use it to grease their heads and bodies." It is believed that this was a petroleum spring in Alleghany county, New York, the water of which flows to the Alleghany river.

In 1665 Father Allouez established a mission at a place called La Pointe, on Lake Superior, near where Ashland, Wisconsin, now stands, and while there he wrote of the great river under the name it now bears—"Messipi"—that being the Indian word meaning great water.

And then came La Salle. Rene Robert Cavalier, Sieur de la Salle was born in Rouen, France, on November 21, 1643. He attended a Jesuit school there until 15, and then went to Paris and prepared to join the Order; but after taking preliminary vows left them, and, according to the best authorities, came to Montreal in the spring of 1666.

Montreal was then the frontier settlement of New France, and the prowling Iroquois often murdered Frenchmen within the shadows of its forts. Nevertheless La Salle, having a small capital, bought a tract of land at the head of the rapids now called La Chine. Here he laid out a palisaded village, and built for his own use a comfortable log house. He intended, at that time, to make a considerable settlement and a trading

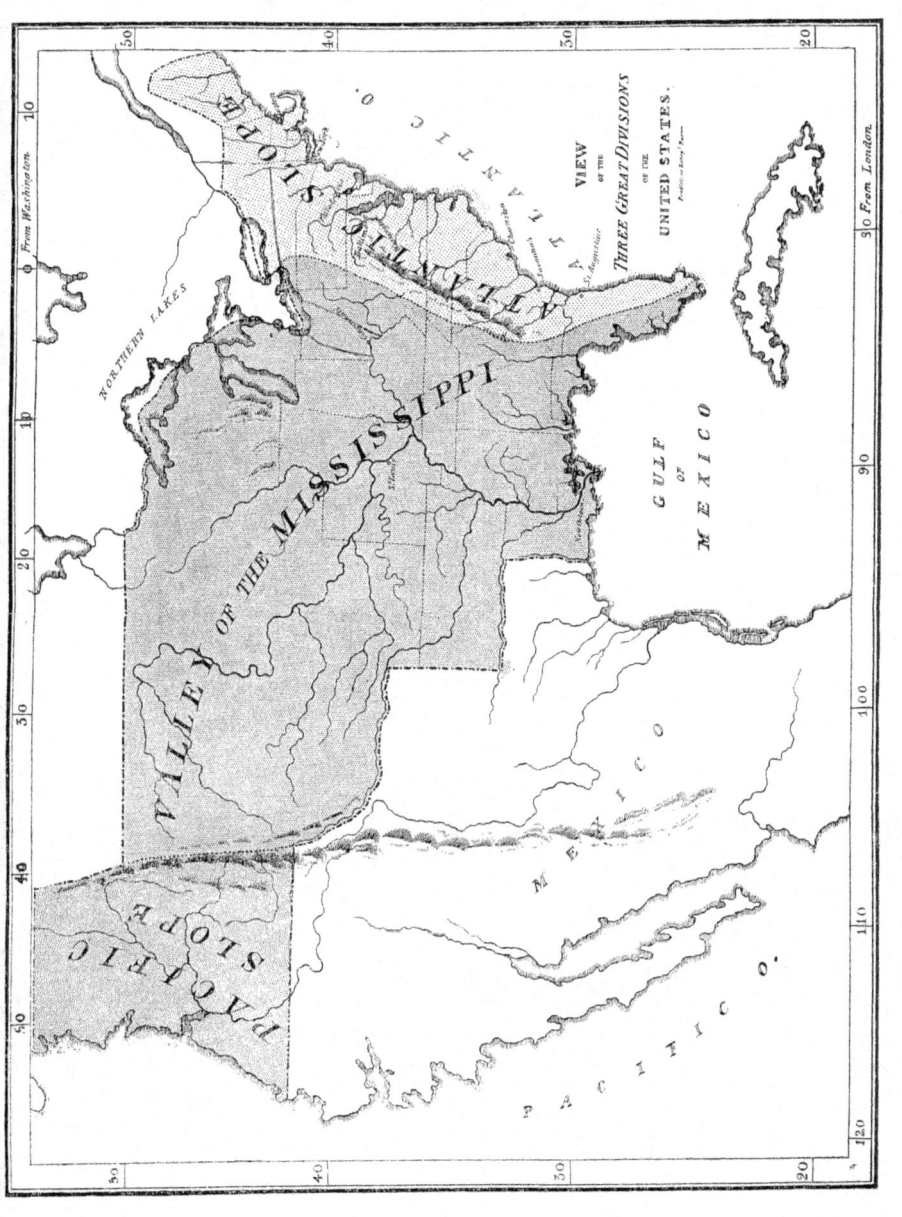

station on his land; and it was then one of the best sites in America, for such an enterprise.

For his house stood at the foot of a long still water in the St. Lawrence and it was but a step to the Ottawa. Whether the Indians and *coureurs de bois* came with their furs by one route or the other, La Salle offered them what our mine saloonkeeper called the "First Chance."

At the same time, however, this was probably the most dangerous spot in New France, for if the fur sellers found there their "first chance" so, too, might the blood-thirsty Iroquois. It was characteristic of the man to select the most advantageous point regardless of its dangers.

La Salle, as eventually appeared, had a mind for other work than that of trading hatchets and brandy for furs. In the fall of 1668 some Seneca Indians came to his station, remained with him on the most friendly terms all winter and told him of a great river to the south of their country which ran away to the west and south, and finally emptied into the salt sea.

"La Salle's imagination took fire." He supposed the river emptied into the Pacific. In the spring he sold out all his holdings, went to Quebec, applied for a commission to go exploring, and got it. It was in the days when Jean Baptiste Talon was "Intendant"—a sort of deputy governor of Canada—and Talon was determined that "the lilies of France must go wherever man could carry them."

La Salle hoped to carry them to China, by the way of the Seneca's great river, and he was willing to pay his own expenses. He was therefore just the kind of a man that Talon was looking for.

How La Salle bought an outfit that loaded four canoes, and hired fourteen men, and on July 6, 1669, started for Lake Ontario need not be told in detail. But it is worth mention that at the head of Lake Ontario he met a woods ranger named Louis Joliet who had been hunting for Etienne Brule's copper mine on the shores of Lake Superior.

The copper mine was not found, but Joliet had come down from Mackinac by way of the Detroit river and Lake Erie, and was the first white man to pass that way.

From the head of Lake Ontario, La Salle went to Onondaga, where he obtained a guide, and thence to a point on a branch of the Ohio river supposed to be "six or seven leagues from Lake Erie." This he followed into the "the Beautiful River" itself, and eventually reached the falls where Louisville now stands.

At this point he was obliged to turn back because his men had deserted him. It was an ominous beginning of a great life work.

La Salle's reception when he returned to Montreal alone, was humiliating. In establishing the post at the head of the rapids above Montreal he had incurred the bitter enmity of all the traders doing business from Montreal to Quebec. They cowered in the shadow of the forts; he had dared to build his store leagues away in the wilderness. His bravery made conspicuous their cowardice; his position enabled him to secure the very cream of the trade. The enmity had been intense, but now, here was the Sieur de la Salle, back

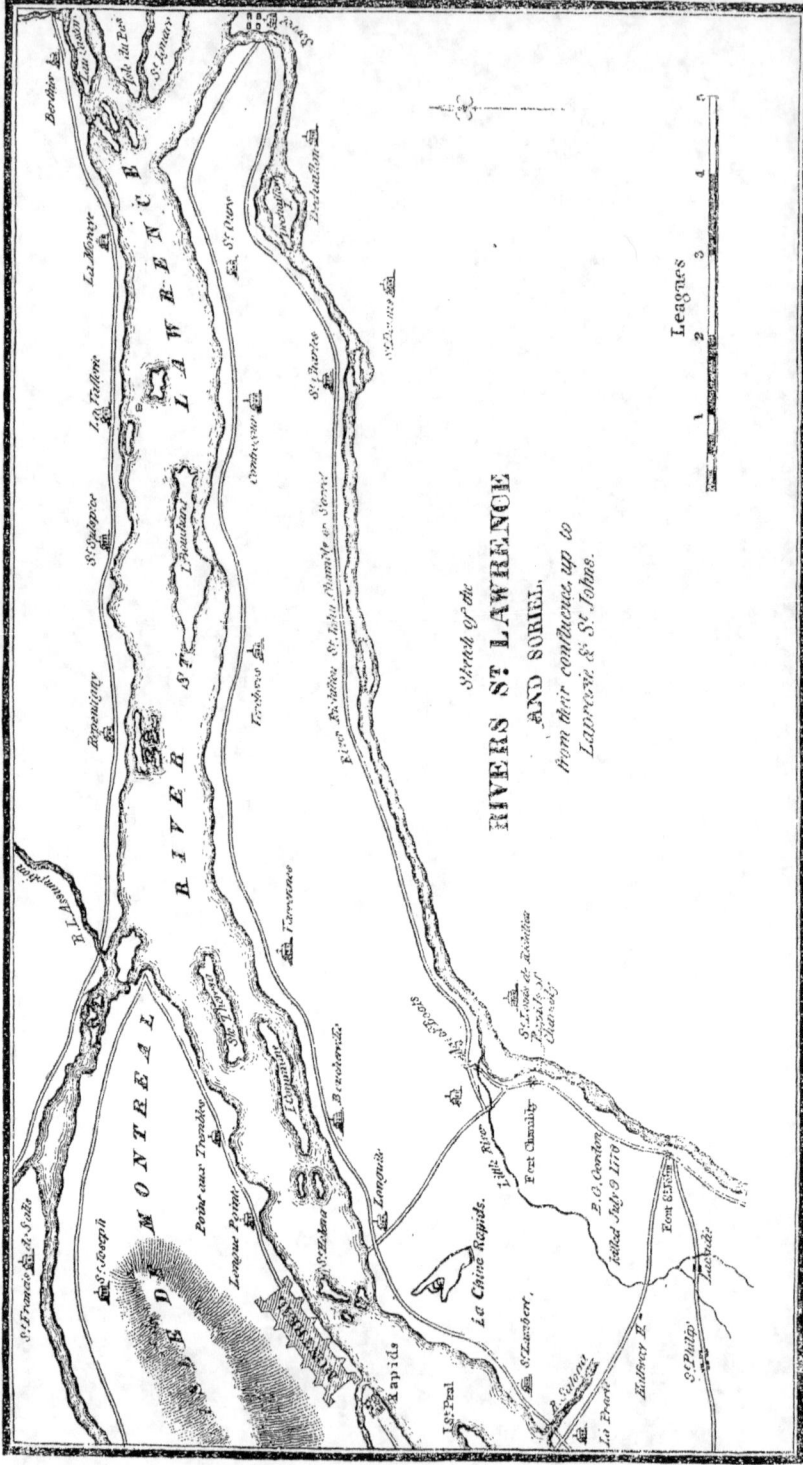

The La Chine Rapids. Ancient Names of Settlements on the St. Lawrence Are Here Shown.

from a voyage in which he had hoped to reach China, baffled, and not with a franc left of all that he had obtained from the sale of his well-located trading station. The tumble of water over which his lost home looked was the only China he had discovered. It was a good joke on La Salle. They would, and they did, call those rapids China—"La Chine"—to irritate him. And as La Chine they are known to this day.

Nevertheless, while the traders sneered, Jean Baptiste Talon, the intendant, saw that the man who would sink his all in such an expedition, was worthy of consideration; and he enabled the discomfited La Salle to try once more. But for this expedition, few words will suffice. La Salle went up to the head of Lake Michigan and crossed to the water shed of the Mississippi. The account of the journey says he went to a river "which flowed from east to west"—presumably the Kankakee. He followed it until it was joined by another river coming from the northwest. This was probably the Des Plaines. La Salle, like Grosseilliers and Radisson, viewed a part of the great valley, but so far he had accomplished nothing toward settling it.

Comparisons are instructive, however odious. In 1634 when Champlain sent Nicolet to visit the Indians on the west side of Lake Michigan, the inhabitants of Massachusetts thought they had shown great enterprise in establishing a trading station on the Piscataqua river where Dover, New Hampshire, now stands; while the Virginia settlers had recently sent an exploring expedition to learn whether a river emptied into Delaware Bay.

JEAN BAPTISTE TALON.
Intendant of New France. From the portrait by Hamel.

II

FIRST EXPLORATION OF THE MISSISSIPPI.

The Facts about Joliet's Expedition Down the Mississippi with Father Marquette as Chaplain of the Company—The Kindly Illinois Indians and Their Calumet—Two Views of a River "Monster"—Tennessee Indians Whom White Men Had Visited—Fate of the Valiant Quapaws—A Far-Reaching Mishap to Joliet.

To the honor of Jean Baptiste Talon, Intendant of Canada from 1665 to 1675, (save for a few months), be it remembered that he not only saw the value of the broad western domain where Grosseillier and Radisson first carried French trade, but he took steps to possess it.

In 1670, when he sent La Salle on the voyage by the way of Lake Michigan and the Illinois, toward the Mississippi, he sent Daumont de Saint-Lusson to Lake Superior to hunt for the copper mine that Joliet had failed to find, and further than that to take formal possession of the upper lake region in the name of the king. Saint Lusson was in command, but the experienced Joliet was guide, and without mishap they reached the Sault Sainte Marie, erected a cross on a hill, blessed it, sang the Vexilla Regis, planted a cedar post to which was attached a metal plate bearing the royal arms, sang the Exaudiat, and then Saint Lusson, with a sword in one hand and a fresh sod in the other, uttered a fierce gust of words by which he said he took possession not only of the upper great lakes, but of "all countries, rivers, lakes and streams contiguous and adjacent thereunto," including not only those his countrymen had already discovered, but "those which may be discovered hereafter."

This was done on May 5, 1671. It had taken the French government thirty-seven years to follow the trail of Nicolet as far as the Sault Sainte Marie.

On the return of this party to the lower St. Lawrence, Talon determined on one more exploration of the region; and Louis Joliet was chosen to lead the expedition.

In order to show that Louis Joliet and not some other man was chosen to lead, we will quote the original sources of information. It is a matter of great importance because it was this expedition that did first *explore* the Mississippi.

Among the Paris documents printed in volume ix. of the "New York Colonial Manuscripts" are found

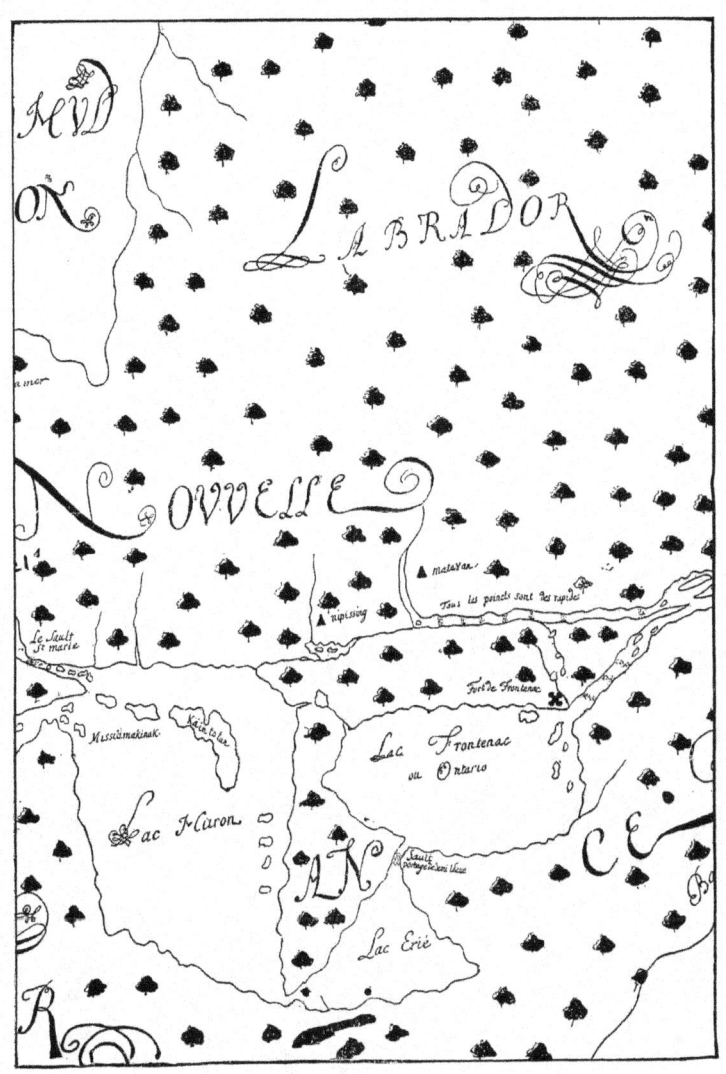

THE EASTERN PORTION OF JOLIET'S MAP, SHOWING GREAT LAKES. (1674).

(pp. 90-94) some "Extracts of the Memoirs of Monsieur de Frontenac to the Minister," Frontenac being Governor of Canada and Colbert the "minister." On page 92 is this sentence regarding an act of the Governor: "He has likewise judged it expedient for the service to send Sieur Joliet to the country of the Maskouteins, to discover the South Sea, and the great river they call the Mississippi."

In volume lviii. of Thwaite's edition of the Jesuit "Relations," pp. 93, 95, is a letter from Father Claude Dablon, the Superior of the Order at Quebec, dated August 1, 1674, which says that "two years ago" it was "decided that it was important * * to ascertain into what sea falls the great river, about which the Sauvages relate so much. For this purpose they could not have selected a person endowed with better qualities than is Sieur Joliet, who has travelled much in that region, and has acquitted himself in this task with all the ability that could be desired."

In the introduction which Father Claude Dablon wrote to Marquette's journal of this expedition, as printed in the "Relations," vol. lix., pp. 87, 89, are these words:

"In the year 1673, Monsieur The Count de Frontenac, Our Governor, and Monsieur Talon then Our Intendant, Recognizing The Importance of this discovery * * * these gentlemen, I say, appointed at the same time for this undertaking Sieur Joliet, whom they considered very fit for so great an enterprise; and they were well pleased that Father Marquette should be *of the party.*"

Let there be no mistake about Father Marquette.

He was the friend and companion as well as the assistant of Joliet. They had often consulted about this expedition before Joliet obtained his commission, and it had been fully understood that Joliet should take him along. But one might as well give the credit of the battle of Manila to the chaplain of the flagship as to give Marquette the credit of the first exploration of the Mississippi River. The man of the expedition was Joliet. And yet a statue has been erected in the capitol at Washington to the honor of the chaplain.

With his outfit in two canoes, and five able *coureurs de bois* to help him, Louis Joliet left Quebec on an unnamed day in the fall of 1672, and on December 8 arrived at the mission of St. Ignace, in the strait of Mackinac, where he found Father Marquette and the Indian converts celebrating the feast of the Immaculate Conception.

At this mission the winter was passed, because the journey was to be made by water; but on "The 17th of May, 1673, we started," and "the joy that we felt animated our courage and rendered the labor of paddling from morning till night agreeable." So wrote Father Marquette. "We were going to seek unknown countries." They crossed Lake Michigan and visited the wild rice Indians on Green Bay, who, when they learned the object of the expedition, "were greatly surprised." The route lay through "Nations who never show mercy to strangers," they said; moreover "the great river" was full of monsters that destroyed canoes and men together, and there was one particular demon—when the Indians spoke of him the mere thought made them tremble. And then there was the heat. Even if the Frenchmen's medicine enabled them to dodge the devils the heat would kill them without doubt.

But Joliet had heard Indians talk in that manner before, and he soon passed up the Fox River, and finally reached a village composed of Miamies, Kickapoes and Mascoutens. A most beautiful country was that around the village. "From an eminence upon which it is placed one beholds on every side prairies, extending further than the eye can see, interspersed with groves or with lofty trees. The soil is very fertile and yields much Indian corn. The sauvages gather quantities of plums and grapes."

It is a far cry to the day of Joliet, but the region is as beautiful and as productive now as when it delighted the eyes of these explorers, for it is that lying west and south of Lake Winnebago.

The kindly Indians gave the party two guides who showed the way "to the portage of 2,700 paces" to "a river which discharged into the Mississippi," and helped them to carry their canoes across the land. Portage City, Wisconsin, a railroad centre of importance, now stands on this crest between the waters of the great lakes and those of the Mississippi.

After "a new devotion to the blessed Virgin immaculate," they launched forth on the Wisconsin river, which they called the Meskousing. It was "full of islands covered with vines." The banks were of "fertile land, diversified with woods, prairies and hills." There were "oak, walnut and basswood trees," and another kind very interesting to them for it was "armed with long thorns." And there were the deer, and herds of huge wild "cattle," as they called the buffalo.

For "40 leagues on this same route," as Marquette estimated the distance, they paddled with the current, and then "We safely entered Mississippi on the 17th of June, with a joy that I cannot express."

To the right was "a large chain of very high mountaines," or so they seemed in the sunlit air; to the left were "beautiful lands." The stream was "divided by islands." And as they "gently followed its course" the mountains fell away, the islands became if possible "more beautiful," and "covered with finer trees, while the prairies were fairly covered with deer and Cattle," and the waters swarmed with "bustards and Swans."

Then there were the monstrous fish, one of which "struck our Canoe with such violence that I thought it was a great tree, about to break the canoe in pieces."

Quite as interesting if less dangerous was another "monster, with the head of a tiger, a sharp nose like that of a wildcat, with whiskers and straight erect ears," which they saw swimming.

To the eyes of this wondering Frenchman it was a land of enchanting beauties. For over "one hundred leagues" they paddled "without discovering any thing except animals and birds," but they kept a good lookout, nevertheless, building only small fires when cooking their food, (Indian corn, fish and dried meat), and sleeping in their canoes anchored in the river "at some distance from the shore."

Finally they saw a "somewhat beaten path leading to a fine prairie." This, Joliet and Marquette fol-

Mississippi Valley.

lowed, leaving the canoes afloat, until they saw three villages, and were so near to one that they could hear the voices of the inhabitants. Then they stopped and shouted as loud as they could.

At that "the sauvages quickly issued from their cabins," and stopped and gazed for a time in wonder at the white men. Then four old men advanced, two of whom "bore tobacco pipes, finely ornamented and adorned with various feathers. They walked slowly, and raised their pipes toward the sun, without saying a word"—a method of worship not without one commendable feature, although Marquette does not say so.

It was soon learned that these Indians were of the Illinois tribe. They took the strangers to their village, and when the chief met them he held up his hands as if to shade his eyes and said, with a grace that even men of "the most polite nation" could not have exceeded: "How beautiful the sun is, O Frenchmen, when thou comest to visit us! Our village awaits thee, and thou shalt enter all our cabins in peace."

Learning that the Frenchmen were to explore the full length of the river, these Indians gave them a pipe of peace—the Calumet—which Marquette describes in detail. It had a stone bowl with a reed stem which was ornamented with the most beautiful feathers and bird heads obtainable. In their way the Indians used the Calumet, when worshipping the sun, as Father Marquette used the Host in his church ceremonies. The chief elevated the pipe before the sun and the people as the priest elevated the Host in the communion services.

The special value of this pipe to the Frenchmen

was in its use as a symbol of peace. They were going into a country where the red inhabitants would drop their weapons, even during the most desperate battle, if the calumet were displayed; and with this to protect them the explorers left their new friends "at the end of June, about three o'clock in the afternoon."

Very soon they came to the great Missouri, with its dominating, debris-laden current, and then on a precipice that towered high on the eastern bank—a precipice that by its "height and length inspired awe"—they found the monsters, the mere thought of which had made the Indians of Green Bay tremble with fear. So terrible were these monsters, says the priest, that they "at first made Us afraid." "They are as large as a calf; they have horns on their heads as large as a deer, a horrible look, red eyes, a beard like a tiger's, a face somewhat like a man's, a body covered with scales, and so long a tail that it winds all around the body, passing above the head and going back between the legs, ending in a Fish's tail."

However, if afraid of it "at first," Marquette recovered his courage far enough to make sketches of the monsters, and was even able to praise them, at last, saying, "those two monsters are so well painted that we cannot believe that any sauvage (*sauvage,* i. e., wild man) is their author." He adds that "green, red and black are the three colors that compose the picture."

To Joutel, who wrote the story of La Salle's final exploring expedition, these famous monsters were by no means fearsome. His account speaks of them as Marquette's "pretended" monsters, and says that they

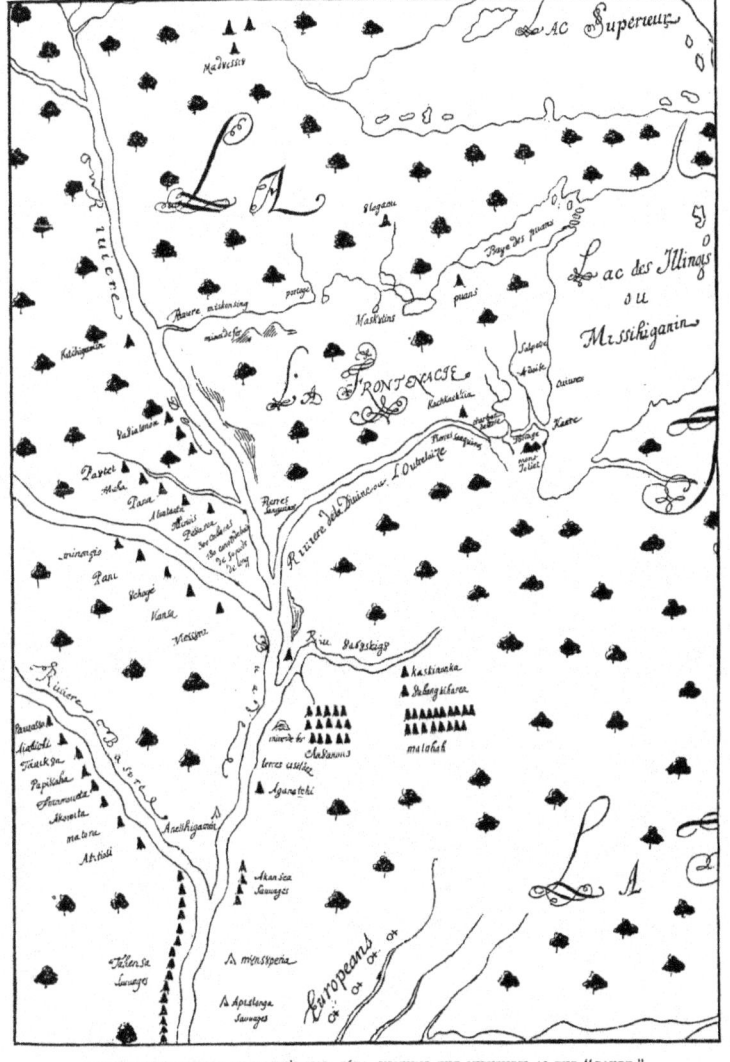

THE CENTRAL PORTION OF JOLIET'S MAP, 1674, SHOWING THE MISSISSIPPI AS THE "BAUDE."

consist of "two scurvy figures drawn in red, on the flat side of a rock, about ten or twelve feet high, which wants very much of the extraordinary height that Relation mentions."

These pictures were painted on the rocks on the east side of the Mississippi, just above Alton, Illinois. The paint was worn away long ago, and in 1867 the owner of the land was quarrying out the rock to supply the needs of the growing community.

One statement made by Marquette regarding the Missouri must be considered. He said he learned from the Indians that a stream rising near its source flowed "towards the west where it falls into The sea." He thought it must empty into the Gulf of California. We know now that the head waters of the Platte, a tributary of the Missouri, lie near the head of the Colorado, which flows to the Gulf of California. And at the head of Jackson's Hole, in Wyoming, is a tiny stream called Two-Oceans Creek, which rises high on a mountain, and flows down to a saddle-back ridge where it divides, the one part running down to Snake River, whose waters reach the Pacific, and the other part running down the Missouri, whose waters reach the Gulf of Mexico.

They found at one point above the Ohio (which appears on his map as the Ouabouskigou), a whirlpool that was dangerous, and that was the "monster" that drowned canoes as well as men; but this expedition crossed it without mishap.

Below the Ohio the explorers saw, on one unnamed day, some Indians on the east bank of the Mississippi, who were "armed with guns." More interesting still, when the explorers landed, they found "hatchets, hoes, knives, beads and flasks of double glass, in which they put Their powder."

"They assured us," writes Marquette, "that they bought Cloth and all other goods from Europeans who lived to The east, that these Europeans had rosaries and pictures; that they played upon instruments; that some of them looked like me, and had been received by these sauvages kindly."

This statement, which is found in Marquette's own story of this exploration (p. 149, vol. lix Thwaite's Jesuit "Relations"), seems plain and easily understood. The fact that the implements made by white men were found in considerable numbers and variety among the Indians confirms the statement. "Europeans (traders) had been received by these sauvages kindly."

"This news animated our courage, and made us paddle with Fresh ardor," writes Marquette. They passed cottonwood, elm and basswood trees that were "admirable for Their height and thickness." They saw "Quail on the water's edge." They heard the bellow of the buffalo. They killed a paroquet that was very beautiful. And then they "perceived a village on the water's edge called Mitchegamea."

This is said to have been located at the mouth of the St. Francis River, that empties into the Mississippi near Helena, Arkansas. The people of it were at first hostile. They came well armed to the bank, yelling, the while, in fearsome fashion, embarked in great dugouts, and surrounded the canoes. They even came swimming to board the Frenchmen, and one warrior hurled his club with deadly force, but when they saw

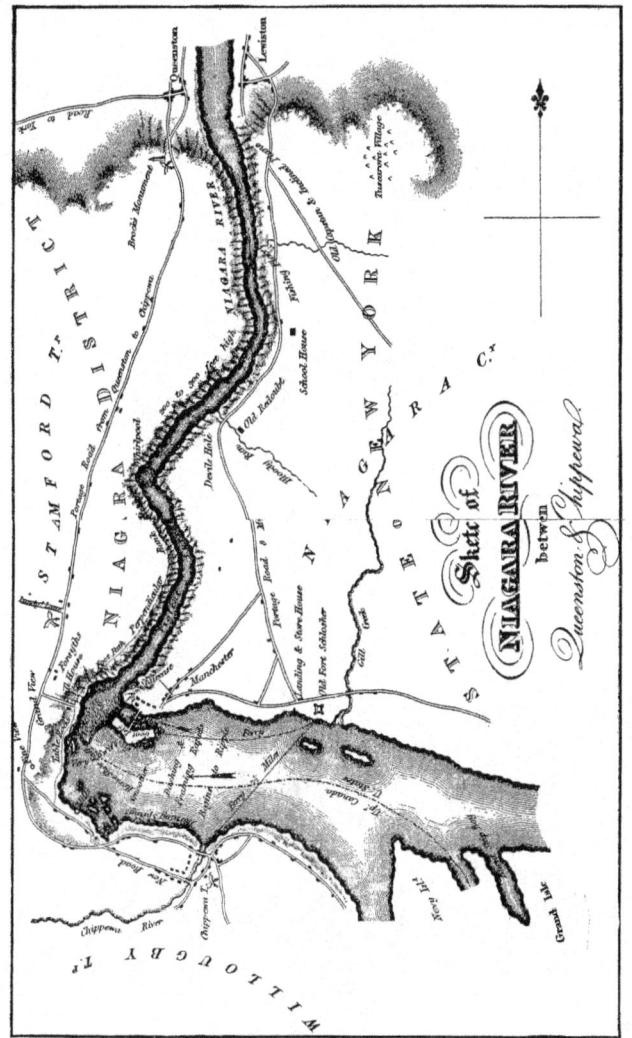

THE OLD FORKES ARE HERE SHOWN.

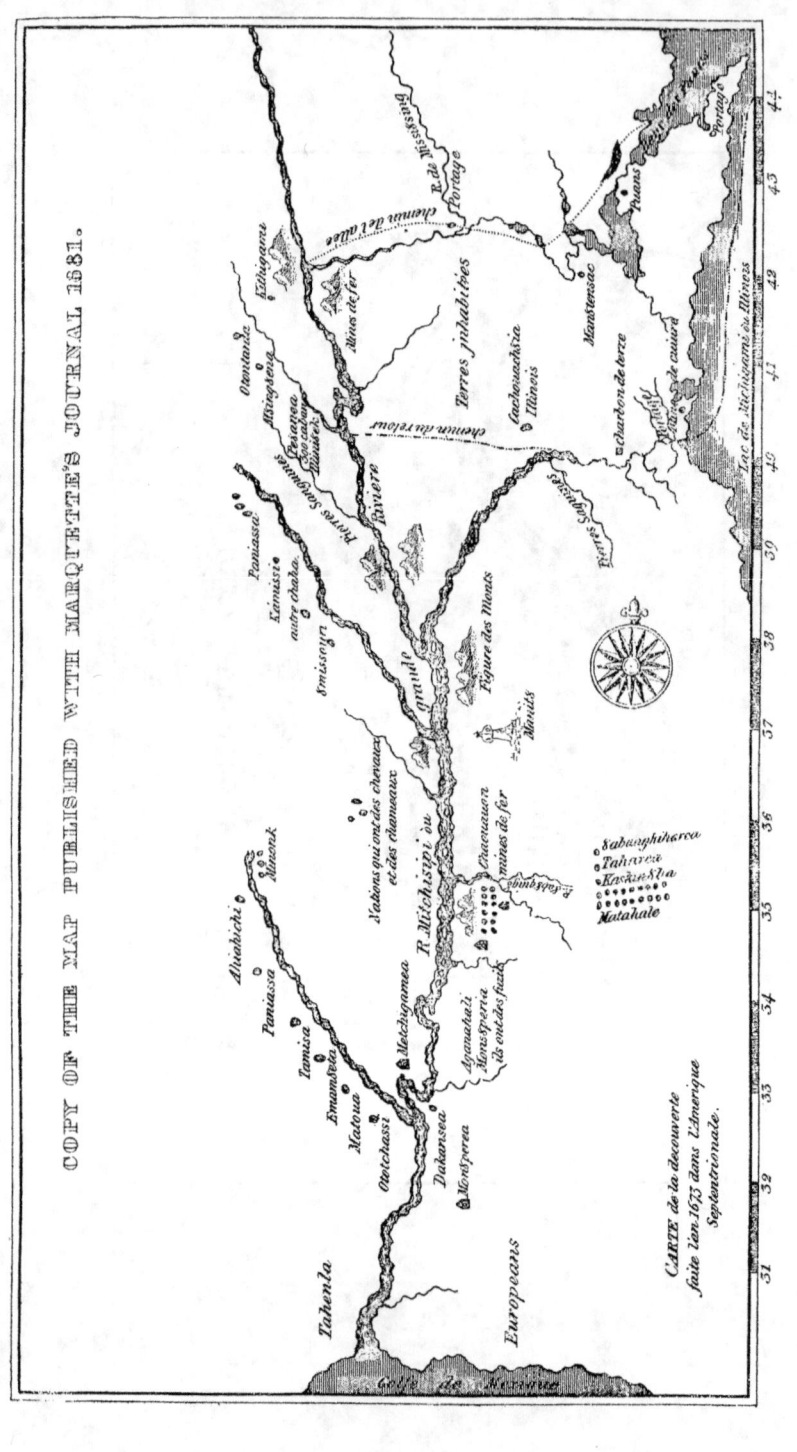

the calumet their passions passed away instantly, and they conducted the explorers to the shore where a dinner of boiled corn and fish was prepared.

A most interesting tribe was that. They worshipped the sun because it was a beneficent mystery. They were ruled by a clan supposed to be descended from the sun. They had a temple in which a sacred fire was kept burning. They lived in adobe houses. They cultivated the earth successfully. They were valiant warriors, but they were, at this particular time, in no little trouble because the Illinois Indians from the north, and the tribes east of the Great River, were well supplied with guns and often came to the Arkansas region searching for slaves.

In after years they, too, obtained guns, and then they promptly recovered the standing as warriors, which they had held before their enemies procured guns. Of the Indians of the Mississippi Valley there were no more generous or capable warriors than these.

Their descendants are now known as the Quapaws, who live on the reservation at the extreme northeast corner of the Indian Territory—a most pitiful remnant, that in 1900 numbered 251, chiefly of mixed bloods, of whom twenty-five were "engaged in civilized pursuits."

At a village "8 or 10 leagues lower down," Joliet turned back. He learned that the Gulf of Mexico "could not be more than 2 or 3 days journey" away to the south, but he did not go to it because he feared he would be captured by Spaniards, and thus be unable to make a report of his discoveries.

He started home on July 17. On the way the

party passed up the Illinois River, "which greatly shortens our route," as Marquette writes. How they knew that it would shorten their road is not explained. The soil and the beauty of the country, and the wild animals found there aroused the enthusiasm of the travellers. "Even beaver" were found here, and what was better, the portage into the lakes watershed was, in spring and part of the summer, but half a league long. The Indians along the route received them with pleasure and helped them on their way; and at the end of September they were back in Green Bay.

It had been a most pleasing and successful voyage thus far, but it was marred by one serious accident ere Joliet reached Quebec. In passing down the St. Lawrence his canoe was upset, and for four hours he fought for his life in the tumbling waters. He finally escaped, but his papers were lost forever. It is chiefly because historians have had to take the story of the exploration from Marquette's account, that the intrepid leader of the expedition has been usually treated as a mere assistant to the chaplain.

BLOCK HOUSE
1779

ROBERT CAVELIER, SIEUR DE LA SALLE.

III

LA SALLE AND LOUISIANA.

The Splendid Record of the Greatest of French Explorers—The Fort Above Niagara Falls—A Gale that Showed the Metal of One Good Salt-Sea Sailor—Mutinies Under La Salle and Their Origin—At the Mouth of the Mississippi at Last—The Sixth Fort in the Chain—La Salle Received at Court—Assassinated in the Texas Wilderness—The Highest Tributes of Honor Paid to La Salle Found in the Deeds of His Enemies.

When in the fall of 1672, Joliet started on his expedition to the Mississippi, the unfortunate La Salle was trading on borrowed capital to make a living. He had done nothing better, in the eyes of his countrymen, than to throw away an excellent estate and give the derisive name of La Chine to the rapids over which that estate looked. He had done worse, in fact, according to their thinking, for while a Government expedition was on its way to explore the great river, this bankrupt was meditating schemes for colonizing the vast region drained by the stream! He—La Salle—was to *do* this! The cackle of his countrymen, as they talked of his audacity in proposing such a work, never reached the stage of the horse laugh—their throats were not built that way—but it was becoming incessant, when it was suddenly cut short and turned into snarls of rage.

Though a bankrupt, and the laughing stock of the traders sitting beside the forts of Montreal and Quebec, La Salle had attracted the attention of the new Governor, Count de Frontenac. Frontenac, as a soldier, had won by good fighting, the rank of brigadier general when only twenty-six years old. Now, at the age of fifty-two, he had come to Canada bearing laurels but recently earned in Candia. "He was a man of excellent parts," by whatever standard tried—one of the few who raised the French in New France above utter contempt. (Parkman).

When Frontenac looked over the land he had come to cultivate, he saw, as Intendant Talon had seen, that it was worth while to add the unoccupied land lying to the west and south-west. He saw, too, as Talon had seen less clearly, that among the cackling mass of citizens, La Salle towered high, and "he often took council" of him. To Count Frontenac, the schemes of La Salle were not visionary. They showed the way to add glory to the crown of Louis XIV, and at the same time gain great wealth for the promoters of the

Mississippi Valley.

scheme—a matter of no small consequence to both Frontenac and La Salle, for both were bankrupts.

La Salle, backed by Frontenac, purposed building a line of forts from Lake Ontario to the mouth of the Mississippi. It was a magnificent conception for territorial aggrandizement. He also purposed controlling the trading stations at each fort—to make of them a source of wealth "beyond the dreams of avarice," and to carry on this trade by the way of the Gulf of Mexico.

When on May 17, 1673, Joliet left Mackinac, bound on the exploring expedition down the Mississippi, La Salle was among the Iroquois inviting them to come to the bay at the northeast corner of Lake Ontario, where Kingston now stands, to meet Count Frontenac, Governor of Canada. They called that bay Cataraqui, then.

On June 28, about the time that Joliet was leaving the Illinois village at the mouth of the Desmoines, Frontenac left Montreal with "400 men and 120 canoes, besides two large flat boats, which he caused to be painted red and blue, with strange devices intended to dazzle the Iroquois by a display of unwonted splendor."

No idle commander was Frontenac. "Without a cloak and drenched to the skin" he directed his men as they toiled, neck deep, up the rapids, or "tracked" along the banks in the midst of pouring rains.

And then on July 13, while Joliet was among the Arkansas Indians, Frontenac first met the Iroquois. Lines of soldiers—some of them veterans—were stationed from Frontenac's tent to the Indian camp.

Between these lines the sixty chiefs were conducted to the tent, and when they arrived, stolid and self-possessed at they naturally were on such grave occasions, they "ejaculated their astonishment" at the gorgeous array of uniforms on the Governor's guards. And they found in the Governor a man with a dignity and a command of language equal to their own, and a graciousness withal that was as winning as his bearing was in other ways commanding.

It has been often said that the the gunshots of Champlain, near Ticonderoga, gained for the French people the everlasting hatred of the Iroquois. It is not true. No white man ever won the hearts of the Iroquois as Frontenac did at Cataraqui, until Sir William Johnson came among them.

For while he talked to the chiefs in flowing language, and gave overcoats, and caressed their babies, he built a fort under their eyes without ever exciting a word or a thought of protest. It was the first of the chain of forts that La Salle had planned. At a single stroke Frontenac made peace with these most formidable enemies, and placed French guns where they would command the Indian trade of the great lakes. The further truth is that in the years immediately preceding the advent of Frontenac the Iroquois had held no special *hatred* against the French, but had *despised* them as easy victims of plundering raids. And it may be added here that the power of the Iroquois nation waned steadily, if slowly, from the day that Frontenac met them.

Having secured a post on Lake Ontario, Frontenac sent La Salle to France. La Salle asked the king for "a grant in seigniory of Fort Frontenac, for so he called the new post in honor of his patron," and for "a patent of nobility, in consideration of his services as an explorer."

Both petitions were granted, and La Salle returned to his new wilderness post a feudal lord, and the head of the best fur trading station in the world. The price he had agreed to pay for these great acquisitions was moderate. He was to return to the king the cost of the fort—10,000 francs,—maintain a garrison equal to that of Montreal, employ at least fifteen laborers, build a church, support a Recollet friar, form a settlement of friendly Indians, and replace the wooden walls of the fort with stone—all of which he did in good faith.

But there was an additional cost, not down in the contract, and this he was compelled to pay, even with his heart's blood—the losses and costs due to the envy and malice of those who had sneered and cackled when he was down, and who now writhed and screamed when they found him planted in the current of beaver skins coming from the upper lakes. In establishing this trading station Frontenac and La Salle had taken in as partners a half dozen of rich traders of the St. Lawrence. All Canada besides these and their friends, turned, like Indians in the bush, upon this monopolizing aggregation.

Nor was that all. Frontenac hated the Jesuits. His quarrels with them over matters of precedence in public functions were most virulent, for that was the day when Louis XIV ruled "the politest" nation. Frontenac also quarrelled with the seminary priests of Montreal. In all these matters La Salle openly "declared himself an adherent of the Governor." Time had been when La Salle would avoid trouble by what the French called "address," but now he stood by his patron, man-fashion. And for a time his manliness and ability prevailed.

A settlement came into existence at Cataraqui. Four sailing vessels of from twenty-five to forty tons each, were built to gather furs around the lake. The vast commerce of the great lakes began at Kingston. For the trade on the rivers, canoes were used, and in managing these La Salle's men "were reputed the best in America." His soldiers were well disciplined. His farm hands raised good crops. And the trade of the fort soon amounted to a profit of 25,000 livres a year.

This success exasperated the opponents of La Salle to the last degree. Nothing but his death would satisfy them, and their efforts to accomplish this were characteristic. One merchant, says Parkman, while pretending friendship, compelled his wife to attempt the act of Potiphar's wife, while he (the merchant), well armed, waited in an adjoining room for a signal. He thought he should have excuse for killing an unarmed man, but La Salle put the woman out of the room at the first advance, and then discovered the scoundrel in waiting outside the door. And another pretended friend mixed verdigris and water hemlock in a salad, of which La Salle ate a portion; but he recovered from the effects of the poison.

In the meantime the Jesuit missionaries among the Iroquois told them that La Salle was building stone walls at Fort Frontenac in order to make it a base for an aggressive war against the Five Nations.

Mississippi Valley.

In the midst of such contests with his enemies, La Salle, not at all daunted or discouraged, went to France once more, obtained a new commission, and came back not only to explore the whole length of the Mississippi, but to build the chain of forts and trading stations already mentioned along the route to the mouth of the Great River. He was particularly anxious for an establishment at the mouth of the Mississippi because he could there rule and trade free from the attacks of the hosts on the St. Lawrence.

This great work was to be done, however, without any financial aid from the government, and one gets a curious view of La Salle's character, and of the business methods of the day, from a statement of the way he raised money for the enterprise. He borrowed 11,000 livres from a merchant named Francois Plet, agreeing to pay forty per cent interest, and he pledged Fort Frontenac, the magnificent establishment yielding 25,000 livres annual income, for the paltry loan of 14,000 livres, on which, presumably, he paid the same deadly rate of interest.

La Salle returned from France late in 1678. Having obtained the needed loans he sent fifteen men to the Lake Michigan region to trade with the Indians in order that he might make the money to pay the enormous interest on his loans. On November 18, another party, under an assistant named La Mott sailed for Niagara river (where they arrived on December 6), to build a fort that would control the portage around the Niagara Falls, and a ship with which to navigate the lakes above.

This fort was the second built according to La

Salle's plan for adding the Mississippi Valley to the dominions of France. The point selected was at the little hamlet called La Salle opposite Cayuga Island in the Niagara River. The Seneca Indians "betrayed a sullen jealousy." They had been in trade themselves. They were middlemen between the western Indians and the settlements on the Hudson. Among them were two missionaries from Quebec who were sided with the enemies of La Salle, and who did all they could to excite the astute chiefs still further. But La Salle went to the principal village and soothed them into consenting to his work.

Then a disaster came on the heels of this success. A vessel loaded with rigging for the new ship La Salle was building above the falls was wrecked. It is charged that the pilot wrecked her in the interests of La Salle's enemies, and it is certain that his enemies were eager and unscrupulous, while he never had the skill to bind his men to him.

Out of the wreck La Salle saved but little. Meantime his men were in a turmoil. Under the strain La Salle's health failed, but he kept the work moving, being aided by a most capable lieutenant named Tonti, a notable man in a variety of ways—a man who had placed an iron hand on the end of his arm because his natural hand had been shot away in battle, and who had a will to match the new member thus obtained.

La Salle, being obliged to go back to Ft. Frontenac for more rigging, left Tonti in command. The work went on more smoothly thereafter, for Tonti kept the gang in awe by a free use of his iron fist.

Accordingly, when the ice broke up in the spring

FORT NIAGARA.
Taken from the British side of the river in 1813. This plate illustrates frontier fort building, stockades, block-houses, etc.

of 1679, the new ship—the first ever placed on Lake Erie—was launched, and fitted with the rigging and five small cannon which La Salle brought for her. She carried as a figure head a rudely carved griffin, and she was named the Griffin, because Frontenac's coat of arms bore a griffin.

"La Salle had often been heard to say that he would make the griffin fly above the crows"—would "make Frontenac triumph over the Jesuits." He got the ship ready for her voyage, but he had to tell his company, meantime, that all his property in Canada, including Ft. Frontenac, had been seized by his creditors, who had become frightened by the persistent rumors kept going by his enemies, that the enterprise was visionary, and that La Salle would never return. Those whom he called "the crows" were enemies not to be despised.

Though in a most desperate condition of affairs, La Salle pushed on. A storm on Lake Huron frightened all hands save one, until they all knelt to pray. But the pilot,—wicked, capable sailor that he was—held her nose to the wind and cursed the sniffling mob that grovelled at the foot of an image of St. Anthony of Padua.

A Recollet friar, named Louis Hennepin, was chaplain of the expedition, and its historian. He says he bribed St. Anthony into stilling the tempest, but we will believe that the good salt sea sailor who stood at the helm, brought the Griffin out of the trouble.

La Salle escaped the gale, but only to find more trouble. Mackinac was then the resort of the unlicensed traders and *coureurs-de-bois* who bought and sold where they could. They carried their furs to Albany quite as often as to Quebec; for Dutch rum would exhilerate as well as French brandy, and Dutch maidens were not to be ignored or despised. Moreover furs bought more of the joys of life in Albany than in Quebec.

These reckless woods rangers saw that La Salle would interfere with their Albany trade, and probably with their other trade. With one accord, therefore, they conspired to ruin the trade of the fifteen advance agents of La Salle who had stopped there on their way to the tribes furthest west. And they succeeded well. It was a mission station, but it was also a trading station, and the dwelling place of many Indians. "Brandy and squaws abounded," says an old account. Aided by the Indians the *coureur-de-bois* persuaded several of the fifteen to dispose of La Salle's goods in ways that profited him not a sou. Others took the goods to the wilds and went trading on their own account—stole the goods outright.

La Salle was anxious to return to Ft. Frontenac, and leave Tonti to go ahead and build a fort among the Illinois Indians, but the desertion of these advance agents compelled him to remain with the expedition to reprieve the loss their treachery had brought upon him. So he sailed over to Green Bay, where he found that an unnamed remnant of his fifteen had been faithful, and had collected a "large store of furs."

Encouraged by this good fortune, for the profit on the furs would partly repair his losses, La Salle took four canoe loads of supplies from the Griffin, and loading her with furs sent her back to Niagara, while

THE COURSE OF THE MISSISSIPPI AS SHOWN BY DE LISLE, 1703.

he went forward with the four canoes to build a fort among the Illinois Indians. The Griffin was to bring, for a return cargo, besides ordinary supplies, the rigging for another ship which La Salle purposed building for use on the Mississippi.

On September 18, 1679, the Griffin made sail for the East. La Salle, on the same day, paddled away toward the head of Lake Michigan, and after a journey that was made most woeful by the mutinous conduct of his men, he reached the St. Joseph's river.

Because La Salle's men were always mutinous it may be well to consider here the reason for the trouble. The words of the man, uttered when his friends accused him with harshness, tell the whole story. He said:

"The facility I am said to want is out of place with this sort of people, who are libertines, for the most part; and to indulge them means to tolerate blasphemy, drunkenness, lewdness and a license incompatible with order. The debaucheries, too common with this rabble, are the source of endless delays and frequent thieving; and finally, *I am a Christian, and do not want to bear the burden of their crimes.*"

A chief characteristic of this man is therein portrayed. He was sincere.

On reaching the St. Joseph this much harassed, most unhappy but conscience-clear La Salle found relief in the work of building a fort not far from the modern town of St. Joseph, Mich., near the mouth of the stream. It was the third of the line of forts that he intended to stretch to the mouth of the Mississippi. Others had proclaimed the sovereignty of France—had written a title in the air—but La Salle was taking actual possession, and it was work worth while.

From this fort, named Miami, La Salle went up the St. Joseph to the site of the present city of South Bend, Indiana, where a portage led him to the Kankakee river. It is to be noted that in crossing this portage one of his men tried to shoot La Salle in the back, but was stopped in time.

On January 5, 1680, the party crossed Peoria Lake and found an Indian village where Peoria, Ill., now stands, and with these people—members of the Illinois tribe—La Salle easily made peace.

And yet, though hundreds of leagues from Quebec, La Salle found he was not wholly beyond reach of his enemies in that town. While he negotiated for permission to establish a trading station and build a ship, an emissary of the enemy—a chief known as Monso, with five Miamis, came to the village by night, and told the Illinois that La Salle was a spy of the dreaded Iroquois. And still greater trouble followed, when six of his men deserted, and another gave him a dose of poison.

Nevertheless La Salle persevered. The poison did not kill him. The emissaries of his enemies fled, and he was able to secure the confidence of the Illinois. Then he went to a point below the camp where he found a low hill with a deep ravine on each side, and a marsh, 200 yards wide, between it and the river. There he built a stout palisade fort, with musket-proof houses in the angles for his men. For himself and Tonti he provided tents in the open center of the fort.

Two facts about this fort are remarkable. He

named it Crevecoeur—Broken Heart—and he lived in a tent while he lodged his men in comfortable, musket-proof barracks. Moreover it was the fourth fort in the long line from Montreal.

And it is not to be forgotten that when the fort was done La Salle began the work of building a forty-ton ship for navigating the Mississippi, and he himself, to animate his men, took hold of the back-breaking whip-saw to cut the logs into planks. It was characteristic of the man. By February 1, 1680, the hull of the new ship was half done.

And all this was done in spite of the fact that nothing had been heard from the Griffin, with her precious cargo of furs to be carried down, and her equally precious up-cargo of rigging that was imperatively needed for the new ship. For La Salle had determined not only to load this ship with skins on the Mississippi, but to sail in her to France.

And not only did La Salle keep working on; he sent, on the last day of February, 1680, an expedition to explore the Mississippi from the mouth of the Illinois up, in order that he might learn its resources, and give some of his men the experience necessary to make them pilots.

Michael Accau was in charge of this expedition, and he was assisted by one Du Gay, but the priest Hennepin was sent along to write the account, and he wrote it as if he was the leader.

Hennepin's account occupies much space in the histories of the French in America. But the expedition did little that was more important than to visit and name the falls of St. Anthony. Hennepin described the country, and the Sioux Indians among whom he was a prisoner for a time, but he strove to obtain honors that he had not earned by asserting that he went to the mouth of the Mississippi, and he is now known to have been a most "impudent liar." (Parkman.)

Meantime the Griffin with her cargo of rigging for the new ship did not come. La Salle had hoped for her coming even after the lake froze over, but she had gone where he nor "the crows" would ever see her. Her fate is a mystery. Some think she foundered in a gale, others that Indians captured and destroyed her with all hands, and a few supposed that the pilot ran away with her and tried to carry her cargo to the English at Hudson's Bay. But we will not believe that the salt sea sailor who stood firm at the tiller openly cursing the cowards who grovelled in abject terror—we never will believe that such a man was a traitor. The Griffin foundered, with the pilot standing at the tiller, looking the gale in the eye with full confidence that the God of the gale would do what was right.

Having at last lost all hope of the Griffin, La Salle started (March 1, 1680), with five companions back to get another outfit. In that journey wherein the waters were covered with ice "too weak to bear them and too strong to permit them to break a way with their canoes;" where the temperature was often low enough to freeze their clothing stiff as they emerged from a ford; where they waded day after day through knee-deep crusted snow, there is one memorable fact. La Salle led the way, breaking the path that the journey might be easier for the others. He would never shirk any labor helpful to his purpose. He was, too, a man of such marvelous physical powers that he reached his fort on the Niagara River in good condition, although four of his companions had been obliged to stop by the way, and the last one was left at Niagara while La Salle went on.

La Salle had not only lost the Griffin; a consignment of goods worth 22,000 livres, that was on the way to him from France, was lost, through the stranding of the ship. Worse yet, two *coureurs-de-bois* brought a letter from Tonti (whom he had left in command at Ft. Crevecoeur), saying that all the garrison but four or five men had mutinied, destroyed the fort and stores, and had fled.

Nevertheless La Salle enlisted twenty-five new men, obtained another outfit, and in August, 1680, started again. Having learned that several of the mutineers were coming east by the way of the north shore of Lake Erie, and that they had determined to kill him, if they could meet him, La Salle was careful to meet them. Two of them he killed, and the others he sent as prisoners to Montreal.

Without further incident worth mention La Salle arrived at the point on the Illinois river where Utica now stands; but instead of finding a plain "swarming with wild human life," he found charred remains of burned cabins, and the ground between strewn with the remains of human bodies. Flocks of ravens and buzzards rose, and "wolves in multitude fled," when he landed.

The Iroquois had come, (sent by Jesuit priests,

Parkman says), and failing to capture as many of the Illinois as they hoped, had not only destroyed the huts and caches, but had ravaged the nearby cemetery, to set up the dry skulls on poles and scatter the other bones to the winds.

Tonti, and the faithful four or five could not be found. The hull of the new ship was not destroyed, but all the iron bolts and spikes had been carried away. So La Salle turned back to pass the winter at Ft. Miami, on Lake Michigan.

As a side light on the character of this man La Salle, it must be told that while he was in the midst of his search among the ghastly relics of Iroquois barbarism for traces of his missing friend and companion, night came on and an enormous comet was seen flaming in the sky. The pious Increase Mather of Boston on seeing it "thought it fraught with terrific portent to the nations of the earth," and nearly all men cowered at sight of it; but La Salle "coolly noted down the phenomenon as an object of scientific curiosity."

As a small relief to his ever present burden of disappointment, La Salle found "allies close at hand," during the winter. The Puritans of Massachusetts had fought out King Philip's War, and a band of Abenakis had fled for refuge to the Miamis of the region where Ft. Miami stood. A small village was close at hand. The New England refugees, "with one voice promised to follow La Salle, asking no recompense but to call him their chief, and yield to him the love and admiration which he rarely failed to command from the hero-worshiping race." So says Parkman. Few passages of higher praise can be found in the story of La Salle.

Mississippi Valley.

It is equally honorable to the refugees. But it does not read so well in the story of the Puritans.

A treaty pledging the allegiance of the Miamis to the French interests was easily made, but before La Salle could start again for the Mississippi he was obliged to return still once more to the St. Lawrence "to appease his creditors," and "collect his scattered resources."

"Any one else would have thrown up his hand and abandoned the enterprise; but, far from this, with a firmness and constancy that never had its equal, I saw him more resolved than ever to continue his work," wrote a friend.

La Salle left Ft. Miami at the end of May, 1681, and in due time reached Montreal. There, in spite of two years of disaster, and in spite of debts that bore interest at forty per cent., he once more obtained the means for a voyage. How it was possible for him to do so under the circumstances is worth consideration. The explanation is given in a memoir written by La Salle in 1684, and now to be found in vol. ix. pp. 216-221, "New York Colonial Documents." It is a statement of the profits made in the trade with the Indians. He says:

To drive a profitable trade, 20,000 livres must be expended in France in the purchase of the following assortments:

Five pipes (tonneau) of brandy at the rate of two hundred livres the pipe; five pipes (tonneau) of Wine at 40 li. the pipe; 2,000 ells of blue poitou Serge at 2 li. the ell; 1,000 ells of Iroquois blanketing at 2 li., 10s. the ell; 1,800 white shirts (chemises) at 30 sous; five hundred pairs stockings at 1 li., 5s. the pair; 2,000 pounds of small kettles at 1 liv., 5s. the pound; two hundred pounds of large black glass beads at 10s. the pound; a thousand axes for the trade at 7 and 8 sous the pound; 4,000 pounds of powder at 10 and 12 sous the pound; 7,000 pounds of ball and 3,000 pounds of lead at 120 liv. the thousand; 1,200 guns at 10 liv. each; 2,400 *flattins* at 30 sous the dozen; 100 dozen steels (*Battes-feu*) at 1 liv. 5s. the dozen; 50 dozen of large tinned looking glasses (mirrors fer-blanc) at 1 liv. 10s. the dozen; 50 pounds of vermilion at 3s. the pound; 250 ells of scarlet stuff (*ecarlatine*) at 4 liv. the ell; and 400 pounds of tobacco at 17 sous.

These things, carried to the Indians, will produce as follows:

They get a pint of brandy for a beaver; and consequently, were only two and a half pipes (tonneau) of it sold, allowing the remainder for the expense of the fort and the pay of the soldiers and sailors to whom it is sold at one hundred sous the quart, the ten barrels, retailing to the Indians at the rate of one hundred quarts to the barrel and of four beavers per quart, would produce four thousand beavers, at four livres a piece, or an equivalent in other peltry, which would amount to sixteen thousand livres, and leaves, consequently, fifteen thousand livres profit.

The wine would also serve to pay the expenses of freight and wages at the rate of 40 sous the quart.

The ell of Poitou serge sells for six francs to the Indians, and that of Iroquois blanketing for eight livres, and consequently on these two articles there would be a profit of thirteen thousand livres.

The shirts sell for at least one hundred sous, and the stockings for eight livres, so that on these two articles there is more than four thousand livres gain.

Kettles sell at four francs the pound, and consequently there would be 5,500 livres profit on that article.

Glass beads sell at eight francs the pound, and axes at thirty sous apiece, so that these two articles would leave a profit of two thousand livres.

Powder sells at 40 sous the pound, and lead at twenty sous, which would make on these two articles over thirteen thousand livres.

Guns sell at 24 livres each, and therefore would produce 2,400 liv. more than their cost.

Tobacco sells at eight francs per pound, it would therefore give over 2,000 liv. profit.

On the scarlet stuff (*ecarlatine*), one-half would be gained, which would be worth one thousand livres.

> The profit is proportionably greater on the other articles, such as knives, vermilion, steel, etc.

He showed conclusively that for every franc invested the trade would yield an ecu, or about sixty cents net profit per year, or say, 300 per cent. 'His Canadian supporters were all practical traders—they knew that he was within the facts in this statement of the profits in the trade with the Indians, and they, of course, endorsed it when he sent it to France.

Accordingly, in September, 1681, he was found in the harbor where Toronto now stands, making the portage to Lake Simcoe, in order to go forward via Georgian Bay, and while there he wrote:

"I hope this business will turn out well; for I have M. de Tonti, who is full of zeal, thirty Frenchmen, all good men, without reckoning such as I cannot trust; and more than 100 Indians, some of them Shawanese and others from New England, all of whom know how to use guns."

They were at Ft. Miami in December and on the 21st the party began crossing the south end of the lake to the Chicago river. There, where many things are made in this day, they made sleds on which they placed their canoes and baggage, and dragging these, they passed over the route of the great modern drainage canal, and followed down the frozen Illinois till they found open water in Lake Peoria. Here they embarked and on February 6, 1682, floated out on the broad Mississippi.

It was late in La Salle's day of life, but for a brief time the sun broke through the clouds. For a few days he was to travel with the tide unbuffeted.

On February 24 a landing was made at the Third Chickasaw Bluff, (in the northwestern part of Shelby county, Tennessee), and the party encamped to hunt for game. Here one Pierre Prudhomme was lost in the forest. Signs of Indians had been seen in the vicinity, and because of this fact La Salle with part of his crew built a wooden fort while the others hunted for the lost man. And when he was found at last, his name was given to the fort to commemorate the successful result of the search. This was the fifth fort in the line which La Salle was building between Montreal and the mouth of the Mississippi.

Again La Salle embarked "and with every stage of his adventurous progress the mystery of this vast new world was more and more unveiled." He met the Arkansas and the Natchez Indians, and took possession of their lands with the usual ceremonies, while the Indians looked on with pleasure because they did not comprehend the meaning of the ceremonies.

Then on April 6, 1682, they reached the place where the mighty stream divided itself into three channels and flowed away into the Gulf of Mexico.

For three days the party cruised about the verge of the Gulf and then going to a low dry hillock, on the bank of the river, they erected a wooden column, on which they carved the arms of France, and these words:

Louis le Grand, Rey de France et de Nevarre, Regne:

Le Neuvieme Avril, 1682.

Then in the usual form the whole magnificent basin of the Great River was claimed for the crown of "Louis le Grand," and named Louisiana in his honor.

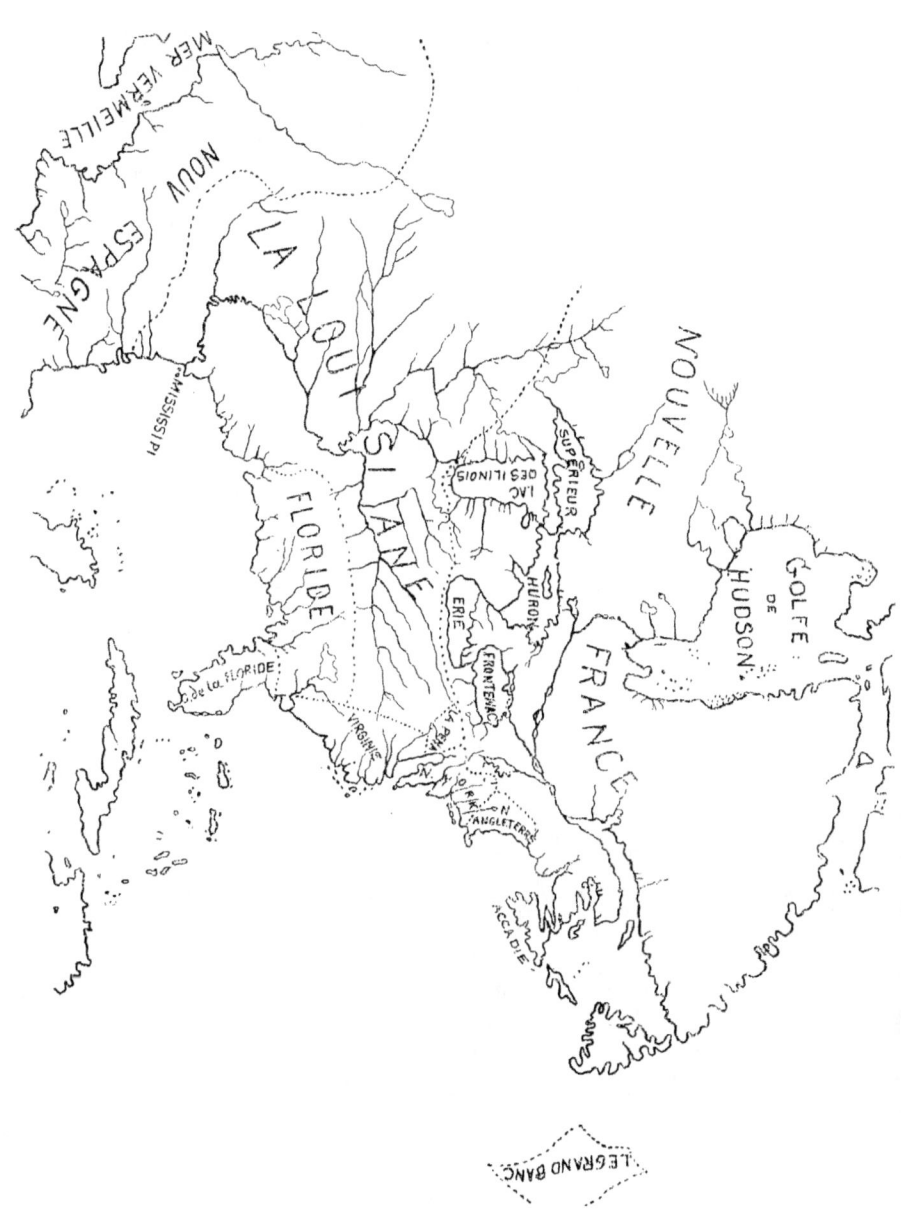

FRANQUELIN'S MAP, 1684.

La Salle had reached the river's mouth. He was the first to explore the land there, and the first to claim the whole watershed of the great river. He had also built a fort on the bank of the river, and another fort on one of the tributaries. By these things done he had filed in the name of France, a good preliminary claim on the whole magnificent valley. From the oil spring in Alleghany County, New York, to the dividing of the waters of Two Oceans Creek in Wyoming; from the Wisconsin lakes where the honking wild goose nested and the Sioux ranged free, to the tide swept marshes of the Gulf of Mexico, Louis the XIV now reigned by virtue of the work of Rene-Robert Cavalier, Sieur de la Salle.

Fortunately for American civilization there was no other Frenchman in America equal to this one, and not from all France, was his equal to follow him to America.

Few words are needed to tell the remainder of the story of La Salle. He returned up the river, and at Starved Rock, on the Illinois, near the modern village of Utica, built another fort which he called St. Louis. It was the sixth of his chain. Here he gathered a colony of Indians of various tribes and granted lands to his followers, as he had a legal right to do. But in the meantime the enemies of the enterprise had succeeded in having Frontenac recalled. A Governor, La Barre, was appointed who antagonized La Salle as much as he could. In desperation La Salle left his colony and went to France.

There "he found himself famous. He, the poor boy, the ignoble by birth, was presented to Louis XIV amid all the splendors of the court. That Jupiter among the Kings of the earth had a smile to bestow upon the humble subject who came to deposit at the foot of the throne the title deeds of such broad domains."

An expedition of four ships was fitted out to make a permanent settlement near the mouth of the Mississippi. There were material for forts, and men for garrisons; materials for plantations and men to work them; a marquis for social elegance and girls to marry the young men—very attractive girls, too, it would seem, for the marquis wanted to marry one of them, later on, in spite of her ignoble birth.

The ambition of La Salle—the one man who stands forever conspicuous in the New France of his day—seemed realized.

Nevertheless the fates had in his hour of triumph, tangled the lines of his life. It was only after much bickering that the expedition sailed. In the West Indies La Salle was stricken with fever, one of his ships was captured by the Spanish and his men were debauched by the buccaneer hordes. Worse yet, when he recovered and sailed on, the squadron overstood the mouth of the Mississippi, and landed in a bay—supposed to be Matagorda—on the coast of Texas.

La Salle was now, at last, fatally enmeshed. A store ship was stranded and lost because her captain persisted in coming into the harbor under sail contrary to orders. There are good reasons for supposing he deliberately wrecked her. Another small store ship was brought into the harbor, but she, too, was lost. The last one, a frigate, sailed away to seek a harbor with sufficient depth of water in which some needed supplies, then stowed down under all, might be broken out, and brought back to La Salle, but she was unable to return.

As theretofore, in the face of every discouragement, La Salle continued to work. He built his fort and planned his settlement. He went exploring to find at what point the great river entered the bay and learned that the river was nowhere in the region. His people were as a whole the scum of Paris. Many died and the living became mutinous. Their clothes wore out and were replaced by others made of the sails of the last ship that was wrecked.

Finally at the end of 1686 it was seen that a journey to France for another outfit must be made, else all would die there in the wilderness, and La Salle determined to go by the way of Quebec. On January 7, 1687, he left his fort with sixteen white men and two Indians, hoping to find his way to the Mississippi, and then by way of the Illinois, where Tonti was yet in command, to the St. Lawrence. He left behind twenty people of whom seven were girls who had come hoping to find husbands and homes in the New World.

The company on leaving France had comprised 100 soldiers. "thirty volunteers including gentlemen," "several families as well as a number of girls," and six priests. Only thirty-seven, all told, were now left, and seventeen of these, in suits made of skins and old sails, were starting on the long journey to Quebec, though they did not know anything about the country between them and the Mississippi, and had only an indefinite idea of the direction.

Until the month of March they struggled on their

way and finally reached the Trinity river. A mutinous spirit had grown steadily, and on March 15, while encamped on the Trinity, some of the men quarreled over marrow bones and other choice bits of two buffaloes killed by a small hunting party that was camped at some distance from the main body. It was a quarrel, naturally, between men who were friendly to the leader and those who were not, and on the night of the 17th of March the friends of La Salle, (three in number, including Nika, an Indian,) were murdered while they slept.

This party should have returned to the main camp on the night of the 17th, and their failure to do so caused La Salle no little uneasiness during the next day. To his Lieutenant, Joutel, a fellow townsman, and the historian of the expedition, La Salle showed a marked "presentiment of what was to take place," as Joutel writes. "He asked me if I had heard of any machinations against them, or had noticed any bad design."

On the morning of March 19, 1687, La Salle started to find the wandering hunters. He took with him Father Anastase Douay and an Indian. On the way "he spoke to me of nothing but matters of piety, grace and predestination; enlarging on the debt he owed to God, who had saved him from so many perils during more than twenty years of travel in America. Suddenly I saw him overwhelmed with a profound sadness, for which he himself could not account. He was so much moved that I scarcely knew him," wrote the priest.

But that feeling passed wholly away when he arrived near the camp of the mutineers. One of them had been placed in view as a decoy while two hid in the grass. The decoy replied "with a tone of studied insolence" when La Salle hailed him.

Full of anger La Salle started forward to punish the scoundrel, but when he was passing the ambushed conspirators they fired, and La Salle fell dead, shot through the brain.

No praise of La Salle is so sincere and emphatic as that of his enemies, unwitting though it has been always. The traders who from the safe shadows of the St. Lawrence forts jeered him; the Jesuits who sent the Iroquois to destroy the Illinois Indians about Fort Crevecoeur; the assassins who shot him from ambush—all these stand forth in history and say:

"There was a man."

For not one of them, nor all combined, ever dared to oppose him, face to face, man fashion.

Six of La Salle's party of seventeen eventually reached Quebec, whence five sailed to France. Two of the three who ambushed La Salle were shot by their companions in a quarrel over the trade goods La Salle had carried, the third lived to reach the Spaniards in Mexico. The remainder of the party were nearly all killed by the Indians, but "Gravier's Voyage" as found in the Jesuit "Relations" (vol. lxv) says that two of them were delivered to the Spaniards and were afterward able to reach "fort Bilocchi." The fort built by La Salle at Matagorda Bay was raided by the Indians, and fourteen out of the twenty that remained in it were killed. Two of these who were spared were the children of a man named Talon, and these eventually reached France.

In all fourteen of La Salle's party are accounted for in the settlements of the French, and of these seven returned to France. All the others died on the way or perished in the wilderness.

JEAN BAPTISTE LE MOYNE, SIEUR DE BIENVILLE.
Governor of Louisiana, 1718.

IV

FROM LA SALLE TO NEW ORLEANS.

Work of a Backwoods Naval Officer—Tales of a Blue Capote, a Piece of Speaking Bark and a Red Tree Trunk—When the Frown of the King's Favorite Sent a Prime Minister Waltzing Into Outer Darkness—The Notable Journeys of Henri de Tonti—A Story of Misplaced Love—Starving, Though Located on the Richest Land in the World—The Founding of New Orleans.

In the journal of the Jesuits for October 26, 1645, is this paragraph:

An order was given at the same time to Monsieur de Chesne, uncle of Charles le Moyne, for 20 ecus, which we were giving his nephew for four years' service rendered among the Hurons. He was clothed and decently supplied with linen, and was sent to Three Rivers as soldier and interpreter.

This Charles le Moyne, then twenty-one years old, is to be remembered here, because he was afterwards the father of fourteen children, "most of whom achieved distinction in military or civil affairs," and among whom were Iberville and Bienville, who gave to France the undisputed de facto possession of the lower end of the vast territory of the Mississippi Valley, to which the work of La Salle had given her the legal right of pre-emption. If Bienville is to be regarded as "the father of New Orleans," Charles le Moyne was its grandfather.

La Salle's plans for settling the lower end of the Louisiana territory did not die with him. Tonti, who remained in command at the fort on Starved Rock, on the Illinois, (a "privileged character," he, and "respected by Indians and whites"), applied in 1694, for a commission to carry on the work, and failed to get it. Two other officers made further application in 1697 without success, but in 1698, when Le Moyne d'Iberville offered to plant a colony in Louisiana, his plans were accepted.

For this youth from the backwoods of Canada had become a noted man. He had entered the French navy, and by good work, had risen, until at the end of the Seventeenth Century he ranked as a post captain. While in command of the frigate Pelican, of but forty-four cannon, he met in Hudson's Bay the British frigate Hampshire, of fifty-two guns, the Daring, of thirty-six guns and the Hudson's Bay of thirty-two— a fleet rated at 120 guns to his forty-four. In spite of the odds, this man, who had been trained in the backwoods of North America, cleared for action, ranged up

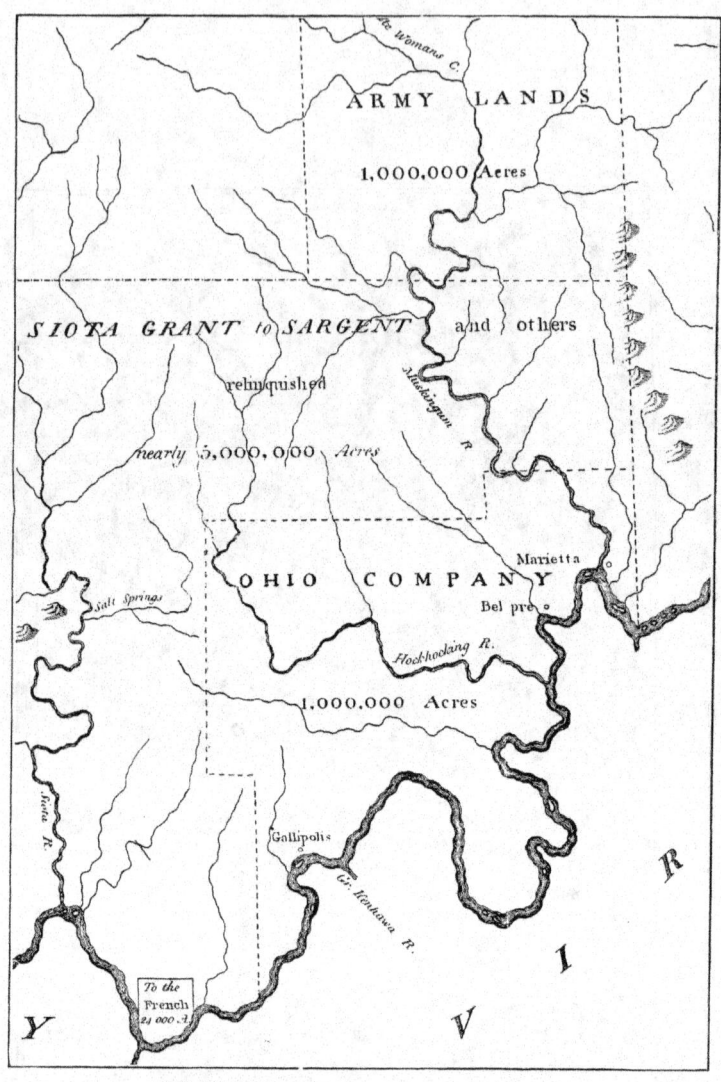

FROM THE MAP OF LEWIS, 1796, SHOWING LAND GRANTS IN OHIO.

Mississippi Valley.

alongside the Hampshire and sank her. Then he captured the Hudson's Bay, and drove the Daring into a flight that belied her name.

The record says the Hampshire sank because of the shot she received between wind and water. Iberville had taught his gunners how to aim their guns, and history shows that naval officers who have done that have achieved, as well as earned, fame whenever opportunity came to them; it shows further that, with rare exception, only naval officers with backwoods experience have fully understood the value of accuracy of aim.

And yet the success of Iberville in obtaining a Louisiana commission but deepens the gloom about the heroic figure of La Salle. For the Le Moyne family had been among the most powerful of his opponents. While La Salle's bones lay scattered on the Texan plain, one of his persistent enemies was to reap where he had, by infinite labor and with life itself, prepared the ground and sowed the seed.

Iberville, in his Louisiana work, had international conditions in his favor. Spain had reached out to settle the Gulf coast, and a company had been formed in London to establish a colony on the Mississippi. A rumor prevailed that a company of Pennsylvanians had settled on the Wabash. The French Government cared very little about the territory for itself, but to prevent its becoming English territory Iberville was sent to colonize it. French jealousy of the English has had much influence on American affairs.

With the war ships Badine and Marin, and a number of transports, Iberville sailed from Brest on

October 24, 1698. On December 4 he arrived at Cape Francois, San Domingo. There he added some buccaneers to his crew, (the notable career of the buccaneers was then just ending), and he was joined by the fifty-gun frigate Francois.

After sailing thence along the south side of Cuba and north past Cape San Antonio, the coast of Florida was seen on January 23, and on the 26th they discovered two Spanish ships in Pensacola harbor. The Spanish "had not been settled [there] for more than three weeks," according to Gravier's Voyage. But the first settlement they made there was in 1696. Leaving the Spaniards unmolested Iberville continued his westward course until, on February 10, he furled sail in what is now the well known road behind Ship Island; and they gave the Island its name because it afforded a safe anchorage.

From this place Iberville and his men went exploring the region in small boats. They found one island well strewn with human bones and named it Massacre Island, but afterwards changed the name to Dauphin. They found another island thickly inhabited by raccoons and named it Cat Island.

On March 2 Iberville's boats rowed into a strong current of fresh muddy water sweeping across the salt sea from among the marshes. Up this current the explorers hastened as well as they could, eventually finding banks more or less firm, and finally some Indians, among whom was one who had a blue hooded cloak. He said a white man had given it to him. At a village of 200 cabins built around a temple, they found a glass bottle left by the man who had owned the blue capote. They saw also a red tree trunk on which the Indians had made rude pictures of a bear and a fish. This red tree marked the boundary between two tribes, and Baton Rouge, (i. e., a red staff or stake used by surveyors) is the name of the city standing where the tree stood.

On returning down the river Iberville sent his younger brother Bienville back by the main stream, and the young man found an Indian who had a piece of "speaking bark." A most wonderful medicine the Indian thought it, but Bienville bought it for a hatchet. It was a letter written by Henri de Tonti to La Salle.

Thirteen years before while in charge of fort St. Louis, on the Illinois, Tonti had heard that La Salle had sailed from France to form a settlement at the mouth of the Mississippi. As soon as possible thereafter he started to visit his friend—to travel in a canoe from Utica, Illinois, to the Gulf of Mexico, in spite of the physical hardships and the hostilities of Indians along the route—that he might make a friendly call on an old comrade. He reached the Gulf while La Salle was struggling in the Fates' mesh on the plains of Texas, but there was no way for Tonti to learn where La Salle was, and after a weary wait, he gave the chief of a near-by Indian village some presents, (among the rest the blue capote), and a letter to be delivered to La Salle whenever the expedition should arrive. It is a picture of early life in the great valley that is worth preserving.

From the Mississippi, Iberville himself returned by the way of Bayou Manchac and Maurepas and Pontchartrain, naming these lakes as he came. Both lakes were named for families that produced prime ministers of France. Some Cyclopedias omit the name of Pontchartrain but all contain that of Maurepas. He was a "nimble old man, who for all emergencies has his light jest; and even in the worst confusion will emerge, cork-like, unsunk," until "fixed in the frost of death," in 1781. His name is "fixed" in the cyclopedias for a number of reasons. He was not only a prime minister of France, but a most capable writer of literature of the class now excluded from the mails. He wrote a description of Madam Pompadour in this vein, and she was so much offended that the king, Louis XV., dismissed him from office. Recalling the conditions prevailing in the court of old France helps toward a comprehension of the history of New France; to see "a lightly-jesting, lightly-gyrating M. de Maurepas" sent waltzing into outer darkness by the frown of the king's favorite explains much—as shall appear in more detail further on. This is not to say that the lake was named for the "nimble old" Maurepas. It was named for his family.

It is well to note here that Iberville's instructions commanded him "to seek out diligently the best places for establishing pearl fisheries." He was also to "look for mines," the finding of which would be "the great business." (Parkman)

Iberville finally settled where Biloxi now stands, choosing that location partly because of the lovely little bay, and partly because the Biloxi Indians (a stray fragment of the great Sioux family), from whom the bay was named, were a very friendly people. "On the east side, at the mouth of the bay, there is a slight swell-

JEANNE ANTOINETTE POISSON, MARQUISE DE POMPADOUR.

ing of the shore, about four acres square, sloping gently to the woods in the background, and on the right and left of which, two deep ravines run into the bay." Here, in April, 1699, the French built a palisaded fort and log houses. Sieur de Sauville, a brother of Iberville, was placed in command, with another brother, Bienville, then a youth of 18, as second, after which Iberville sailed for France to get further supplies and more colonists.

Bienville was then once more sent exploring the region, and he learned soon that the English from the Atlantic coast were in constant communication with the Chickasaw Indians, the most aggressive tribe of the region. The Chickasaws even came to Lake Pontchartrain, soon after the French settled at Biloxi, and with the aid of Englishmen fought a battle with other Indians there. It was an ominous piece of news, exceedingly ominous if considered in connection with the English goods that Joliet had found among the Indians on the banks of the Mississippi during his exploration. The tide of English enterprise had risen so high as to find the passes through and around the Alleghany range of mountains.

A little later Bienville saw some of the English. While floating around the sharp bend of the Mississippi where it passes near to and just west of Lake Borgne he met an English ship commanded by one Louis Bank, (or Bar, as Gayarre writes it). Bank said he was bringing a company of Englishmen and French Huguenots to settle on the Mississippi, and that another detachment of the settlers was coming overland from the sea under the guidance of the Chickasaws. Bienville protested. He said that this river valley had been settled by the French for many years, and that a large force was near at hand. In proof of his assertion he called attention to the fact that he was there roaming about in a row boat. The Englishman blustered a lit-

MOLL'S MAP OF 1710.

tle but turned back to the Gulf; and that bend in the river has been known as the English Turn ever since.

When, in the following December, Iberville returned and heard of this incident he immediately determined to build a fort on the river bank. Leaving Biloxi on this errand on January 8, 1700, he began work on the fort at a spot about 18 miles below the present site of New Orleans—perhaps on the Scarsdale plantation. He named the fort La Boulaye.

While engaged in this work Henri de Tonti came paddling down the river. He was still in command on the Illinois, where he held the privilege of sending two canoe loads of beaver a year to Montreal; but he thought he might find a better market by way of the mouth of the Great River, as La Salle had hoped to do. He had come down to see about the matter. A canoe journey of more than 1,500 miles through the wilderness, in the interest of trade, was no more to him than a ten-mile trolley ride is to a modern commercial traveller.

Iberville and Bienville were so glad to meet their old friend that when he started home, three days later, they went along as far as the village of Natchez Indians, standing where Natchez, Mississippi, is found now. As it happened a thunder storm was raging, when they arrived, and the lighting had just set fire to the temple wherein these Indians worshipped the sun. The Indians were insane with fear and excitement, for they believed the disaster was due to the anger of their god, and to appease him, five infants were thrown alive into the flames, at the commands of the medicine men. The incident seems to have given the Frenchmen a strong prejudice against these Indians.

In the year of 1700 a notable voyage was made on the Mississippi by one La Sueur, a man who had led an adventurous life on the great lakes, and had come to Louisiana with Iberville in December, 1699. With a felucca, a small two-masted coaster, rigged with lateen sails, and a crew of 25 men, he made his way up to Lake Pepin. There he built a fort, killed 400 buffaloes, lived on the flesh all winter, drove a good fur trade with the Indians, and carried back a cargo of earth stained blue with silicate of iron, thinking it a valuable ore. It was this blue earth that gave a name to Blue Earth River. And the Sueur's felucca was the first decked and ship-built vessel to make a voyage on the Mississippi.

In 1701 Iberville moved the larger part of his colony to Mobile Bay (named from a clan of Indians), and placed Bienville in command of the colony, Sauville having died meantime. Settlements had already been made on Dauphine and Ship Islands. The Spanish at Pensacola protested that Florida extended to Mexico, but the matter was referred home to the two Governments, and the Spanish King yielded the land to his uncle, Louis XIV.

As the King's colony these settlements existed until 1712. For about two-thirds of this time Bienville was Governor and was second in command during the remainder of the time. A few extracts from the records will sufficiently portray the ways of life in those days.

In 1705 the arrival of a party of seventeen Canadians is mentioned in the records as a matter of importance because they "came with the intention of making a permanent settlement, and had provided themselves with all the implements of husbandry." All the other settlers had come hoping to get rich quickly and then return to France. It is reasonable to infer that the Canadians raised considerable crops of corn, for in 1706 one of Bienville's despatches says:

Mississippi Valley.

"The males in the colony begin through habit to be reconciled to corn as an article of nourishment; but the females, who are mostly Parisians, have for this kind of food a dogged aversion. Hence they inveigh bitterly against his Grace, the Bishop of Quebec, who, they say, has enticed them away from home under the pretext of sending them to enjoy the milk and honey of the land of promise."

The usual cargo of a ship from France in this period, contained (to quote from the manifest of one of them), "goods, provisions, ammunition; Flesh-pots of France, rivalling, to a certainty, those of Egypt; sparkling wines to cheer the cup; twenty-three girls to gladden the heart; five priests to minister to the soul and to bless holy alliances; two sisters of charity to attend on the sick, and seventy-five soldiers for protection against the inroads of the Indians. This was something to be thankful for." (Gayarre).

As in Canada the Louisiana colony was governed by an Intendant as well as a Governor, the Intendant's chief business being to spy on the deeds of the Governor. In a letter dated December 7, 1706, Intendant Nicolas de La Salle says that the Le Moyne brothers were guilty of "every sort of malfeasances and dilapidations. They are rogues who pilfer away his majesty's goods and effects."

A partisan of Bienville writes that among men "none was better calculated than La Salle to personate the toad. His mission was to secrete venom. Fat, short, sleek, with bloated features and oily skin. * * * Puffed up in conceit, an eternal smile of contentment was stereotyped on the gross texture of his lips."

The Curate de la Vente, the leader of the priests, was opposed to Bienville, and Bienville wrote that La Vente "has tried to stir up everybody against me by his calumnies, and who, in the meantime, does not blush to keep an open shop, where his mode of trafficking shows that he is a shrewd compound of the Arab and the Jew."

Even one of Bienville's own family helped to stir up strife. A nephew, Major Boisbriant, fell in love with the lady who was in charge of the girls brought out, at the King's charge, to marry colonists. She returned his passion, but Bienville refused to allow them to marry, on the ground that the lady was of a lower social rank. Thereupon the lady wrote the story of her woes to the Colonial Secretary, and ended it by saying: "It is therefore evident that he has not the necessary qualifications to govern this colony."

It was in the condition of things that the troubles with the Indians should be never ending. The colony was weak in numbers. There were but 279 people all told in 1708—and yet they were full of arrogance in dealing with the Indians. The Chickasaws, being allies of the English, were steadfast enemies. The Choctaws, as enemies of the Chickasaws, were encouraged to go hunting both Chickasaws and English, but their friendship was not always to be trusted. The Alibamons (from whom Alabama was named), though nominally at peace, frequently waylaid and murdered the French for the sake of the plunder. And when they heard the French boast of the greatness and power of the French King, these redmen asked with unconcealed contempt, how it happened then that this great king did not send soldiers to avenge the many murderous aggressions under which the colony had suffered. "The very existence of the colony is daily threatened by the Indians," says one account.

But a worse picture than that remains. In 1709 provisions became so scarce that the colonists were reduced to a diet of acorns, and Bienville reported that he had been obliged to send half his soldiers among the Indians because he could not obtain enough food for them in any other way.

For ten years these people had been in the country. They had come there not merely to man forts but to people the region—to create a new French empire. They were at the gateway of the most wonderful farming region of the world—a valley that can readily support 200,000,000 people. And yet here they were in more desperate straits than the Indians whom they despised.

Few words suffice to tell of the actual work in the interior of the great valley by the French people. Late in 1702, Juchereau, of Montreal, established a fur-buying station near, if not exactly, where Cairo, Ill., now stands. He helped to make a profit from copper and lead ores that had been found not far away. In the course of two years he built a tannery, made some leather, shipped out a few furs and accumulated a stock of 30,000 buffalo skins. Then he fled through fear of the Indians, (whom he had wronged, no doubt), leaving the huge store of skins to waste.

Some prospectors went up the Missouri river, in 1705, and built a small fort above the Ossages, but it was afterward abandoned. Explorers went above the Natchitoches on the Red River. The *coureurs de bois* from the upper lakes region, in some numbers, brought their furs to Mobile, but Bienville himself describes them as Canadian vagabonds leading a wandering and licentious life among the Indians, rather than additions to the new settlements. The indefatigable Tonti came to live at Mobile, but soon (1702) died of the yellow fever. In short it was, as a whole, a colony of paupers.

Finding that his politicians were unable to make the colony self-supporting the King, on September 14, 1712, turned it over to Anthony Crozat, a wealthy merchant who undertook the task of managing it on business principles for fifteen years.

Crozat was to have the exclusive privileges of the Louisiana trade, all mines of precious metals to be discovered were his on payment of a royalty of one-fourth of the yield; he was permitted to import one ship load of negroes per year; the King was to pay $10,000 a year toward the expenses of the garrison, for nine years. In return Crozat was to send out "two ship loads" of colonists a year, and pay all the expenses above the King's contribution.

La Mothe Cadillac, who, for a number of years had been the governor of Detroit, (at which point the French located on July 24, 1701), was made governor of Louisiana, where he arrived May 17, 1713. The instructions from Crozat to Cadillac were brief in substance, if multitudinous in words. He was to search "diligently" for mines, and to open a trade with Mexico—with the consent of the authorities, if that were

Mississippi Valley.

possible, but without it if they refused. He was to trade with the Indians, also, of course.

From the settling of Biloxi, the French had traded

A SECTION OF JOUTEL'S MAP, 1713.

with the Spanish of Pensacola, contrary to law, but now smuggling was to be part of the business commanded by the ruler of Louisiana.

The population at this time, it is said, included one hundred soldiers, seventy-five Canadians in the pay of the King, twenty negro slaves and 300 plain citizens, who were much scattered, owing to the famines that had prevailed.

Cadillac wrote a frank description of his colony, on January 1, 1714, saying, as quoted by Gayarre: "The inhabitants are the scum and refuse of Canada; ruffians who have thus far cheated the gibbet of its due; vagabonds who are without subordination to the laws, without any respect for religion or the government; graceless profligates who are so steeped in vice that they prefer the Indian females to French women. * * * But what shall I say of the troops, who are without dicipline, and scattered among the Indians at whose expense they subsist?"

To learn the ways of life under this commercial regime we need only read the complaints of Governor Cadillac, as set forth in his despatches. He quarrelled with the soldiers because they were "without discipline," and with their officers because they refused to apply to the priests for the holy sacrament, "even at Easter." "He complained bitterly of one officer, Capt. Richebourg, of the dragoons, (an officer who came to the colony in the ship with Cadillac) because he "seduced most of the girls" sent over by the King to become wives of the colonists. These girls, Cadillac says, very justly, "ought to have been respected," but he quarrelled with them also, on arrival, because they did not at once find husbands. He says they were left on his hands because of Richebourg, but Duclos, the commissary, whose despatches also show an all-absorbing interest in this matter, wrote that the girls were "so ugly that the inhabitants are in no hurry to take them."

Then came the priests who "insisted" that he expel out of the colony two women of bad character. "I have refused to do so," he wrote, "because if I sent away all women of loose habits there would be no females left, and this would not meet the views of the government. Besides, one of these girls occupies the position of a servant in the household of the King's commissary, who will, no doubt, reclaim her from her vicious propensities."

There is but one reason, of course, for making these quotations from the official despatches. It is to show clearly the character of these so-called settlers and their habits of thought while engaged in founding a French empire in America.

However, Cadillac did try to open trade with Mexico. In the voyage which Iberville made to Louisiana, in 1699, he brought an adventurous youth named Juchereau de St. Denis. After his arrival, St. Denis was a good soldier. He obeyed orders; avoided the ever present disputes between those over him as much as possible; made friends with the Indians, and went exploring the region west of the Mississippi, especially along the Red River.

In 1714, Cadillac sent him to Mexico. He went up the Red River as far as the Natchitoches, and thence struck out on the route to the Spanish settlements lying along the Rio Grande, where he arrived in August. It was an eminently successful expedition, for St. Denis. He fell in love with the daughter of the Spanish Governor, was arrested as a smuggler, refused splendid offers to enter the Spanish service, escaped from prison, served as peacemaker between the frontier Spaniards and plains Indians, married the lovely senorita, and returned safe to the French settlements. A subsequent expedition made by St. Denis was not so fortunate even for him. He barely escaped from Mexico with his life. Every sou of Crozat's money spent in the two expeditions was lost, and large quantities of goods sent out in anticipation of a successful smuggling business were wasted.

The search for mines had a similar result. As a rule Cadillac employed *coureurs de bois* as prospectors, and they proved to be the fore-runners of the "grub stake eaters" of modern days. They accepted their supplies of food and instruments, and going to some favorite Indian village gave their goods to their friends, and remained there until the time came to report progress, when they returned to Cadillac for further supplies.

Lead ore was found in southeastern Missouri. The lead and zinc mines in Missouri have been, and are now, the source of immense wealth. The French began working the "prospect" and established a supply station for the miners, but they were incapable of making the ore profitable.

Crozat's commercial agents did something in the way of establishing trading stations. Natchez, Mississippi, and Nashville, Tennessee, have grown where trading stations were built in 1714. In 1717 Cadillac sent a force to occupy the land of the Natchitoches Indians, on Red River, and in 1719 Bernard de la

Harpe built Fort St. Louis de Carlorette near where Natchitoches now stands.

Before Cadillac's time (in 1700), a mission for the Illinois Indians had been established where Kaskaskia, Ill., now stands. It was in 1717 a considerable settlement. Under the influence of the priests ploughs had been introduced, windmills erected and horsepower tread-mills constructed.

Crozat finding no returns even from the trade in furs, which lesser merchants had found so profitable, remonstrated, and Cadillac replied:

"What! Is it expected that for any commercial or profitable purpose boats will ever be able to run up the Mississippi, into the Wabash, the Missouri, or the Red River? One might as well try to bite a slice off the moon."

One quotation from the despatches will suffice for Cadillac's Indian policy. He wrote:

"I have persuaded the brother of the great chief of the Choctaws to kill his sovereign, and brother, pledging myself to recognize him as his successor. He did so and came here with an escort of 100 men. I gave him presents and secured from him an advantageous peace."

On June 22, 1716, Cadillac wrote a despatch saying:

"Decidedly this colony is a monster without head or tail, and its government is a shapeless absurdity." The minister of the colonies department, for a reply, added a postscript to a letter from Crozat, saying:

"The Governor, La Mothe Cadillac, and the commissary, Duclos, whose intellects are not equal to the functions with which His Majesty has instructed them, are dismissed from office."

On August 13, 1717, Crozat, having concluded that his intellect was not equal to the task of managing Louisiana on business principles, surrendered his contract to the King.

John Law, with his wondrous schemes of finance, then took hold of the colony through what he called the Mississippi company. Law at 23 years of age, fled for his life from England. By his love for deep play and his gallantries "he had squandered a fortune." In a duel he had killed a man—unfairly, it is presumed,—for he was tried, convicted and sentenced to be hanged, on a charge of murder. On the continent he introduced the game of faro, and won large sums—more than 2,000,000 francs, it is said. He established a private bank in Paris, (May, 1716), that received Government support. Louis XIV. had died on Sept. 1, 1715. Louis XV. was then a child of five years, and the Duke of Orleans ruled as Regent. Louis XIV. had left France with a debt of 80,000,000 livres, while the new ruler could, at best, raise 9,000,000. Law proposed solving the difficulty of paying eighty millions with nine by issuing notes based on the real estate of the nation—a million in paper money for every two millions assessed valuation of the real estate. The scheme was accepted. There was soon an abundance of "money" in the nation. Prices rose steadily; with each issue of "money" prices rose in geometrical ratio. Fortunes were made in a day. Law became such a favorite with the Regent that he "was admitted into all the licentious privacies of the Palais Royal."

LOUIS XV., KING OF FRANCE.

Mississippi Valley.

On September 6, 1717, when his schemes were dazzling all France, he floated the Mississippi company. This company was to develop the boundless resources of the great valley—to take up the work in which Crozat had failed. The valley was to be peopled; a great commerce between it and France created; the smuggling trade with Spanish-America was to be promoted; mines of gold and silver were to be discovered and many of those of the Spanish were to be appropriated, while the fur trade, already established, was to be greatly enlarged. And all this for the benefit of Law's bank. England had, just then, a South Sea bubble. That company (it was established in 1710), did not fail until 1720, and it was therefore reaching its greatest reputation when Law floated his Mississippi scheme. Law was familiar with the plans successfully used by the South Sea Company to "boom" their shares, and his Mississippi company was managed in much the same way.

Pamphlets were distributed setting forth the wonders of the Mississippi Valley. The deposit that could be filtered from the water of the river yielded gold in immense quantities, said these pamphlets, and bars alleged to be of this gold were placed in the shop windows of Paris. The liquid found in the cup of a certain flower, in Louisiana, turned to a diamond in a single night, at a certain season, and diamonds from these flowers, as alleged, were also on exhibition.

Men of money fought for place in the line when the books of the Mississippi company were opened for subscriptions.

For a time, too, people—especially those of broken

fortune, and all who were of undue greed—flocked to the company's ships that were sent to the Mississippi; but this human tide began to ebb within a year; for they learned the truth, on landing, of course, and they found means to tell the facts in France where their stories of hardship were exaggerated as much as the real productiveness of the region had been.

Then the company, under due license, resorted to press gangs to fill the necessary quota of emigrants. These gangs swept the beggars from the streets, the tramps from the highways, the vile from the houses of correction. With these were taken some whose sole offence was the mistake of having offended people of influence, while others were carried to the shipping ports in order to extort blackmail.

In spite of these frauds and outrages, however, some real work was done in Louisiana. Even John Law, though a thief and a murderer, was to leave his mark on the Mississippi River.

When Law's company took charge of Louisiana, Bienville, who was really the only man of notable ability in the colony, was made governor once more, and his first work under his new commission was to be of lasting importance to the Mississippi Valley.

The fort built by Iberville on the bank of the Mississippi had been abandoned. Bienville had wished to build a new one at a point higher up the river, while Cadillac ruled, but Cadillac refused permission. Now Bienville could do as he pleased, and the new fort was at once planned.

The point at which he determined to build is of special interest. In his travels through the neighborhood Bienville had observed that two bayous running from Lake Pontchartrain were "navigable by small sea-going vessels to within a mile of the bank of the

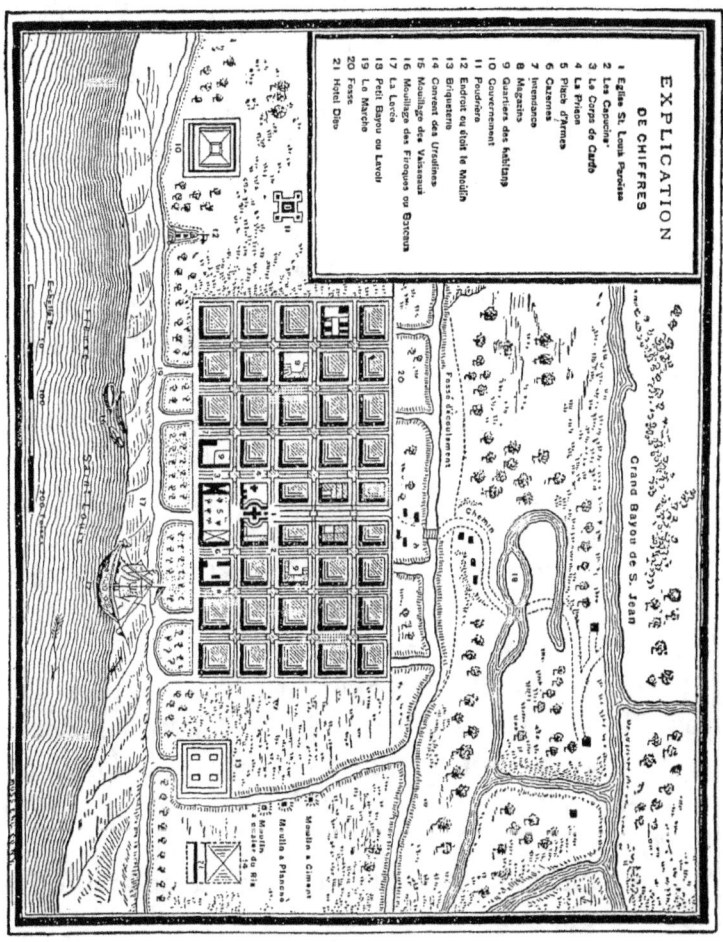

NEW ORLEANS 1728.

Mississippi." There was an Indian portage from one of these bayous to the great river. Bienville had passed his youth in Canada—he saw that a trading station built where this trail reached the Mississippi would have communication with all points on the Great River and its tributaries, and at the same time, would, by the back door of Lake Pontchartrain, reach with equal ease the region to the east. A fort there would command the river, and, in a way, Lakes Pontchartrain and Maurepas, and the waters beyond.

On an unnamed day in February, soon after the arrival of his commission, Bienville sent "twenty-five convicts, and as many carpenters, with some *voyageurs* from the Illinois," to the river end of that portage trail. A narrow strip of dry land was found there. It lay about ten feet above the ordinary stage of the river surface, but had been formed by deposits of sediment made when the river was flooding high. This bank was plainly subject to overflow, and the slope toward the lake reached the swamp level a mile back of the river. But Bienville was willing to risk the damage that extra high water might do, and the convicts and carpenters he sent there, cleared away the moss-covered trees and underbrush.

Then they built on the height of land a straggling row of houses having log walls that were not snake proof, bark roofs that were not rain proof and chimneys—fire places—made of sticks plastered over with thick masses of clay. And to these shelters came "three companies of infantry and a small body of colonists," on March 9, 1718.

In such fashion was the great city of New Orleans founded.

LOUIS XIV., KING OF FRANCE.

V

INDIANS OF THE MISSISSIPPI VALLEY.

The Pathetic Story of a Race of Children Who Were Taken from Their Play and Set at the Work of Butchers and Scalp Hunters—Indian Motives Compared with Those of the Whites—Story of a Kansas Real Estate Agent and Charlie Quapaw—The Moravian and the Quaker Methods of Treating Indians Considered—The Most Important Statement in This Book.

With the founding of the city of New Orleans the movement which was to people the valley of the Mississippi with the white race and displace the red men, was fully begun. For while Father Gravier was making ploughs and horse-power tread-mills at Kaskaskia, and Bienville was working after a fashion at New Orleans, the British colonies were spreading to the Alleghanies. Gov. Spotswood of Virginia, with fifty followers, "Knights of the Golden Horseshoe," and "an abundant variety of liquors" went (1716) to the crest of the Blue Ridge, where with his eyes to the west "he took possession of this place, in the name and for King George the First, drank the King's health in champagne, and fired a volley." From this height, or some other, he saw that "the British plantations are surrounded." The French are in position, he said, not only to "engross the whole skin trade," but to "send such bodies of Indians on the back of these plantations" as might "greatly distress his Majesty's subjects here."

The remedy for these well-seen evils was to form settlements beyond the range, and in saying so Gov. Spotswood voiced the sentiment of nearly all the thinking people in the British colonies.

Therefore mighty hosts were to gather, later on, at the passes of the Alleghanies—mighty, if few by count, and sometimes not well ordered. The volley which Spottswood fired while on the crest of the Blue Ridge, though fired with powder only, and heard no further west than the springs that fed the Shenandoah, —was in a way the first in the conflict that drove the foolish cackling French from their stations in the Great Basin, and with many whirligigs of dust and smoke, swept the red nations into the refuse heaps, unpleasant enough to look at, that we call reservations.

It seems necessary, therefore, to stop here and consider what manner of men these Indians were originally; what influence the white men had upon their character; what rights they had in the land, and in what ways and how far their rights were violated.

In the days between Champlain's battle on the outlet of Lake Champlain, (1610), and the founding of the city of New Orleans, (1718), the important families or "linguistic stocks" of Indians occupying the Mississippi Valley were the Algonquian, the Siouan, the Iroquoian, the Muskhogean and the Cadoan. They covered the whole region save only for six spots, relatively very small, that were occupied by small communities, having languages of their own, the remnants, very likely, of ancient tribes that had been reduced to insignificance by the inexorable law of the survival of the fittest.

The location of these families are shown at a glance in a map prepared by Major J. W. Powell ("Linguistic Stocks of American Indians North of Mexico").

Of the different tribes into which the families were divided, some account may be given here. Along the Alleghanies were the Cherokees, Chickasaws, Choctaws and Creeks, though the Creeks were mainly found in what is now Georgia, and had an offshoot in Florida, called Seminoles. In 1785 they were supposed to number 70,000 souls. The Cherokees were Iroquoian, the others Muskhogean. One writer believes there were 9,500 warriors among the Southern Indians.

Northwest of the Ohio, in the 18th century, were the Shawanees, Delawares and Miamis, of Algonquian stock, with the Wyandots, (a remnant of the old Hurons), and as years passed, many of the Iroquois confederation who were here called Mingos. Mingled with these, when the whites came to the Ohio, were individuals from further west—Pottawattomies, Ottawas, Chippewas and Foxes. Andrew McFarland Davis, of the American Antiquarian Society, estimated, (Winsor's "History of America"), that "there were about 35,000 warriors east of the Mississippi, in the United States and across the straits at Detroit," at the time of the war of the Revolution. The Shawnese, at that time, had about 300 warriors, the Delawares 600 and the Wyandotts 200—all northwest of the Ohio. The Iroquois had 2,000 warriors. What was known as the "Ottawa Confederation"—a loose aggregation of western tribes—had 8,000 warriors, of whom 3,000 lived near Detroit," (Winsor).

Most interesting is a study of the characteristics of the red people as they existed before they came in contact with white men. Let the reader who is not familiar with the matter forget what his school histories taught him, put aside his prejudices, whatever they may be. Above all let him put aside for the present what the men who have lived among modern Indians have to say about them. Parkman, for instance, thought he had learned the characteristics of the *aborigines* by living among a tribe that had been trading with white men for more than 200 years. Let the judgments of such men be put aside, and then consider what the scientific ethnologists have learned and printed, after long and patient labor, about the American aborigines. The reader who has seen the modern Indian and like Parkman, has lived among them, should be especially careful not to allow prejudice to influence him. For it has been shown that the dog soup, dirt and carnivorous insects of the wigwam and tepee almost invariably prejudice a clean man's mind so that he is incapable of rendering a fair judgment.

Mississippi Valley.

Scientific investigation has learned first of all that it was not a roaming or nomadic people. It is true that a party of the Siouan people had gone away from the original family home to settle at Biloxi. Another party had become Catawbas living on the east side of the Alleghanies. The Shawnees had lived in various localities. But these were migrations of sedentary people,—migrations due to family quarrels—and were not the wanderings of nomads. The nearest approach to a nomadic life was found on the plains where such tribes as the Pawnees followed migratory herds of buffalo for limited distances.

Being sedentary, the tribes were, as a whole, developing into agriculturalists—becoming farmers. "They were fast progressing from the hunter state," says Powell in "Indian Linguistic Families." Corn was the chief of their cultivated foods. In the Jesuit "Relations" one of the missionaries speaks of a Huron chief who had two caches of corn, each containing 125 bushels. That was in Canada. In the south the corn crop reached tens of thousands of bushels.

More notable still some of the Indians were on the threshold of taming wild animals for domestic use. The Creeks of each village refrained from hunting over certain tracts of land where products of the forest relished by bears, abounded, until the bears there became both fat and tame. Then when meat was needed a bear was quietly killed. Precautions were taken to keep the bears tame, that is to say, and the range well stocked.

To say that the tribes were sedentary implies that they had dwellings of more or less substantial character. The Iroquoians and other northern tribes built great shelters of poles covered with bark. The Dacotah Sioux covered the poles with buffalo skins. The Pawnees built houses with sod walls. The Natches and the Quapaws built houses with a latticed frame covered with adobe clay. The Cherokees and Muskhogean built good log houses. It is a right curious fact that the red men learned to build thick dirt walls to keep out heat before they learned to use such walls to keep out cold.

Of the Indian canoes and dugouts as means of transportation only mere mention seems necessary.

The Indian had developed the art of making pottery, baskets and cloth. They made sufficient tools of stone, shells and wood. Some that had native copper had learned to beat it into ornaments with a skill that the whites who first came to America were unable to surpass. They had, indeed, begun to develop the higher talent of the artist and they had made the first steps toward a written language.

There is, perhaps, nothing more interesting in the story of the red American than the few facts we know about their culture of the higher faculties—their groping after something that was not a necessary of life.

Consider their first steps in the development of a written language. One may presume that their attempts to write out ideas grew out of their sign language, or were suggested by it. And it is not difficult to think that the sign language was developed before articulate speech.

Many ideas were conveyed by movements and

postures of the body—by living pictures, that is to say. A Dacotah standing on one bank of a river saw strangers on the further side and held aloft his left hand to ask, "Who are you?" And one of the strangers put two fingers of each hand up above his head in a way to suggest the sharp, peaked-up ears of the wolf, and thus replied, "We are wolves—Pawnees."

From making these living pictures it was but a short step, easily taken, to the painting or carving of pictures that would convey ideas. They had learned to paint and carve some pictures of their sign language on their pottery, on wood and on smooth stones. Most remarkable are some of the rock carvings that are yet to be found along the Mississippi and its branches. Pictures of men, beasts, birds, reptiles and insects abound. With these are found pictures of the tracks of men and animals, and of figures and lines oft repeated that represent nothing to our minds.

Many essays and books have been written about the picture writing of American Indians—works that usually describe rather than explain the Indian pictures—but some advance in comprehending this red literature has been made by the scientific specialists. Says Mr. James Mooney, (Seventeenth annual report Bureau of Ethnology):

"It is known that our own tribes had various ways of depicting their mythology, their totems, or isolated facts in the life of individual or nation, but it is only within a few years that it was even suspected that they could have anything like *continuous historical records*, even in embryo.

"*The fact is now established*, however, that pictographic records, covering periods of from sixty to perhaps 200 years or more, do or *did exist among several tribes*, and *it is entirely probable that every leading mother tribe had such a record of its origin and wanderings,* the pictured narrative being compiled by the priests and preserved with sacred care through all the shifting vicissitudes of savage life, *until lost or destroyed in the ruin that overwhelmed the native governments at the coming of the white men."*

Time was when all of these tribal histories might have been gathered, or copies made. The white men might have learned exactly what ideas the Indians intended to convey when making some of the noted pictures now called petrographs. For when the first missionaries and the first traders went among the Indians the art of stone writing was at its best. But because Indian art work or culture was commonly found in connection with Indian religion, our missionaries were shocked by the "idolatrous exhibits," and strove in earnest, well-meaning fashion, to turn the Indian thoughts from pictured totems, and dreams of happy hunting grounds, to a conception of a cubical city built of jewel stones, and having streets paved with gold.

As for the traders who might have learned something about this latest development of Indian culture—this picture writing—it is enough to say that the one thought constantly animating their minds was to exchange a pint of rum, or six cents' worth of red paint, for a beaver skin worth ten dollars in the white settlements. The poet-naturalist of Concord wrote that "trade curses everything it handles," and no men in the history of civilization and commerce have been so fully engrossed or so utterly degraded and deeply cursed by their trade as those who have dealt with the aboriginal inhabitants of the earth. With them even a thought of fair dealing was, (and is), a manifestation of contemptible weakness; the ability to over reach the *sauvage* was the only feature of mind worth praise or cultivation.

In short, through egotistical prejudice and foul greed, we threw away—refused to gather—the full knowledge of how men in the stone age of the world began to develop their higher faculties.

Nevertheless some knowledge remains. A glance at the arrow heads with notched edges; at the baskets and pottery, illuminated with the lightning flashes from the thunder god, and at the ornaments of beaten copper, shows unmistakably that a love of the beautiful was growing among them, and that many of their products portrayed the joy of the artist in his work.

Consider next the subject of aboriginal warfare. It is in connection with this subject that one needs to forget what his school histories teach him. Says Major Powell in "Indian Linguistic Families"; (p. 39):

"Altogether the character of the Indian since the discovery of Columbus *has been greatly changed,* and *he has become far more war-like and predatory.* Prior to that time, tribes seem to have *lived together in comparative peace,* and to have *settled their* difficulties *by treaty methods.* Their accumulations were not so great as to be tempting, and their modes of warfare were not exceedingly destructive. * * * *Battle for plunder, tribute and conquest was almost unknown.* Such intertribal wars as occurred originated from other causes, such as infractions of rights relating to hunting grounds and fisheries, and still oftener prejudices growing out of their superstitions."

For the sake of emphasis let this be repeated.

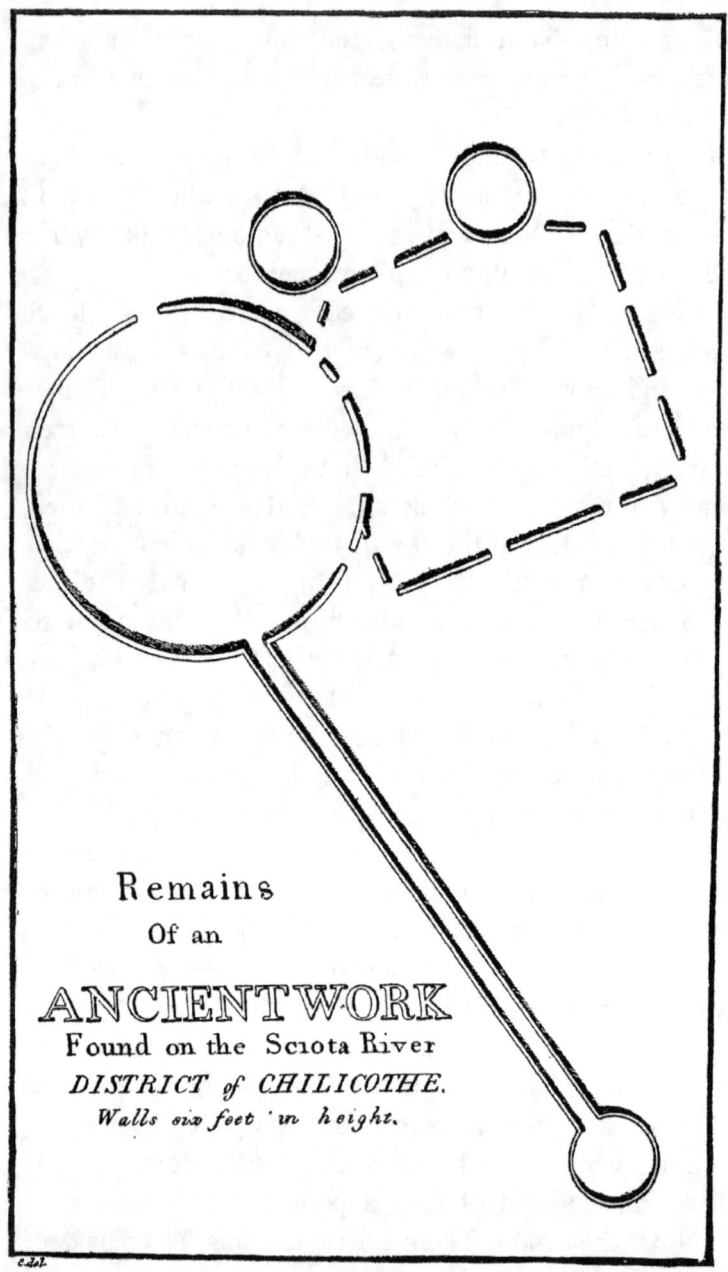

Although the red men "had not yet entered completely into the agricultural condition," they "were fast progressing from the hunter state." "Battles for plunder, tribute and conquest were almost unknown."

War never was and never will be advantageous to mankind as a whole, however necessary at times between nations; but for the red men such wars as occurred before the whites came were not an unmixed evil. For they fought hand to hand, or at close range; they fought for the love of their country and for glory. Thus they learned to face death with unruffled minds, and to covet something higher than physical wealth.

Then, too, through wars they built fortifications—they became mound builders, though their mounds were also erected for the purpose of worship. Many earthen forts were found in the Mississippi valley, and we know, now, that it was not some prehistoric tribe of superior intelligence that built them. Nothing proves the white man's lack of intelligent observation so conclusively as does this now abandoned notion about a prehistoric tribe of superior attainments.

Consider one of these Indian fortifications—that one built where Marietta, Ohio, now stands. There was one square fort, fifty acres in extent (one authority says forty), and another twenty-seven, (or twenty) large. The walls were from twenty to thirty feet wide on the base when surveyed. It is fair to presume that these earth walls were originally surmounted by palisades, for wooden forts were common enough.

There were other works of less extent, in and near these two, including elevated mounds within the squares, a guarded passage way, 680 feet long, to the

Muskingum river, a well-protected cemetery, an enclosed field, a large camp ground, &c.

At least ten thousand cubic yards of earth were piled into the walls of the passageway that led down the hillside toward the Muskingum, and how many thousands in the remaining walls need not now be calculated. What should be considered is the fact that the Indians had neither shovels nor wheel barrows when they built these walls. How many days, therefore, did they labor in digging the earth with their rude tools and carrying it up by hand to build those walls? And yet we have been told in our school histories that the Indian was by nature lazy!

Huge mounds were built for graves, as well as for war. The structure that gives its name to Moundsville on the Ohio, is as interesting as any. It is one hundred feet in diameter at the base, sixty-eight feet high and fifty-five in diameter at the top. The mound was tunneled at the surface of the earth, in 1838, and a shaft was sunk from the top down to the tunnel. Thirteen skeletons, with shell beads, copper rings and plates of mica for ornaments, were found in two vaults that had been lined and covered with timbers.

It is evident that the Indian would work when he had a motive that he considered adequate, but his motives were not always those of the whites. The white man who turned the tunnel in Moundsville mound into a lager-beer saloon, some years ago, was, doubtless, animated by some motives which the red builders of the mound could not have comprehended. And that white man undoubtedly held the entire red race in contempt.

We have now arrived at what really is the red

man—that is, at the *motives that inspired him to action;* for all men should be judged, at last, by their aspirations.

To learn what the Indian motives were, consider first that every red settlement was literally a community, especially in the food supply. "The hungry Indian had but to ask to receive * * * it was *his right to demand"* a share.

"Indiscriminate hospitality" followed. We see herein one feature of Indian life that attracted many white men. The white visitors might eat, even though they could not provide food for themselves or others. With men of the habits of thought of the white race, this "indiscriminate hospitality" would, and does, destroy industry and thrift. Free food at the kitchen door adds to the number of tramps. It is believed by some philosophers that the selfish love of money—the desire to get rich—is all that sustains the push of enterprise.

But among the Indians, game was killed and shared, corn was cultivated and shared, and clothing, tools and weapons were made and shared, year after year, without pauperizing the race. The race made progress, in fact, in spite of the influence of a custom that would, it is alleged, pauperize the white race.

How did it happen, then, that work was done, and progress achieved without the spur of greed? Says Powell: "The peculiar institutions prevailing in this respect gave to each tribe or clan a profound interest in the skill, ability and industry of each member. He was the most valuable person in the community who supplied it with the most of its necessities. For this reason the successful hunter or fisherman *was always held in high honor,* and the woman who gathered great store of seeds, fruits or roots, *was one who commanded the respect and received the highest approbation of the people.*

A desire for honor among his people was the chief motive that inspired the Indian. And the Jesuits in their "Relations" tell of Indians who, in the pursuit of game, continued the chase until death from exhaustion overtook them. *For the sake of standing well in his community the Indian would sometimes work till he died.* For killing game was unquestionably work with the Indians; it required much more strength and endurance than digging ditches or building forts.

But the common motive of the white man made no appeal to him.

A Kansas real estate dealer was once good enough to go with the writer of this chapter into the Quapaw reservation. There, as it happened, we met Quapaw Charlie, the Indian chief. And as the real estate dealer and the Indian looked at each other, a feeling of contempt, deep and unrestrained, appeared in the face of the white man, and found expression in his words. That Indian had a thousand acres of the fattest land of America. If he would but cultivate it he might sell the produce for $5,000 a year, clear profit, and rapidly accumulate those evidences of wealth for which the white race strives. But there he lived in a little log hut with its acre or two of corn and vegetables. He killed rabbits, quails and prairie chickens, now and then, and he often fished in the nearby stream;

Mississippi Valley.

but his food was coarse and his clothing worse. The Kansas man did not believe God meant that such beings should cumber the earth.

But while the Kansas man talked the Indian gazed back at him with a feeling of contempt equally deep and hearty. The Kansas man had been "booming" a townsite. He had been working day and night. His eyes were red from lack of sleep. His hands trembled from nervous exhaustion. The "boom" had "gone broke." Rest and peace were words but dimly understood by this feverishly energetic man of business. Could he have come into the possession of Charlie Quapaw's acres he would have obtained less comfort from them than the Indian did, for he would have surveyed a town site immediately, and started another "boom," with all its deadly nervous exhaustion.

Quapaw Charlie was not condemned by this white man for failing to use his abundant leisure in the study of literature, or the study of art, or the study of nature. He was not condemned for any ill use of leisure. He was condemned for having leisure. Why didn't he plow and sow and reap from sun to sun, and do the chores by lantern light? That was the query of the indignant man from Kansas.

The bald truth is that the Indian's habit of thought was in exact accord with the Christian precept which says; "Having food and raiment be ye therewith content." And he used some of his abundant leisure in ornamenting his weapons, and in making petrographs.

The Indian government was, perhaps, the loosest bond that ever held peoples together. It was a simple democracy so far as it was like anything called govern-

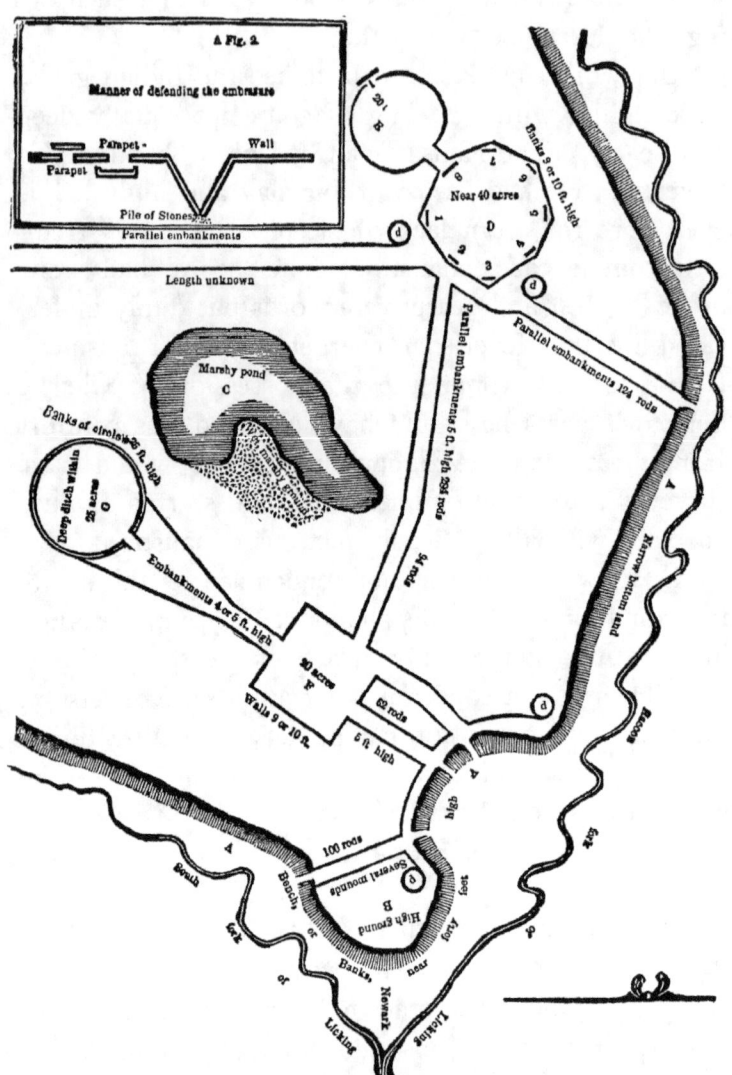

Ancient Fortifications near Newark, Licking County, Ohio.

ment among the whites. Important matters were considered by the whole people in open council, and in these councils the women often had a part, and their advice was considered. The majority of the whole tribe decided to follow this or that course; in many cases a tribe would unanimously agree on some important matter. But when a majority considered one course advisable the minority was free to follow its own course; and even when all were agreed, their fickleness soon divided them.

As for the chiefs, the whole community constantly weighed the merits of each member of it, and the individual's influence was in exact proportion to his abilities. A war chief was an able fighting man; the sachems were the most astute statesmen and diplomats. But the ruler ruled only by influence—by advice and example—not as a despot. Each individual might do as he pleased even to making war when peace had been declared by the chiefs.

By dwelling on the good qualities only of the Indian, one easily comes to believe that he was, if a "little lower than the angels," not far from as good as the white man. It is worth while to remember that he was of a lower race—one far less developed than the white race. In ferocity the American Indians were unsurpassed. They continually acted on the theory that "hanging was too good" for certain offences. They burned captured enemies to death, and prolonged the torture. In doing this they were animated by various motives; they did it for revenge and to awe the tribe to which the prisoner belonged, hoping thus to prevent future aggressions in the same direction.

That is to say they tortured a prisoner to death—burned him alive—in order "to protect their homes."

They sometimes tortured prisoners at the stake through religious motives—as a duty to their gods—but never to make converts, or restrain conscience.

But behind all these motives was the pleasure which undeveloped men, and degenerates, feel when they see another in pain. As a race these undeveloped men found intense delight in the prolonged suffering of their victims. When La Salle's agents went among the Iroquois to get permission to build a fort at Niagara, a victim was burned by way of entertaining them.

It is asserted by some writers that ferocity was cultivated as a virtue, and pity condemned as a vice by the Indian. It is certain that in their gatherings each man rose to his feet and boasted of his deeds of prowess—of the scalps he had taken, and the tortures he had inflicted. It was not idle boasting either. The scalps were in evidence, the audience knew the statements to be true. And when they approved the boasting words the hearts of the boys burned with an eager ambition to do deeds of which they might boast in like manner. Red boys were taught to hunt for scalps. But in the course of nature—of evolution—the harvesting of corn, and the making of copper ornaments, and the carving of petrographs, were coming to occupy much more time than the gathering of scalps. They were taming themselves while they tamed wolves and made preserves for bears.

The Indian's idea of love has been much discussed, but we will never doubt that red mothers loved their children as white mothers love theirs. In the relations between the sexes, however, it seems impossible that what we call heroic unselfish love, (such, for instance, as Ruskin bore for his unworthy wife), was ever known among them. Passion was unrestrained. Indulgence was no cause for shame. The unfaithful wife was sometimes punished. Grosseilliers and Radisson "observed with much admiration," says a Jesuit writer, "that one tribe of Indians cut off the noses" of unfaithful wives. The unfaithful man was, of course, never punished. The man without sin could not be found to cast the first stone. The Indians had no conception of what we call sexual morality. The girls might do as they pleased. The guests of the tribe—even the white trader who came to swindle them, in after years—received not only his food, but a wife. And when the Indian came to visit the whites he was, at times, not a little astonished and indignant because they were not equally hospitable. In short, the Indians were wholly unmoral in sexual matters. In some tribes they were too vile to be discussed by self respecting men.

In other morals they were little better. They would lie for fun, and for gain. It is true that treaties between the whites and the Indians were usually broken by the whites. It would have afflicted an Indian with syncope had he moved swiftly enough to get ahead of the whites in breaking treaties. Nevertheless, it is certain that the aboriginal Indians would strive by lying and deceit to gain advantages over their neighbors. And all of this but proves that he was a lower race of men—that is, not so far developed as the whites.

In religion the Indian believed in many supernatural beings or spirits. He did not believe in one supreme Gitche Manitou until the white man came. The early missionaries were led into error, in this matter, by asking leading questions. The religion of the Indian was, in short, a belief in devils—a belief quite as sincere and as intelligent as that of Milton, however. Among the Natchez, and apparently among some Arkansas Indians, they had arrived at that state of mental development where men were employed continually as priests. It was a cruel priesthood. The whole system of Indian worship was, essentially, a series of attempts to bribe the gods into granting favors and withholding evils, but their fear of devils was very much stronger and more influential with them than their hope of pleasures.

Nevertheless, if approached with sympathy, instead of prejudice—if the student is not quite sure that he has a monopoly of the knowledge of God—the Indian religions, so far as known, are worth study. The Indians saw in the blossoms of spring "the power that catches out of chaos charcoal, water, lime, or what not, and fastens them down into a given form," and they called that power a spirit. "And we shall not diminish but strengthen our conception of this creative energy by recognizing its presence in lower states of matter than our own," for it is "properly called spirit." He saw that the bird "is little more than a drift of air brought into form by plumes," and that "in the throat of the bird is given the voice of the air." A spirit was made tangible in this drift and voice of air. A god that was not always evil was found "in that running brook of horror on the ground,"

Mississippi Valley.

the serpent. They believed gods move in a mysterious way their wonders to perform, and plant their footsteps in the sea and ride upon the storm. As they gazed into the glories of the sunset they thought and said they "could almost see, through opening vistas into heaven." And when the milky way lay white across the vault of the purple night they said with hushed voices, "it is the pathway of the departed souls."

They had an unquestioning faith in the immortality of the soul. Whenever a Natchez chief died, says Father le Petit, (Jesuit Relations, vol. xlviii), "the women (wives) are always strangled to follow (him), except when they have infants at the breast, in which case they continue to live for the purpose of nourishing them. And *we often see many who endeavor to find nurses, or who themselves strangle their infants so that they shall not lose the right of sacrificing themselves.*" Neither by argument or force could the French keep these wives from following their dead chiefs. They had never heard of a city whose walls were made of diamonds and whose streets were paved with gold, but they dreamed of a land where lakes and streams and prairies and forests and hills and mountains forever charmed the eye; where the ills of life were unknown; where peace reigned; where friends gathered; where joy was untainted. And to that land they fain would go.

Unfortunately for the race the Indians saw the work of an evil spirit and nothing else in almost every case of sickness. The work of their medicine men was horrible and destructive. Their practices killed where rational nursing would have saved. The villages of the

Indians generated diseases because of the utter lack of knowledge of the proper way to dispose of offal. They were inexpressibly filthy. They were worse even than the modern white villagers who dig wells between barns and cesspools, and ascribe the subsequent cases of sickness to the providence of God.

We think of the Indians as a healthy race, made robust by hardships endured in early life. It is a savage as well as an erroneous idea. The Indian suffered hardships and tortures voluntarily in order to toughen his fibre, and such acts helped him mentally, very likely, but they weakened his body. The lack of sanitation, the hardships of unsheltered lives, the practices due to superstition, and famine due to thoughtless indulgence, were the chief causes of death among the Indians. Inability to cope with disease, and to look ahead to a time when food would surely be scarce, were the causes that exterminated some tribes, rather than war—that is to say, in the days before the whites came. Other tribes survived because their habits and practices were less destructive.

As one reads of the life of the Indians when the whites first saw them, and as one gains a knowledge of their lives as seen by whites among them, even in the modern days, it becomes evident that the red men were in many ways merely a human race less developed than the whites, and with a smaller capacity for self-development. "They are like children," has been said by a thousand white men who knew them well. The words are accurately descriptive. They were, and they are children. In their villages they drummed and sang and danced, day and night; they played tricks and

A TYPICAL INDIAN VILLAGE.

cracked jokes and told stories that made the audiences shout with laughter.

To these tribes of undeveloped men—of children—came the whites bringing a book which, they said, (and believed), contained the Word of Life. Two courses were then open to the whites in their treatment of the Indians, and very good directions for following each course were to be found in their Word of Life. There was the method of dealing with men which was laid down in the Sermon on the Mount. A notable command, (not yet fully comprehended), that was found in connection with the Sermon on the Mount plan said, "Thou shalt love thy neighbor as thyself," and the context of this command explained that *it was to be applied more particularly to inferior people*. The white men might have followed this plan, if they had comprehended it, but they didn't comprehend it. The story of the Son of God coming to the earth to serve *beings lower than angels* was as pearls under their feet.

The other plan was found in the account of the Israelitish invasion of Canaan. The whites who came to America comprehended that plan very well, but they didn't adopt that either. They believed themselves the true and only accepted children of God, and that a Canaan was before them, but they could not bring themselves to wage a war of extermination against the red inhabitants. For they had left their homes proclaiming in one way and another that the first object of their migration was "to preach and baptize into the Christian religion, and by the propagation of the Gospel, to recover out of the armies of the devil, a number of poor and miserable souls wrapt up unto death in almost invincible ignorance, * * * and to add our myte to the Treasury of Heaven." They did not wish to add their "myte" by immediately exterminating all the Indians.

Carlyle said that "true Guidance [is] properly, if he knew it, the prime want of man." It was the prime want of the red men, (and of all undeveloped men), beyond question, and it ought to have been given to him in a way that would have enforced "loving obedience." The thought is idle now, but suppose the whites had asked the Indians for pottery or baskets or corn, instead of furs, offering in exchange household implements and tools as well as the harmless if silly mirrors, beads and trinkets. It is almost conceivable that all whites, being professed Christians, might have treated all Indians as the Quakers did some, or as the Moravians treated the Delawares in Gnadenhutten, (the story of which shall be told)—might have turned the wildmen into industrious, peace-loving agriculturists, thus deciding the land question before it arose.

It is conceivable that the whites might have given the Indian herded cattle and tame fowls, in time, and thus have fixed him in his sedentary pursuits, while they promoted his mental powers by a demand for the simple goods and ornaments he was able to make. *They might have made a Gnadanhutten of every Indian village in the land.* This is the most important statement in this book. The Moravians took wild Delawares—Indians who lived wild lives, and were, moreover, exasperated at ill treatment received from

Mississippi Valley.

the whites—and out of them made sober, earnest, stump-grubbing farmers.

There is even a practical side to this idle fancy. By adopting the Quaker and Moravian ideas, all the merciless slaughter, and, (here we are practical), the greater part of the infinite waste and expense of the Indian wars, would have been saved. We hope that this practical consideration may excuse the mention of such a sentimental proceeding as the application of Christian principals to a business transaction.

Sad to relate the white man did nothing like this. On the contrary the two white peoples who came to America in the Seventeenth Century utterly checked and turned back the Indian's natural current of evolution.

In proof of this assertion consider the effect of the rum—how the squaws with trembling limbs hastened to hide all weapons when the trader arrived. Consider the smallpox and other diseases which the whites introduced among the red men.

Consider the effect of what is called the innocent trade that the whites established. The whites offered a variety of goods that were always tempting, and in some cases very useful to the Indians. But the whites wanted furs only in exchange and in order to get the goods offered for furs, the Indians abandoned all other pursuits to go hunting. The Indian had been "fast progressing from the hunter state," but the white demand for skins stopped that progress and turned him back to the slaughter of wild beasts. From 1610 until long after the end of the Eighteenth Century the whites assiduously cultivated the fur trade, and then won-dered why it was the Indians preferred the hunter's life to that of a stump-grubbing farmer! They made liquor the chief article of exchange, and yet the whites —even the historians—were disgusted because the Indian became a drunken beggar.

Consider the effect of the guns which were sold to some tribes and not to others. Says the Jesuit Relation for 1659-60:

"The Dutch took possession of these regions and conceived a fondness for the beaver * * * and in order to secure them in greater number they furnished those people with firearms, with which it was easy to conquer; * * * *it has also put into their heads that idea of sovereign sway to which they aspire,* mere barbarians although they are, with an ambition so lofty."

But the posession of arms and the greed of dominion were only the beginning of the cultivation of the red man's ferocity. In the journal of Father Le Moyne, written while on a mission to the Onondagas, in 1654, he describes at length a speech which he made to the Indians on August 10. This journal can be found in the Jesuit Relation for 1653-54, Thwaite's edition, p. 111.

"I opened the proceedings with public prayers," says the Father and when that was ended, "I told them that in my speech, I had nineteen words to lay before them." That is, he had nineteen propositions and statements to make, each of which was emphasized by a present. Of the first seven of these, nothing need be said here, but to quote the words of the father, "the purpose of the eighth, ninth, tenth and eleventh presents was to give each of these Iroquois Nations a hatchet to be used in the new war in which they were engaged with the Cat Nation."

A white missionary sicked on the Iroquois dogs to devour the unfortunate Eries. And the Abbe Piquet was the most active and the most influential man in Canada in instigating those bootless raids made by the converted Abenakas and Mohawks on the helpless settlers of New England previous to 1750.

Even that does not tell all the story. Read the following from Winsor's "Mississippi Basin," (pp. 242-243):

"The several governments of the English Colonies," writes Colonel Stoddard at this time (1747) to Governor Shirley, *"had for three years* been persuading the Iroquois *'into a war* wherein they had not any concern but to serve their friends, and *they have left their hunting and other means of living and exposed themselves and families for our sakes,* only to be *left in the lurch.'* * * * This failure of the English to support the Indians in *wars which the savages undertook for the defence of the Colonies* was nothing new."

This is a most important matter in any consideration of the character of the red Americans. Before the white men came "battle for plunder, tribute and conquest was almost unknown," says Powell, the best authority on the history of the red race. But from the time the whites came until the French rule in America was ended, the most conspicuous feature of the history of the white dealings with the Indians is found *in the oft-repeated offers of rewards for scalps.* The whites steadily incited the Indians to fight, and buying scalps did not cease until the last remnant of European power was swept from the Mississippi valley.

One reads much about the wickedness of robbing

the Indian of his *hunting* grounds—as if that were the great wrong done him. It is all nonsense. The one injury done him that is worth remembering—the injury that was deadly to the white race as well as to the red—was in persuading him to abandon his self-acquired opportunity to develop himself, and go hunting for skins and for scalps.

The *hunting* grounds of the Indians should have been taken from him to the last acre. The writers who have bewailed his loss of hunting grounds do but show how much they, not the Indians, are to be pitied. And it is chiefly because the white race is still blind to the real wrong done the red that this wretched story is worth some consideration here. It is never in vain to remember that the whites, while boasting of their Christian religion, sowed saltpetre and sulphur, and were inexorably obliged to reap hell-fire.

It is a most pathetic story—a story of children taken from peaceable play and set to the bloody work of butchers. And when New Orleans had been settled the time was at hand when the English and the French would grasp each other in mortal combat to determine which should have sole opportunity of robbing the unfortunates—with such results as we shall see.

JOHN LAW.
Projector of the Mississippi Scheme.

VI

WORK OF THE FRENCH IN THE VALLEY.

Law's Mississippi Company and Law Himself Did Something—Bienville's Way of "Booming" a Town Site—Character of the French-Americans Described by a Candid Priest—Indians Burned Alive by the French at New Orleans—A Southern Gentleman's Opinion of Such Deeds—Reasons for the French Failure as Colonists Plainly Stated by French Priests and Soldiers.

Stories of the work of the French in the Mississippi Valley, after the founding of New Orleans in 1718, are by no means uninteresting, nor are they without significance. John Law's company began work very earnestly. In June, after the founding of New Orleans, three ships brought out "colonists, convicts and troops, in all 800 souls." Of the colonists, 148 were sent up to Natchitoches, on the Red River; 82 were sent to the Yazoo, and 68 remained in New Orleans. There were, it is seen, only 298 colonists among the "800 souls," and Bienville wrote that very few carpenters and plowmen were to be found among the colonists. The number of convicts is not stated, but the fact of their presence is significant.

In October, 1719, 200 Germans came to settle on a tract of land, twelve miles square, that belonged to Law. Others followed. It was in making a settlement of Germans that Law left a permanent impression on the Mississippi Valley. For these Germans could and would work. When Law, after having flooded France with 3,000,000,000 livres of paper money, fled for life with only 800 livres in coin, the Germans were evicted from the land he had owned. But other land was given them on the river. There they thrived by good work, and to this day the settlement is known as the German coast.

Besides the Germans the only valuable accessions to the population in 1719 were 500 negro slaves—the first importation of any size. This is not to commend slavery, but to point out the fact that in such a country as Louisiana was then, any workers were better than idlers. Hard manual labor had to be done in unhealthy localities, and the slaves did it then, and they were found equally serviceable in later years, even though slavery was a curse to the whites in the long run.

In 1721 Bienville sent surveyors to lay out "a suitable site for a city worthy to become the capital of Louisiana," and Louisiana in those days included the

A Portion of Labat's Map, 1722.

whole Mississippi valley except some of the extreme upper part which was governed from Canada. He wished to remove the seat of government from Mobile to the new city, but, partly from a love of opposing the Governor, his associates refused to do so. What Bienville did at New Orleans, then, is worth remembering. By his orders streets were cut through the brush, and were ditched; palisades were erected around the town; a levee was made (the first attempt to confine the Mississippi to its channel), and warehouses were built to accommodate trade. By practical, permanent improvements, Bienville brought all the traders of Mobile to the new town site, and the Government officials were obliged to follow to the new center of population.

In 1724, a company of Jesuits came bringing orange trees, fig trees, and indigo plants. They also gave attention to the native myrtle bush that produced a valuable wax. On April 11, 1726, Bienville gave them a tract of land, 3,600 feet front on the river and 9,000 feet deep, where now is found the heart of the city, together with enough slaves to work the tract; and here they made a plantation that was in its day a sort of agricultural experiment station and therefore valuable.

In 1727, a company of Ursuline nuns came to open a school for girls—the first of the kind in the valley—and to attend to the sick in the hospital that was built soon after the settlement was made. A letter written by sister Hochard, of this company, soon after her arrival, contains the following description of life as she saw it in times of plenty among the official and wealthy class in the young city.

"Although I do not as yet know perfectly the province called Louisiana, still I will attempt, dear father, to give you some details about it. I assure you that I can hardly realize that I am on the banks of the Mississippi, because there is here, in certain things, *as much magnificance as in France,* and as much politeness and refinement. *Gold and velvet stuffs are commonly used,* although they cost three times as much as in Rouen. Cornbread costs ten cents a pound, eggs from forty-five to fifty cents a dozen, milk fifteen cents for a measure that is half that of France. We have pine apples—the most excellent of all fruit—peas and wild beans, watermelons, potatoes, *sabotines*—which are very much like our gray renette apples—an abundance of figs and pecans, walnut and hickory nuts, which, when eaten too green, act as astringents on the throat. There are also pumpkins. I do not speak of many other kinds of fruit of which I have heard, but with which I am still unacquainted.

"As to meat, we live on wild beef, venison, wild geese and turkey and a sort of swan, hares, chickens, ducks, teals, pheasants, partridges, quails, and other game. The river abounds in monstrously large fishes, among which the sheepshead must be mentioned as excellent; and we have also rays, carps, and an infinite number of other fishes unknown in France. A great use is made of chocolate and coffee with milk. We eat bread made of half rice and half wheat flour. We have wild grapes larger than those of France. They do not grow in bunches, but are put on the table in plates in the fashion that prunes are served.

"The dish most in favor is rice boiled in milk, and what is called *sagamite,* which consists of Indian corn pounded in a mortar and boiled in water with butter or lard. The whole people of Louisiana regard as most excellent this kind of food." (Translated from the Catholic World by Charles Gayarre. Italics not in original.)

Meantime there was some little growth of population elsewhere in the valley. In 1720, Major Pierre Dugue Boisbriant, (he whose wish to marry had been thwarted by Bienville), went up the river with 100 men and at a point sixteen miles above Kaskaskia built a fort which he named Chartres. The river channel has changed to and fro since then, but Chartres Landing still perpetuates the memory of this fort. In 1721, Kaskaskia became a parish, and in 1722, Boisbriant, who ruled as commandant of the region, issued the first land warrant known to the records of what is now the state of Illinois.

In 1721, a capitalist named Philip Francois Renault brought 200 miners and 500 slaves to the point where Galena now stands, and opened the lead mines found there. In this year, also, the Jesuits established a college and monastery at Kaskaskia, and "Fort Chartres became not only the headquarters of the commandant in Upper Louisiana, but the center of life and fashion in the West," as Monette says.

The details of this "life and fashion," (as he got them from Martin, Flint and Stoddard), are given by Monette, who, it should be said, is a most sympathetic recorder of the annals of the French in Louisiana. For the sake of comparison with a frontier manner of life to be described in another chapter the following is worth reading:

"The early French on the Illinois were remarkable for their *easy amalgamation in manners and customs and blood*" with the red men. "Their villages sprang up in long narrow streets," with each family homestead so contiguous that the merry and social villagers could carry on their voluble conversation "each from his own balcony."

"Each homestead was surrounded by its own separate enclosure of a rude picket fence. The houses were generally one story high, surrounded by sheds (verandas) or galleries; the walls were constructed of a rude framework, having upright corner posts and studs, connected horizontally by numerous cross ties, not unlike the rounds of a ladder. These [cross ties] served to hold the 'cat [straw or moss] and clay' of which the walls were made and rudely plastered by hand.

"The chimney was made of similar materials, and was formed by four long corner posts, converging at the top to about one-half, or less than the space below."

A large field nearby was fenced for the common use of the villagers. "The season for plowing, planting, reaping and other agricultural operations in the 'common field' was regulated by special enactments, or by public ordinance, and to take place simultaneously in each village. Even the form and manner of door yards, gardens and stable yards were regulated by special enactment."

"The winter dress of the men was generally a coarse blanket *capote* drawn over shirt and long vest," which served both as cloak and hat, "for the hood, attached to the collar behind, hung upon the back and shoulders as a cape, and, when desired, it served to cover the whole head from intense cold. In summer, especially among the *couriers de bois,* the head was enveloped in a blue handkerchief, turban like."

A handkerchief of "fancy colors, wreathed with bright colored ribbons, and sometimes flowers, formed the head dress of females on festive occasions." "The old fashioned short jacket and petticoat, varied to suit the diversities of taste, was the most common over dress of the women. The feet in winter were protected by Indian moccasins, or the clog shoes; in summer they were all barefooted, except on festive occasions," when they wore "light moccasins, gorgeously ornamented with brilliants of porcupine quills, shells, beads, lace, ingeniously wrought" over the whole above the sole.

The traders kept a heterogenous stock of goods in their largest rooms, where the assortment was fully displayed to the gaze of the purchasers. "The young men who wished to see the world sought occupation as *voyageurs* and their return was greeted with smiling faces, and signalized by balls and dances at which the whole village assembled."

"The commandants were invested with despotic authority." "Learning and science were terms beyond their comprehension." "The priest was their oracle in matters of learning as well as in the forms and observances of religion." "On politics and the affairs of the nation they never suffered their minds to feel a moment's anxiety." "Day after day passed by in contentment *and peaceful indolence*." (Italics not in the original.)

And yet, being agriculturists, they did raise food for export. In 1745 the Illinois country sent 400,000 pounds of grain to New Orleans, the French population being then not far from 900 souls, all told.

Other villages near Chartres were Prairie du Rocher, with twelve dwelling houses in 1770, and St. Phillippe with sixteen dwellings. Cahokia (called Kaoquias by the French), was at this date a long straggling village of forty-five dwellings and a church.

A trading post was established at or near the site of New Madrid as early as 1740 (according to tradition). The region was notable for its number of bears, and the "principal occupation" of the inhabitants "was the chase of that animal, and the preparation and sale of bears' oil." Hence the *voyageurs* named it "L'Anse de la Graisse"—Grease Bay.

St. Genevieve was not established in Missouri until about 1755.

Following the Illinois settlements came the occupation of the Wabash country. The Fox Indians living around the Wisconsin River proved implacable enemies to the French, in the Eighteenth century. Neither blandishments, nor attacks that drove them temporarily from their homes, could bring these Indians to the French interests, and the portages at the Fox River and the Chicago River, and the St. Joseph-Kankakee portage became, in spite of fortified posts, so dangerous that the *voyageurs* from the St. Lawrence began, as early as 1705, to use the portage from the Maumee to the Wabash.

This portage had been avoided in the Seventeenth century because of fear of the Iroquois. The route led up the Maumee to the St. Mary's branch, the present site of Ft. Wayne, Indiana. A portage of three leagues brought the *coureurs de bois* to a branch of the Wabash. According to Father Marest, a stockade was built on the upper Wabash previous to 1712, but it appears that the route was not popular previous to 1716. The post on the upper Wabash was called Ouiatanon. Lafayette, Ind., stands on the site of Ouiatanon. It stood at the mouth of Little River. In 1705 some enterprising *coureurs de bois* collected 15,000 skins on the Wabash and took them to Mobile, where they were received joyously, because it was the first arrival from the Wabash.

The fortified trading post of Vincennes was established where Vincennes, Indiana, now stands, by Monsieur Vincennes in 1722. But Vincennes did not become a settlement, properly so called, until 1734 or 1735, when a number of families made homes there.

Father du Poisson, describing what he saw in a journey made from New Orleans to the Arkansas, beginning May 25, 1727, says (Jesuit Relations, vol. lxvii) :

"A tract of land granted by the company of the Indies to a private individual, for the purpose of clearing that land and making it valuable, is called a concession. * * * The concessionaries are, therefore, the gentlemen of the country. The greater part of them are not people who would leave France, but they equipped vessels and filled them with superintendents, stewards, storekeepers, clerks, and workmen of various trades, with provisions and all kinds of goods. They [these workmen], had to plunge into the woods to set up cabins, to choose their ground, and burn the cane brakes and trees. This beginning seemed very hard to people not at all accustomed to that kind of labor; the superintendents and their subordinates, for the most part, amused themselves in places where a few Frenchmen had already settled, and there they consumed their provisions. The work had hardly begun when the concession was ruined; the workmen, ill-paid or ill-fed, refused to work, or himself took his pay; the warehouses were pillaged. *Do you not recognize in this the Frenchman?*"

"There are also people who have no other occupation than that of roving about: 1st. The women or girls taken from the hospitals of Paris, or from the Salpetriere, or other places of equally good repute, who find that the laws of marriage are severe, and the management of a house too irksome. A voyage of 400 leagues does not terrify these heroines; I already know of two of them whose adventures would furnish materials for a romance. 2nd. The travellers; these for the most part are young men sent to the Mississippi 'for various reasons' by their relatives, or by the law, and who, finding that the land lies too low for digging, prefer to hire themselves to row and ply from once shore to another. 3rd. The hunters," who supplied New Orleans with dried buffalo meat, skins and bears' oil, a class of men not reprobated by the father, though most of the writers speak harshly of these wood rangers.

In the course of forty years after Iberville came to Louisiana, the French, by an unhurried progression over easy water routes, made settlements at Natchez; at Natchitoches, on the Red River; on the Mississippi, near the Arkansas; on the Yazoo; in the region around Kaskaskia and Fort Chartres (five villages there); on the Illinois River above Lake Peoria; at Vincennes, and near the Wabash-Maumee portage.

In all these years they suffered but one serious attack from the Indians, though many small ones were endured. On November 29 (one account says 28), 1729, the Natchez arose and wiped out the French inhabitants and garrison at the village of Rosalie that stood where Natchez now stands. Five men escaped, and two, a tailor and a wagon maker, with the attractive women, and the children were kept alive.

Aided by the Choctaws, the French took ample revenge, and Governor Perier wrote on August 1, 1730, concerning some of the red prisoners captured:

"Laterly I have burned here four men and two women, and sent the rest to St. Domingo."

Charles Gayarre, the New Orleans historian, himself a Frenchman, says of this burning. "It was not only an act of useless cruelty, but of exceedingly bad policy. * * * It must have looked, in the estimation of the Indians, as an approval of their national custom. * * * But what is remarkable *and characteristic* is the *cool, business-like indifference,* and the matter of fact tone *with which Governor Perier informs his government of the auto-da-fe which has taken place by his orders."*

These words are worth remembering because they show how all Southern gentlemen regard such atrocities. There is a very great difference between the Southern gentlemen and the upstarts, (sons of former overseers, in many cases), who describe themselves as "leading citizens," and are found heading the mobs that burn negroes alive.

On November 15, 1731, Law's Mississippi Company took final leave of Louisiana by turning the country over to the King. It is a curious fact in French history that this company continued to exist long after every other scheme planned by Law failed. Being freed from the grasp of private monopoly the young city was now able to open free commerce with the French West Indies and the home country. By the labor of slaves the colonists were producing indigo, rice, tobacco and lumber for export. The tobacco is worth special notice because at a point fifty-five miles above New Orleans a kind of tobacco is yet produced, (400 pounds to the acre, at that), which is famous as Louisiana perique.

And yet when Bienville left Louisiana in 1743, the whole province had a population of only 4,000 French and 2,000 negroes, and but for the supplies of food sent down the river from the Illinois, New Orleans would have been starved from the face of the map. In 1730 Bienville reported that for three months the colonists had "subsisted on the seeds of reeds and wild grass." The Marquis de Vaudreuil, who succeeded Bienville, "notified his home government in 1744, that if an importation of flour had not arrived he could not have controlled his famished garrison." (Winsor.)

In a letter by Father Vivier, written from the Illinois country, November 17, 1750, he says, "Wheat, as a rule yields only from five to eight fold; but *it must be observed that the lands are tilled in a very careless manner,* and that they have never been manured during the thirty years while they have been cultivated."

Father Gravier describes one method of curing the sick which he practiced, (Jesuit Relations, vol. lxv, p. 109):

"A small piece of Father Francois Regis's hat, which one of our servants gave me, is the most infallible remedy that I know of for curing all kinds of fever."

Said Bienville in a letter written on April 15, 1735:

"I neglect nothing to turn the attention of the inhabitants to agricultural pursuits, but in general they are worthless, lazy, dissolute." And of a company of soldiers that had arrived a short time before writing another letter, he said:

"There are but one or two men among them whose size is above five feet; as to the rest, they are under four feet ten inches. With regard to their moral character it is sufficient to state that out of fifty-two, who have lately been sent here, more than one-half have already been whipped for larceny."

During the summer of 1754, some soldiers of a garrison kept on Cat Island, when exasperated beyond endurance by the cruelty of their commander, killed him, and started through the woods toward South Carolina, but were all captured by Indians sent after them. One killed himself. Two were broken upon the wheel, and one, who was a Swiss from the regiment of Karrer, was placed alive in a wooden coffin, and by two sergeants sawed in two with a whip saw.

Father Etienne de Carheil in a letter regarding the work of missionaries at French forts in the interior, (Jesuit Relations, vol. lxv) says: "These [missions] are reduced to such an extremity that we can no longer maintain them against an infinite multitude of evil acts—acts of brutality and violence; of injustice and impiety; of lewd and shameless conduct."

As a final view of those Frenchmen who were ostensibly striving to make a great colony of the Mississippi valley, take this from the "Present State of the Country and Inhabitants, Europeans and Indians, of Louisiana," by "An Officer of New Orleans to his

Mississippi Valley.

Friend at Paris," as translated and printed in London in 1744, (page 11 et seq).

"Every one studies his own Profit; the Poor labour for a Week and squander in one day all they have earned in six; from thence arises the profit of the Public Houses, which flourish every day. The Rich spend their time in seeing their slaves work to improve their land and get money which they spend in Plays, Balls and Feasts; but the most common pastime of the highest as well as the lowest, and even of the slaves, is Women; so that if there are 500 women, married or unmarried in New Orleans, including all ranks, I don't believe, without exaggeration, that there are ten of them of a blameless character; as for me I know but two of those, and even they are privately talked of. What I say of New Orleans I say of the whole province without being guilty of Slander or Calumny."

"Laws are observed here much in the same manner as in France, or worse. The rich man knows how to procure himself Justice of the Poor, if the affair is to his advantage; but if the poor man is in the right he is obliged to enter into a composition; if the rich is in the wrong the affair is stifled. They deal fairly with such as are very sharp sighted. As the King is at a great distance they make him provide Victuals, Arms and Clothing for troops, which those who keep the offices or magazines sell and put the money in their own pockets; the poor soldier for whom they were designed never so much as seeing them."

With patient persistence and unsurpassed endurance the austere La Salle staked the trail from Montreal to the mouth of the Mississippi. Iberville, a hero of the French Navy, came to possess the land. The populations that followed were composed of convicts, male and female; soldiers "under four feet ten inches" in body, mind and morals; colonists whose highest ambition was to find a gold mine, and whose pastime among the "highest as well as the lowest, and even of Slaves, is women."

The Goths and Vandals who swarmed through the gates of degenerate Rome "did not come a day too soon." The swelling tide from the British colonies that was already trickling through the passes, and washing around the ends of the Alleghany range, had something in it as harsh and bitter as the brine of the sea, but it was to descend on the valley of the great river with the cleansing power of the flood of Noah.

VII

THE FRENCH EXPELLED FROM THE VALLEY.
PART I.

This is to Tell How the Corruption of the French Court Spread Until it Blighted French Trade Among the American Indians and How the French Resorted to Inhuman Warfare to Retain Their Trade—Celoron's Expedition—The Remarkable Attitude of the British Colonists After Celoron's Warning—Work of the British Traders Brings Another French Irruption—First Gun in the War that Ended on the Plains of Abraham.

The war that destroyed the French power in the Mississippi Valley began, strictly speaking, in an attack on Indians, (friendly to the British), who lived on the banks of the Scioto river in the present state of Ohio; it ended, so far as America was concerned, when Wolfe scaled the Heights of Abraham at Quebec. But this war was, after all is said, only an outbreak of a chronic state of conflict that had grown out of the earliest efforts of the British to extend their "peaceful commerce" in beaver skins.

To understand the conditions under which the British colonists drove the French from the Mississippi Valley it is necessary to consider briefly this chronic state of conflict growing out of the competition for furs—especially to consider what the French did in that conflict and their avowed object in fighting.

As has been noted already, the British were in no degree as venturesome as the French in the fur trade, but the British trade, especially at Albany, grew in spite of the greater enterprise of the French traders. In fact a time came when *coureurs-de-bois* carried packs of furs down the Mohawk instead of down the St. Lawrence.

The reason for this growth of trade is readily found. The British undersold the French merchants. As one French merchant said in a letter yet preserved, the Albany traders gave a silver bracelet for two beaver skins where the French trader would have charged ten.

This difference in price is accounted for by the enormous burden of taxes which the French King laid upon his people, and by the utter dishonesty of the French officials in America. The practices of the French court, so graphically described by Carlyle, necessarily spread through all the French domains. "Monsieur the Count de Maurepas [the "lightly gyrating" Prime Minister] is right when he says that the officials

Mississippi Valley.

in Canada are looking not for the Western sea but for the sea of beaver," wrote Father Nau, on October 2, 1735.

To preserve their fur trade in spite of prices that amounted in a moral point of view to sheer robbery, the French resorted to inhuman warfare. They set the Indians raiding the New England settlements. Said Charlevoix regarding one of these raids:

"Monsieur de Vaudreuil formed a party of these savages to whom he joined some Frenchmen under the direction of the Sieur de Beaubassin, when they effected some ravages of no great consequence; they killed, however, about 300 men." To this he adds the very significant remark: *"The essential point was to commit the Abenakis in such a manner that they could not draw back."*

The Abenakis, and the Iroquois converts known as the Caughnawagas, (in the Eighteenth Century French diplomacy had fully established priests in the Iroquois villages), were sneaking away from the shadow of the altar to buy goods at Albany; and the French persuaded them to raid the British settlements in New England on the theory that no raider would dare to go to a British town to trade. Every New England settlement within reach was raided by order of the French, and French officers went along to see that the raiding was thoroughly done. Women were slaughtered, parents saw the brains of their babes dashed out against rock or tree, prisoners were tortured in ways so shocking that a detailed description cannot now be printed; and all this was done "to commit the Indians in such fashion that they would continue to buy French goods at prices rendered excessive by the bald stealing of which French officials were guilty."

It was New England alone that suffered from the early raids for the preservation of the French trade. The Caughnawaga Iroquois, (located on the St. Lawrence), could not be trusted to raid toward Albany, because their relatives lived in the Mohawk valley; and the Abenakis could not be sent there alone because that would rouse the resentment of all the Iroquois.

In consequence of this freedom from raids, New York's population spread slowly up the Mohawk. The Lutheran Palatines, fleeing from religious persecution in Europe, came nearly 3,000 strong, to New York, and were sent by the wily authorities to settle west of Schenectady, because they would serve as a buffer in case of French-Indian invasion over the route lying west of the Adirondacks. Their plantations were extended as far as where Rome now stands. Some of them went also to the frontier of Pennsylvania and Virginia.

In 1727 Governor Burnet, of New York, built at his own expense "a stone house of strength," where Oswego now stands, in order to fend off the French. Here a lively trade was established.

The French fumed over the advancing settlements of Englishmen, but instead of attacking this "house of strength," they built a trading station where Toronto now stands.

Meantime, (1726), Joncaire, a Frenchman living among the Iroquois, had re-established on Niagara River the post La Salle had built, while in 1731 Fort

Mississippi Valley.

Frederick was built at Crown Point, on Lake Champlain. Both patriotism and private greed urged the French to establish new posts; for by so doing they hoped to wall in the British, and they knew by experience that every post was a source of wealth to its officers.

During all the early years of the Eighteenth Century, while British settlers and stations spread westward through New York, the British traders of Pennsylvania, Virginia and the Colonies to the South, had been working across and around the Alleghanies, while their stations were eventually established in the mountain passes, and beyond them. Col. Thomas Cresap, whom Winsor calls "a vagrant Yorkshire man, then near forty years old," built, in the winter of 1742-43, a hunting and trading cabin near the upper fork of the Potomac in the extreme west part of what is now Maryland. In 1745 a British trading post was established on Sandusky Bay, Lake Erie, near the site of the present city of Sandusky, Ohio, and as many as 300 traders are said to have gone to the Ohio country every season thereafter, for several years. If anyone wishes a more detailed story of this growth of colonial trade it can be found in Walton's "Conrad Weiser."

In 1748, the Ohio company was organized in Virginia for trade and colonization in the Ohio Valley. They applied to the King for a grant of 500,000 acres in that valley, (which Virginia claimed), and they received, by the royal order of May 19, 1749, 200,000, on condition that they settle 100 families on the tract, each year, for seven years, and build a fort to protect them. This done they were to receive an additional

300,000 acres. This company did a little memorable work. They contracted with Col. Thomas Cresap "to lay out and mark a road" from Will's Creek, (now Cumberland, Md.), to the forks of the Ohio. Cresap, with the aid of an Indian named Nemacolin, marked the trees along an old trail that had been occasionally used by the Indians, and created a path fit for surefooted pack horses. It lay not far from the route of the old National Road, as now found there.

In 1736, Col. William Mayo from a head spring of the Potomac passed over to the head of a tributary of the Monongahela with a party of surveyors. In 1748, Dr. Thomas Walker, "a genuine explorer and surveyor, a man of mark," reached the Cumberland River, and in 1750, passed through and named the Cumberland Gap, after the Duke of Cumberland.

The British population that was crowding westward toward the Great Lakes and swelling to the crests of the Alleghanies, occupied a territory of 514,416 square miles, (Census Report of 1850), and numbered 1,160,000. The French who were to try to stop the westward movement of the British, numbered no more than 80,000, and they claimed in addition to all Canada, the entire Mississippi Valley with its area of 1,217,562 square miles. If the French were to hold their claims to the Mississippi Valley, they needed to bestir themselves—and that they did.

But before telling what they did to rivet their claims to the Great Basin, it seems worth while to consider whether the British ought to have respected the claim of the French.

The French claim was based on the work of La

Salle in discovering the mouth of the Mississippi, and in building forts within the watershed of the Great River. Under the law and practice of nations, this certainly gave them what is now called the right of preemption to the whole basin. They had the right to establish a great French colony there. But when that much is conceded, the fact remains that the French nation had failed to do anything in furtherance of this right—they had failed to colonize the region. The widely scattered posts that had been established could no more be called lasting or sufficient "improvements on the claim," than the planting of an apple seed would have been, in recent years, sufficient to give an American settler a right to a quarter section of land in Kansas as a timber claim. The Mississippi Valley, with its capacity to support 200,000,000 people, in the middle of the 18th century contained less than 7,000 Frenchmen, including slaves; and more than half of these were concentrated around New Orleans. The whole region was an unscarred wilderness.

Although there were no statutes or treaties that covered the condition of affairs in the Mississippi Valley, the French law governing individual settlers at the posts is a strong point to urge against the French claim to the whole valley. To any French settler of good standing in the church the King would concede a reasonable tract of land on condition that he improve it within seven years. If within seven years he failed to improve the claim to the satisfaction of the commandant of the post, the land could be taken by another. The Mississippi Valley, in the middle of the Eighteenth Century, was by the French standard, wild land, because they had not made the proper improvements; and it was therefore open to the claims of whomsoever would improve it.

To look at the matter in another point of view, the French were trying to take the wild region for a vast game preserve, wherein to gather furs, while the British were trying to get it for home sites. The quarrel was somwhat like that between actual settlers and cattlemen on the wild land west of the Mississippi after our Civil war. Exact justice always gave the actual settler his claim wherever he chose to stake it.

But laying aside all such arguments as these (although an international court would consider them), there is one more point to be made for the British, and it is one that is decisive. The argument is as follows:

For more than fifty years the French, in order to preserve their trade with the Indians, had deliberately waged an inhuman warfare on the British settlements that were within convenient reach of the French posts. In due time they determined to monopolize the trade of the Mississippi Valley, as they had tried to monopolize that of the St. Lawrence. To do that they began attacking the British traders found west of the Alleghanies, and then they established forts in that region. The British colonists were fully justified in believing that raiders would be sent from the French posts west of the Alleghanies as they had been sent from the posts on the St. Lawrence.

It is especially important to note that the raids against New England were not made to preserve Canada from invasion; the British colonies had no thought of pushing settlements to the Canada line at any time before or during these raids. The raids were made solely to protect a trade that in a moral point of view was robbery; and they were made at times when the French and British kings were nominally at peace. Therefore to drive the French from the region west of the Alleghenies was an act of self defence. Let it be repeated for the sake of emphasis, that during fifty years the French had relentlessly pushed their inhuman warfare, and the British were then justified in sweeping such neighbors from the continent.

With his sympathies excited by the magnificent achievements of La Salle, and his prejudices aroused against the British for the arrogance and oppression with which they treated the United States, more than one American writer has said the Mississippi Valley was rightfully the property of the French, and that predatory aggression took it from them. But it is not so. For, even though it be allowed that the Great Basin was rightfully French land, it was not predatory aggression that took it. It was an aggression in self defence.

In fact, as shall appear, the French shifted the war from New England to a point back of the Alleghanies. They made an attack on British traders who were in the Ohio country, where they had a right to be under the treaty last made by the two nations (Utrecht). It shall further appear that when the British colonies expressed a fear that if French posts were established west of the Alleghanies, the raiding that had been done in New England would be continued in Pennsylvania and Virginia, the fear was fully justified. The truth is that in the state of civilization then prevailing the continent was not large enough to hold the two peoples, and a war that would expel or subjugate one of them was unavoidable.

In a larger view this war was but an incident in a prolonged conflict between rival races which is yet waged, though at present not with guns.

The first French move into the Alleghany region was made in 1749. On June 15 Monsieur Celoron de Bienville (commonly called Celoron only), left La Chine with a party that included fourteen officers, twenty regular soldiers, 180 Canadians, a band of Indians, and a priest, all in twenty-three canoes. Going to the mouth of the creek that empties into Lake Erie, near Westfield, N. Y., they passed over to Lake Chautauqua, and thence to the Alleghany river, which they reached on July 29. There Celoron began the particular work of his mission. Drawing his forces up in lines he buried a plate of lead in the south bank, and further down the stream he attached the royal coat of arms (painted on tin), to a tree. After that was done a notary public, brought for the purpose, made a formal written statement of what had been done.

The lead plate was inscribed as follows (translation by Parkman):

Year 1749, in the Reign of Louis Fifteenth, King of France, We, Celoron, commanding the detachment sent by the Marquise de la Galissonnière, commanding general of New France, to restore tranquility in certain villages of these cantons, have buried this plate at the confluence of the Ohio and the Kanaouagon (Conewango), this 29th July, as a token of renewal of possession heretofore taken of the aforesaid River Ohio, of all streams that fall into it, and all lands on both sides to the source of the aforesaid streams, as the preceeding Kings of France have en-

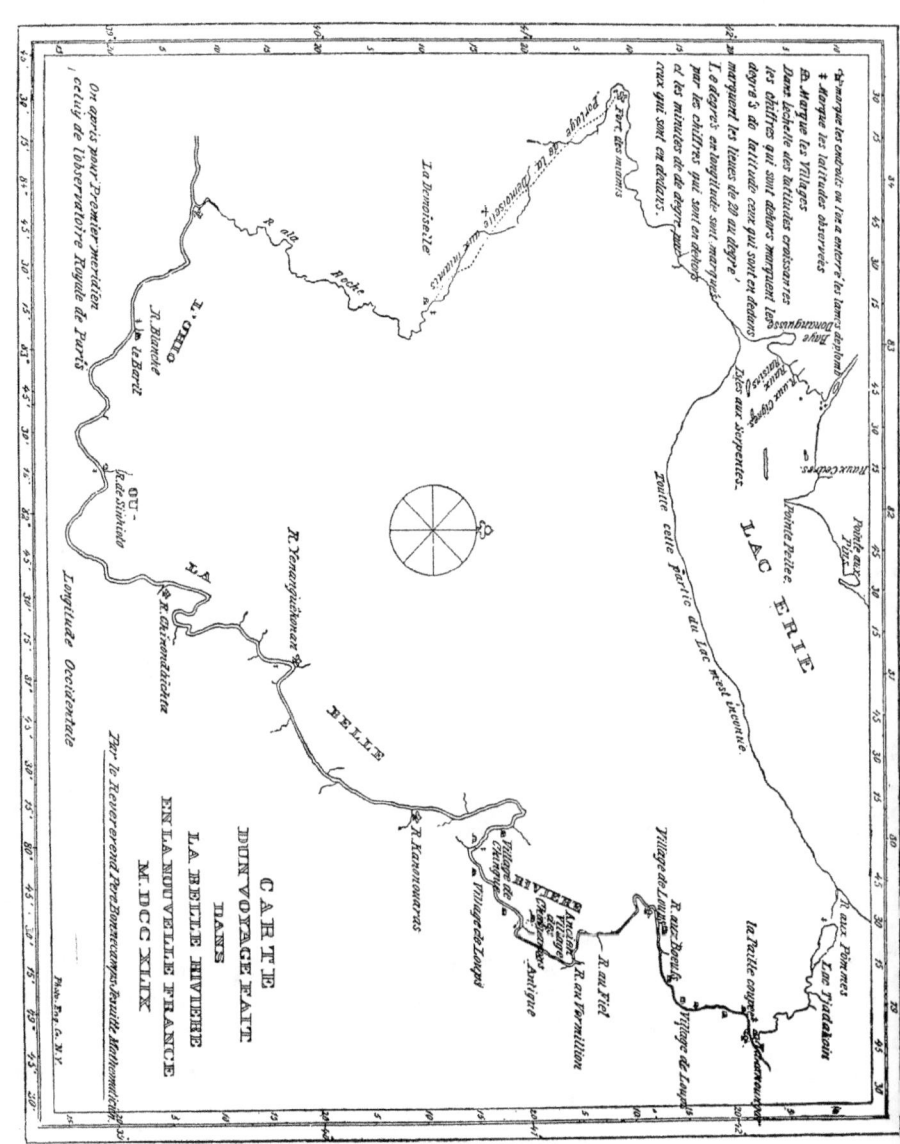

MAP OF CELORON'S EXPEDITION, 1749.

joyed or ought to have enjoyed it, and which they have upheld by force of arms and by treaties, notably those of Ryswick, Utrecht and Aix-la-Chapelle.

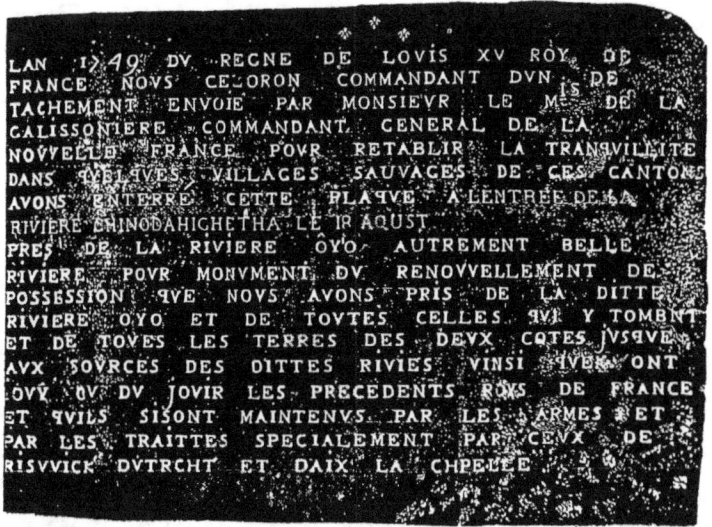

This Shows the Inscription on One of the Two Plates Which Have Been Found.

It was by such idle displays as this that the French then expected to stop the onflow of British settlers.

Celoron was under orders to expel all British traders that he might find, but the further they travelled down the river, the more threatening became the bearing of the Indians, who had found British goods better as well as cheaper than those supplied by the French.

On reaching the Scioto the expedition turned north, and at the mouth of the Laramie creek had a talk with a chief the French called La Demoiselle, though he was known to the British traders as "Old Britain," because of his friendship for all things British. Old Britain accepted the presents offered, but when asked to remove his people to their former dwelling place, near a French post on the Maumee River, he said he would do so "at a more convenient time." What he did do was to increase the population of Pique Town, or Pickawillany, as his village was called, and make it a stronghold for British traders. This village gave its name to the modern town of Piqua, Ohio, which, however, stands some distance south of the mouth of Laramie creek.

At the head of the Scioto, Celoron burned his canoes, and marched overland to the Maumee, whence he returned home by way of the lakes. He had accomplished nothing but to give the British warning that the French were going to claim everything back of the Alleghany mountains.

In view of this warning, the attitude of the British colonists in the three years after 1749 was most remarkable. Not only did they ignore the threat of French occupation of the lands claimed by Virginia and Pennsylvania; they even neglected the Indians on those lands, and allowed "the chain of friendship to rust; and then to break."

Several causes united to create this singular attitude. In Pennsylvania the people and the proprietors were quarreling over the expenses incidental to Indian affairs. The assembly wished the proprietors to bear part of the expense and the proprietors refused. It was a question of principle rather than of cash apparently, for the Quakers, who refused to vote money when they thought the proprietors ought to give it, were always ready to give liberally, and their time also when treaties were to be held with the Indians.

GEORGE WASHINGTON.

This portrait was presented by Washington to his niece in 1757, when he was twenty-five years of age. Braddock's defeat was in 1755, and the surrender of Fort Duquesne in 1758.

Mississippi Valley.

In other colonies, too, the people were too busy with a growing struggle they were maintaining against the encroachments of their governors, to give adequate attention to either the Indians or the French.

Further than that there were jealousies between the colonies, while the French were one people with a single head, and a single purpose. There were also divisions among the Indians. Time had been when the Iroquois nation controlled all the Indians of the Ohio region, but in the middle of the Eighteenth Century the Delawares were asserting independence once more, and there was talk of making an alliance of the tribes in the West somewhat similar to the confederation of the Six Nations. Even the Iroquois were divided. The Onondagas were selling land to Pennsylvania and ignoring the Mohawks altogether in the transaction, while the Senecas, the most warlike of the six tribes, having a natural liking for the aggressiveness shown by the French in those days, were, to a large degree, won over to the French interest.

Nevertheless the British traders kept the grass out of the trails leading to the Ohio country. More than fifty of them were found gathered at Old Britain's, on more than one occasion, and they reached out for the trade of the Indians living with the French on the Wabash, the Maumee and at Detroit. This activity stirred the French to make an advance, in spite of the failure of Celoron's expedition. Commandant Raymond, commanding the post on the Maumee, wrote, (quoted by Parkman):

"All the tribes who go to the English at Pickawillany come back loaded with gifts. I am too weak to meet the danger. Instead of twenty men I need 500. * * * If the English stay in this country we are lost. We must attack and drive them out." The time for something more than an idle display of forms had come.

An attempt to incite the Indians about Detroit to go on a raid to Old Britain's town developed the fact that they were "touched with disaffection." But Charles Langlade, a French trader at Green Bay, came down to the Maumee with 250 "Christian Ottawas and Ojibwas, and passing through the dense forest, reached Old Britain's town at 9 o'clock on the morning of June 21, 1752. The stockade gates were immediately closed by traders, and a short resistance was made, but the Green Bay Indians triumphed. Two traders escaped. One who was wounded was murdered after the surrender. The Miamis lost fourteen killed and among these was Old Britain. And him the "Christian" Green Bay Indians boiled and ate, while the French looked on without protest, if not with entire approval.

The Marquis Duquesne de Menneville had just become governor of Canada when the report of Langlade's victory reached the St. Lawrence. In spite of the terms of the Treaty of Utrecht he asked the minister to pension Langlade.

The first gun in the war that ended on the Plains of Abraham was fired, with the full approval of the French authorities, by Charles Langlade on the banks of the Scioto.

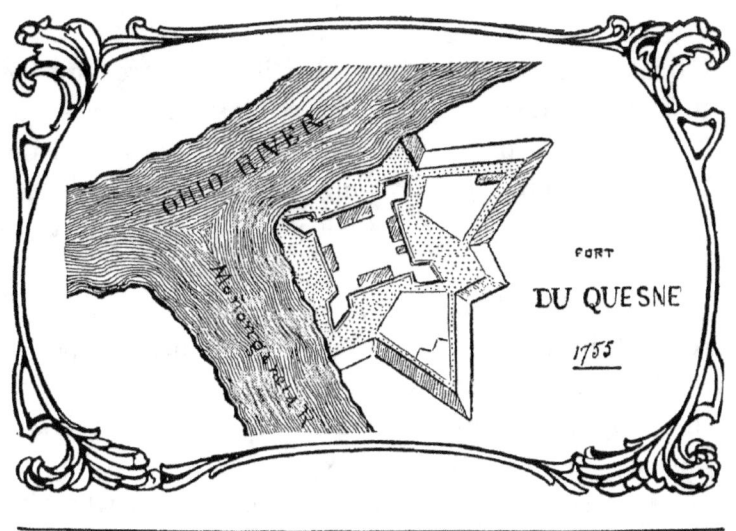

VIII

THE FRENCH EXPELLED FROM THE VALLEY.
PART II.

When the French, with Their Silks and Velvets, Came to the "Belle Riviere"—Washington's Journey into the Wilderness—Virginia's Efforts to Repel the French—Washington's First Battle—The Power of Madam de Pompadour—The Story of Braddock's Expedition—The French King Approved Indian Raids on the Home-Makers—It Was in Accordance with an Inexorable Law of Nature that the Man with an Axe Should Supplant the Vagabond with a Sword.

To follow up the successful work of Langlade on the Scioto, Gov. Duquesne, of Canada, determined to occupy all the passes of the Alleghanies, and support them by building a strong fort at the forks of the Ohio. In this plan, contrary to the usual condition of affairs in

Canada, the Governor was heartily supported by the Intendant, Francois Bigot. To establish new posts was to give new opportunities for enriching himself to the Intendant, and Bigot was an official with whom forgery and perjury, for the concealment of theft, were common acts.

To further show the character of the Canadian officials it must be said that Governor Duquesne appointed Pierre Paul, Sieur de Marin, (described as a gruff, choleric old man of sixty-three, but full of force and capacity), to lead the new expedition to the Alleghanies because of the charms of Madam Marin, who was much younger. At the request of Intendant Bigot the Chevalier Péan was made second in command, and Bigot made the request because Madam Péan was young and charming.

In the fall of 1752, Marin, with 250 men, went to the bay where Erie, Pennsylvania, now stands, and built a fort of chestnut logs to guard the harbor. A road over a newly-discovered portage was then cut to where Waterford, Pennsylvania, now stands on French creek, a distance of twenty-one miles. Here they built a fort and named it Le Boeuf.

Over this route they carried their baggage consisting of "velvets, silks and other costly articles sold to the king at enormous prices as necessaries of the expedition," and then the force sat down for the winter.

It was not until the next spring, when reinforcements were sent up the lakes to this new post, that the English heard of the new movement. On May 15, 1753, Capt. Benjamin Stoddart wrote from Oswego to Col. Johnson saying: "Yesterday passed here thirty odd French canoes, part of an army going to Belle Riviere, to make good their claim there." He thought the whole army numbered 6,000. There were near 1,500 all told.

When the reinforcements reached Le Boeuf they fortified the trail and spent so much time in useless work that they did not reach and fortify the site of Venango, (on the way to the forks of the Ohio), until August. Meantime sickness had appeared among the loitering throng, and so many of them died, (including Marin), that the project of going to the forks that year was abandoned.

This irruption of the French pleased the Indians, as a whole, in spite of their previous regard for the British traders. The British colonial officials had neglected them. The neglect offended them. The French came with a threat of war in one hand and many presents as a reward for help in the other, and the Indians, having the character of children, grasped eagerly at the presents. The old Iroquois chief Half-King went to Marin with a protest, but Iroquois, Delawares and Shawnees helped the French carry their goods, (more "velvets, silks and other useless and costly articles"), over the portage, and even the Miamis came with the scalps of two British traders. The memory of Old Britain, boiled and eaten, was gone. Pottawattamies and Ojibways also came from the West as a part of the French force.

In spite of this ominous condition of affairs but one man in the British colonies did anything to avert the danger. Governor Robert Dinwiddie, of Virginia, wrote a letter of inquiry and protest to the commander of the French forces, (for Virginia claimed all the Ohio region under her charter), and sent it by the Adjutant General of the Virginia militia, George Washington, then twenty-one years old, to the French. Christopher Gist, who had been prospecting the Ohio country in the interests of the Virginia land speculators called the Ohio Company, went along as guide.

The story of this journey into the wilderness—Washington's first notable public service—is told in his journal and has been so often retold that it need not be repeated here in detail. At Venango Washington was received with every form of civility. He noted that at dinner wine was served in abundance, and that the French officers, (the notable Joncaire was in command), drank enough to loosen their tongues.

"They told me it was their absolute design to take possession of the Ohio, and by G— they would do it," writes Washington. They said also that the British colonies were too slow in making retaliatory movements to stop the French. And in this statement the French were very nearly but not quite correct.

Washington went on to headquarters at Le Boeuf, and delivered (December 11, 1753), his message. He found Legardeur de St. Pierre in command. Legardeur replied, "I do not think myself obliged to obey" your summons to leave the country.

Nevertheless Washington accomplished the chief object of his journey. He learned the French plans, and he brought back a statement of the number of French in the Ohio water shed, and the number of canoes built and building for use in the next forward movement. He also noted that in the forks of the

Ohio the land lay well for the site of a fort. He reached home in January, 1754.

In the meantime a letter was received from the British King commanding Dinwiddie "to drive them (the French) off by force of arms." To obey, however, was to prove a hard task. For, first of all, the colonists were not greatly interested in the matter. Even some Virginians argued that the Great Valley really belonged to the French, while others believed the anxiety of Dinwiddie to drive off the French was due to his interest in the Ohio Company that purposed settling lands on the Ohio river. In fact in all the Colonies the one man in official position who would make a definite move to stop the French advance to the forks of the Ohio was Governor Dinwiddie. But for him the French would have established themselves where Pittsburg now stands without any opposition other than written words. And once they had been thus established who can say when or how they would have been routed out? It was fortunate for the future of the Mississippi valley that Dinwiddie "had enthusiasm, persistence, and a hatred of the French."

By thorough, enthusiastic and persistent effort, Dinwiddie persuaded his legislature to offer 200,000 acres of land west of the Alleghanies to any men who would fight to perfect the title to it. The legislature also voted 10,000 pounds for the purpose of perfecting that title. Meantime Dinwiddie raised 300 militia —"raw recruits." Joshua Fry, "bred at Oxford," was made Colonel, Washington was promoted to the rank of Lieutenant Colonel, and with half the force was sent forward to Will's creek, an upper branch of the Potomac, (Cumberland, Maryland). William Trent, a trader, with a gang of backwoodsmen, was with Washington, and when Washington stopped, under orders, at Will's creek to build storehouses for a base of supplies, Trent's men went on to the forks of the Ohio and began to erect a fort on the point between the rivers. Here the command devolved upon Ensign Ward, who began work on the fort on an unnamed day, early in April, 1754.

Dinwiddie had hastened forward this force because he believed the French would come down from Venango, early that spring, and his belief proved well founded, for on April 17, six flat boats, carrying eighteen cannon, and 300 canoes, came down the Alleghany river, bearing 500 Frenchmen under Captain Claude Pecaudy de Contrecoeur.

Ward, having but forty men, and an unfinished fort for shelter, was obliged to leave. The French then completed the fort, (it was 120x150 feet large), and armed it with "six pieces of cannon of six, nine of two, and three pound ball." They named the fort Duquesne.

The station that Washington was building on Will's creek was 140 miles from Fort Duquesne, by the usual trail. At the mouth of Redstone creek, (a branch of the Monongahela), a point that was half way between Will's creek and Duquesne, the Ohio Company had built a stone house. Dinwiddie, on hearing of the French arrival at the forks of the Ohio, ordered his forces forward to the stone house on Redstone creek, and Washington at once began to cut out the Old Indian trail that had been marked by the Ohio Company, and made a wagon road of it. And this "was really the first wagon road into the Great Valley from the Atlantic slope." Traces of this old trail can still be found though it was abandoned in 1818, when the National Road was constructed.

Late in May, Washington reached a natural opening in the woods in the valley of the Youghiogany, known as the Great Meadows, and there he cleared away the brush in front of a small ravine, which he turned into a fortification. Meantime, the French had sent out thirty-three men under Ensign Coulon de Jumonville, to attack Washington. But, finding his force too small, Jumonville hid in a dense wooded ravine to await reinforcements. While the French lay hid, Washington learned from his old guide, Gist, that the party was out, and determined to defend himself by attacking them. The Iroquois Half-King and others of his tribe guided Washington to the ravine on May 28, 1754. The French were surprised in their camp. They jumped to get their guns, and Washington ordered his men to fire. Jumonville and nine Frenchmen were killed, (which shows the accuracy of the British-American aim, even though Half-King did claim that his Indians did most of the killing), and twenty-two were captured. One Canadian escaped by running.

The French who for more than fifty years had been raiding the back settlements of the British colonies, slaughtering women and babies whom they dragged from their beds at night—these Frenchmen called, and yet call, the killing of Jumonville an assassination. They wrote the tale in verse, and they screamed it into all the courts of Europe.

Washington returned to his camp at the Great Meadows, after the attack on Jumonville, and made an entrenchment which he named Fort Necessity. It was on a small branch of the Youghiogany, in Fayette county, Pa., four miles east of Laurel Hill, and 300 yards south of the old National Road. Here some reinforcements joined him, and here Washington learned that he was in supreme command, (though but twenty-two years old), through the death of Col. Fry.

On July 1, 1754, Washington was attacked by 700 Frenchmen and an uncounted number of Indians, under the command of Coulon de Villiers, a brother of Coulon de Jumonville. Villiers had come from Canada especially to avenge the "assassination" of his brother. To defend his fort, Washington had 350 men.

The French, sheltered by forest trees standing from sixty to 100 yards from the fort, opened fire at 11 o'clock in the morning and for nine hours they worked their guns with "zeal and ardor." At the end of that time "the detachment was tired and the Indians sent me word that they would depart next day," as Villiers reported. Moreover, the French ammunition was almost exhausted. The attack had failed.

But what he could not get by force of arms, Villiers obtained by finesse. "A cessation of arms was proposed to the English," and when the cessation had been accepted, Washington sent his Dutch-French interpreter, Van Braam, to learn what the French would propose.

It was now that French finesse succeeded. The French proposed that the English march out with colors flying and drums beating, and take a swivel with

Mississippi Valley.

them. The French were to have back the prisoners taken when Jumonville was killed, and Washington was to give two hostages for the fulfillment of this condition.

This proposal Washington accepted, for he was in straits for food and ammunition and he signed a paper which purported to contain those conditions and nothing else. But the finesse of the French had gone still further. Taking advantage of the ignorance of Van Braam, Capt. Villiers had scrawled the conditions in a well-nigh illegible hand, and had inserted therein an acknowledgment that Jumonville had been assassinated in the previous fight. This paper was wet and badly blotted, as well as badly written. When he had written it, Villiers read it over to Van Braam, and there is every reason to believe that in so reading it, Villiers used the words "death of Jumonville," instead of "assassination of Jumonville." For Major Adam Stephen (second to Washington), in describing the paper says: "No person could read them [the words of the articles of capitulation], but Van Braam, *who had heard them from the mouth of the French officer.*"

This acknowledgment, which was in effect a forgery, was published and screamed throughout all Europe, and the French to this day believe the forged statement.

In the face of the dangers which threatened them, now that the French were fully seated at the forks of the Ohio, the citizens of seven colonies sent delegates to a Congress which met at Albany, and appointed a committee to consider the trouble further. They were still unable to agree to do any real work.

In Europe, the matter received more practical consideration. The reader who would like to learn what was done in Europe, in connection with this war, is advised to read Carlyle's "Frederick the Great," first of all. For the war that followed between France and England was a part of the great "Seven Years War," that is so fully treated in Carlyle's "Frederick." And Carlyle is one of the two British writers of the Nineteenth Century whose works are all worth oft-repeated readings.

The British King ordered two regiments of redcoated regulars (500 men each) to sail for Virginia, under command of "our trusty and well-beloved Edward Braddock," whose instructions were dated November 25, 1754. These soldiers sailed in January, 1755.

On hearing of this move the French government ordered 3,000 men to Canada under Baron Dieskau. But as the Rev. Mr. Parkman says, "In France the true ruler was Madam de Pompadour, once the King's mistress, now his procuress, and a sort of feminine prime minister." Men were appointed to office for pleasing her, regardless of their lack of other abilities, and Dieskau did not sail until May 3, 1755. Thus the British had time to learn all about the expedition, and to send a squadron to intercept it.

Braddock arrived at Hampton, Va., on February 20, 1755, and an intercolonial conference was convened on April 14, at Alexandria, where the two regiments were encamped. Here attacks were planned on Acadia, Crown Point, Niagara and Fort Duquesne. Braddock, with his two regiments of regulars, chose

FREDERICK THE GREAT.
From the engraving in the Encyclopedia Londinensis.

to lead the force against Fort Duquesne. He reached Will's Creek on May 10. Washington, with some hundreds of Colonial militia, had been at work there during the preceding winter, and had built Fort Cumberland where Will's Creek entered the Potomac, (Cumberland, Md.). A month later, June 10, the force moved forward with three hundred axemen, cutting a road twelve feet wide ahead of all. There were about 1,200 soldiers in the command, besides officers, teamsters and workmen. The line stretched out to a length of four miles—"a thin, long, party-colored snake, red, blue and brown, trailing through the depth of leaves." They were able to advance but a trifle more than three miles a day.

On July 7, Braddock with eighty-six officers and 1373 men reached Turtle creek, (eight miles from Fort Duquesne), having decided to leave his heavy baggage under a guard in order to advance more rapidly with a fighting force. Here he crossed to the southerly side of the Monongahela, continued down stream, and on the 9th crossed back again by a ford that lay near the dam at the present village of Braddock, Pa.

At this time Contrecoeur commanded Ft. Duquesne, with a force of something over 250 white men and nearly 800 Indians. The approach of Braddock had created not a little excitement in the fort, and there were two British Colonials there, (James Smith and Robert Strobo), to take note of what was done. The Indians at first refused to fight the British, but when they had seen how the red coats marched in close order, and that it would be possible to shoot them "like pigeons," as one said to Smith, they decided to try it.

Accordingly, when Capt. Daniel Liénard de Beaujeu was placed in command of the regulars and Canadians, on the 9th, with orders to ambush Braddock at the ford of the Monongahela, the Indians raised the war whoop.

Barrels of gun powder, bullets and flints, were opened at the fort gate, and the Indians helped themselves. Beaujeu dressed himself like an Indian, (a common habit of the French at the time), and with 108 officers and regulars, 146 Canadians, and 642 Indians, (one account says 637), he started at 8 o'clock for the ford. It appears, however, that they were in no haste to reach the ford. A man could walk the distance in two hours, but Braddock crossed unmolested at 1 o'clock. Even when the British sat down and ate a luncheon no attack was made. But when Braddock's advance guard had passed a ravine in the hills a mile from the ford, they met a man "dressed like an Indian, but wearing a gorget of an officer." This man—Beaujeu, no doubt—stopped at sight of the British, gave an Indian war whoop, waved his hat and jumped for a tree. The French regulars, Canadians and Indians were then seen coming behind him. The greater part of the Canadians fled crying, *"Sauve qui peut,"* but the regulars and Indians "treed" themselves, and stood still while the British advance guard fired three almost harmless volleys into the tree trunks—almost harmless, but not quite, for Beaujeu was killed by the third.

Then the French and Indians began to shoot from their safe shelters; and the range was short. No braver regular troops than those red coats had ever marched into such a battle, but their bravery was their

THE BRADDOCK CAMPAIGN.

destruction. They stood in place in solid masses, scorning shelter, and fired back—uselessly as before. But a time soon came when flesh and blood could not stand the unseen death that pelted them from the brush, and they gave way just as Braddock arrived to support them with the main part of his force, shouting, "God save the King."

The fresh troops, on meeting the retiring vanguard, were thrown into some confusion, but were rallied by their officers, and formed into solid masses; and there, with few exceptions, they stood, facing the lead-laden storm, and firing back exactly according to the manual.

The Virginians, almost to a man, took to the trees like Indians. Braddock, with vigorous British profanity, ordered them back into line, and even killed one of them, it is said, with his sword, (see Gordon's "Pennsylvania"). A few of the red coats, who also sought shelter were beaten back into line or killed by the exasperated general. No flinching would be permitted by this commander. He crowded them together until they were as close together as wild pigeons on a roost, and they were slaughtered like the pigeons, as the Indians had foreseen. It was an army of disciplined Englishmen, Irishmen and Scotchmen. As firmly as their native islands, they withstood the storm until half their number were down—"stood panting, their foreheads beaded with sweat, loading and firing mechanically,"—and then they broke and fled. A moment later Braddock fell, shot through the lungs—"bleeding, gasping, unable even to curse." He was shot down by Thomas Fawcett, whose brother Braddock had cut down for seeking a tree, says Gordon.

The retreat at once became a panic, but Washington, with his sheltered Virginians, covered the flight, and the Indians turned from slaughter to the gathering of plunder, and finally went back to Fort Duquesne, "driving before them twelve British regulars, stripped naked, and *with their faces painted black."* They were to be burned.

Said James Smith who, from within Ft. Duquesne, saw the victorious mob return: "The savages appeared frantic with joy, dancing, yelling, brandishing their red tomahawks and waving scalps in the air, while the great guns of the fort replied to the incessant discharge of the rifles without. The most melancholy spectacle was the band of prisoners. They appeared dejected and anxious. They were led to the banks of the Alleghany" and there each was "tied to a stake with his hands above his head," and then they were "burned to death." The Frenchmen made no efforts to prevent these tortures. There is every reason to suppose that the French approved them. The French had, on several occasions, burned Indians to death, and the instances where any Frenchman actually interfered in behalf of a British prisoner are so rare that one is fully justified in believing that the tortures at Fort Duquesne had their full approval.

It seems proper, therefore, to call attention to the fact that in all the wars between the British Colonies and the Indians, and between the United States and the Indians, no captured Frenchman was ever burned to death, nor was any captured Indian. Our people saw their wives and children outraged, murdered and tortured by the Indians, but there was never a case where

FALL OF BRADDOCK.

our men so degraded themselves as to burn to death one of the inferior race in retaliation. One may remember this with some satisfaction, even in the midst of the unspeakable humiliation which has been brought upon our nation by the burning of members of an inferior race during recent years.

Braddock's wound was mortal. He had faced the enemy he justly despised with vigorous, voluble energy and courage; for four days he faced death with silent resolution. Once, as he recalled the rules his teachers had given him, he said aloud, "Who would have thought?" And then at 8 o'clock in the evening of Sunday, July 13, having seen, at least, that tactics in war, as in all other matters, must be adapted to the circumstances, he said, "We shall know better how to deal with them another time," and then died.

Out of eighty-six officers in the British force, sixty-three were killed. Washington had two horses shot under him, and several bullets pierced his clothing as he fearlessly exposed himself. Twenty years later, an armed host of Americans who had gathered around the port of Boston and were staggering beneath a burden of war that was yet too great for them to carry, remembered that battle on the bank of the Monongahela, and sent word to the Continental Congress that they would "rejoice to see this way the beloved Colonel Washington."

Out of 1373 privates and non-commissioned officers, 459 only escaped unhurt. Among those who escaped was a teamster who was to achieve fame in after years. His name was Daniel Boone, and he was then twenty-one years old.

The French had three officers killed and two officers and two cadets wounded. Of their regular privates four were hurt. The Canadians lost five wounded, and the Indians twenty-seven killed and wounded.

In its immediate result, the victory seemed almost decisive for the French, for the whole frontier, from Pennsylvania south, was left unguarded, and every tribe of red men, save only the well-settled portion of the Iroquois at the eastern end of their "long house," was fully committed to French interests.

And yet the success of the French here led them ultimately to their downfall. For as soon as they learned that the British were fully defeated, they began raiding the British frontier, and the devilish cruelty of these raids united the colonists and brought them into the field in overwhelming numbers.

The orders to raid the home makers on the British frontiers were issued in France—"manage on occasions in which there may be acts of violence *in such a manner as not to appear the aggressor,*" said a letter to Duquesne dated September 6, 1754, but *"if you consider it necessary to make the Indians act offensively against the English, his Majesty will approve of your using that expedient."*

As a matter of fact little effort was made to avoid appearing as aggressors. Captain Dumas succeeded Contrecoeur at Fort Duquesne, and he immediately began sending parties of Indians under French officers to raid the Pennsylvania frontiers. In speaking of these raids Father Godfroy Cocquard, S. J., in a letter to his brother, written early in 1757, said:

"The Indians do not make any prisoners; they

MODERN SCENE OF BRADDOCK'S DEFEAT.

kill all they meet, men, women and children. Every day *they have some in their kettle,* and after having *abused the women and maidens, they slaughter or burn them."* (N. Y. Colonial Manuscripts, vol. x, p. 528.)

"The upper country Indians have really laid waste Virginia and Pennsylvania," wrote Montcalm in 1756. The Indians on the Upper Lakes heard of the vast amount of plunder gathered when Braddock fell, and they came to get more by raiding the undefended colonists.

"In April [1756] there had been in those parts twenty detachments of Delawares and Chauanons [Shawnees]; these were joined by more than sixty Indians from the Five Iroquois Nations who have committed frightful ravages. The only resource remaining to the inhabitants was to abandon their houses and to remove to the sea coast. Three forts have been burnt, among the rest one containing a garrison of forty-seven men. The garrison was summoned to surrender, but having refused, the fort was set on fire in the night. The garrison attempted to escape, and *the Indians gave no quarter,"* so says "Abstract of Despatches from Canada, Vol. x, N. Y. Colonial Documents. M. Douville comanded the last named assault, and was killed.

Parkman notes that Dumas gave to each French officer in command of a party of raiders a *written* order to keep the Indians from torturing prisoners. Parkman thinks these orders were sincerely given. But the student of history may reasonably ask why were the orders *written* in every case? An officer obeys an oral order as carefully as a written one. One of these written orders was found on Douville whose forces "gave no quarter." The French commander not only knew that the Indians would give no quarter, but he knew that "every day they have some in their kettles," as Father Cocquard wrote. If the French King, in his orders to Duquesne was careful to say that "acts of violence" must be managed so as not *"to appear* the aggressor," is it too much to suppose that Dumas was animated by the same regard for *appearances,* and the same disregard of the infinite horrors of Indian atrocity?

The extent of the country raided is shown by the fact that on August 2, 1756, the Chevalier Villiers burned the log fort called Grandville on the north bank of the blue Juniata, a mile west of the present town of Lewiston, Mifflin county, Pa. He was but sixty miles from Philadelphia.

The French officers, in their reports on aggressions very often used the term "disgust the English." What they meant to say was that they believed the raids would intimidate the Colonists—fill them with the sense of inferiority to the French.

During the years 1756 and 1757, (called by Winsor the two dismal years), and in a part of 1758, the state of affairs seemed to justify the French hope. To keep back the Indians the Governor of Virginia built a fort, (1756), on the Holston river about thirty miles above the present site of Knoxville. Colonel Bird built another in the same county in 1758. Both were well garrisoned and mounted cannon, but both were whelmed by Indians and the garrisons forced by heavy losses to leave. A line of forts was built along the frontier. At the demand of the backwoodsmen, and in

Mississippi Valley.

spite of Quaker protests, a reward of 136 Spanish dollars was offered for every scalp of a male Indian, over twelve years of age, and fifty dollars for a squaw scalp. "John Potter, sheriff of Cumberland County, declared that the only way to prevent slaughter and destruction on the frontier was to send a strong force into the center of the Indian stronghold. His words are worth further consideration. While it is true that the friendship of the Indians might have been retained had they been treated on all occasions with Quaker kindness and justice, it is equally true that when war had been precipitated by wrong treatment, the quickest and therefore the most merciful way to end it was to send a *strong* force under a *strong* man into the center of the Indian country. The advice of John Potter cannot be emphasized too much. If a people are attacked, the best method of self-defence is to strike into the heart of the enemy's country. The Governor of Virginia refused to heed John Potter. He built a chain of forts instead. So the raiding continued unchecked.

In August, 1756, the French captured Oswego, "using in the operation the cannon Braddock had lost on the Monongahela." On July 6, 1758, Abercrombie was defeated at Ticonderoga.

Then the bloody tide was turned. At the end of July, Amherst, seconded by "the slender, nervous and almost dying Wolf," captured Louisburg. Coming thence to Lake Champlain, Amherst brought victory with him. Lieutenant Colonel John Bradstreet, with "an amphibious little army" of 3,000 men, crossed Lake Ontario, and captured Fort Frontenac on the morning of August 26, 1758. Nine armed vessels were in the harbor. Seven of these were destroyed, and two loaded with supplies needed for a new fort building on the site of Oswego, which the French had abandoned.

By this success Bradstreet gave the French power in the Mississippi Valley a serious wound. Their command over Lake Ontario, and so over their highway from Montreal to the southwest, was gone. Supplies could still be sent up the river from New Orleans, and from Illinois, but the chain of French posts, stretched first by La Salle, was broken.

Meantime General John Forbes left Philadelphia, (end of June, 1758), with an army to take Fort Duquesne, and on November 5, he was on Loyal Hannon Creek, in the town of Ligonier, Westmoreland County, Pa., fifty miles from his destination. He had advanced by slow but sure stages; and having studied well Braddock's disaster, he had trained his force, (between 6,000 and 7,000 men, of whom 5,000 were from Pennsylvania, Virginia and South Carolina), to meet the French and Indians in their own manner of warfare.

It was an efficient force, but the Quakers of Philadelphia forestalled it in its work. They opened the way so effectually that Fort Duquesne might have been taken without firing a gun in the whole campaign. And none was fired in the vicinity of the fort.

That the Quakers had no direct influence on the French scarcely need be said. But while Forbes was on the way west they persuaded the Governor of Pennsylvania to send Christian Frederick Post, a Moravian preacher, with a pipe of peace from them to the Indians beyond the Ohio. Post had earned the confidence of the Indians by his sincerity when a missionary among them, but he took his life in his hands when he accepted this task, for it was certain the French would have him assassinated, if possible. However, he reached his red friends in November, and they accepted the pipe of peace the Quakers had sent them.

Sufficient credit has not been given to this mission of peace, in our histories because, probably, the writers have supposed that Forbes and his force frightened the Indians into submission. But a careful reading of Post's second journal, (see the "Olden Time"), shows clearly, first, that Post was entirely truthful, and, second, that the Indians changed their allegiance from the French to the British (in spite of every opposition on the part of the French officers), because of the message Post carried to them. They did this in the face of the overwhelming defeat of a detachment of Forbes's army, 800 strong, under Major Grant, wherein nearly 300 men were lost, (Sept. 15, 1758).

Forbes, after a council of war, had determined to proceed no further than Loyal Hannon Creek, and he would have persisted in this determination, but for the defection of the Indians from the French interests after they had seen the Quaker pipe of peace. And the French would have stood firm at Fort Duquesne but for this defection. French officers were present at the public councils Post held with the Indians, but on the night of November 22d, 1758, "the Indians danced around the fire until midnight for joy of their brethren, the English coming," and the next day the French gave up hope.

Returning to Fort Duquesne, on the afternoon of

the 23d, De Ligneris, who was then in command, and who had been watching Post, prepared his forces for embarkation. All the buildings and the fort were fired. Under the ominous shadow of the smoke the French divided themselves into two companies, and at daylight, one under De Ligneris went up the Alleghany to Venango. The other paddled down the Ohio to Fort Massac, a station not far from the Mississippi, left there a small garrison, and then went on to Fort Chartres.

On November 25, General Forbes entered Fort Duquesne, and having repaired it, he renamed it Fort Pitt, from which we have the name of the modern city of Pittsburg.

How the British won at Fort Niagara and at Lake Champlain in 1759; how and why Wolf on the Plains of Abraham said, "Now, God be praised, I will die in peace," need not be recounted here, even though these victories shut out forever the French from the Great Valley which La Salle had given them. But a word regarding French official life in America during the last days will prove instructive. To quote the words of Parkman, ("Wolf and Montcalm"):

"A contagion of knavery ran through the colony. . . . Conspicuous among these military thieves was Major Pean. 'La Petite Pean' had married a young wife, famed for beauty, vivacity and wit. Bigot [the Intendant] who was near sixty, became her lover; and the fortune of Pean was made. . . . He had bought as a speculation a large quantity of grain with money of the King, lent him by the Intendant. Bigot then issued an order raising the commodity to a price far above that paid by Pean, who thus made a profit of 50,000 crowns. A few years later his wealth was estimated at from two to four million francs. Madam Pean became a power in Canada, the dispenser of favor and offices. Pean, jilted by his own wife, made prosperous love to the wife of his partner, Penisseault, and after the war took her with him to France; while the aggrieved husband found consolation in the wives of the small functionaries under his orders."

And while Wolf was before Quebec, and food was so scarce that the people were placed on a ration of two ounces of bread a day, "fowls by the thousand were fattened on wheat," that Bigot and his followers, male and female, might have delicate food for their carousals.

After the fall of Quebec, the remainder of this war—the great Seven Years War—was fought out in Europe. In November, 1762, the plenipotentiaries of England, France and Spain, at a meeting in Paris, agreed to make peace. One condition of the treaty was that Canada should be ceded to Great Britain, with all of the French claim east of the Mississippi. Fearing that, in the negotiations, he would have to give the whole valley to the British, the French King forestalled such a disaster by a secret treaty, (dated Nov. 3, 1762), in which he gave to Spain the island on which New Orleans stood, and all the French possessions west of the Mississippi.

Robert Rene Cavalier, Sieur de la Salle, by honest work, filed a claim in the name of France, on the broad basin of the Mississippi. Honest work only was needed to secure to that nation the full title in fee simple. But those whom France sent to complete her title took for a pattern of life the example found in the King's court. From first to last the most exciting theme among them—the theme that created deadly quarrels most frequently—was the matter of precedence in social and public functions. From the first to the last they sought the sea of beaver instead of the South sea. In gathering wealth they flung honor to the winds, where they had any to fling, and when they had accumulated a store, they spent it as their King was spending the whole French nation. It was because the dominant French in America were foul exudations of the Court over which the Pompadour ruled, that the French nation was driven across the Atlantic. When ten righteous men could not be found in all the plain, the fire of God swept it. It was in accordance with an inexorable law of nature that the man with the axe should at last supplant the vagabond with the sword.

HERNANDO DE SOTO.
The spelling of his given name is as varied as his biographers.

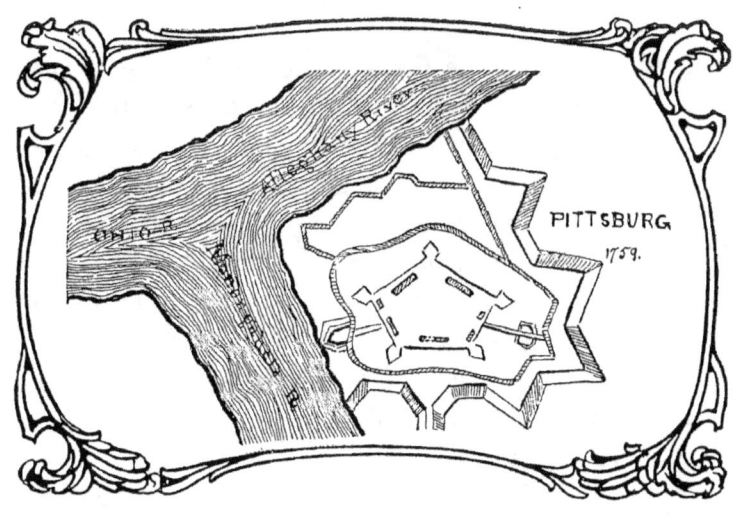

IX

THE SPANISH IN THE GREAT VALLEY.

De Soto's Character as a Highway Robber Plainly Described—Raids through the American Wilderness that turned an Army of Glittering "Knights" into Wilderness Tramps—The splendid Courage of an Explorer compared with the stubborn folly of a Highwayman—The first thought of Proclaiming an American Nation—A peep into the Bed Chamber of a French Lady—"Ca ira, les Aristocrates a la Lanterne."

Brief shall suffice for the story of the first Spanish expedition to the banks of the Mississippi, for the men in it were animated by the spirit of highway robbers, and nothing came of their work.

It was on April 6, 1538, that Hernando de Soto sailed from Spain on the expedition that led him to the banks of the Mississippi River, and gave him the credit of being the first more or less civilized man to see the stream and explore any part of the mighty basin. The story of this expedition has fascinated more than one poetic mind. "It was poetry put into action; it was the knight-errantry of the Old World carried into the depths of the American wilderness," says one writer. A calm study of the facts, however, shows that the work was detestable. Hernando de Soto had been a follower of Pizarro, and had enriched himself by the merciless slaughter and robbery of the Peruvians. Returning to Spain he was greatly honored because of his success, but neither his vanity nor his greed was satisfied.

"De Soto burned with ambition to signalize himself equally with Cortez and Pizarro;" the region north of the Gulf of Mexico was the only one left to explore; this region was supposed to hold as much gold and silver as the countries to the south, and to Florida De Soto would go.

In all, 1,000 men, of whom 350 were mounted, sailed from Havana on May 12, 1539, to Florida. "They provided everything which the experience of former expeditions could suggest, or avarice or cruelty dictate * * * chains and fetters for the captives, and even blood hounds to assist in drawing them from their hiding places."

The soldiers were completely covered with armor that was trimmed with gold, and they were armed with swords, spears and cross bows, only eighteen having arquebusses, as the rude muskets of the period were called. They were gay "as if it had been an excursion of a bridal party." Whether awake or asleep,

Mississippi Valley.

they dreamed only of finding cities of red men, with gold-filled temples devoted to the worship of the sun. These temples were to be robbed. The red men were to be set to work as slaves in the mines, with armed men to keep them at it, and priests to baptize them as they expired under the lash or by more cruel torture.

Having landed at Espiritu Santo Bay, Florida, De Soto led his "steel clad cavaliers" on their "prancing steeds" into the wilderness of Florida. Thereafter, until the spring of 1541, this "glittering host" with their waving plumes ranged the interior in search of gold. The red men were slaughtered in open battle, and by deliberate butchery after they had surrendered as prisoners. They were maimed and they were tortured, because they had no gold or silver. A thousand, chiefly women and children, were burned alive in a huge public wigwam at one village, after one battle. But the Indians were not cowed, for they never ceased to hover around and fight back.

The Spaniards had come to take gold from its rightful owners, but they never saw a color in the pan. Instead of finding gold they lost what they had brought with them. Their waving plumes were broken in the brush. Their glittering armor was rusted in the swamps, and battered by the impetuous red home-defenders. Their clothes were worn out. Their horses were killed. A time came, (it was in the second year), when they were glad to use rawhide shields in place of glittering steel, and the skins of wild animals in place of velvets and laces. With the war whoop of the red man ever sounding in their ears, many of them came at last to long for a speedy return home.

But the vanity of De Soto held them fast. Others might return and admit defeat, not he. The poet says that ambition fired his fortitude, but in cold fact, it was sheer vanity, what would have been called splendid courage in an explorer, was stubborn folly in him. The motive made the difference. So he led his drooping, fagged followers away from the port, (Bay of Achusi), where ships were awaiting to carry him to Cuba, and continue on through the wilderness.

It was now that De Soto found the Mississippi. On April 13, 1541, he reached a stream which he named Rio Grande because it was so large—the Mississippi of modern days. Up this stream the expedition toiled for four days to an open country. There they encamped for twenty days while they built boats to carry them over, and, presumably on May 7, they crossed the river—fought their way across, for armed red men stood on the western bank and came afloat to meet them.

A local historian (Monette) thinks De Soto crossed "within thirty miles of Helena," but he adds that "the changes of the channel in the lapse of 300 years may have been such as to defy identification."

From the Mississippi, De Soto marched west and north to a mountainous region—the Ozarks—and then gave up hope. Turning around he came once more to the Great River. He arrived in the spring of 1542, at the village of Guachoya, located on the Mississippi, twenty miles below the Arkansas river. Here, while building vessels, "the incessant fatigue of body and anxiety of mind, together with the influence of climate, brought on a slow, wasting fever; and here, on June 5, 1542, De Soto died."

Mississippi Valley.

It had been the habit of the near by Indians, (Quapaws they, and a fierce nation when defending their homes), to dig up the body of every buried Spaniard, quarter it and hang the pieces on trees and posts, as a warning to the predaceous host. To save the body of De Soto from such a fate, his followers made a coffin of a green oak log, placed the body therein, and, carrying it to the center of the Great River, sank it "in nineteen fathoms of water."

It was for an end like this that vanity and greed had carried De Soto into the American wilderness. His followers, under Luis de Mascoso, made another trip into the wilds to the west of the river, but returned in fewer numbers and with fewer arms and less clothing. No leader now had any thought but to escape the wilderness, and building such boats as they could, they launched forth on the Great River, on July 2, 1543, a remnant of 350 squalid, ragged wilderness tramps out of the plumed, glittering "knight-errants" that had come to fatten on blood and gold. So they reached Panuco, Mexico, and disappeared in the armies maintained in Spanish America by the throne of Spain.

If a first view of the mouth of a river gave its water shed to the nation whose explorers obtained such a view, then the Mississippi Valley was rightfully Spain's. Don Alonzo de Pineda discovered the mouth of the stream in 1519, and named it Espiritu Santo. In 1528 Cabeza de Vaca crossed the river, and then De Soto explored, after a fashion, a considerable portion of the valley. Spain might, indeed, have said that De Soto's expedition "took out the first papers" for a claim, if we may use the homesteader's vernacular. But De Soto's expedition completely satisfied the Spanish in one sense; they would have no more of that region for more than 100 years. But it was a copy of the Spanish history of this region that inspired La Salle in his work.

When, in November, 1762, the peace commissions gathered at Paris to end the Seven Years War, France was not only anxious to thwart as far as possible the British ambition for territorial expansion, but she was willing to get rid of the burden involved in supporting a governor in Louisiana. The last Governor, (Kerlerec), had used 10,000,000 livres in four years—ostensibly in preparing for war. Spain therefore once more sent a soldier of repute to the banks of the Mississippi.

The treaty by which Spain acquired Louisiana was completed on November 13, 1762, but for a time the French retained control, and the people of New Orleans knew nothing of the transfer.

It was during this period of Spanish ownership and French control that St. Louis was founded. Pierre Liqueste Lacede obtained a charter which gave "the necessary powers to trade with the "Missouri river Indians, and "as far north as the river St. Peters." On August 3, 1763, Laclede, with August and Pierre Choteau, members of his family, (sons of his mistress), left New Orleans. He reached St. Genevieve on November 3. Finding no houses large enough to hold his goods, he went on to Ft. Chartres, where he remained for the winter, spending the time in exploring the Mississippi for a site for a trading station.

DON ANTONIO DE ULLOA.
Governor of Louisiana, 1764.

At a distance of eighteen miles below the mouth of the Missouri river he found, on the west bank, "a growth of heavy timber, skirting the river bank, and behind it, at an elevation of some thirty feet," a "beautiful expanse of undulating prairie." To this spot he brought his party and possessions on February 15, 1764, and laying out a town site, he named it St. Louis.

Meantime M. D'Abbadie was sent out by the French government to rule New Orleans. He took command June 29, 1763, knowing nothing of the sale to Spain, but during the summer rumors of the sale came and in October the Government confirmed the rumors. Meantime D'Abbadie died and one Aubry succeeded him.

The French inhabitants were excited and alarmed. Commissioners were sent to Paris to petition for the repurchase of the territory, but in vain. In 1765 a letter was received from Don Antonio de Ulloa, a commodore in the Spanish navy, and a man of letters as well. It was written at Havana, on July 10th, and announced that he had been appointed governor and would "soon have the honor" to come and render "all the services the inhabitants may desire."

He arrived at New Orleans on March 5, 1766. He was a man of learning and an author of wide repute, but he was coldly received. A committee of merchants presented a petition that seemed to Ulloa to be "insolent and menacing" in its tone. The superior council, a legislative body, demanded the exhibition of Ulloa's commission. The French troops declined absolutely to enter the Spanish service, although the agreement with Spain had provided that they should do so.

Because of the mutinous spirit of the people "the really mild and liberal Ulloa" did not show his commission, or take formal charge of affairs, but managed matters as well as he could through Aubry. He began a series of concessions for the benefit of trade. He allowed the French flag to fly. He did more to conciliate the people than he should have done, for his mildness was misunderstood, and as time passed, advantage was taken of it to create an insurrection. "Now it was that a deficiency in habits of mature thought and self-control, and, in that *study* of *reciprocal* justice and natural right, became to the people of New Orleans and Louisiana a calamity." (Cable.)

On October 25, 1768, a great mob from the Acadian and German coasts entered the city. They were armed with fowling pieces, with muskets and all sorts of weapons." The cannon at the gates of the fortifications had been spiked during the night. The people of the city rose in a body. Ulloa and his family were obliged to board a Spanish frigate to escape the mob. The superior council at a meeting, the next day, adopted a report demanding that Ulloa leave the colony, and on October 31, he did leave, "enduring at the last moment the songs and jeers of a throng of night roysterers."

The leaders of the mob at first thought to set up a new nation, and they applied to the British of Pensacola for help. But failing to get help they abandoned this early thought of American freedom, and begged Louis XV. to take them back. "Great King, the best of Kings, father and protector of your subjects, deign, sire, to receive into your royal and paternal bosom the children who have no other desire than to die your subjects!" said the petition sent to Paris. Nevertheless here was the first colony in America that *entertained the idea* of proclaiming her independence.

But both the thought of liberty, and the petition to "the father and protector of your subjects," failed. On August 18, 1769, Don Alexandre O'Reilly, landed at New Orleans with 600 picked soldiers, from a fleet of twenty-four ships, that lay at anchor in the Crescent. The jeers that filled the ears of the departing Ulloa were hushed. In place of them were heard the cheers of the thronging soldiers. But when the flag of France came down, and that of Spain arose, the people wept aloud in spite of bayonets.

O'Reilly was Irish by birth, but by long training had become a Spaniard in his mental characteristics. He had come to punish the leaders of the insurrection, but he concealed his thoughts. On August 31, he invited, with "professions of esteem and friendship," the leaders of the insurrection to attend a levee at his official residence. They accepted, and "while enjoying the hospitality of his house, were invited by O'Reilly himself into an adjoining apartment," where they were arrested by armed soldiers. (Monette.) The men so arrested were Focault, former commissary-general; De Noyant and Boisblanc, of the superior council; La Freniere, attorney-general, and Braud, public printer; Marquis, an officer; Doucet, a lawyer; Villiere, Mazeut and Petit, planters. John and Joseph Milhet, Caresse, and W. Poupet, merchants, were arrested several days later. "The trials which followed were hasty, arbitrary and tyranical in the extreme."

De Noyant, La Freniere, Marquis, Joseph and Caresse were convicted and sentenced to die, with confiscation of property. They were shot to death on September 28.

In connection with the execution of these French mutineers Gayarre gives us an interesting, and perhaps not impertinent peep into the bed chamber of a grand lady of the day. The property of the executed men having been confiscated, an inventory of the household effects of each was taken. In the bed room of Madam Villiere the confiscators found a "cypress bedstead, three feet wide, by six in length with a mattress of corn shucks and one of feathers on the top; a bolster of corn shucks, (split fine and curled, without a doubt), and a coarse cotton counterpane; six chairs of cypress wood, with straw bottoms; some candle sticks with" candles made of the wax of the myrtle bush. It was a bed room in marked contrast to "the hooped petticoat, the brocaded gown, the rich head dress;" and other fine clothing of the lady.

O'Reilly came to enforce the submission of the people. His power was ample and his methods effective. Having shot five, he sent four more to Morro Castle, at Havana, where they were imprisoned one year. That ended the insurrection spirit.

Martin says the population of Louisiana, at this time, was estimated at 13,540 souls. New Orleans held 3,190, of whom 1,803 were free whites, 31 free blacks, 1,225 slaves. Martin gives St. Louis a population of 891, meaning thereby, apparently, the region of which St. Louis was the chief settlement.

The pictures of life under the early Spanish rule are interesting. "I found the English in complete pos-

Mississippi Valley.

session of the commerce of the colony. They had in this town their merchants and traders, with open stores and shops, and I can safely assert that they pocketed nine-tenths of the money spent here," reported O'Reilly. But he soon "drove off all the English traders," and all other individuals of that nation.

The British having, meantime, come into control of West Florida, and the east shore of the Mississippi above the Bayou Manchac, and having moreover, the right of free navigation of the big river, had not only established trading posts on their own territory, contiguous to the French domain, but during the rule of D'Abbadie and Aubry had entered the city itself, obtaining permits, no doubt, by bribing the officials.

When driven out by O'Reilly the British merchants, knowing that they had the right to the free navigation of the river, built "two large floating ware houses, fitted up with counters and shelves, and stocked with assorted merchandise"—the first houseboat of the Mississippi known to the record. These were moored at Gretna, opposite the city, a good part of the time, but where poled (pushed), up stream when the exigencies of trade among the "Cajuns" or at the German Coast demanded. "Anything offered in trade was acceptable, revenue laws were mentioned only in jest, profits were large, credit was free and long, and business was brisk."

Martin makes an estimate of the business of Louisiana province, at this time, and places the annual exports at: Indigo, $100,000; deer skins, $80,000; lumber, $50,000; naval stores, (resin, etc.), $12,000; rice, peas and beans, $4,000; tallow, $4,000—a total of

$250,000. The smuggling trade done with the Spanish colonies before O'Reilly's time reached $60,000 a year.

"The indigo of Louisiana was greatly inferior to that of Hispaniola; the planters being quite unskillful and inattentive in the manufacture of it."

The culture of sugar cane, introduced by the Jesuits, had not flourished. A M. Dubreuil, in 1758, had erected a sugar mill in the lower part of the present city, and a cargo of soft sugar was exported to France in 1765. But half of it leaked from the barrels during the voyage, and the sugar made thereafter, for a long time, was consumed at home.

Some time after O'Reilly arrived at New Orleans, a fleet of transports came up the river bringing 2,600 Spanish soldiers. The ships with food supplies failed to arrive in time, and provisions became so scarce that the price of flour quickly rose to $20 a barrel. In this condition of affairs came Oliver Pollock, a Baltimore merchant, with a ship load of flour which he offered to O'Reilly for the use of the soldiers, and the people, at his own price—a notable incident in the history of American commerce. O'Reilly declined to fix the price and Pollock put it at $15. Then O'Reilly bought it and "granted to Pollock the free trade of Louisiana" for life—a privilege worth much more than five dollars per barrel on one cargo of flour.

O'Reilly sailed from New Orleans on October 29, 1770, leaving Louis de Unzaga, with 1,200 soldiers, to rule. O'Reilly having pacified, Unzaga was to conciliate, the people. How he succeeded he tells in a letter to the Bishop of Cuba (1773), in which he says there are not in New Orleans and its environs 2,000 souls of all professions and conditions. Many Creoles (that is, as Cable says, "the French speaking ruling class"), had emigrated to St. Domingo, taking with them mechanics and other valuable citizens—a movement which those who lived long enough, greatly regretted, less than twenty years later, when the negroes arose."

In place of these emigrants came many Spaniards, and in one respect the Spanish families were better for the country than the French had been, for they came to make Louisiana their home, where the French had, to a great extent, looked upon the country as an abiding place where those with sufficient influence could accumulate wealth. But not all the French emigrated, and in consequence two social communities were created in one town—an official Spanish community, and a land-owning, French-speaking aristocracy.

A curious result followed. Many Spanish officials, including Gov. Unzaga, who succeeded him, married French ladies. But "in the society balls when the uncompromising civilian of the one nationality met the equally unyielding military officers of the other, the cotillion was French or Spanish, according to the superior strength of the Creole or Spanish party." And "more than once" there was "actual onset and bloodshed," to determine which was the stronger, with duels a plenty next day.

Spanish Ursuline nuns, brought from Havana to teach Spanish, "found themselves compelled to teach in French, and to content themselves with the feeble achievement of hearing the Spanish catechism from girls who recited it with tears rolling down their cheeks" (Cable).

"I cannot flatter his majesty so much as to say that the people have ceased to be French at heart," wrote Unzaga in 1773, and Bishop Penalvert in 1795 repeated the same thought.

Not only did Unzaga fail to make Spanish of the Creoles; he and his successors failed absolutely to create a colony worth comparison in any respect, save one, with the Anglo-Saxon communities at the Northeast. When a stranger passed the thresholds of New Orleans he was "welcomed with such manners as were habitual in the most accomplished court of Europe." In "artificially graceful deportment" (Gayarre), and in that only, this Latin-American colony led all other American colonies. In all practical matters, the Louisiana territory was sunk into the rich soil of the valley by its official incubus.

The local historians tell of the convents, the churches, the hospitals and the fortifications that were built in New Orleans, but the most careful search of all that they have written shows but one indication or promise of the magnificent future that awaited the city. It was this—When the French Republic arose to "fire the Creoles' long-suppressed enthusiasm," the "Marseillaise was wildly called for in the theatre; and in the drinking shops was sung defiantly the song, '*Ca ira—ca ira, les aristocrates a la lanterne.*'" A thought—even a hope of self-government, ill-conceived, and dimly seen, indeed, and yet unmistakable, was in the hearts of this people. They were lying in the cradle of a paternal despotism, but by and by they would walk.

X

PONTIAC'S WAR AS SEEN IN THE VALLEY.

The True Cause of Pontiac's War Considered—The Savage Victories at Erie, Le Boeuf and Venango—Fort Pitt twice Besieged—Saved by the First Armored War Ship known to American History—The Desperate Fight at Bushy Run—A Comparison of Losses—The Universal Law of Compensation has been Written in Blood from the Blue Juniata to Jackson's Hole.

To learn the origin of Pontiac's war, one must go back to the evacuation of Fort Duquesne, November 24, 1758, because the Indians began to grow angry very soon after that event; and they were angered because of what followed naturally (alas!) as a result of British domination. As soon as Fort Duquesne came into the possession of the British, the traders began to stream through the passes. These traders had, in former times, defrauded the Indians by finesse. The French traders had made more than 700 per cent. profit (La Houtan), but both the British and French had always made many presents to the influential members of the tribes. When the French government could no longer assist the French trader, however, the British traders had almost a monopoly of the Indian traffic, and the one brutally odious characteristic of the Anglo-Saxon—his contemptuous disregard of the rights of inferior races—displayed itself. Where the traders had bribed, they now bullied, the Indians. Whom they had caressed, they now kicked from their path. Instead of adroit swindlers, they became highway robbers without masks.

Even the officers and the soldiers who replaced the French in the frontier posts after the fall of Quebec (1760), forgot, if they ever learned, that soldiers are trained solely to protect the weak. The Indian had been received at the stations with flattery and feasting; he was now, with undisguised disgust, kicked from the premises.

This matter seems important because the Indians, as a mass, were not incited to go to war under Pontiac by any encroachment of settlers actually made in the territory France had surrendered. The prime moving cause of this war was the bearing of the traders and soldiers who came to and were stationed among the Indians. Pontiac and his long-headed sachems saw, indeed, that British colonial farmers would follow the soldiers to the British forts, and would there clear away the forests—destroy the hunting grounds—but

MAJOR ROBERT ROGERS.
Indian fighter, ranger, English spy, etc. From an engraved portrait of 1770.

they were not aroused to a point where they would resent the foreseen intrusion until the aggressive arrogance of the British forerunners became unbearable.

In 1760 Pontiac, the chief of the Ottawas, was willing to be the friend of the British. Major Robert Rogers, while on his way to take over the French forts at Detroit and Mackinac, met Pontiac where Cleveland, Ohio, now stands. It was a meeting of two able warriors. Pontiac, on learning the mission of the British forces, not only bade them go on, but he sent messengers who shielded them from the attack of Indians along the Detroit river. And that he remained neutral, if not friendly, for some time after the British took possession of all the French forts is manifest from the fact that several small conspiracies were created among the Indians living between the Alleghanies and the Illinois, in which Pontiac did not appear.

Pontiac might have been made the firm friend of the whites—he would have been made a friend had he been treated with kindly consideration. The historians rail much at the "stubborn Quakers" of Pennsylvania for refusing to vote supplies during Pontiac's war, but they omit the fact that if Quakers had been employed to deal with the Western Indians, there would have been no war with Pontiac. The Pontiac war was due to outrageous doings of white men in contact with the red, and the utter neglect of the authorities in the seats of government. As the time passed, Pontiac saw the trend of British domination—that the red men were to be subjugated by a race whose arrogance and insolence were unendurable, and then he prepared for war.

Pontiac knew that the French had been defeated at Niagara and Quebec, but he did not know that the French nation was staggering to its knees under a weight of corruption too great to be borne. He supposed that if the red men were all to unite they would be joined by the French, as of old, and that with one mighty upheaval those united powers could sweep the British into the sea. With shoulders humping and hands chopping the air, the French vehemently encouraged this view, and Pontiac determined to try.

The writers speak of this war as Pontiac's "conspiracy." They call the artifices by which he and his men strove to get advantages over the white soldiers as treachery. In like manner Indian warriors have been styled horse thieves. But remembering that civilized naval officers have disguised warships as merchantmen, and that civilized governments, long after Pontiac's death, authorized private armed ships to prey on the unarmed merchantmen of the enemy, we will speak of Pontiac and his men as wild men—*savages* only.

How Pontiac fasted and prayed and dreamed dreams; how he gathered the tribes to a great council, and fired them with his own mad enthusiasm; how the Frenchmen helped on the combination, and promised to take part in the actual war; how the red sweetheart of the commander at Detroit betrayed the plot in time to save the garrison there; how Pontiac and his sixty warriors, with sawed off guns under their blankets, and a lie on their lips came to the fort, to stagger with astonishment as they saw the troops under arms and heard the drums roll; how they struck on May 10,

1763, nevertheless; and how until October 12, the incongruous forces were held to the work of besieging the British fort, and finally gave up only when Sir Jeffrey Amherst compelled the French commandant at Fort Chartres to send a message to Detroit calling off the red warriors, can have only mention here. Of the fighting that was done within the watershed of the Ohio, however, some details may be given.

On May 18, the Indians in a great mob made a furious attack on the fort at Le Beuf (Waterford), Pennsylvania. The assault failed. At night they fired the wooden structure, and then danced before the gate, as they looked to see Ensign Price and his thirteen men come out to die fighting. But Price and his men cut their way through the rear wall and escaped to the woods. By a circuitous route they reached French Creek, and passing down arrived at Venango.

In place of a stockaded fort they found there a heap of hot ashes and a few smoking logs. A party of Seneca Indians (the Seneca tribe only, of the Six Nations, joined Pontiac), had entered the fort professing friendship, and then had tomahawked all the garrison save Lieut. Gordon, commanding. Him they burned in Seneca fashion, keeping him alive for three days.

By following the river, Price and seven of his men reached Fort Pitt, on May 26. Six had dropped on the trail through exhaustion. On the same day a soldier named Gray arrived from Presqu' Isle, (Erie, Pa.), with a story of the slaughter of all but himself and one other man of the garrison there, although the Indians had promised them a safe conduct to Fort Pitt.

A day later (May 27, 1763), the Indians were

prowling around Fort Pitt, killing stragglers. A delegation came to the Fort and demanded that it surrender, promising, the while, a safe conduct to all within its walls to the settlements in Pennsylvania. They pretended to be friendly and anxious only to keep the people in the fort from the hands of Pontiac and his Western Indians, who, they said, were on the way. Capt. Ecuyer thanked them and in return warned them to flee quickly because, he said, an army of 6,000 men was coming to Fort Pitt, and 3,000 more were going up the lakes.

It is an interesting fact that while the Indians were trying to deceive Ecuyer they were themselves deceived, and fled. They went east, instead of west, however, and they ravaged the frontiers, as they had done when incited by the French. Thus they learned that no army was coming to Fort Pitt, and on July 26, they came back to the fort.

Shingiss (a notable leader), Turtle Heart and another chief were admitted to a conference, when they asked for it; and Shingiss made a speech which unfortunately has not been preserved—unfortunately because it was a fierce statement of the real wrongs the Indians had suffered at the hands of the whites, with special emphasis on the supposed wrong of taking their hunting grounds. It was a speech to make a patriot wince, but Capt. Ecuyer's reply was still more painful to the patriot heart, for it was a lie. He said the British posts were maintained in the Indian country solely to protect the Indians from the French. And yet, while he talked, there were 100 women and children of would be settlers, within the walls of the fort.

A siege followed that is memorable for one event. The Indians, by creeping under the shelter of the banks of the streams, found a safe lodgment under the walls of the fort, and were able to shoot flaming arrows to the roofs of the fort buildings in a way that was exceedingly dangerous to the whites. A rude fire engine was constructed, but only constant and most wearying vigilance saved the buildings from destruction; and finally it appeared that the garrison would be exhausted by the struggle.

In this extremity some bright intellect planned relief. A flat boat, with wooden walls that were bullet proof, was built and mounted on rollers. A crew, well supplied, was placed in it, and it was then rushed through a gate and down a steep slope into the Monongahela. The crew then anchored off the point where they could fire through their ports and rake the Indians concealed in little caves under the banks. "Whereat," as a soldier who was present says, "they set up the most diabolical yells I ever heard, retired up stream, and never again ventured so close to us" in daylight. The success of this, the first armored American warship, was manifest from the first run.

It is estimated that 20,000 people were driven from their homes in Virginia by the red raiders. In Pennsylvania the red fire swept eastward until the smoke was seen from the mountains around Carlisle. In Virginia a thousand riflemen were enrolled, and these beat back the raiders. In Pennsylvania, Col. Henry Bouquet, a native of Berne, Switzerland (a soldier of fortune), was placed in command of 500 men, the remains of two regiments of regular troops, and sent with supplies, toward Fort Pitt. He left Carlisle on July 19, with what seemed a most forlorn hope. For the force was inadequate in number, the soldiers were not frontiersmen, and many of them were sick. But it is recorded of Bouquet that "he was enthusiastic in the *study* of his profession," and such a leader could not fail altogether.

Fort Bedford and then Fort Ligonier were reached without mishap. The Indians about each place fled when Bouquet came, but it was only to gather in force further on.

Leaving Ligonier on August 4, Bouquet camped within eighteen miles of Bushy Run. The next day a forced march was made over a dry trail for seventeen miles—a distance that was covered by 1 o'clock in the afternoon—and the tired and thirsty soldiers were hastening forward, hoping for rest and water on the shaded banks of the run, when the brush ahead of the advance guard began to spit flames, and in a few moments the whole force was surrounded by a whooping, merciless horde of Delawares, Shawnees and Mingoes. The Indians that had been foiled at Fort Pitt came to seek revenge on the troops of Bouquet.

Lining up in a circle around the supplies and baggage, the little force of white men stood in their places, and fired back at the gun flashes of the Indians who kept well-hid behind rocks and trees.

It was a most unequal conflict. The troops by companies charged the concealed Indians, and with the bayonet drove them hither and thither at every charge. Only a temporary relief was thus attained, however, for the Indians turned around and fought with as much determination as ever, the moment the pursuit stopped. But in spite of discouragement; and in spite of fatigue, heat and thirst, the men, inspired by their leader, fought until night came, and then with their mouths as dry as ashes, they took posts as guards, or lay down to sleep around the wounded, who were suffering from tortures only a trifle less than the Indians would have inflicted at the stake. It is a story worth telling chiefly because of the magnificent endurance of these men.

At daylight the Indians came with renewed fury, and then Bouquet provided a trap for them. He ordered the two companies in advance to fall back hastily as if a retreat of the whole force was contemplated, while he concealed other squads where they could cover with their muskets the space abandoned. The Indians were deceived, and with yells of joy rushed in a thick mob after the companies that seemed to retreat. At the right moment the ambushed squads opened fire on the flanks of the mob, and then charged them with the bayonet.

That work won the victory. The Indians fled in a panic, and Bouquet was able to reach Fort Pitt without further mishap. But while the Indians lost near sixty killed, the white force had 116 privates and eight officers killed.

The much greater loss of the whites in this victory is worth a word aside. Consider the losses at Venango and Presqu' Isle; consider the losses at the other posts. To these add the losses (nowhere stated, unfortunately), that were suffered during the raids. It is a most important consideration. Definite figures are unattainable, but Roosevelt says that "in Braddock's War the borderers are estimated to have suffered a loss of fifty souls for every Indian slain; in Pontiac's war they had learned to defend themselves better, and yet the ratio is probably ten to one." In Lord Dunmore's war the ratio did not rise to more than three whites killed for every Indian life taken, but to sum up all the slaughter of whites, in occupying the Mississippi Valley, it is fair to suppose the losses of the whites out-numbered those of the Indians, by at least four or five to one. The whites paid a frightful price for the negligence and brutal greed they exhibited in dealing with the Indians. The universal law of compensation has been written in blood from the Juniata to Jackson's Hole beside the Tetons. We will but mention the penalty the whites have paid in money—the annual fine, as one may say, that amounted in the year ending June 30, 1900, to $10,175,106.76, that sum being the amount expended for "Indian Affairs."

It was Emerson who wrote an essay on the Universal Law of Compensation, and it was Carlyle who said of a certain part of the great Anglo-Saxon race that they numbered 27,000,000, and were "mostly fools." The truth of this last statement is never plainer than when considering the story of the Indian—unless, indeed, it be when considering what our present-day critics say of that dour old Scotchman.

The relief of Fort Pitt by Bouquet, and the failure of Pontiac at Detroit disposed the Indians to peace, though peace was not made immediately. The raiders in Pennsylvania retired to the Muskingum. A royal proclamation was issued forbidding absolutely all white settlements in the Indian country; forbidding the purchase of Indian lands by private persons, and ordering that all Indian traders take out licenses and give bonds that they would observe certain regulations providing for honest dealing with the red men.

Nevertheless the Indians began the war once more in the spring of 1764. Pontiac besieged Detroit, and the raiders came to the frontier homes with renewed fury.

Accordingly a force was sent up the great lakes under Col. Bradstreet, who did nothing but allow the Indians to deceive him with idle promises. Another force, under Colonel Bouquet, marched to Fort Pitt. Three wily chiefs came to meet him, bringing such promises as had deceived Bradstreet, but Bouquet arrested them as spies, and then sent one home to tell the tribes that only sincerity would save them. As a test of their sincerity he sent two messengers through the wilderness to carry letters to Bradstreet, at Detroit, and he told the Indians that if these messengers did not return safely, at the end of twenty days, the two chiefs held as hostages would be killed.

Then to emphasize his words, Bouquet marched his whole force, (1,500 men), through the wilderness to the Muskingum River, where he arrived near the middle of October, 1764. There he met the red peacemakers.

Bouquet was a sincere man, and because he was sincere and firm, the keen-eyed Indians saw their doom, if they failed to obey his will. The terms he imposed upon them were strictly fulfilled—the promises the Indians made to him were kept to the last letter, and that is a most important fact in the story of the Indian. A clear-eyed, very bad child was the Indian of 1764—bad enough to seek every advantage by indirection, and to revel in cruelty, but clear-eyed enough to know a man at a glance; and good enough, withal, to meet sincerity with sincere compliance.

The terms imposed were simple. The Indians were to give up all prisoners, first of all, and then send a deputation of chiefs, fully authorized to make a treaty with Sir William Johnson in the Mohawk Valley.

The prisoners were promptly delivered, and a most remarkable gathering they made. For some were wild with joy, and others who had become true children of the forest, were sullen and exasperated. There were white wives who, with unspeakable joy, were taken in the arms of their husbands who had come with Bouquet to find them. There were others who, with downcast eyes, because of half-red children, appealed for pity. There were white girls who were leaving red lovers whom they loved, and with whom they fain would stay, and there were white boys who watched for a chance, sure to come, at last, for a return to the wild free life of the wilderness. But all together were taken to Fort Pitt, and the war was ended.

The good work of Col. Bouquet, a sincere man, firmly established the British power over the Indians in the Mississippi Valley, and thus opened the way for British settlers.

DANIEL BOONE.
From an original portrait by Harding.

XI

CROSSING THE RANGE.

The Origin and Character of the Home makers who first Passed the Alleghanies—Cumberland Gap Named—Work of the Ohio Company—George Croghan as an Explorer—Kentucky Purchased from the Iroquois—Washington as a Speculator in Ohio River Lands—Daniel Boone and His Adventures—When the "Divine Right of Self Government" was first Exercised West of the Divide—Slaves in Great Demand.

At the end of Pontiac's war, the British colonists no longer feared either French or the Indians. Their migration across the range was therefore to grow in volume with an increasing ratio from the day peace was announced. But before relating the interesting facts of this migration it is well worth while to consider how it happened that such a westward movement came into existence in the first place. The fact is a consideration of the causes of this migration gives one a key to some of the most prominent characteristics of the settlers in the Mississippi Valley—and of their descendants.

In any study of this matter it is learned first of all that the people who were found flocking to the mountain passes were for the greater part, either emigrants, (with little money), from the old country, (or the immediate descendants of such emigrants), and they landed in ports south of New York. They came from countries where the land was in the possession of the gentry—where the possession of land, in fact, created a class distinction—gave the land owners social superiority. In the old country the emigrants had learned that the possession of land not only gave social elevation; it was the basis of physical comfort and mental ease. But toil as they might, they could not hope to obtain possession of so much as a single acre in the land of their birth.

Over the sea, however, in America, there was wild free land in breadths beyond their comprehension. It was to be had by any one who would take it and work it, and they came in ship loads to the ports of the colonies—25,000 of them arrived in Delaware Bay, in the course of two years—in order to secure this land.

They were thinking people or they would not have seen and comprehended the advantages connected with the ownership of land. They were ambitious, energetic and enterprising, or they never would have left their old homes and surroundings to migrate to a new country.

When they landed in America they showed forth other admirable characteristics. There were breadths of unoccupied land—wide breadths a plenty—east of the mountains, but these sturdy migrants would not take it. They landed in the Delaware or the Chesapeake, and a brief examination of the people and the conditions along shore showed them that an aristocratic class dominated that region—landed gentry very much like those left behind in the old country, even though there were neither dukes nor lords to be found. Under the gentry in Virginia were negro slaves. Under the gentry in Pennsylvania were a "boorish people—good farmers who cared more for their pigs than their own comfort, uniting thrift with habits that scorned education." That these migrants would not associate with either the negroes or the boorish people who scorned education was a matter of course. Having no means to buy estates it is plain that they could not have joined the landed gentry, but it is also a fact that they would not have done so even if it had been possible. For in Virginia the dominant people were Episcopalians; in Pennsylvania they were Quakers, and the migrants were Scotch Presbyterians who were ready to give reasons for the faith that was in them. Not all the migrants were Scotch Presbyterians, of course. There were some Huguenots and Palitinates, and many were without religious scruples; but the important fact is that these people as a whole were driven by their land hunger and religious peculiarities—by their ambition and their determination to think for themselves—away from the coast, where they landed, to the freedom of the wilds.

And if we look at the American born people, (men like Robertson and Boone), who flocked across the mountains, we will find that the feelings which urged them to seek homes in the wilderness were akin to those of the migrants from over the sea.

Rightly considered, this westward movement marks one of the most important epochs in the development of the race. The migration was due to the sprouting belief that all men were born free and equal, and were endowed with inalienable rights. It was a manifestation of the spirit that gave the world the American Nation.

There was, indeed, one slight obstacle in the way of the home seekers as they toiled through the passes—the King's Proclamation forbidding it, and forbidding also all private purchases of lands from the Indians. The real objects of this proclamation, as explained by Lord Hillsborough, President of the Board of Trade, were as follows:

"We take leave to remind your Lordships of that principle which was adopted by this Board, and approved and confirmed by his Majesty, immediately after the Treaty of Paris, viz.: the confining the western extent of settlements to such a distance from the seacoast as that those settlements should lie within easy reach of the trade and commerce of this kingdom, . . . and also of the exercise of that authority and jurisdiction which was conceived to be necessary for the preservation of the colonies in due subordination to, and dependence upon, the mother country. And these we apprehend to have been the two capital objects of His Majesty's proclamation of the 7th of October, 1763. . . . The great object of colonizing upon the continent of North America has been to improve and extend the commerce, navigation and manufactures of this kingdom. . . . It does appear to us that the extension of the fur trade depends entirely upon the Indians being undisturbed in the possession of their hunting grounds, and that all colonizing does in its nature, and must in its consequences, operate to the prejudice of that branch of commerce. . . Let the savages enjoy their deserts in quiet. Were they driven from their forests the peltry trade would decrease."

It had been openly asserted in England that if the Colonies were relieved from the fear of Indian aggressions they "would cover the continent, become a great nation, manufacture their own goods, and eventually declare themselves independent."

In the colonies, however, the proclamation was not taken seriously. It was considered as a collection of soft words intended to allay the irritation of the Indians. Washington said of it, that it was not intended as a permanent law governing the territory west of the Alleghanies.

Therefore, obeying the impulse of a dominant race, the British-Americans moved on. We can see now that the race progress through the valley of the Mississippi was inevitable—not to be stopped by any earthly power. A little consideration of the history of man shows that the spread of a dominant race is not only inevitable, but that it ought to be so if man is to continue to elevate himself.

And yet, in spreading through the Mississippi Valley—in spreading over every part of the continent, in fact—the white men wronged the red men beyond the power of words to describe, and thereby inevitably injured themselves vastly more than they injured the red men.

If a brief consideration be given to this matter, it will appear that the spread of the white men over the Great Valley was not necessarily in itself an injury to the Indian. The whites did necessarily take from the

Indian his hunting grounds, but enough has been said, already perhaps, to show that the Indian ought to have been kept out of hunting grounds from the earliest possible moment.

In short it was not in the taking of lands that the Indian was wronged, it was in the *manner* of the taking.

We are venturing once more on an idle speculation, but recalling the fact that at Gnadenhutten (and elsewhere by the Quakers), wild Indians were turned into peace-loving, stump-grubbing farmers, we can see now that the white men, if united in the project, might have made a Gnadenhutten of every red village on the continent. Let this statement be considered without prejudice. Bad as the Indians had become after 150 years association with the worst men of the white race, it was possible, by united and sincere efforts, even in 1764, to make a Gnadenhutten of every Indian village in the land. Because the white men were of a superior race, they were the natural guardians of the red men. These words are, perhaps, the mere prating of a sentimentalist, but because the whites were of a superior race, it was their duty to place the red men, at whatever cost, in permanent homes as corn-growers. But they shirked their duty—they refused to take up the "white man's burden"—and they have been compelled to pay for their neglect a price in blood and treasure so great that words are inadequate to tell how great the price is. Indeed, instead of trying to settle the Indians on farm lands, there are records showing that punishments were provided for subjugated Indians who failed to bring in certain stated quantities of skins of wild animals. It is a matter worth repeated considerations, when we think of the inferior peoples over whom we are yet guardians.

But this is not to withhold sympathy from the frontier home maker in his battles; his sufferings were often heartbreaking. He was only fulfilling the destiny of his race, for in him the forward impulse was strongest. The frontiersmen were the instruments by which the race worked out its destiny. It was their part to meet and push on the red men, to endure the hardships of forest life, and to turn the wilderness into home lands for a more (if not wholly), civilized people. They were the advance guard sent ahead of the main army; they were to be sacrificed—shot down—for the good of the many. How they did their duty shall now be told.

Few of the explorers need be named. It was in 1748 that Dr. Thomas Walker, "surveyor and man of mark," reached the head of Cumberland River, and two years later he passed through the Gap. His party killed "thirteen buffaloes, eight elks, fifty-three bears, two deer and 150 turkeys." The abundance of all kinds of game found is, perhaps, the most important feature of the story of Walker's expedition, and of others like it; for every frontiersman knew that these wild animals swarmed only where their food was abundant, and that their food was abundant where the land was rich.

It was in 1749 that the Ohio Company of Virginia, the organization of capitalists already mentioned, who had tried to acquire a half million acres of land on the Ohio River for the purpose of speculation, now did some work. They employed Col. Thomas Cresap, a frontiersman and trader living on the headwaters of the Potomac, to mark a trail fit for pack horses, from where Cumberland, Md., now stands, over the mountains to the forks of the Ohio. A friendly Indian named Nemacolin, who lived with Cresap, did the work. He blazed the trees along the route followed by the Indians when crossing the mountains by that pass; that is the Indian with a tomahawk, cut patches of bark from all the trees along the route. It was this path that was eventually opened as a road fit for wagons by the axemen with Braddock's army, and it was thereafter known as Braddock's Road. The great National Road, made the next century, followed this trail in part.

On September 16, 1750, Christopher Gist, a notable Indian trader, was commissioned by the "Ohio Company" to go over the range and prospect for lands on which they could locate their claim for 200,000 acres. His journey took him through the central and southern part of the State of Ohio as far as the mouth of the Scioto, whence he crossed to the Kentucky side, went up the Licking, climbed over the divide to the Kentucky River, up which he traveled to the Clinch, and so home by the way of the New River, and the head of the Roanoke. As a result of his explorations, the Ohio Company determined to locate their claims on the south side of the Ohio, and Gist was sent, in April, 1752, among the Indians to induce them to move their villages to the lands which the company purposed securing from them. In a dim way, this company saw the right method of dealing with the red men. They meant to turn him from a roving to a sedentary life, for the purpose of trade first, of course, but ultimately that he might become an agriculturalist and a citizen.

Dr. Walker, who named Cumberland Gap for the Duke of Cumberland, explored a part of the Kentucky River in 1758, as agent of a British land company, of which the Duke was chief patron, and he gave this river the name of Louisa in honor of the Duchess—a name that is perpetuated only by the name of the Kentucky town of Louisa.

After this, Virginia sent Joshua Fry, Lunsford Lomax and James Patton, with Gist, to Logstown, when a treaty was made wherein the Indians agreed not to molest any settlements that might be made on the Virginia side of the Ohio. Then Gist was ordered to build a fort and lay out a town site on the Virginia side of the river, two miles below the forks, but before this work was accomplished, the French advent on the head of the river stopped all further progress toward settlement.

After Pontiac's war ended, and while yet the French were in possession of the Illinois posts, George Croghan, now deputy Indian agent under Sir William Johnson, was sent through the country northwest of the Ohio River to prepare the red men for British domination. It was known to be a dangerous mission, for Pontiac was still alive and unappeased, and the French residents of the region naturally hated the British.

The party left Fort Pitt on May 15, 1765, and without adventures worth noting here, passed down to the mouth of the Wabash River, where they arrived on June 6, and camped in a fortification that Croghan supposed to be of Indian origin. There, at daylight, on the morning of the 8th, they were attacked by a party of Kickapoo and other Wabash Valley Indians, two white men and three Indians of Croghan's party were killed and everybody else wounded (including Croghan), except two white men and one Indian. The Kickapoos then rushed in and plundered the camp.

When told that the Iroquois would come to take vengeance, they excused themselves by saying that "the French had spirited them up," and they appeared to be alarmed, but they kept the plunder they had taken.

After some discussion of the matter, the Kickapoos took Croghan and his party as prisoners to Vincennes, where "about eighty or ninety French families" were "settled on the east side of the river, being one of the finest situations that can be found," to quote one of Croghan's journals. They were "an idle, lazy people, a parcel of renegades from Canada, and much worse than the Indians," in Croghan's opinion. He had little reason to think well of them, for, before Croghan's eyes, they traded baubles and red paint to the Indians for the tools and other valuables of which Croghan had been robbed, including gold and silver coin. One trader sold a pound of vermillion paint for ten of Croghan's half johannes (a gold coin worth $8.25), and jeered at Croghan after the trade was completed.

However, Croghan was released, after a time, and was able to hold a number of important councils with the Indians, including one with Pontiac, who then agreed to keep the peace. Pontiac had raged to and

GEORGE III., KING OF ENGLAND.
From a portrait made just before his accession to the throne (1760).

from Detroit to Ft. Chartres in a vain effort to rouse the Indians and French to make war again. He had "sent an embassy of warriors down the Mississippi, with an immense war-belt, with instructions to show it at every Indian village on the river," and to get aid of the French at New Orleans; but all in vain, for the French had made peace with the British. It was when this last hope had expired that Pontiac made peace. It was on August 28, 1765, at Detroit, that this council was held. Pontiac made a speech, in which he said: "Father, we have all smoked out of the pipe of peace. It's your children's pipe, and as the war is all over, and the Great Spirit and Giver of Light, who has made the earth and everything therein, has brought us all together * * * I declare to all nations that I had settled my peace with you before I came here." (N. Y. Colonial Mems., vii., p. 783.) In 1768 the aggressive old chief was assassinated near St. Louis by an Illinois Indian who had been hired by a trader named Williams to do the deed. The price paid was a barrel of rum.

At the treaty meeting which followed the Pontiac war (held by Sir William Johnson, at the German Flats, Herkimer Co., N. Y.), the Indians proposed that the Alleghany River be established as a definite and permanent boundary between the white men and the red. This offer was evaded, but on October 24, 1768, delegates from the Six Nations, the Delawares and the Shawnees, met at Ft. Stanwix (Rome, N. Y.), and here a boundary line was agreed upon. It began in the Ohio River at the mouth of the Tennessee, passed up the Ohio to Ft. Pitt, up the Alleghany to Kittanning, and thence across to the Susquehanna. These Indians abandoned all claim on the land lying south and east of that line. The Six Nation deputies signed the treaty for all Indians, but, the Shawnee and Delaware chiefs, while orally agreeing to it, held a mental reservation in the matter that was troublesome later. The price paid the Indians for the cession was £10,430, 7s, 6d—200 boat loads of goods brought up the Mohawk. It was by this payment that the Indian title to Kentucky, a slice of Tennessee, and the Ohio water shed of Virginia was extinguished, save only as the Cherokees claimed part of that region. The Cherokees did not sell out until 1775, though it is worth noting that the Cherokees made a treaty at Hardlabor, S. C., on October 14, 1768, by which they ceded the lands between the Great Kanawha and the Ohio.

When Pontiac's warriors came to Fort Pitt, 100 women and children, the families of home makers, were within, as already noted. When this war ended the blue smoke was already rising serenely from the stick-and-mud chimneys of the cabins they had built at Redstone (now Brownsville, Pa.), on the Monongahela. The King's proclamation, limiting the colonial settlements to the slope east of the mountains, had ordered all settlers west of the mountains to return to the east side. The Pennsylvania legislature passed bills for the removal of these settlers, and sent commissioners to enforce the acts. One bill provided the death penalty for all who should fail to remove as ordered. These acts were passed in sincerity, and the commissioners tried to enforce them. But it was work against a law of nature, and it failed, as all such work must fail. Even the Indians interfered to keep white settlers west of the mountains.

The purchase of lands by the treaty of Fort Stanwix (November 5, 1768), was the first act in the gate-opening that let the white settlers legally across the mountains, to make homes in the Ohio Valley. A number of companies were formed, about this time, to acquire lands in the Ohio Valley and people them. Franklin was interested in one. Washington, the Lees, and other prominent people were in another that absorbed the old Ohio company. Not one is worth more than mention here, because none of them accomplished anything beyond advertising the desirability of the lands of the Ohio Valley. Still, the agitation created by the application for grants evolved one practical Act in Council known as the Walpole Grant, by which the King gave, on August 14, 1772, a large tract of land west of the Alleghanies, which was to be erected into a new colony. Sir William Johnson, the Indian Agent, was instructed to inform the Indians that a new colony was to be formed in the Ohio Valley. This colony-on-paper (for it was never organized), is commonly called Vandalia. Its capital was to be located on the Great Kanawha. It was to be organized to give a definite western limit to the seaboard colonies that were already in the ferment which led to the War of the Revolution. But before the work of organization could be completed, a plan for placating the French inhabitants of Canada was turned to the purpose of limiting the seaboard colonies.

The French had petitioned, from time to time, for a restoration of their old-time laws and religious privileges. By an act of Parliament, approved June 22, 1774, known as the Quebec Bill, these privileges of law and religion were granted, and a vast region west of the Alleghanies was made a part of the Royal Province of Quebec. The Bill was to take effect in 1775, but the work of George Rogers Clark in the Revolution, following on Lord Dunmore's war, to be described further on, ended that business.

In the meantime (1767 and 1770), Washington had gone down the Ohio twice to prospect for good land, and with such success that he eventually acquired through his claims as a soldier, and by the purchase of other claims, no less than 32,373 acres of land in great plots, besides a small plot of 587 acres located fifteen miles below Wheeling. He had a total water front of sixteen miles on the Ohio, and forty miles on the Great Kanawha. He estimated the value of this land at $3.33 per acre, but it is to be noted that he had great trouble to keep squatters off his holdings.

But the man whose name is best known in connection with the movement of settlers across the Alleghanies was Daniel Boone. Daniel Boone, the fourth son of Squire and Sarah Boone, was born on November 2, 1734, in Oley Township, Berkes County, Pa. The father owned 250 acres of land on Owatin Creek, "some eight miles southeast of the present city of Reading." (Thwaite's "Daniel Boone.") It was then a frontier region. In 1750 the Boones sold out their holdings in Pennsylvania and moved to the Yadkin Valley, in North Carolina, where they arrived after a leisurely, halting journey, in the fall of 1751.

On their way they stopped at a small settlement

Mississippi Valley.

made on New River, just west of the Alleghany divide, but well within the limits of Virginia. Some Pennsylvanians had staked claims there in 1748. They had gone at about the time Dr. Walker was exploring the Cumberland Gap, and they made the first settlement west of the divide, though by no means west of the Alleghany mountain system.

In 1755, Daniel Boone joined as a teamster, a party of neighbors who went up to Pennsylvania, to help Braddock drive the French from the forks of the Ohio.

It was during this campaign that young Boone met John Finley. Finley, as a fur buyer, had been in the Kentucky region, and as far down the Ohio at the falls. His stories of the game to be found there greatly interested young Boone, for he was already a notable woodsman and hunter, and his interest was the greater because Finley told him that the Kentucky grounds were to be reached easily by following the well-known buffalo trail through the Cumberland Gap. Accordingly, after Boone reached home he extended his hunting trips westward, but it was years before he went to Kentucky, for on reaching home he was married to a handsome, black-eyed Irish girl named Rebecca Bryan.

As early as 1760, however, he had hunted on a branch of the Watauga, now called Boone Creek, where a beech tree was marked:

```
                    D. Boon
      CillED A. Bar      on
                        tree
      in    THE
      yEAR
              1760
```

In 1761 he accompanied an expedition under Capt. Hugh Waddell that went into the Cherokee country to avenge raids on the whites. In 1766 Benjamin Cutbirth, John Stuart, John Baker and John Ward, all neighbors of Boone on the Yadkin, crossed the Alleghanies on an exploring expedition, during which they reached the Mississippi, and this was the first expedition to do that of which there is any record. They gathered a harvest of skins, bear's oil and dried meat, which they sold at good prices in New Orleans. It was the first cargo of Kentucky produce sent down the Great River by British-Americans.

In the fall of the same year Boone and William Hill "crossed the mountain wall, were in the valleys of the Holsten and the Clinch, and reached the head waters of the West Fork of the Big Sandy," (Thwaites). The winter was passed at a salt lick ten miles west of the site of the modern town of Prestonburg, Kentucky.

In the autumn of 1768 John Finley came to the Yadkin as a peddler and remained all winter with Boone. Boone had found game a plenty in the water shed of the Big Sandy, but the forest was not to his liking. In talking the matter over with Finley, however, the latter proposed an expedition to the country further west, to be reached by a well-worn buffalo trail through Cumberland Gap, and after the crops had been planted in the spring of 1769, Boone, Finley, John Stuart, Joseph Holden, James Mooney and William Cooley, with the best outfit known to the frontier, went to a tributary of the Kentucky River, called Station Camp Creek, (Estill County, Kentucky), and built a camp. They were there, not as explorers, but as skin hunters. They were very successful until December 22, when Indians captured and robbed them, and then, after warning them to leave the country, set them free.

All but Boone and Stuart left. These two who remained were afterwards joined by Squire Boone, a brother of Daniel, and Alexander Neely. Eventually, (February, 1770), Stuart failed to return to the Camp —just why is not known,—but Daniel Boone found his skeleton in a hollow sycamore tree five years later. He may have been wounded by Indians from whom he escaped only to die in his hiding place. His skeleton was identified by his powder horn.

Being frightened by Stuart's disappearance, Neely went home. The Boone brothers remained until May, when Squire went to the settlements with their accumulated skins, and Daniel remained alone for three months, sleeping in caves, in the cane-brakes, or wherever a good hiding place could be found. After Squire returned with fresh supplies, the brothers killed another lot of skins which Squire carried to the settlements, leaving Daniel alone in the woods once more. In fact it was not until the spring of 1771 that Boone returned home. He had been for two years in the Kentucky wilderness, and had explored the fertile region as far as the falls, (Louisville).

It was the adventurous spirit of Boone, thus shown, rather than what he accomplished during these two years, that gave him immediate fame. For the Indians, as Boone's experience proved, were hostile, in spite of the treaty of Fort Stanwix. Boone for two years braved their wrath, and for months at a stretch, he was absolutely alone in the wilderness. It was an adventure that made the strongest possible appeal to the daring spirits among the frontiersmen on the east slope of the Alleghanies. That his accounts of the number of wild animals he had seen stirred the people who heard them scarcely need be said.

Daniel Boone, it may be said here, was the typical frontier explorer, rather than the typical home-builder. He was one of many good explorers. He founded Boonesborough, as the agent of Col. Richard Henderson, as shall be told further on, but he did not settle down permanently, either as a farmer or a village resident. He moved on, and died at last in Missouri—on the frontier—in 1820 (September 26). As one who blazed the trail he deserves fame. And having found a biographer (John Filson),—a reporter, literally, who took notes at various interviews, and published the story in 1784—Boone attained the recognition he deserved.

The home-builders, however, were among, or on, the heels of the explorers, and none of them was more notable than James Robertson. A North Carolinian, he, and his parents were so poor that they had been unable to send him to school. He could not read or write when he married, but he got a wife who would teach him, and in every way take part in his career. Finding few chances of rising in the world among the settlements of North Carolina, Robertson, early in 1770, took his rifle and a bag of corn, and went afoot over the range.

On reaching Boone's Creek, he found one William Bean making a home. Bean had been of the party in that hunting trip when Boone "CillED A. Bar" in

1760, and had liked the country so well that he had come with his family to make a home there.

Robertson selected a home site not far from Bean's, cleared a patch, planted it with corn, attended it until ripe, (living, the while, on game), harvested it, and having thus prepared in the wilderness, sufficient food for a small party of friends, as well as for his own family, he stored it away and went to his home in North Carolina. The next spring, March, 1771, he came back to the Watauga with a party that numbered eighty men, women and children—sixteen families. These people were going into the wilderness, trusting in the corn Robertson had stored, and in their rifles, for their food, until another crop could be harvested. They were looking for no other neighbor than William Bean, already there, but as they descended the western side of the range, they found ten cabins scattered along the stream, with men swinging the axe in the forest round about, or planting corn, while the women sang songs over their house work, and the children played at the work of clearing the land by gathering brush and building fires. A party had come from Fairfax County, Virginia, and seldom have home-builders been more joyfully surprised than those under Robertson.

This settlement was made near where Elizabethtown, Carter County, Tenn., now stands. Robertson's house stood near the head of the long island found there in the Watauga. Though not the first west of the divide, by many years, it was one of the most important in the history of the valley.

These pioneers had come to make homes about 300 miles from the "settlements." They supposed they were yet in Virginia, but when the Virginia line was surveyed out by Anthony Bledsoe, in 1771, they found themselves in a legal no-man's land. For North Carolina was then in a state of anarchy, owing to the revolt of the people against Governor Tryon, and they were beyond the bounds of the lands bought of the Indians at Fort Stanwix.

Something of the story of this No-Man's settlement must be told. The settlers soon found frontier desperadoes coming over the range—men who fled from the old settlements to escape the penalty of crime.

Loving order and hating anarchy, the settlers got together and exercised the "divine right of self-government." This right was exercised for four years before the Declaration of Independence. In 1772 they held a convention, signed articles of association for good government, and elected thirteen commissioners to enforce these self-made laws—"the first written compact for civil government west of the Alleghanies." It was an efficient government, too, in spite of the fact that it had no legal existence. It was good, that is to say, because the men who governed were entirely sincere in their desire to promote the *public* welfare, and they did not mistake selfish or private ends for the public good. To secure order they regarded justice, but not the forms found necessary in older communities. A horse thief, for instance, was hanged four days after his arrest. Enough time was taken to definitely ascertain the facts, but no time was wasted, once the facts were learned. This self-organized government, being honestly administered, preserved order and compelled justice in this community in spite of criminals and vagabonds that fled to the mountains from the alongshore settlements. The love of order shown by these frontier home-builders has been deemed worthy of the highest praise. No one has ever denied the praise due, and no one is likely to do so. But it may be worth while pointing out to the lynch-law loving people of the United States that the praise given to Robertson, Sevier and Campbell has been ill-considered in that it was unmodified. Preserving order by lynch law was praiseworthy only because it was the only resource of the order-loving frontiersmen. Such a use of the rifle or halter was a frightful necessity, and it carried in its wake the long line of disgraceful outrages on human rights that have blackened the history of the Nation since that time. Let it be repeated for the sake of emphasis that the Americans are the only nation of lynchers, because they were obliged, during the Revolution, and at times on the frontier, to disregard the forms of Law in the search for Justice; they thus acquired the lynching habit. It is because of the success of the Deckhard-rifle government of the early days that we now see mobs of enraged men lynching supposed offenders in the midst of communities where the laws might be enforced in orderly fashion.

It is most important to observe that even when an innocent man is lynched the victim is less to be pitied than the lynchers. For the degradation they inflict upon themselves and the comunity is far worse than death.

The Watauga people on learning that they were beyond the limits of Virginia, themselves made a treaty with the Cherokees by which they leased the lands they occupied, thereby evading the king's proclamation, forbidding the private purchase of Indian lands. But on March 17, 1775, when Henderson bought his Transylvania tract of the Cherokees, the Watauga people made another treaty, and bought their tract, paying £2,000 in goods for it. It was during those treaty-making days that the leading Cherokee chief, Oconostota, spoke of the Kentucky region as a "dark and bloody ground," and another chief said to Boone:

"Brother, we have given you a fine land, but I believe you will have much trouble in settling it," (Imlay, p. 361).

In 1770 Ebenezer, Silas, and Jonathan Zane came to Wheeling Creek, and where the city of Wheeling now stands, made a "tomahawk claim." Blazing a tree they marked on it, (engraved on it with a knife), the extent of land claimed, with its river boundary. There was no law authorizing such an "entry" of land, but it was a method usually (not always), recognized by the home makers, and such claims were commonly made valid by legal process afterwards. The Zane claim was a fine townsite, for to this day it is at the head of deep water navigation on the Ohio. The Zanes were pioneers on that part of the river, and Zanesville, Ohio, perpetuates their memory.

On October 18, 1770, at Lochabar, the Cherokees signed a treaty locating the Indian boundary line between a spot on the south branch of the Holston, six miles east of Long Island, and the mouth of the Kanawha, a confirmation of the treaty of 1768. Thereafter the Virginia Legislature offered every actual settler on the western lands, 400 acres of land free, save for the

AN INDIAN SURPRISE.

expense of registering the claim, with the privilege of buying 1,000 acres adjoining it, at a price but little above the cost of surveying the claim and filing the papers.

About this time good inducements were offered to people who would emigrate to the British territory on the lower Mississippi between Natchez and the Manchac Bayou. To this region went many people, including not a few New Englanders. They usually passed the Alleghanies in companies to the head waters of the Tennessee, where they usually arrived early in the spring. On the Holston or the Clinch they squatted down and passed the summer in raising corn, hunting and building boats. When the corn was harvested they went afloat with their families and corn; braved the terrors of the Boiling Pot, the Suck and the Muscle Shoals; fought the Indians as the occasion required; and finally reached the promised land. These were the first house boatmen of the Great Valley, properly so called. The village of Boatyard, in Sullivan County, Tenn., got its name from the fact that it was the point from which most of these voyagers took their departure.

In 1773 General Lyman, of Connecticut, and some military friends, laid out several additions to the old French settlement at Natchez, and to that point no less than 400 families emigrated during the year named, passing down the Ohio in flat boats, while an unrecorded host traveled by way of Boatyard.

In February, 1764, Capt. George Johnson arrived at Pensacola to take possession of the Territory which had been acquired by the treaty with France. He soon sent detachments of soldiers up the Mississippi to Baton Rouge and Natchez. A fort was built on the Bayou Manchac, a short distance from the Mississippi, and named Fort Bute, in honor of the Prime Minister. Meantime, on February 27, Major Loftus and a force of 400 men were sent up the river in ten barges rowed by sixteen oars each, to take command of the Illinois country, with head quarters at Fort Chartres. At the end of three weeks the force was toiling around the base of the bluff where Fort Adams landing is now found, (ten miles above the mouth of the Red River), when a host of Tunica or Yazoo Indians attacked them, and inflicted such severe loss that the force turned down the river, abandoning the enterprise.

On securing peaceable possession of the territory along the lower Mississippi, the British first of all opened a smuggling trade with the people of New Orleans. Fort Bute was built for a smuggling station, no doubt. Trade flourished so well there that when the Spanish came into power at New Orleans they built a fort opposite and about 400 yards from Fort Bute as a check on the smugglers, though without materially hurting the trade.

The slave trade was the most important branch of the business. The slavers of Newport, Rhode Island, competed with those from Bristol, London and Liverpool, in supplying the demand for ignorant black laborers. Moreover a demand for slaves grew up in the British territory. It is a notable fact that the pioneers of the Ohio watershed hewed their homes out of the solid green woods with their own strong arms, while the lands on the lower Mississippi were developed chiefly by slave labor. The emigrants who made homes below Natchez appear to have been wealthier, as a class, than those locating in Kentucky. Among the old land grants of the time, yet to be found on file in the Natchez district land office, (Washington, Miss.), is one of 25,000 acres to Amos Ogden, dated October 27, 1772. Another for 20,000 acres was granted to Thaddeus Lyman, of Connecticut. Many others of varying size are to be seen.

These people cultivated sugar cane and cotton, and lived such quiet lives that no record of their doings is found in history, save only that when the Atlantic colonies revolted under the oppression of the British Government, they remained loyal to the King, but were not sufficiently numerous or aggressive to take any material part in the struggle.

Fort Chartres was surrendered by the Commandant, (St. Angé), early in 1765, to Captain Sterling, who came by the way of Detroit. It was then, and continued to be, the head post of all the western territory while the British ruled there.

Meantime many surveyors came into the Ohio Valley, among whom none was more notable than Capt. Thomas Bullitt. Bullitt laid out a town, (1773), where Charleston, West Virginia, now stands —an excellent location because at the head of the deep-water navigation of the Great Kanawha. Then he went to the falls of the Ohio, and in August laid out a townsite where Louisville, Ky., has since developed. The first house was built on this site by John Cowan in 1774.

In 1773 James, George and Robert McAfee, with Hancock Taylor, went to the Kentucky River, and on July 16, surveyed a plot of 600 acres where Frankfort now stands. In 1774 James Harrod with a party of forty men went to the spot where Harrodsburg is found, and beginning on June 16, built a log house—the first house of any kind erected in Kentucky. They also planted corn—made a cornpatch claim—and that was a claim no one would dispute. During that season the woods were full of homeseekers, speculators and surveyors, but another Indian war was to interrupt their work, and to that the next chapter shall be given.

SIMON KENTON.

The companion of Boone in many of his enterprises. A portrait from life, by Morgan.

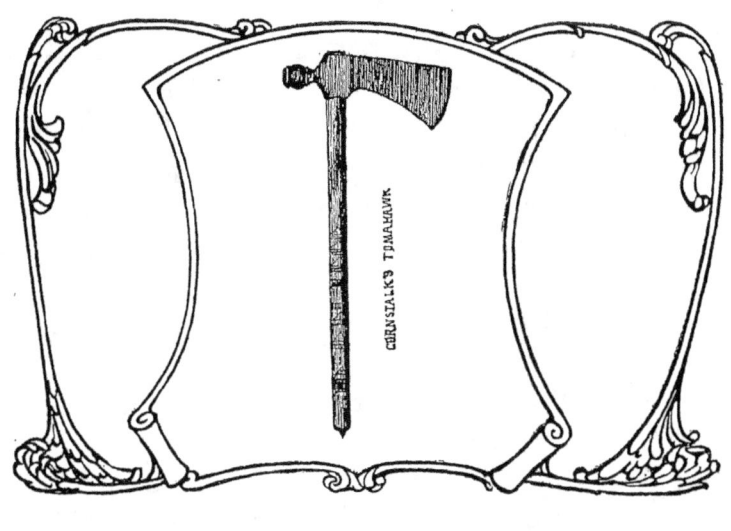

XII

LORD DUNMORE'S WAR.

An unfair Distribution of Goods was one Cause of the Trouble—Men who Delighted in Murder and Theft—Robbed Soldiers and White Home Makers as well as Indians—Desired an Indian War as an aid in Settling a Colony's Boundary—An Official Letter that Turned the White Desperadoes Loose on the Indians—The Battle of Point Pleasant—The True Story of the Famous Speech of Logan.

The brief and decisive conflict known as Lord Dunmore's war was brought on partly by the heedless ignorance of the Indian ways which the whites have always displayed, and partly by the devilish depravity of some of the white men on the frontier. At the treaty of Fort Stanwix the whites paid $50,000 to the Indians for the lands on the southerly side of the Ohio River as far as the Tennessee. The goods were delivered to the representative chiefs gathered at Fort Stanwix. The Six Nations chiefs so far dominated at that treaty that they signed it for the Delawares and Shawnees, and it was therefore but natural that they should dominate in sharing the goods received for the land. To the Delaware and Shawnee chiefs a small portion was given and they went away partly satisfied. When they reached their homes in the Ohio country with their attenuated share of the goods they divided with their immediate relatives and friends. The masses of the Delawares and Shawnees did not get so much as a smell of the Fort Stanwix rum, or more than a long range look at the arms, tools and good cloths dealt out there. The lands, where the buffalo and the deer ranged in herds almost as tame as the white men's oxen, had been sold; the white man would soon kill off all that game and make farms of the lands, and not one glass bead were the masses of these Indians to get in return.

The thought of it was maddening. Worse yet, the white man, having spread to the Tennessee, would cross the Ohio as he had crossed the Alleghanies. The Indian foresaw that event very clearly, and even the chiefs who had been bribed at Fort Stanwix soon realized that they had resigned a lasting heritage for goods that, at best, were soon worn out and lost. It was in this kind of bargaining that the whites were heedless.

Following the Zanes to Wheeling came many people, of whom the majority were the homemakers whom

Mississippi Valley.

we cannot sufficiently honor. But along with these came others whom we cannot sufficiently detest. In our later history, when our frontier was far beyond the Mississippi, the existence of frontier desperadoes was well known, and vigilance committees were necessary, perhaps, to rid the fair earth of their depraved presence. The existence of this class, when the Ohio country was the frontier, seems not to be so well known, but they were there in force. They were men who sought the frontier because government among the whites there was about as loose as among the Indians at all times. They not only robbed the white homemakers, but they even formed widespread organizations for that purpose. They were so bold, in fact, that they would rob a Government expedition in the wilderness. When in 1785 General Butler went down the Ohio river with a force of national soldiers to establish posts and make a treaty, these desperadoes robbed the expedition.

"I find we are infested by scoundrels more unruly and unprincipled than the savages, and who wish to frustrate the treaty," wrote Butler in his journal.

They were men who delighted in theft and murder, and who thrived best when there was open war between the whites and the Indians. But while many of them were lynched for stealing horses from white men, their disregard of Indian rights was considered very lightly by the homemaker who had suffered or seen his neighbor suffer from Indian raids.

Early in 1774 Virginia's claim to the land in the forks of the Ohio added to the trouble. Dr. John Connelly came to Fort Pitt, (then grown to be quite a settlement), and as a representative of Lord Dunmore, governor of Virginia, issued a proclamation calling the people there and at Redstone to meet at Fort Pitt and organize themselves as Virginia militia. Connelly was arrested by Arthur St. Clair, who represented Pennsylvania, but a mob gathered in answer to the proclamation, and after drinking freely, fired at an Indian village across the Alleghany.

When Connelly was released, (on bail), he determined to precipitate a war with the Indians because such a war would give excuse for Virginia's governor to call out all the militia, when, with an overwhelming force, he could settle the disputed boundary. To this end, on April 21, 1774, Connelly wrote a circular letter to the white settlers down the Ohio, warning them to prepare for a Shawnee outbreak.

Coming from a man set in authority, though by unrighteous means, this letter was sufficient for the purpose intended. The peaceable homemakers fled by thousands to Fort Pitt and Redstone for safety. Daniel Boone ranged through Kentucky and warned the people there to fly through the Cumberland Gap.

But the desperadoes did not flee immediately. Instead of that they sought for scalps, knowing that the Indians were not expecting trouble, and that attacks could be made in safety on the unsuspicious.

It was in vain that the trader, George Croghan, then living near Fort Pitt, gave warning. "There is too great a spirit in the frontier people for killing Indians, and if the assembly gives in to that spirit, no doubt they will soon have a general rupture," instead of a conflict with the Shawnees merely, he said.

Mississippi Valley.

A copy of Connelly's letter reached the Zane settlement at Wheeling, and fell into the hands of Michael Cresap. This Cresap was a son of Col. Thomas Cresap, the "vagrant Yorkshire man" previously mentioned as a settler in Western Maryland. Young Michael had been trained on the frontier, and had been a trader, like his father; but he had become bankrupt, and was now on the Ohio, hoping to recruit his fortunes by land speculations. To Cresap the letter of Connelly was a sufficient warrant for any deed of blood. According to George Rogers Clark, who was present, "the war post was planted, a council called, the letter read, *the ceremonies used by the Indians on so important an occasion acted*, and war was formally declared."

These civilized white men, before going out to kill Indians, went through with the ceremonies used by Indians. They circled around the war post, and each struck his tomahawk into it, while all gave the war whoop repeatedly.

Clark adds: "The same evening two scalps were brought into camp." The story of these two scalps is interesting. Word reached the settlement that a canoe with two or three Indians in it was coming down the Ohio. Cresap gathered a party and started up the river in a canoe to meet them, sending another party to lie in ambush in the weeds of the river bank, meantime.

This canoe contained a white man named Stevens, a friendly Delaware and a friendly Shawnee, all in the employ of a Pittsburg trader named Butler. They were coming down the river to get some furs belonging to their employer, which had been lost by other employees of the trader in a brawl with a party of Cherokees some days earlier.

On seeing Cresap's canoe, Stevens thought from the way it was handled that it contained the party of Cherokees that had made trouble on the former occasion, and he steered for the bank. This brought his canoe within range of the men Cresap had placed in ambush, and they, although they could see that Stephens was a white man, shot the two Indians dead.

These Indians were murdered on April 26, 1774. On the 27th, (one account says the 26th), a man named McMahon brought word to Cresap that fourteen Indians had passed down the river. Cresap, with a party of fifteen, pursued and overtook them at Grave Creek. Having heard of the aggression of Cresap the day before, the Indians, when Cresap opened fire, returned it, and then they fled into the woods, leaving one of their party dead. It appears that others were mortally wounded. Cresap brought but one scalp to Wheeling, but the Indians said afterward that "several" were killed. George Rogers Clark, then a youth of twenty-one, but afterwards a noted military officer of the frontier, was with Cresap. In after years Clark tried to excuse this attack by saying that these Indians acted in a suspicious manner when going down the river,—that is, they passed on the further side of an island in order to keep clear of the whites; and he adds that "we found a considerable quantity of ammunition and other warlike stores," in their canoe when they fled. What Cresap actually did find was "sixteen kegs of rum, two saddles and some bridles,"—and nothing more. The idea that Indians would leave ammunition behind on such an occasion is pure nonsense. But even if they had been supplied with enough to leave some behind, the fact would have shown only that they were going hunting.

On returning to Wheeling, Cresap organized a company to go up the river and attack an Indian village, under the famous chief Logan, at the mouth of Yellow Creek, opposite a trading station belonging to a man named Joshua Baker. The company marched five miles, and then abandoned the plan for reasons not fully known. Clark's statement that these men "argued the impropriety" of the attack, and abandoned it on humane grounds, is unbelievable. They were frontier toughs, and it is likely that the revulsion of feeling often seen in such characters—a panic of fear following murderous deeds—came upon them. At any rate Cresap and more than half of the gang immediately fled to safety at Redstone, on the Monongahela. A few continued on to Baker's, being determined to slaughter the red people at all hazards. A man named Daniel C. Greathouse now took the lead, and gathered a gang of thirty-two. On April 30, he went across to Yellow Creek alone, pretending friendship for, but really to count, the Indians. He found them too numerous even for a night attack, although thirty-two white men had been induced by love of blood and the hope of plunder to make the attack.

While he was still among the Indians a friendly squaw, (a relative of Chief Logan), told Greathouse that her people had heard of the deeds of Cresap, and were meditating revenge. She advised him to leave, and he did so, after inviting, as he left, a considerable number of Indians to cross to Baker's and get some rum as a treat.

Accordingly several Indians did cross to Baker's. The accounts vary as to the number, but it appears that four red men, three squaws and a little girl went. Definite statements are made that one of the squaws was Logan's mother, that another squaw, (one who carried the little girl), was his sister, and that one of the red men was his brother. Two Indians got drunk, and two refused to drink, but these two were induced to shoot at a mark, after the other two were helpless.

When the Indians had fired their guns, and were thus incapable of defending themselves, the thirty-two white men attacked and slaughtered the party all but the child. The man who killed Logan's sister boasted that he shot her at a range of six feet. He was then going to "dash out the child's brains," but on seeing the little thing fall with her mother, "felt some remorse," and desisted. The Indians over at Yellow Creek, on hearing the reports of guns, sent a canoe with five warriors to learn why the guns were fired. These were ambushed and four, (or perhaps but two), were killed, while another was wounded.

It was during these days that John Heckwelder and David Zeisberger, Moravian missionaries, animated by a feeling which frontier writers have ever since, with lofty contempt, called "Quaker sentiment," were teaching the Ohio Indians to grub stumps and dig the ground and plant corn, and adopt a new religion—they were building Gnadenhutten, of which something more shall be told.

Logan had been the friend of the whites, but now the red blood in his veins boiled. Three separate raids were made by parties under him into the Monongahela valley. In the first of these he alone took thirteen scalps. What other raiders did is told only in general terms. It was a war on the Virginians, and the whole Virginia frontier blazed, and ran red with blood, the innocents suffering, as always, for the crimes of desperadoes, who sneaked away to safety when the danger became great. But when Logan took a prisoner, as happened on one raid, he saved the man from the stake at the risk of his own life.

But the story of the white treachery is not yet complete. The traders then among the Indians fled for their lives and were helped from the country by personal friends among the red men. Some of these friendly Indians went as far as Fort Pitt with the traders. And while these friendly Indians were at Fort Pitt, Connelly tried to imprison them, but Croghan, the trader, foiled him. Then finding that they were getting away, Connelly sent men who waylaid and shot three of them from ambush.

An old account says that "the character developed" by Connelly on this occasion was such as to draw down "the reproof of Lord Dartmouth."

The Ohio Indians had been restless for months. They had been expecting large quantities of goods in payment for lands that were to be organized as the colony of Vandalia, and had been disappointed. They were angered because they had been driven from the lands within the forks of the Ohio. They were alarmed and angered by the influx of whites that had followed the treaty of Fort Stanwix. The devilish work of Connelly, Cresap and Greathouse came just at the right time to rouse them to the point where almost to a man they would dig up the hatchet, as Logan had done.

To meet the overwhelming red force thus turned loose on the Virginia frontier, Gen. Andrew Lewis, with 1,100 or 1,200 men (of whom fifty came from the Watauga settlement, under Capt. Evan Shelby), marched from Virginia over the range to and down the Kanawha. Lord Dunmore himself, with another force, announced that he would join Lewis at this point, and the united forces were then to cross the Ohio, and lay desolate the Indian villages.

When Lewis reached the Ohio, on October 9, 1774, however, Lord Dunmore was nowhere near. Instead of Dunmore came Cornstalk, the Shawanese, with 1,000 warriors, to fight these white men on their own ground. Cornstalk had learned Dunmore's plan of bringing the Virginians in two bodies to unite on the Ohio, and, with admirable tactics, determined to attack and destroy the smaller force first. The Indians knew all they needed to know, as they crossed the Ohio above the Kanawha, about the position of the Virginians. The Virginians knew nothing of the coming of the Indians.

At four o' clock next morning, October 10, the Indians came gliding through the woods to surprise the white man's camp, and they would have succeeded, but for the lack of discipline in the camp! The General had ordered the poorest of the cattle, driven along to supply the men with beef, to be killed and served. Men who didn't like this beef left camp without permission, to go and kill game. Several men were going out hunting in pairs, that morning, before daylight. One pair, whose names were Mooney and Hickman, met the Indians about a mile from camp, and were fired on. Hickman was killed. At about the same time James Robertson and another Watuga man met the Indians, but both of these escaped, and with Mooney ran to camp.

It was a camp of frontiersmen. They were asleep, but the shouts of the hunters and the rolling of drums brought them to their feet, gun in hand. And leaping behind trees and logs they were instantly ready for the conflict.

It began in the dusk of morning. The commanding general thought only a scouting party had been seen, and sent out a detachment with two scouts leading the way—two to serve as a sacrifice that the men might not be surprised. The two were soon killed. The attack on the detachment soon followed. Reinforcements came swiftly to support them, but the Indians took position on a commanding piece of ground, and before the sunlight brightened the tops of the trees, the two hosts were spread out in lines more than a mile long, facing each other at a range that never exceeded twenty yards. They crouched behind trees, and looking up or down the line, fired at glimpses of white or red flesh, or coon skin caps or disordered plumes. They leaped from shelter, and with jeers and taunts invited assault, only that the assaulters might be decoyed into exposing themselves to those lying in wait. Indians were never more aggressive in open battle. They repeatedly called the whites the sons of female dogs, and shouted "why don't you whistle now?" (referring to the fifes), and "we'll learn you to shoot." They even charged on the whites, singly and in squads, and with knife and tomahawk, fought it out, hand to hand, man fashion. Many men with mortal wounds fought on until death froze the look of hate on their faces.

And through it all old Cornstalk raged up and down his line, shouting in a voice heard above the roar of guns:

"Be strong! Be strong!"

GEN. WM. HENRY HARRISON'S RESIDENCE.
(FROM A CONTEMPORARY PRINT.)

They were strong. Indians never were braver. Here was the best fight ever made by our red men. Two white colonels were killed and one wounded. The whites became discouraged under the prolonged assaults of the red men. As the sun went down defeat stared them in the face.

But when they would have wavered Gen. Lewis sent Capt. Evan Shelby, with his Watauga men, under the bank of the Kanawha to a ravine, through which

MAJ. GEN. WILLIAM HENRY HARRISON.
From an original portrait by Lambdin.

they were able to flank and get in rear of the Indians. And then when Shelby opened fire there, the Indians fled in spite of the storming Cornstalk.

The white men lost seventy-five killed and 140 wounded. The Indians lost only thirty-three killed, so far as known, but they were disheartened.

Among the men who took part in this fight was one Benjamin Harrison, whose name is not unknown to American history. He was a captain under Lewis. Isaac Shelby, afterward Governor of Kentucky, was a lieutenant of the company of Capt. Evan Shelby, his father. James Robertson was a sergeant in this company, and all its members came from the Watauga country.

Lord Dunmore had taken his force down the Ohio to the Hockhocking River, where he built a wooden fort. Thence, after Lewis won the battle of Point Pleasant (as the fight at the mouth of the Kanawha was called), Dunmore marched to the Scioto, camping on Sippo Creek, about eight miles from the modern town of Westfall, O. There he met Cornstalk and made peace.

Cornstalk, with all his eloquence, strove to rouse the Indians to another battle. He taunted and implored, and finally proposed that they kill their women and children, and then fight until they themselves died free, rather than yield before the advancing whites; but nothing could move them. With the feeling that he was the chief of a band of cowards, he met Dunmore. He accepted Dunmore's terms, but he did it "with words and bearing that roused the admiration even of the Indian haters among the whites."

To this conference Logan refused to come. He "disdained to be seen among the suppliants." But he was willing, for the sake of his people, that peace should be made. John Gibson, an interpreter with Lord Dunmore (Gibson was a general in the war of the Revolution), was sent to the Indians, at their request, during the negotiations. Logan met Gibson, took him a little away from the other Indians, sat down among the bushes near the camp, and there, "after shedding abundant tears," dictated the message that is one of the most striking outbursts of red oratory known to the annals of the race:

"I appeal to any white man to say if ever he entered Logan's cabin hungry, and he gave him not meat; if ever he came cold and hungry, and he clothed him not. During the course of the last long and bloody war Logan remained idle in his cabin, an advocate for peace. Such was my love for the whites that my countrymen pointed as they passed and said, 'Logan is the friend of the white men.' I had even thought to have lived with you, but for the injuries of one man. Col. Cresap, the last spring, in cold blood, murdered all the relations of Logan, not even sparing my women or children. There runs not a drop of my blood in the veins of any living creature. This called on me for revenge. I have sought it. I have killed many. I have fully glutted my vengeance. For my country I rejoice at the beams of peace. But do not harbor a thought that mine is the joy of fear. Logan never felt fear. He will not turn on his heel to save his life. Who is there to mourn for Logan? Not one."

BENJAMIN FRANKLIN.
From a portrait published in the "Portfolio" in 1818.

XIII

THE HOME MAKERS IN KENTUCKY.

The Story of Pennsylvania and Boonesborough—The Frontier Forts and Frontier Houses Described—The Old Fashioned Log-Rolling and Other Bees—The Deckhard Rifle—Frontier Clothing—Contrast Between the Dominant People of Louisiana and Those of the Ohio Watershed—A Government Established at Boonesborough.

When Lord Dunmore dictated peace to the Indians on the bank of the Scioto, he opened wide the road for the home-seekers who had thronged to the passes of the Alleghanies. In cowing the Indians he had strengthened Virginia's claim to lands west of the mountains far more than the Quebec Bill had injured it. The story of the home-makers who came to the wilderness, after this war ended, is, therefore, now to be told.

And it may be observed that no chapter of American history is better worth the attention of young Americans than this, for these home-builders were emphatically men who could and would *work*—the men after God's own heart, who had learned "the infinite conjugation of the verb *to do*."

Winsor notes in his "Westward Movement" that 25,000 Scotch-Irish Presbyterians arrived in the Delaware from 1771 to 1773, and he adds that such of this element as came to the frontier had no better use for an Indian than to make of him a target for their rifles. Any study of the history of the region shows that settlers of the Ohio Valley were of Protestant extraction, and to a large extent Presbyterians. It is easy to see, now, that their kind of Presbyterianism, and their other isms, were not like modern views of Christianity. It is a matter worth consideration, because, as Carlyle points out, a man's real creed, the one by which he lives, is the most important fact about him. But if these home-seekers were not men who obeyed the Sermon on the Mount, it promotes one's optimism to note that they were distinctly better men than the people who came to Virginia in 1609. They did not profess one thing and do another. They might and they did shoot the red men, but they did not preface the killing by publishing drivel about coming to the frontier "to recover out of the arms of the Devil a number of poore and miserable soules."

In spite of their professions, the Virginians of 1609 had "no talk, no hope, no work, but to dig gold, refine gold, loade gold." The emigrant to the Ohio River frontier of Virginia had "no talk, no hope, no work"

Mississippi Valley.

but to make a home; and that was the public profession as well as the creed of his heart that he expressed in his daily life. "God never intended this fair land to remain a wilderness," was his oral and written creed, and the one under which he acted. Church rites and ceremonies received very little attention during the days when the "boom was on."

The home-makers came to the frontier usually in small companies, but sometimes in single families. Individual men also came. They selected the bottom lands and low ridges covered over with giant walnuts, maples, oaks, sycamore, shell-bark hickory and other trees known to grow on rich soil, until all readily reached lands of the kind were taken up. The beech grove lands were held in less esteem.

Consider as a sample, and the best one of many such settlements, the founders of Boonesborough. During the years that Daniel Boone was going to and fro between the hunting grounds of Kentucky and his home on the Yadkin, he was very well acquainted with Col. Richard Henderson, "one of the principal judges in North Carolina, a scholarly, talented man, eminent in the legal profession," (Thwaite's "Boone"). Boone's stories of the game and other evidences of the fertility of the Kentucky soil greatly interested Col. Henderson, and he eventually resolved to establish a colony in the new country. When the company was organized they adopted Transylvania as the name of the colony. After some delays, the chief of which was due to Lord Dunmore's war, a grand council was held (March, 1775,) at Sycamore Shoals, on the Watauga, with 1,200 Cherokees, who were gathered there by Daniel Boone, as the agent of the Transylvania Company. When there, the Cherokees, "for $50,000 worth of cloths, clothing, utensils, ornaments and fire arms," ceded to Henderson "all the country lying between the Kentucky and Cumberland Rivers; also a path of approach from the east, through Powell's Valley."

To show how far such bargains benefited the Indians, Thwaites points out that the goods in bulk "filled a large cabin." When distributed "there was but little for each warrior, and great dissatisfaction arose. One Cherokee, whose portion was a shirt, declared that in one day, upon this land, he could have killed deer enough to buy such a garment," and yet the chiefs had given the land away for all time for such a trifling return. It "seemed to him a bad bargain."

Boone, with near thirty woodmen, was sent from the treaty grounds to clear a path to a spot on the Kentucky River. The trail thus made entered Kentucky by the Cumberland Gap, and came to be, at one time, the chief route south of the Ohio River. It was, in fact, traveled by more people, in war times, than the Ohio was. It was called the Wilderness Road.

As Boone's trail-making party traveled through the woods the rougher obstructions were cleared away in order to make a passable pack-horse route for others who were to come. At night the party slept without sentries, a fact that shows better than any other the intrepidity of their hearts. But one morning a band of Indians charged the camp at daylight, killed a negro slave (a few slaves came thus early to blight the land) and Capt. Twitty, besides wounding Felix Walker. Then the whites rallied and beat off the Indians, and they kept on to the site selected for Boonesborough, in spite of another attack, when two men were killed.

The site selected, (Big Lick, just below the mouth of Otter Creek), was reached April 6. "The site was a plain on the south side of the Kentucky." As the party entered the natural opening they startled a herd of 200 or 300 buffaloes "of all sizes," that "made off from the lick in every direction."

Naturally, their first care was to provide a shelter —one that would keep out Indian bullets as well as rain and snow. They marked off a rectangular piece of ground 165x250 feet large, and, although they were a long time completing the structure, at each corner of it they built a two-story house of squared logs. The upper story was made to project several feet beyond the walls of the lower, and it was floored with puncheons, (or split planks), thick enough to be bullet proof. In the parts of this floor that projected beyond the lower story they cut holes through which they could shoot down at an enemy beneath, and there were a plenty of port holes in the walls of these houses, to cover the space around and between them.

Between these corner houses, (called block-houses), and along the lines of the rectangle they built twenty-six log cabins, each about eighteen feet square. The outside wall of each was laid on the line of the rectangle, and was built up smooth and solid, (so that no Indian could climb it), to a height of twelve feet. It contained no door, window or other opening. The inner wall was eight feet high, and in this were cut two openings for windows, and one for a door. The roof was laid in a single flat slope from the outer to the inner wall, and was covered at first with bark, but afterwards with long shingles that were held in place with thick poles.

The rows of cabins did not quite reach the block-houses, a space being left so that if one of the rows was burned, the adjoining block-house, might be saved. But a palisade wall filled these spaces.

In the center of each of the long sides was a heavy, solid gate. One opened toward the river; another inland. The gates were defended by rows of palisades. The loop holes of the block-houses commanded them, and so did loop holes in the adjoining cabins.

The Indians had but one hope of capturing a fort like that. The roofs were easily fired.

James Harrod and his associates built a fort like this at Harrodsburg beginning in March, 1775. In fact forts of the kind were scattered all over the region. In Imlay's "Topographical Description of the Western Territory" (published in 1793), is a "Map of Kentucky" by John Filson. It shows all the settlements and outlying posts and homes. The fortified stations are represented by marks well worth note.

But there were also many single cabins built in this region far beyond the protection of the forts. They were without exception of log walls. An ax and an auger were the only tools needed for building such a house. The logs were notched together at the corners. The rafters were held together and to the tops of walls by pegs driven through auger holes. Thick boards called puncheons, were split from logs and laid for floors, if any floor was laid. Round logs served to support such a floor. Doors were made of puncheons also,

Mississippi Valley.

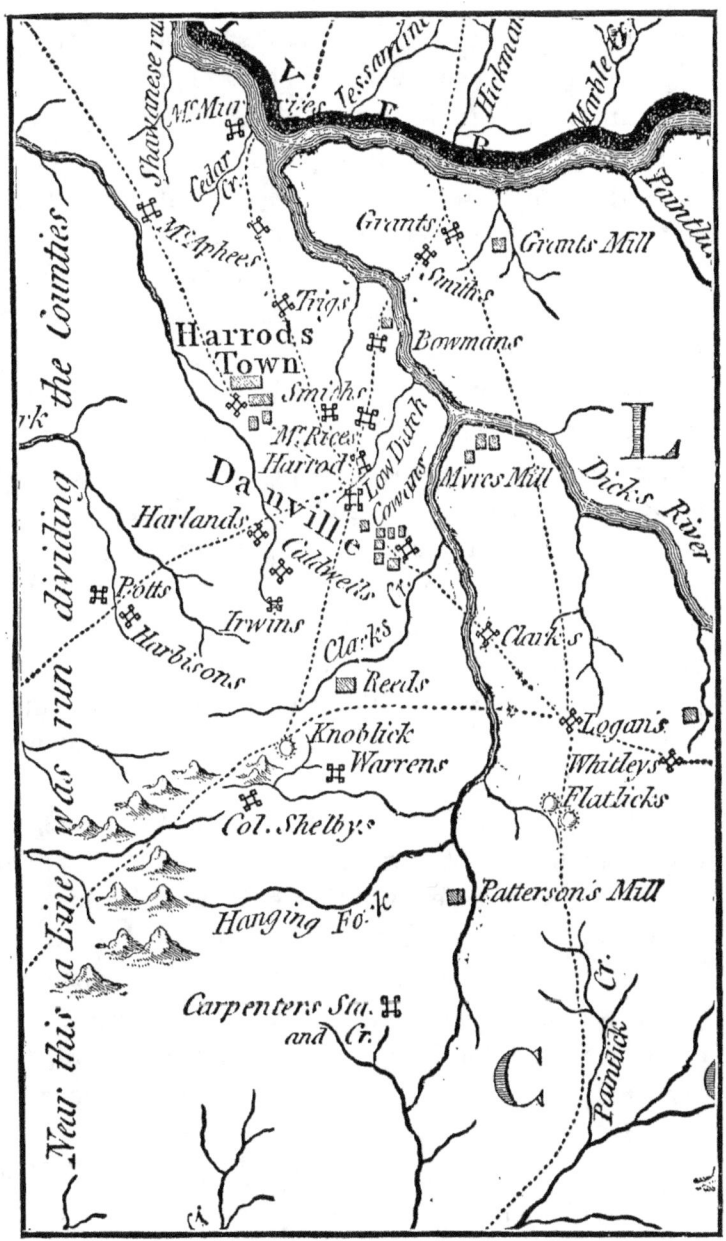

A Portion of Filson's Map of 1785, with Harrodsburg.

and these were hung on wooden hinges, and barred at night with heavy pieces of timber. The doors were sometimes made in two parts, upper and lower, and it was the custom to open the upper half only, in troublesome times in answer to a hail, because an enemy could not readily charge over the lower half. Windows were not put in, at first, because the home builder could defend but one aperture, but for years after peace came, the only window was a square hole, closed at night by a heavy puncheon shutter. Neither glass nor iron was used in those houses. The huge fireplaces were made of sandstone where it could be found; elsewhere of split sticks thickly covered with clay. The shingles on the roof were held in place by straight logs laid on each row; but it should be noted that the log house at first was roofed with bark. Says a journal written by one Calk, of Boone's early settlement, (Roosevelt), "we git our house kivered with bark and move our things into it at Night, and begin Housekeeping." That was on April 29, 1775.

The spaces between logs were filled with moss, or clay or both, but not always. There is a story of a man whose arm was severely bitten by a wolf because, as the hungry beast prowled near the cabin, at night, the man in his sleep happened to thrust his arm not only out of bed, but out through the space between the logs on a level with the bed. Another man lying with his head near such an opening had his scalp badly torn by a wolf.

In Mansfield's "Life of Dr. Daniel Drake" is a letter written by Drake to describe a Kentucky home built in the forest in 1788. It was one of a group of

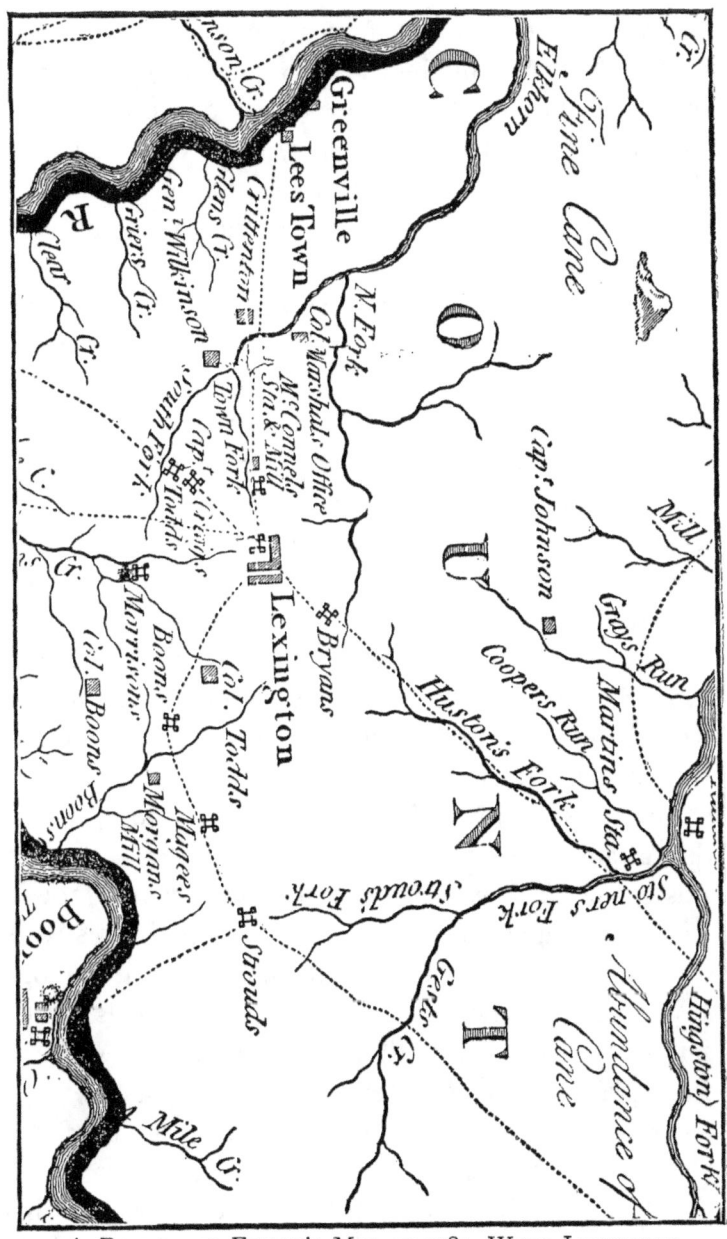

A Portion of Filson's Map of 1785, with Lexington.

five and all were located so that "no house, in the event of being attacked by the Indians, would be unsupported by some other." When the parents of Drake moved into their cabin it was "one story high, without a window, with a door opening to the south, a half finished wooden chimney, and a roof on one side only, but without any upper or lower floor." There was a puncheon door, however, and it could be secured by a stout bar. The sills for the floor were also in place, and Drake recalled his playing on the ground between these sills, while the father and mother stepped from one sill to another while arranging their scant household goods. He adds that each cabin had port holes in the walls. They always kept the axe and scythe under the bed to use in case of attack by Indians; and before opening the door in the morning the father always climbed up the log wall to an unchinked crack between the logs through which he peered to see whether any Indians were in waiting to rush into the house when the bar was removed from the door.

For descriptions of the furniture of those homes, the unfailing resource is Dodridge's "Notes." A table was made of split slab and supported by four round legs set in auger holes. Some three-legged stools were made in the same manner. Some pins stuck in the logs at the back of the house supported clapboards which served for shelves for the table furniture. A single fork, placed with its lower end in a hole in the floor, and the upper end fastened to a joist, served for a bedstead, by placing a pole in the fork with one end through a crack between the logs in the wall. This front pole was crossed by a shorter one within the fork,

Mississippi Valley.

A Portion of Filson's Map of 1785, Showing Louisville.

with its outer end through another crack. From the front pole through a crack between the logs at the end of the house, (split) boards were put on which formed the bottom of the bed. Skins of animals, especially bear skins, made excellent substitutes for blankets.

A hollowed log—a round-bottomed trough—served for a cradle. They had the rudest furniture ever seen, but also the strongest. Fancy the possibilities before him who was rocked to sleep in a hollow log, and was taught to read, and imbibed ambition, by the flames of a roaring fire-place!

The furniture of the table consisted of a few pewter dishes, plates and spoons; but mostly of wooden bowls, trenchers and noggins, (cups). If these last were scarce, gourds and hard-shelled squashes made up the deficiency. The iron pots, knives and forks were brought from the east side of the mountains on pack horses. When china ware came it was not liked because it dulled the edge of the scalping knife.

They had neither closets nor trunks. Their clothing hung from pegs driven into the wall. All the possessions of the entire family were under the eye of every visitor. This people did not cultivate the habit of concealment. They were frank and open-hearted.

But a more important—on the whole probably the most important—feature of the frontier was the bee habit—the custom of gathering in companies whenever opportunity offered. The individual settler girdled the trees on the patch of land he wished to clear, and when they were dead, he felled them. Then by building little fires at intervals of twelve or fifteen feet along the trunks—fires of small sticks, oft replenished,

ANDREW JACKSON.
From a portrait by Jarvis, in 1815.

and held down by a chunk of a log called a niggerhead—the trees were divided into logs. A time came when the whole patch was strewn with charred logs, much too heavy for one man to handle alone readily, even with a team of horses; and yet it was necessary to pile them up and burn them before the land could be cultivated. To get those logs into a heap was the hardest physical toil known to the frontier, and yet for the frontiersmen it was literally a whooping joy. For food in huge quantities (and, if possible, rum in sufficient quantities), was procured by the land owner, and then the neighbors—all who lived within twenty miles—were invited to a log rolling bee. A man who was not invited felt seriously offended. By the dozen —sometimes by the score—they came to the new home. Those who could do so brought horses; some brought oxen, some brought their wives and children. In troops they flocked, to the log-strewn patch, and then with hilarity, energy and muscular exertion never surpassed, if ever equalled, they dragged and flung the logs into heaps.

The children piled on the limbs and brush, and bringing brands from the fire-place in the house, started fires whose smoke darkened the heavens.

At noon the company ate dinner with a relish, now unknown, save only to a few (chosen of God to enjoy life), who sometimes go to the woods. For though only corn bread could be served with the wild meat, they had appetite and freedom from care.

Nor was that all. Though it was the heaviest of work their muscles were elastic, and as the sun went down behind the forest; and the squirrels leaped from tree to tree with mellow crash within sight of the house; and the cardinal and the oriole and the red start flamed and drifted among the leaves, these men bantered each other into wrestling matches and foot races, and the victor in each leaped on a stump, flapped his arms against his sides, and crowed like a rooster. If a fiddle could be had, they ended the lark with a "hoedown"—a dance that made even the log-walled house tremble. When Jackson, the hero of these backwoods men, had beaten the invader at New Orleans, and the people of the city gathered to do him honor at a grand ball, he—tall and lank, and his wife, short and round—danced what a polished spectator called a *"pas de deux."* They danced a backwoods jig to the tune of "Possum up a Gum Tree"—to the intense delight and admiration of the riflemen who shot the invader out of the swamp.

At weddings (and there is scant record of unions without weddings), the neighbors made a bee, and built a house for the new couple in the course of a few hours after the ceremony was ended. And at night they put the young couple to bed with many a sly hint, as well as good wish.

They gathered to husk the corn and to make maple sugar. Whatever could be done well by companies, was done by them in companies. No more independent or self-reliant individuals were ever seen on our soil than these home-makers who peopled the Ohio watershed, and yet never was a better exhibit of the community spirit seen. Each was entirely able to shift for himself, but out of love for his neighbors, each made haste to lend a hand at every gathering.

Absolutely necessary to the outfit of every fron-

MRS. ANDREW JACKSON.

Born Rachel Donelson, daughter of Col. John Donelson of Virginia. In this portrait she wears the head-dress in which she appeared at the ball herein described.

tiersman was the rifle. A gunsmith named Deckhard, living in Lancaster, Pa., at some unnamed period of the border, began making rifles of small bore in place of the smooth-bored musket in common use. The barrel was an iron tube at least thirty inches long, and usually three feet, six inches. The bore was rifled, had twisting grooves cut in it, and the bullet that fit the bore was a round pellet weighing seventy to the pound. In loading the rifle a well-greased linen patch was wrapped around the bullet. The patch fitted into the grooves, and the bullet was not mutilated like the modern rifle projectiles are. It was a remarkably accurate weapon, though one requiring more skill than a modern rifle, for, having a flintlock, there was a marked interval between pulling the trigger and the discharge of the bullet, an interval during which the rifle must be held on the target. But the iron-nerved men of the frontier had the skill. They shot running deer at a range of 150 yards. They killed geese and ducks, and even wild pigeons on the wing. Boys of twelve hung their heads in shame if detected in hitting a squirrel in any other part of the body than its head. Though the bullet was small, it was large enough for any game when fired by the men that knew how. One of the Zane brothers, who went with Gen. Butler down the Ohio in 1785, killed a buffalo that Butler called "a real curiosity for size." The animal was more than six feet tall when it stood erect. Its head, cut off with as little of the neck as possible, weighed 135 pounds.

A time came when the small bullet went out of fashion. Plainsmen, who had horses to ride, wanted a bore that would admit the thumb. But the Kentuckian, who had to "tote" his entire outfit, found the small bullet better; five hundred rounds of ammunition weighed less than ten pounds. And in these last days the armies of the world are armed once more with small caliber rifles, to the entire vindication of the Boone class of frontiersmen.

Says Dodridge regarding the clothing:

"Amongst those who were much in the habit of going hunting, and going on scouts and campaigns, the dress of the men was partly Indian and partly that of civilized nations. The hunting shirt was universally worn. This was a kind of loose frock, reaching half way down the thighs, with large sleeves, open before, and so wide as to lap over a foot or more when belted. The cape (a wide collar) was large, and sometimes handsomely fringed with a ravelled piece of cloth of different color from that of the hunting shirt itself. The bosom of this dress served as a wallet to hold a chunk of bread cakes, jerk (dried meat), tow for wiping the barrel of the rifle, or any other necessary for hunter or warrior. The belt, which was always tied behind, answered several purposes besides that of holding the dress together. In cold weather the mittens, and sometimes the bullet bag, occupied the front part of it. To the right side was suspended the tomahawk, and to the left the scalping knife with its leathern sheath. The hunting shirt was generally made of linsey, sometimes of coarse linen, and a few of dressed deer skins. These last were very cold and uncomfortable in wet weather. The (under) shirt and jacket were of the common fashion. A pair of drawers, or breeches and leggins, were the dress of the thighs and

A HUNTER WITH A DECKHARD RIFLE.
Notice length of same.

legs; moccasins were nicely adapted (fitted) to the ankles and lower parts of the legs by thongs of deer skin, so that no dust, gravel or snow could get within the moccasin.

"The moccasins in ordinary use cost but a few hours' (say two) labor to make them. This was done by an instrument denominated a moccasin awl, which was made of the back spring of an old clasp knife. This awl, with a buckhorn handle was an appendage of every shot pouch strap, together with a roll of buckskin for mending the moccasins. This was the labor of almost every evening. They were sewed together and patched with deer skin thongs, or whangs, as they were commonly called.

"In cold weather the moccasins were stuffed with deer's hair, or dry leaves, so as to keep the feet comfortably warm; but in wet weather it was usually said that wearing them was a decent way of going barefooted, and such was the fact, owing to the spongy texture of the leather of which they were made.

"Owing to this defective covering of the feet, more than to any other circumstance, the greater number of our hunters and warriors were afflicted with rheumatism in their limbs. Of this disease they were all apprehensive in cold or wet weather, and therefore always slept with their feet to the fire to prevent or cure it as well as they could. This practice unquestionably had a salutary effect, and prevented many of them becoming confirmed cripples in early life.

"In later years of the Indian war our young men became more enamored of the Indian dress throughout, with the exception of the match [watch?] coat.

The drawers were laid aside and the leggins made longer, so as to reach the upper part of the thighs. The Indian breech clout was adopted. This was a piece of linen or cloth nearly a yard long and eight or nine inches broad. This passed under the belt before and behind, leaving the ends for flaps hanging before and behind over the belt. These flaps were sometimes ornamented with some kind of coarse embroidery work. To the same belts which secured the breech clouts were attached strings which supported the leggins. When this belt, as was often the case, passed over the hunting shirt, the upper part of the thighs and part of the hips were naked."

The first woman came to Kentucky in 1775. After building the fort at Boonesborough, Daniel Boone went back to North Carolina, and brought his wife, with Mrs. Denton, Mrs. McGarry and Mrs. Hogan. The journey of the family parties into the wilderness usually began at the Holston region. At Watauga, or some other mountain settlement nearby, the horses were fitted with pack saddles, and the goods of the family were piled on these; for families rarely went by this route into the wilderness unless able to afford horses, either of their own or borrowed. As a rule, cows were driven along as well. The older boys had charge of the cattle. "The younger children were placed in crates of hickory withes and slung across the backs of the old, quiet horses," though some found seats on top of the goods on the pack horses. Some of the women rode, some walked and carried their babies, too. The men, with rifles ready, went scouting through the woods in all directions, and looked after the pack horses as well. One of them was always elected captain of the band. "Special care had to be taken not to let the loaded animals brush against the yellow jacket nests, which were always plentiful along the trail in the fall of the year, for in such cases the vicious swarms attacked men and beasts, producing an immediate stampede" that distributed packs and children in disordered condition all over the region (Roosevelt).

"The linsey petticoat and bed gown were the universal dress of our women in early times. A small home-made handkerchief" was worn around the neck. "They went barefooted in warm weather, and in cold their feet were covered with moccasins, coarse shoes, or shoe packs" (Dodridge).

"Until flax could be grown women were obliged to be content with lint made from the bark of dead nettles. This was gathered in the springtime by all the people of a station acting together, a portion of the men standing guard, while the rest, with the women and children, plucked the dead stalks. The smart girls of Irish ancestry spun many dozen cuts of linen from this lint, which was as fine as flax but not so strong" (Roosevelt, quoting from McAfee Mss.).

For a contrast recall Gayarre's description of French life in Louisiana. The Louisiana houses were not pretentious, but a stranger who "passed their thresholds would have been amazed at being *welcomed with such manners as were habitual in the most polished* court of Europe, and entertained by men and women wearing with the utmost ease and grace the elegant costume of the reign of Louis XV.—the powdered head, the silk and gold flowered coat, the lace and frills, the red-heeled shoe, the steel-handled sword, the silver knee-buckles, the high and courteous bearing of the gentlemen; the hoop petticoat, the brocaded gown, the rich head-dress, the stately bow, the slightly rouged cheeks, the artificially graceful deportment and the aristocratic features of the lady."

A most instructive contrast is that between the dominant people of Louisiana and those of the Ohio watershed; it is a most instructive contrast. On the one hand stands the courtier displaying with ease and grace his lace and frills and red-heeled shoes. On the other stands a man dressed in homespun and swinging an ax.

The frontier food is not (and it never was) to be passed without consideration. "The articles of (table) furniture corresponded very well with the articles of diet on which they were employed. 'Hog an' hominy' [hominy is corn boiled in lye to remove the hulls, cleaned, and then boiled till soft in pure water] were proverbial for the dish of which they were component parts. Johnny cake [a corruption of journey cake, a kind of corn bread], and pone [another kind of corn bread], were the only forms of bread in use for breakfast and dinner. At supper milk and mush formed the standard dish. When milk was not plenty, which was often the case, owing to the scarcity of cattle or the want of proper pasturage for them, the substantial dish of hominy had to supply the place of them; mush was frequently eaten with sweetened water, molasses, bear's oil or the gravy of fried meat.

"Every family, besides a little garden for the few

vegetables which they cultivated, had another small enclosure, called the 'truck patch,' in which they raised corn for roasting ears, pumpkins, squashes, beans and potatoes. These, in the latter part of the summer and fall, were cooked with their pork, venison and bear meat for dinner, and made very wholesome and well-tasted dishes. The standard dinner for every log-rolling, house-raising and harvest day, was potpie" [boiled meats, such as chickens, grouse, pigeons, veal, or venison with abundant dumplings]. What was left over was served for supper along with milk to drink. Tea and coffee, were, for a long time, unseen. When introduced, at last, the men thought such "slops" good enough for women and children. As for themselves they preferred something strong enough "to stick to the ribs."

Mention has been made of the form of government organized by the Watauga people. In 1775 there was a similar movement at Boonesborough, Ky. When Col. Richard Henderson was establishing his "Transylvania" colony at Boonesborough, (1775), Lord Dunmore issued a proclamation warning people that the act was contrary to the laws of Virginia, and of the Crown; but Henderson's company followed Daniel Boone to the site of Boonesborough. It was a feudal colony that Henderson purposed organizing—something like the colony that La Salle ruled for a time at Fort Frontenac, and therefore wholly unsuited to Americans—but certificates for more than 500,000 acres of land were issued to colonists by Henderson, (whence followed many a law suit). But the act of this company most interesting here is the fact that, although Henderson did not reach Boonesborough until April 20, he issued a call on May 23d to the settlers of the region asking them to send representatives to agree upon some form of government. And the settlers came to answer the call. They had not finished chinking the walls of their log cabins before they gathered to establish a system of lawful government. *They* were to *establish* a system of government; they were not *to be* ruled over by priest and gold-laced commandant.

On this primitive legislature the Rev. John Lythe asked a blessing, for a preacher came with the other settlers. The acts passed numbered nine, as follows: To establish courts; to regulate the militia; prescribe punishment for crimes; to prevent profane swearing and Sabbath breaking; providing for writs of attachment; limiting the fees of legal officers; preserving the right of free pasture on public lands; improving the breed of horses; for preserving the game. Daniel Boone prepared the statutes relating to the preservation of game, and improving the breed of horses.

There was a creed worth consideration in every particular, but perhaps the first thought in connection with it is that the very first Kentuckians were full of sporting blood. They would preserve the game and improve the breed of horses. And as a matter of fact a race course was laid out at Shallow Ford Station, in that very year. It is no wonder Kentucky horses are famous. It is to be noted, too, that the game laws were aimed against skin hunters—men who came from the settlements east of the mountains and killed the wild animals for their skins. These home makers claimed the wild animals along with the lands. The admirable non-export laws of many of the states at the present time are founded on that old feeling.

The colony of Transylvania as a legal organization failed because the proprietary system was wrong, and because the proprietors did not have a legal title to the lands; but the actual settlers had their titles confirmed, while the company received a grant of 200,000 acres, located on the Ohio, and the thriving city of Henderson, Ky., perpetuates the name of an enterprising and heroic, if mistaken frontiersman.

We get another view of Kentucky life from the records of Henderson's Transylvania company, wherein sales of gunpowder are noted at $2.66 per pound, and lead at 16 2-3. The woods rangers or hunters employed were paid thirty-three cents a day; and they worked from sunrise to sunset, without a doubt. The modern definition of the word strike was unknown; for every man was man enough to "hoe his own row," regardless of bosses, or unions or trusts or other combinations made to wring something from an unwilling somebody.

The fees for acquiring the right to 400 acres of land, under the laws of Virginia amounted to $10, in 1775, but the home maker was obliged to build a log house sufficient for a dwelling, and raise and harvest a crop of corn in addition. Having done this he could acquire 1,000 acres more adjoining his first claim, at a cost of $400.

At the end of 1775 there were 300 men in Kentucky, it is said, men who intended to make homes. A breadth of something more than 200 acres of corn had been harvested. The people had abundant food, vigorous health, and hope that amounted to enthusiasm. There was every needed local indication of a splendid development of the new settlements.

But another war was at hand, and in it these frontiersmen were to have a memorable part. On an unnamed day, while a party of Kentucky hunters camped on a branch of the Elkhorn river near the cabin of a man named McConnel, a messenger brought them a story of trouble between some Massachusetts farmers and a company of British soldiers. The messenger said that the farmers were gathered with arms to resist the soldiers. The commander of the soldiers shouted "Disperse, ye villains! Damn you why don't you disperse?" But the men of Massachusetts instead of obeying the profane tyrant, attacked the soldiers and compelled them to fly so swiftly that when rescued by reinforcements from Boston, their tongues [were], hanging out of their mouths like those of dogs after a chase." That was a story to arouse the enthusiasm of every American—and especially of such Americans as these backwoodsmen—and when the tale was ended they named the spot on which they were encamped *Lexington.*

OUTACITE.

A Cherokee chief. The reader will note the ancient tribal marks upon his face.

XIV

ON THE FRONTIER DURING THE REVOLUTION.

Dunmore's Soldiers Declared They Were Ready to Fight for American Liberties—The Responsibility of the British Rulers of All Ranks for the Indian Raids on the Frontier Home-Makers—The Cherokee Outbreak—The First Kentucky Colonel—Pluck of the Frontier Girl—Life in Harrodsburg During the War—Boone Captured by the Indians—George Rogers Clark's Memorable Plan for Defending the Settlements.

As the soldiers under Lord Dunmore marched home from their conquest of the Indians northwest of the Ohio, late in 1774, they paused near the mouth of the Hockhocking river, and the officers gathered and "held a notable meeting." Before entering on this campaign they knew how the people of Massachusetts, when the written law had failed them, had, in the exercise of "the paramount law of self preservation," assaulted the British ship Dartmouth, on the night of December 16, 1773, and thrown her cargo of tea into the bay. They had learned further that five acts of brutal oppression had been passed thereafter by parliament, and that a Congress representing the colonies had assembled in Philadelphia to consider the situation. They had followed Dunmore to this war cheerfully. They were well enough satisfied with his work as a leader. They were still cherishing a feeling of loyalty to the King, but their hearts were inspired with the feeling which prompted Patrick Henry to say, "Give me liberty or give me death," and they thought they ought to declare their readiness to fight for American freedom "when regularly called forth by the voice of their countrymen," and to say at the same time that this little backwoods army "could march and fight as well as any in the world."

Among these officers was Captain Micheal Cresap, whose murderous assaults on Indians in time of peace had brought on the Dunmore war, and he afterward made good these words by fighting in a way that goes far to redeem him in the eyes of most American students of history.

The five acts of Parliament that followed immediately on the Massachusetts appeal to the "paramount law of self preservation" provided: That the port of Boston should be closed until Massachusetts paid the owners of the destroyed tea its full value; that the charter of the colony should be annulled and an absolute despotism substituted; that any soldier or revenue officer charged with killing a citizen should be tried for the crime in England instead of Massachusetts; that British troops should be quartered thereafter in Boston, and that all of the British territory lying west of the Alleghanies and north of the Ohio river should be added to Canada and "governed by a viceroy with despotic powers." "Such people as should come to live there were to have neither popular meetings, nor *habeas corpus,* nor freedom of the press."

This last act is known in history as the Quebec Bill. When the King, in 1763, by proclamation, set aside this region as a royal domain in which no land could be purchased from the Indians but by royal authority, it is likely that he was moved chiefly by a desire to save the Indians from imposition, and thus preserve peace with them, no matter what the Board of Trade had in view. But the manifest design of the Quebec Bill was to restrict the territorial limits of the colonies; and because it reaffirmed, and was based on the old French claim that Canada extended to and included the Ohio Valley, it is naturally the subject of much comment among critical historians. But because the current of events in the Mississippi was not changed by the Quebec Bill, a mere mention of it will suffice here, and this chapter may be devoted wholly to things done.

It will help to a better comprehension of the things done in the valley to recall the fact that while Henderson was laying the foundation of his Transylvania colony in Kentucky, by buying the land of the Cherokees, (March, 1775), Parliament was raising the number of British regulars stationed in the American colonies to 10,000. In March and April, while Boone was cutting the trail from Cumberland Gap to Boonesborough, Franklin was on his way home from England because he had seen that war could not be averted. It was more than a month after the battle of Lexington, (which occurred on April 19, 1775,) that the frontiersmen met at Boonesborough, and established a form of government.

It is an interesting fact that the rapid growth of population in Kentucky, after Dunmore's war, (1774), was due in part to the migration of Eastern people who were trying to escape the disorders of the growing contest with England. And it is to be noted, by the way, that not a few of these new arrivals were ne'er-do-wells, horse thieves and desperadoes, but in coming west most of these people made a very great mistake, for those that wished to escape war soon found the Indians on their trail, and the desperadoes found that the home makers recognized the right of private war in the interests of order—that disorder would be repressed by the use of noosed ropes or well-aimed rifles.

This brings us to the most important feature of the American Revolution as seen in the Mississippi Valley —the British use of the Indians. Any attempt to gloss over, or palliate the acts of the British in this matter, even though done to promote international harmony, is but a form of foolish lying; and no good can be promoted by a lie.

The first troubles of the people in the Ohio Valley, as a result of the Revolution, came through the successful efforts of the British agents to incite the Indians to attack the home-makers. And their last troubles were due to the same cause. In fact the British made no move in the Great Valley but with the aid of the Indians. In the present state of civilization, it is difficult for many people to believe these facts, but the truth is that the British authorities, from the King down through the ministers, and the local rulers, to the Tory partisans, deliberately approved the use of Indians. In some cases local officials, gleefully approved, incited and took part in Indian raids wherein women were outraged and murdered, little children were slaughtered, and men were burned at the stake. When Col. Henry Hamilton began his work with the Indians at Detroit, it appears that (to quote Winsor's "Westward Movement," p. 111), he "was acting in anticipation of orders *which he had asked of Germain*. These, when received,—dated March 26, 1777—conformed to Hamilton's suggestions, and *directed him to organize Indian raids against the frontier*. We have his own statement (made) in the following July, that he had up to that date sent out fifteen distinct parties on such fiendish errands."

The facts in this matter shall be given as briefly as possible, but to see, first of all, that the humanity of the British *in authority* was on a level where these things were possible, it is necessary only that the reader recall a few such acts of the British troops in the east as the first foray into Jersey, where they "set fire to farm houses, murdered peaceful citizens and violated women;" the acts of Gen. Richard Prescott, who, when he took possession of Newport, "encouraged his soldiers in plundering houses and offering gross insults to ladies;" the capture of Norfolk where "every house was burned to the ground, many unarmed citizens were murdered, and delicate ladies were abandoned to the diabolical passions of the soldiery." The quotations are from Fiske's "American Revolution." One notable British historian, quoted by Fiske, says distinctly that the Americans would have been justified in refusing to give quarter, when Stony Point was taken, and thereby, as Fiske points out, portrays the level of his own civilization and that of people who approve his words.

It is now coming to be understood, even among the most obtuse observers in Europe, that American armies have always shown marvelous efficiency, even after brief training, because *every man in the ranks* has always fully understood the cause of the war in hand, and fully approved the object for which it was waged, and felt and manifested the keenest personal interest in the success of his arms. In other words, American armies have been composed of united thinking men, instead of well-trained, unthinking brutes. But it is not yet understood that this personal knowledge of the causes of the conflict and this personal interest in the result necessarily led to lasting indignation and prejudice. This is not to commend or even excuse lasting anger and prejudice; it is to deplore them and to point out that these are among the chiefest of the inevitable evils of any war involving a thinking people. It is also worth observing that when the cause of ill-feeling is known, a remedy may often be found.

Americans came to feel "a deadly and lasting hatred which their sons and grandsons inherited," not because the Indians were employed to fight American

The above Engraving exhibits a view of the massacre of the family of JOHANNES DEITZ, which took place in the time of the American Revolution, near a place called the BEAVER DAM, some twenty miles west of Albany; the particulars of which are set forth in the following pamphlet. The horses, baggage and Indians as grouped above, show them moving off from the scene of devastation and murder, while the buildings, a log house, log barn, and out houses of the same description, are on fire; the flames of which are seen bursting out from the windows, roofs, doors, &c. The two boys and Captain Deitz, are seen in the foreground; as also an Indian having the eight scalps of such as they had killed, strung out at full length on a stick.

soldiers, as when Carlton employed them to fight Arnold on Lake Champlain. Americans did as much. *It was because the Indians were deliberately sent against women and children.* This point is to be most carefully considered. "God and nature hath put into our hands the scalping knife and tomahawk, to *torture* them into unconditional submission," said the Earl of Suffolk (Almon's Remembrancer, viii., p. 328). A price was put on scalps, and a woman's scalp was purchased as readily as a man's. The Indians received various prices for the scalps brought in, but the white marauders who went on raid with the Indians received "a bounty of 200 acres of land," (Winsor's "Westward Movement," p. 111). The British officers, among whom Col. Hamilton, commander at Detroit was most infamous, sent out the Indians for the deliberate and openly-declared purpose of "driving in" the frontier homemakers and depopulating the newly-settled districts.

"Hamilton and his subordinates. both red and white, were engaged in what was essentially an effort to exterminate the borderers," says Roosevelt in "Winning the West." It was "a war of extermination waged with appalling and horrible cruelty." "It brings out in bold relief the fact that in the West the the War of the Revolution was an effort on the part of Great Britain to stop the westward growth of the English race in America, and to keep the region beyond the Alleghanies as a region where only savages should dwell."

"Few, if any, British officers brought themselves so much under severe criticism for inciting savage barbarities as Governor Hamilton. He sang war songs with the braves, he made gifts to parties returning with scalps. * * * His glee at the successful outcome of savage raids was not unshared by many in the royal service," says Winsor in "The Westward Movement," p. 127.

When Hamilton was captured, he was sent to Virginia, where his conduct was investigated by the Council of Virginia. In their report the Council say: "The board find that Governor Hamilton gave standing rewards for scalps, but offered none for prisoners, which induced the Indians, after making the captives carry their baggage into the neighborhood of the fort, there put them to death, and carry in their scalps to the governor, who welcomed their return and successes by a discharge of cannon."

This was a judicial investigation made by men who were not frontiersmen, to determine what treatment Hamilton should receive as a prisoner. The evidence of Hamilton's inhumanity led to his imprisonment in irons.

In order to palliate these admitted facts, some writers note that even Hamilton was in the habit of telling the Indians, as he sent them forth, that they should spare the women and children. There is no doubt that Hamilton did do that, but when these same warriors returned with the blood of women and children on their tomahawks, Hamilton joined in their rejoicing and rewarded them.

In view of this rejoicing over the slaughter of the innocents, there can be but one interpreting of his habit of telling the Indians, as he sent them forth, not to kill women and children. He did it for the sole purpose of throwing dust in the eyes of critics who might come, eventually, to call him to account for his barbarity. He was animated by a regard for "appearances," as Dumas was, when in command at Ft. Duquesne. Instead of his words palliating his conduct, they do but blacken it; for they show his hypocrisy.

The first outbreak of the savages during the Revolution was in June, 1776, when the Cherokees, on receiving fifty horse loads of ammunition from the British, were induced to go to war. It was an outbreak due solely to the desire to ravage the frontier of the Patriots, for there was no British army in the South, at the time, and no success which the Indians could attain would serve in the remotest degree to return the colonists to their allegiance to the King.

The Cherokees numbered 2,400 warriors at the time, it is said—more than twice the force that Old Cornstalk had in his great fight at Point Pleasant. Dividing this force into large parties (the party that attacked the Watauga settlements numbered 700), they came upon the frontier like packs of wolves. The home-makers fled toward the forted villages, whenever warning came to them in time, but many an unfortunate knew nothing of the danger until the painted warriors were upon him. Cameron, the British agent, and a number of tories were with some of the red bands, but it is likely that their presence added to the horrors of the raids; at any rate the women and children slaughtered outnumbered the men, and many of the men slain were unarmed. That men were burned at the stake scarcely need be said, but it is recorded that one boy was carried from a Watauga home, and at Tuskega was slowly tortured to death; and a woman would have been served in like manner, but for the humanity of one squaw, known as Nancy Ward, who, having great influence in her tribe, interfered with success. Of the cattle that were killed, homes burned and fields wasted, mere mention is necessary.

Naturally the first settlers to strike back were those of the Watauga region. While nearly all of the stockades in that region had no more than men enough for successful defence, that in Eaton's Station had some to spare, and these could not remain cooped up. Sallying out on the morning of July 20, 1776, in a band 170 strong, they found a party of Indians near their Island flats, but failed to get even one of them.

It seemed improbable that any damage could be inflicted on the Indians after they had learned the whites were out, and the whites turned back to the fort. Then the Indians, seeing the whites turn, supposed them panic stricken, and raising the war whoop, came in a mass of a hundred or so, led by the famous chief, Dragging Canoe; they were expecting to slaughter the whole company of whites, but the whites formed in line and allowed the Indians to come until within easy range. Then they opened a shriveling fire which turned the wild war whoops into howls of dismay. Yet the Indians carried off their wounded (among whom was Dragging Canoe), and presumably most of their dead, for the whites got but thirteen scalps. Four settlers were wounded badly, but none killed. It was one of the rare occasions where the Indian losses exceeded those of the whites.

About this time a party from the Wolf Hills Fort took eleven red scalps which they hung above the fort gate, Indian fashion. The Watauga fort, where Robertson and John Sevier were, had no more than fifty men, and remained on the defensive. Some would go forth, however, and three or four were killed, and the boy who was burned at Tuskega, was captured. One girl—Kate Sherrill—"brown haired, comely, tall, lithe and supple," would go down to the stream, one day, and the Indians who were in hiding nearby, dashed forth to capture her.

It was a most thrilling race, for they headed her away from the gate; but nothing daunted, she ran straight to the palisades, leaped up, caught two pointed tops, and drawing herself up, tumbled over, and dropped into the arms of John Sevier, who had shot her foremost pursuer, meantime, and who was standing ready to catch her.

Sevier at this time was a widower, and one of the most popular men of the country. Kate was one of the most charming girls of all the mountain region. So John and Kate were married, and the girl who could mount a twelve-foot palisade became the first lady of Tennessee, for Sevier was elected Governor as soon as the State was admitted to the Union.

One of the most interesting features of frontier life is found in the stories of loves and marriages that followed the gatherings of families into the forts during the Indian raids—raids that were made to depopulate the frontier.

The raids east of the mountains roused the inhabitants. The militia were called out by the thousand,

and then in due course the Cherokee towns were raided in turn. And a Cherokee town was not like a collection of bark shelters found in the north, for the Cherokees built good log houses and cultivated large fields. They were civilizing themselves steadily, if slowly, and the return raids made into their country, inflicted such serious damage that the majority of the Cherokees had to flee for succor to the Creeks and live on charity, during the ensuing winter. They were chastised in a way that compelled the clans to keep the peace for several years.

And yet old Dragging Canoe refused to join in the peace. Going down to the Chickamauga, he gathered the outlaws of every clan and tribe of red men, with bloodthirsty desperadoes from among the Tories, and there established a pirate community. In the course of the fighting, however, the Cherokees lost 200 men killed, while the whites lost as many men, and more than 200 women and children.

Meantime the Kentuckians were organizing their country as a county of Virginia. At a gathering in Harrodsburg, in the middle of June, 1776, they elected George Rogers Clark (the youth who had been under Cresap in the murderous attack on Indians below Wheeling, in 1774), and one other man to carry a petition to the Virginia legislature. This petition was dated June 20, 1776, and the most interesting paragraph in it was that which pointed out "how impolitic it would be to suffer such a Respectable Body of Prime Riflemen to remain in a state of neutrality" while the United Colonies were in a desperate struggle for liberty.

Mississippi Valley.

Clark succeded in his mission. Kentucky was admitted as a county, with Harrodsburg as the county town. The militia were organized, and John Bowman was placed in command with the rank of colonel—the name of the *first* Kentucky colonel is, doubtless, a matter of National, if not of world-wide, interest.

In the meantime, Delaware, Shawnee and Mingo (the Iroquois of the Ohio) chiefs had assembled at the forks of the Ohio, and declared for neutrality in the conflict between the colonies and England, but that was a position they could not hold. Col. Henry Hamilton, with abundant supplies of goods for presents, and money for the purchase of scalps, was at work to incite the Indians to raid the home makers. The colonies had little money for any purpose—they could not compete with this well-supplied official in bargaining for the favor of these red men. Besides the commissioners of Congress were trying to keep them neutral only. Hamilton offered them the still greater delight of shedding the blood of unarmed men, and helpless women and children. After the training which the Indians had received at the hands of the whites, during the preceding 150 years, there could be no question as to the course they would pursue.

During 1776 small parties of the Ohio Indians began making raids into Kentucky and other parts of the frontier. Numbers of Ottawas, Pottawattomies and Chippewas, the *raptores* of the Great Lakes, came to the feasts of blood and plunder.

One story of these raiders in 1776 may be told to show the pluck of the frontier girl. On July 14, five Indians carried off Boone's daughter, Jemima, with

Betsy and Fanny Calloway. The Indians made the girls wade in brooks, and took pains to obliterate the trail in every way, but Betsy Calloway, in spite of the uplifted tomahawks, kept breaking twigs and ripping off bits of her dress to catch the eyes of those she knew would follow. And so a party, led by Boone, and including the lovers of the three girls, came upon the Indians, late the next day, as they were preparing to cook a buffalo calf they had killed, and shot two of them. The three who were untouched fled, almost naked and without any weapon, into the forest and escaped.

The fighting, when a band of 200 Indians came to Wheeling on the morning of September 2, 1777, showed the metal of the frontiersmen. They arrived at daylight, a thick fog aiding them materially. A little later a white man and a negro left the fort to bring in some horses from a pasture. A party of six Indians waylaid the two men and killed one of them. One, it appears, was allowed to escape in order that he might bring out a party to attack the six, with the idea that they were a small band of raiders. Anyway, fifteen men left the fort to hunt the Indians, and before them the six Indians fled until the white men were led into an ambush. Then the Indians in hiding rose up with the war whoop, and closed in. But, although outnumbered more than twelve to one, the trapped men refused to yield. Twelve died fighting, and three escaped by hiding in the brush. A party of twelve that came from the fort to aid the fifteen were also trapped, but of these four escaped to the brush.

The men now remaining in the fort numbered no

more than fourteen, but the Zane brothers, who were too humane and just to take part in the murders preceding Lord Dunmore's War, were among them. The Indians came to the dwellings that stood near the fort and called on the whites to surrender, but the whites replied by firing at every patch of red skin that came in view. The women aided the men by running bullets, by cooling the heated guns and even by taking places at the port-holes to fire at the red men.

Knowing that the force of settlers was small, the Indians came boldly to the fort gate, carrying a log for a battering ram; but their dash failed because of the deadly aim of the defenders. All that day and the following night the Indians raged vainly around the fort. The next morning a small relief party (thirteen or fifteen men), came to the fort by way of the river, and a little later a party of forty men, led by Major Samuel McCulloch, arrived on horseback. As this party approached the fort, McCulloch was cut off from his men. The Indians were so close to him that the only way of escape led toward the top or crest of a "slipbank," 300 feet high, and steep and rocky. But McCulloch galloped to the brink, and plunging headlong down, he reached the bottom safely and crossed the flats to the fort. The precipice is there yet, but the slope is moderate in these days.

Harrodsburg was under fire nearly all the summer of 1777, the besieging parties of Indians coming in such quick succession that the people of the neighborhood were unable to raise any crops, save a few turnips.

On one occasion the uneasiness of the cattle (cattle

always showed fear when they smelled Indians), gave them warning, and they were able to attack a party of Indians who were trying to ambush some men at work in a field. Three of the Indians were killed, one by George Rogers Clark, who was in the fort almost all summer. The plunder these Indians left behind was sold at auction for £70.

The siege here was so close, at times, that the people were at the point of starvation. The most skillful woodsmen tried sneaking away from the fort at night to get game, but so many were caught and killed, that a time came when no more men could be spared. In this emergency, James Ray, a lad of seventeen years, begged permission to try, and because of a previous adventure, he was allowed to go. In the previous adventure, Ray, with two other boys, had been at work, in a field four miles from the fort, when a pack of forty-seven Indians, under a chief named Blackfish, attacked them. The two boys with Ray were killed, but Ray, in a four-mile race for life, fairly and easily outran the whole pack. The hungry settlers in the fort thought that one who could run as he could might escape; so they let him try for game.

In the dark hour just before day, this boy led an old horse from the fort into the river, and then by riding continually in the stream or its branches to conceal his trail, he reached safe hunting grounds and killed a load of meat. This he brought to the fort by the same trail, and so succored the famishing garrison. And these expeditions were made time and again without the Indians learning anything about them.

Nevertheless, Ray was at last to have about the

Mississippi Valley.

narrowest escape of any of the people in Kentucky. A man named McConnel was out trying his rifle at a mark, with Ray beside him, at a time when the people supposed no Indians were near. But suddenly a shot from the brush killed McConnel, and then a great body of Indians leaped out to take the boy.

For 150 yards the boy ran, with the Indians so close to him that the people in the fort were obliged to close the gate lest the Indians enter with him. But as the gate closed, the garrison opened fire, and the Indians stopped, while Ray threw himself flat on the the ground behind a stump, near the bottom log of one of the cabins that formed the fort wall.

His peril, however, was now greater than before, because, on seeing they could not capture him, the Indians opened fire. To try to rise and run for the gate was but to give the Indians a better chance to kill him, and to lie still was to be reached by a bullet, sooner or later.

Nevertheless, his wit was sufficient for the occasion.

"For God's sake, dig a hole under the wall and take me in," he shouted, and in a few minutes the work was done, and he was safe. He lived to be governor of the state.

It was a perilous summer, but in the course of it, George Rogers Clark sent two spies among the French of Illinois, and in a diary that he kept is found this entry:

"July 9—Lieutenant Linn married, great merriment."

Boone says "Col. Harrod's fort was then defended

by only sixty-five men, and Boonesborough by twenty-two, there being no more forts or white men in the country, except at the Falls, a considerable distance from these, * * * but a handful to the numerous warriors that everywhere dispersed through the country."

And yet in spite of the "numerous warriors," a party of forty-five men—home seekers—came in from North Carolina, arriving on July 25, 1777, and a hundred more arrived on August 20.

Early in 1778, while making salt at the Blue Licks, Daniel Boone and a party were captured by a band of eighty Miamis, and were taken to Detroit. Because Boone was such a famous frontiersman, Hamilton tried to ransom him, but the Indians preferred to adopt him, and thus gave him a chance to escape.

This chance came just as the Indians were preparing to start in large force on a raid into Kentucky. Boone traveled 160 miles in four days, eating but one meal during the time. Knowing that Boone would prepare the settlements for the attack, the raiders remained at home.

Boone was raised to the rank of Major in the militia on his return.

On August 8, 1778, the Indians came to Boonesborough with a force of more than 300 under a French partisan named Daigniau de Quindre. There were eleven other French soldiers of fortune in the band.

By asking for time in which to consider a demand for surrender, Boone was able to put the fort into good condition, and then he laughed at the simple Frenchmen. In return the Frenchmen persuaded Boone and eight others to come out and meet nine Frenchmen and nine Indians to discuss a treaty of peace. All met unarmed according to agreement, but the Frenchmen and Indians tried to carry off the Kentuckians barehanded.

Of course they failed, for no two men of any other race could, (or can), carry off, barehanded, an American frontiersman. An effort to run a tunnel under the fort was blocked, and the invaders went away deeply humiliated. Many other stories of raids of similar character are found in the annals, but as they were much alike, and none had any lasting effect on the ultimate isues of the war, no more shall be given here.

In the meantime the spies sent by George Rogers Clark had returned to Harrodsburg with the news that Kaskaskia and other British posts in the Illinois country were but feebly manned, and that the French population had very little love for their British rulers, though they had been taught to believe the American frontiersmen, (known, by the way, as the Long Knives), were devils incarnate for fighting, and monsters for cruelty and rapacity.

To Clark this news was most cheering, for he could now see his way to success in an expedition to the Illinois country. Whether or not Clark then saw the tremendous results involved in the capture of the British posts is a question which has been discussed, but this much is undoubted: Clark saw *that the way to defend the Kentucky settlements from aggression was to capture the British posts from which the raids were made.* One summer passed within the walls of Harrodsburg fort was all of the porcupine style of fighting that he wanted. He determined to fight the wolves in their dens, and what he accomplished shall be told in the next chapter.

But before passing to the achievements of this hero of the frontier it is worth while noting that there were a few wolves among the Americans. While the British were still bargaining with the red men, Old Cornstalk, the red warrior who led his host with consummate skill at the battle of Point Pleasant, and with his words, "Be strong! Be strong!" gave courage to the weak through all that deadly strife, now favored the Americans by speeches in council; and in every way possible, he opposed the British agents. Finally, when he saw that he must fail, he went to Fort Randolph, at Point Pleasant, to give the officers there due warning. A young chief named Red Hawk went with him. In spite of Cornstalk's friendly act he was imprisoned, and when his son Ellinipsico came to learn why the old chief did not return home, he too was held a prisoner.

The next day after Ellinipsico arrived, two men from the garrison, while hunting on the farther side of the Kanawha, were ambushed by Indians, and one was killed. To avenge the death of this man, the militia ran to the quarters where the unarmed Cornstalk and his son, and Red Hawk, were confined, working up their passions the while, with shouts and yells.

The coming rabble frightened the son, but old Cornstalk, whose courage had never faltered, said:

"My son, the Great Spirit has seen fit that we should die together, and has sent you here to that end. It is His will, and let us submit—it is all for the best."

GEORGE ROGERS CLARK.
From an oil-painting in the possession of Vincennes University, Ind., said to be the only portrait from life now in existence.

FORT WAYNE
1794

XV

THE WORK OF GEORGE ROGERS CLARK.

The Expedition that Acquired for the United States All the Territory Between the Ohio River, the Great Lakes and the Mississippi Was Started on a Cash Capital of £1,200—The Lone Stranger that Stood in the Doorway of the Ball Room at Kaskaskia, and the Effect of His Appearances on the Dancers—A Bit of Acting that Was Far More Effective than Gunshots—A Striking Comparison of the "Hair-Buyer" Hamilton with George Rogers Clark.

During all the time that George Rogers Clark was planning, in Harrodsburg, his attack on the British posts of the Northwest, he did not give any one so much as a hint of what was on his mind. Even the spies who went to Kaskaskia thought they were making this adventuresome trip in the interests of trade. With equal reticence he left Harrodsburg on October 1, 1777, and started alone over the Wilderness Road, to Old Virginia, to obtain men and supplies for the meditated expedition.

Clark arrived in Williamsburg, Virginia's capital, at an auspicious time. Burgoyne, through the well-laid plans of Schuyler and the hard fighting of Stark, Morgan and Arnold, had been compelled to surrender his entire army, and "things seemed to wear a pleasant aspect," in consequence.

On December 10, Clark laid his plans before Governor Patrick Henry. The man who had said "Give me liberty or give me death!" was able to appreciate the splendid project, and when Thomas Jefferson, George Mason and George Wythe were called on they also gave it hearty approval.

Only these men learned that such an expedition was contemplated. Clark was made a Colonel in the Virginia militia, and he received £1,200 in depreciated currency for expenses. An expedition to take possession of all the region between the Ohio, the Great Lakes and the Mississippi was started with a cash capital of £1,200 in depreciated currency!

If there is anything in history that can convert the fool who says in his heart there is no God, it is the story of the American Revolution. That pitiful sum was sufficient for George Rogers Clark. What he lacked in cash he made up with his youthful energy and hopefulness, for he was only twenty-five years old. Taking his money he went to Pittsburg, authorized to enlist 700 men, ostensibly to defend Kentucky from invasion, and with his utmost efforts was able to fill three companies of fifty men each. With these, and the rumor that four companies had been raised in Kentucky, he took boats and went down the Ohio River to the Falls, (Louisville), where he landed on Corn Island, May 27, 1778. Instead of four companies, he found less than 100 men, and when, at last, public announcement of the object of the expedition was made, a considerable number of these deserted.

And yet, after building a fort, Clark divided his force in order to garrison the island and protect some settlers who had come down the river with him to make homes there. He was then able to organize only four companies, each having less than fifty men, for the expedition, (he had 175 men all told); but with unsurpassed pluck he launched forth his boats on June 24, 1778, just as an eclipse of the sun was coming on, and in the growing darkness they shot the falls and proceeded on their way. The captains of the four companies were John Montgomery, Joseph Bowman, Leonard Helm and William Harrod.

The river was followed until nine miles below the mouth of the Tennessee, when Clark turned into the mouth of the Massac Creek, that enters the Ohio about 200 yards above the "steep, low hill of iron-stained gravel and clay" on which old Fort Massac was built by the French after they were driven from Fort Duquesne, (Pittsburg) by the Quaker emissary, Frederick Post. Fort Massac was in ruins and without garrison when Clark arrived, and he rested for one night beside the creek. Here he was joined by a party of American hunters who, in ranging over the plains of Illinois, had been to Kaskaskia. They told Clark that Rocheblave, a Frenchman in the British service, had kept the fort at Kaskaskia in good repair, and the militia well drilled and ready for a fight. The Mississippi was carefully watched, and that the French inhabitants hated and feared the Americans, as the Spanish-Americans hated the buccaneers—a story that pleased Clark right well.

Sending out scouts to capture any stragglers from the enemy's camp, and to kill game for the subsistence of his men, (for no pack train encumbered his movements), Clark started overland for Kaskaskia, guided by one of the hunters. After winding his way through fifty miles of forest and crossing the grove-marked plains beyond, he reached the bank of Kaskaskia River, three miles from the fort, on the evening of July 4, 1778. Here the command hid in the forest on the low grounds until night came, when boats enough were procured at a river-side farm to ferry them across the stream.

Then dividing the force, a half of the men were sent to form a cordon around the village, so that no one could escape, while Clark led the remainder silently to a covered gateway on the river side of the fort. Fortunately, no sentinel was on guard, and unopposed, Clark led his force within the walls.

The officials of the post were giving a ball to the inhabitants of the place, that night. A great hall was lighted by many candles, and with torches, here and there, and within were gathered a merry host of creoles, dancing with a glee that was delightful.

Walking to the door of the hall, Clark stopped and "leaned silently with folded arms against the doorpost, looking at the dancers. An Indian lying on the floor of the entry, gazed intently on the stranger's face, as the light from the torches within flickered across it, and suddenly sprang to his feet, uttering the unearthly war whoop.

"Instantly the dancing ceased; the women screamed while the men ran towards the door. But Clark, standing unmoved, and with unchanged face, grimly bade them continue their dancing, but to remember that they now danced under Virginia and not Great Britain!" (Roosevelt.)

And thereafter they never did dance under Great Britain, in that town. For the Americans secured the garrison, including the commander, as Clark gazed on the dancers, and the flag that replaced the British was never lowered. It is plain that Clark understood the French character well when he appeared alone at the door of the ballroom. He could have done nothing else that would have impressed them so deeply.

All night the backwoods Americans patrolled the dark streets of the town in ominous silence, while the French shivered with fear in their unlighted homes to which they were sent as soon as Clark saw that they would dance no more. The tales of bloody deeds done by merciless backwoodsmen from Kentucky, of which they had heard enough, were remembered in detail. When morning came, the French inhabitants were in a state of mind whereupon a deputation, headed by the priest, (Father Pierre Gibault), waited on Clark to beg for their lives. They said they were "willing to be slaves to save their families."

At that Clark, who had cultivated their fears by

night, told the trembling suppliants that the Americans had come to set them free, not to slaughter or enslave them; and that any who wished to take the oath of allegiance to the United States would thereby become American citizens, with all American privileges, while all who preferred to leave might depart in peace.

Hardly crediting his own senses, Father Gibault asked whether the Catholic Church could be opened. Clark replied that the American government had nothing whatever to do with any religion, save only to protect every man in his right to worship God according to the dictates of his own conscience.

The conquest of Kaskaskia was completed by that assurance. The deputation returned "with noisy joy" to the church, where they sang *Te Deum*, and the people made haste to swear allegiance to the new flag. Only Rocheblave remained obdurate. He replied with insulting language to an invitation to dine with Clark, and his slaves were sold for £500, (which was distributed as prize money among the soldiers), after which he was sent to Virginia as a prisoner. When there he broke his parole and escaped. Cahokia, the nearby French settlement, was conquered, on the same terms, by merely sending an account of what had been done at Kaskaskia, and Father Gibault volunteered to go to Vincennes and bring it under the flag, a mission in which he succeeded perfectly.

At once Clark enlisted a considerable body of French youth as militia and spent much time in drilling them and his own men; but a new danger impended in the arrival of a host of red men who came to Cahokia to learn what had happened, and Clark met them there. They were all from the Great Lakes—Chippewas, Pottawattomies, Sacs and Foxes—and there was an insolence in the bearing of a part of them, (known as the Meadow Indians), that might well have alarmed any commander having no more rifles behind him than Clark had.

But Clark was exactly fitted to handle these wild men without bloodshed. The first open aggression came on the third night, when a party forced themselves into the house where Clark had his headquarters. But Clark had suspected treachery, and had a force in waiting that promptly captured and ironed the red men.

The warriors begged for release, saying they were merely trying to see if the French were really friendly to the Americans, but Clark listened with indifference, even when some chief men of other tribes came to beg favor for the prisoners. To make a still deeper impression, Clark "assembled a number of Gentlemen and Ladies, and danced nearly the whole night."

The next day, after some negotiations with the other Indians about the future relations of the various tribes to the "Long Knives," the fettered Indians were brought before the Council. There Clark told them that everybody thought they ought to die for making an attack upon him during the sacred time of council, and that he had fully determined to kill them, but he had learned they were old women and not men, and for their treachery were considered too mean to be killed by a Big Knife. He had therefore decided to take away their masculine garments, clothe them in the appropriate garb of squaws, and then, since women could not hunt, he would give them a plentiful supply of food and send them home.

The punishment thus awarded them was worse than death to these Indians, and when the irons were taken from them a chief came forward with a belt of wampum and a pipe of peace; but Clark refused to listen to his words, saying that he would not treat with squaws. This impressed the guilty Indians so deeply that after a few minutes consultation, it was decided to offer two of their number as a sacrifice to clear away the disgrace they had brought upon themselves. Two youths volunteered to die for the rest, and walking to the center of the council, they sat down, covered their heads with their blankets, and silently awaited the stroke of the tomahawk.

The triumph of the Long Knives was now completed. Going to these youths Clark raised them up, and told them he was glad to find that two men and chiefs were to be found among those he had supposed to be squaws only. He was therefore able to treat with the others through them.

A peace that probably bound all who were present at the council, (though, as usual, not their fellow tribesmen), was concluded, and the name of Clark attained a fame through the Northwest that was better for the preservation of peace than the presence of many soldiers.

The most trying part of Clark's work, however, was yet to be done. Vincennes had surrendered at the request of Father Gibault, and Captain Leonard Helm had been sent there to take command. The news of all the changes wrought in the Illinois country by Clark's

COL. GEORGE CROGHAN.

Son of Maj. William Croghan of the Revolution. His mother a sister of Gen. George Rogers Clark. Received a medal from Congress for distinguished services.

Mississippi Valley.

invasion reached Detroit while Colonel Hamilton was meditating an expedition to the forks of the Ohio, and he at once turned his energies to Vincennes instead.

Colonel Hamilton himself took command of a force with which, on October 7, 1778, he left Detroit. It included thirty-six British regulars under two lieutenants, forty-five French volunteers under Captain Lamotte, and militiamen that brought his white force up to 179. The Indians at first numbered sixty-nine, but they were afterwards increased to 500.

Crossing Lake Erie to the Maumee River, Hamilton poled up that stream past the site of the present city of Toledo to the carrying place, nine miles long, that crossed the height of land where Fort Wayne, Indiana, now stands. The portages ended in what the French called a *flae*—or swampy lake, made by a beaver dam across *Le Petite Riviere*—a tributary of the Wabash that had little water in it below the beaver dam. The Indians and whites alike had preserved the beavers living in this *flae*. By opening the dam a sufficient amount of water was released to carry Hamilton's flotilla down to the deep water of the Wabash; and when the expedition was gone the beavers promptly repaired the dam, and filled the lake again, ready for use of the next expedition.

At this time Capt. Helm, commanding at Vincennes, had but one American in the fort, a private soldier named Moses Henry. He had to depend on the French militia entirely. He had a scouting party of the French up the Wabash, at the time, but Hamilton captured the party, and on December 17, the overwhelming British force entered Vincennes. The poor little Frenchmen promptly went over to the invaders, and Helm was obliged to surrender. Nevertheless he did it in good frontier style. Placing "a loaded cannon at the open gate" of the fort, as Hamilton advanced, Capt. Helm stood by the gun with a lighted match, and" commanded the British to halt. Hamilton demanded the surrender of the garrison. Helm refused and asked for terms. Hamilton replied that they should have the honors of war, and the terms were accepted. The comical aspect of the garrison, consisting of one officer and one soldier, marching out of the fort between lines of disgusted Indians on one side and British soldiers on the other, is happily illustrated in Gay's History of the United States, (Winsor).

When Hamilton reached Vincennes, Clark had about 100 Americans with whom to hold the Illinois country against this hair-buying invader, who now had a force of more than 600. Had Hamilton been half as courageous and resourceful. as Clark, the British flag would have been flying from every post in the region very quickly. But the fact is Hamilton had been obliged to drive his boats through ice, during his descent of the Wabash, and the winter rains and winds of the region had seemed to search the marrow of his bones. A seat by an open fireplace was much more to his liking that an expedition to Kaskaskia. Kaskaskia could wait till the orioles came to weave hanging nests on the tips of the white elm branches. He sent most of his Indians to their wigwams, and most of his militia to Detroit, without even trying to do so much as cut off Clark's communications with Kentucky. He retained for a garrison thirty-four British regulars, forty Detroit Frenchmen, and twelve white associates of the Indians—men fit to send on expeditions for scalping women and children. In fact, while Hamilton neglected to place a force where Clark's communication with the American settlements would be cut off, he repeatedly sent out bands of Indians in charge of these white men to raid, with fire and scalping knife, such lone home-makers as could be found at work in the wilderness, unsuspicious of danger. In nothing that Col. Hamilton did during the American Revolution is his character more accurately portrayed than in his preferring scalp-hunting raids to a war-like attack on Clark's line of communications.

And in nothing that Clark ever did was his character as an American frontiersman set forth better than in his work after Hamilton came to Vincennes. For while Hamilton sat down to plan the uprising of every Indian tribe from the Great Lakes to the Gulf, Clark planned to attack Hamilton.

Clark saw that he was in great danger at Kaskaskia, and *to defend his post he determined to attack the invaders while they were yet at Vincennes.* He did this in spite of his reasonable belief that the British force far outnumbered his, and in spite of a perilous lack of ammunition.

A big row boat was built and armed with two four-pounder cannon and two one-pounders—swivels—and manned with forty men. She was named the Willing. Her he sent around by the Ohio to serve as a ferry and a gunboat in the attack. Then he called for volunteers among the Frenchmen, and the boldness of the plan so roused the enthusiasm of the French girls that scarcely a French young man dared refuse to enlist, and on February 7, 1779, he marched from Kaskaskia at the head of 170 men.

In the annals of American warfare there are no accounts of such another expedition as this. The weather had turned warm, the snow and ice had melted, and nearly the whole route, 240 miles long, was flooded.

Clark himself might face a journey like that with composure. With his iron will its hardships might be turned to pleasure, but the appalling task was to make the hardships seem pleasures to his men, of whom many had been induced to enlist by a passing excitement. Yet here and elsewhere the man was equal to the occasion. He led the way. He kept many hunters out to bring in game, and he had the game served in banquets. At night they kindled huge fires and feasted and danced and sang songs.

At the end of the week they reached the Little Wabash and found the country flooded three feet deep far beyond the channel. But a boat was made by hollowing out a big log, and some men were ferried across to a place beyond the channel where they could be landed in water not more than waist deep. There they built a scaffold on which the baggage was loaded as the pirogue brought it over, and finally the pack horses came swimming across. Three days was consumed in crossing. The horses were repacked as they stood belly deep beside the scaffold, and then away the command all splashed through water and mud, waist high most of the time. They had found nothing worse than mud for beds, hitherto, but on February 17, when Embarras river was reached, they had to huddle on the top of a low hillside that did not afford room for them to make camp.

To increase their misery, the game had abandoned the overflowed land, and moreover they were so near Vincennes that the firing of a gun was likely to give warning to the British.

In fact at sunrise on the 18th, they heard the morning gun in Vincennes. The men began making pirogues, that day, and for two days they worked on the low ridge of ground. But in the meantime they had no food, and the spirits of the French volunteers sank until they begged Clark to return. However, before the night of the 20th, five Frenchmen from Vincennes were captured, and they gave the cheering news that no alarm had been raised in the town. The same day, a hunter, taking chances, killed a deer that gave every body a bit of meat, (the last food they had on the march), and in the morning the force was ferried across the river, leaving the horses behind.

Having landed on a low mound they set forward, (Clark leading), and marched for three miles through water that was up to their chins, part of the time, while a drummer boy "did good service by making the men laugh with his pranks and his jokes." Then they camped on a low ridge for the night—a most wretched night; though a worse was to come.

The next morning there was work for the boats, for the men were giving out under their prolonged hardships. The exhausted were put in the boats and then Clark, having painted his face Indian fashion, gave the war whoop and led the way once more, while some of the bolder men began to sing a favorite song to cheer the others.

But neither war whoops nor songs could strengthen the famished men, and when at night they came to a ridge six miles from Vincennes many were so weak that they fell to the ground.

To add to the misery of the starving host, the weather turned cold and ice formed a half inch thick over all the overflowed meadows around them.

Strange to say, however, no man died, and when daylight came they marched on once more. A prairie four miles wide that was now an ice-covered lake, waist deep, lay before them, but the strong broke the ice for the others, and the boats were paddled to and fro swiftly, to pick up those who fell by the way. A guard of twenty-five men, with orders to put any one to death who might try to desert, brought up the rear. And so they struggled on until an island was reached in the midst of a forest two miles from Vincennes. On the way across, a canoe which some squaws were paddling toward the town, was taken, and in it they found a quarter of a buffalo, some buffalo fat, and some corn —enough to make a good soup for all.

This swallowed, the forces overhauled their rifles and what with the sup of broth, and the prospect of a fight, the little band became as enthusiastic, once more, as it had been at the start. Some scouts sent out brought in a youth from Vincennes, who said that 200 Indians had just arrived; the British force was now very much larger than that of Clark. But instead of growing disheartened, Clark became the bolder. He had hoped, theretofore, to surprise the garrison, but now he determined not only to approach openly, but to release this prisoner with a letter to the people announcing his coming. The friends of the Americans were told to remain in their houses, while others were urged to go into the fort with the "hair-buyer General," and "fight like men."

Resting his men by their fires till sundown, Clark marched from the forest into a prairie in which were a number of low hills and ridges. The prairie was within plain view of the settlement, but by waiting until night was at hand, Clark concealed his force. Hamilton had seen the camp fires of the previous night, and he had sent out a scouting party, but the country was impassable to such men as they were, and they reported that it was impassable for everybody. Hamilton did not so much as know that the Americans were at hand when Clark marched from the woods.

But in the meantime the confident words of the letter sent to the French inhabitants had turned them to support the Americans, while the letter and extraordinary boldness of Clark's raid had turned the hearts of the Indians to water, and they fled; save only a few who determined to join Clark.

At 7 o'clock on the night of March 23, 1779, Clark entered Vincennes and was welcomed by the creoles, who first of all gave him a much needed supply of powder and lead. Fifty men were immediately posted as guards, and then the remainder approached the fort and opened fire.

Clark in his memoirs says that knowing Capt. Helm's habits well, and knowing, too, the building in which Helm as a prisoner resided, the attacking force was ordered to shoot into the stick and mud chimney of that house in such fashion as to knock a shower of dirt and soot down the chimney. The men did this with glee, and the result was that the tumbling dirt fell into and spoiled a brew of fine toddy which Capt. Helm was preparing as usual for the evening. This story seems incredible and "childish" to one modern writer of repute, but the truth is, it was just what the frontiersmen would have done under the circumstances. I have known the woodsmen of the Maumee swamps to do just such tricks in the days before the civil war. Horse play during a siege may be childish but it is common enough, and *not without good effects on the men.*

As soon as daylight permitted, the fire of the backwoodsmen was directed at the loop holes. There were several small cannon and swivels in the upper stories of the block houses on the corners of the forts—enough to knock the village to splinters, in fact—but the British could not serve them. The British regulars had courage enough, but the volunteers weakened as they saw man after man shot dead in trying to serve the guns. Here, as usual, the ability to shoot straight was on the American side, and was the chief factor in the fight.

To Clark's demand for surrender Hamilton replied early in the morning by requesting a truce of three days. Clark, of course, refused this, but he took advantage of the interval made by the request to give his men an ample meal—the first they had eaten in six days.

In the afternoon finding that he was losing men

INDIAN SCALP DANCE.

steadily, while inflicting no apparent damage on the Americans, Hamilton sent word that he would arrange for capitulation, and then he came out and met Clark in the church to discuss the matter. He had terms for surrender already written, but Clark refused them, and in the course of the discussion accused Hamilton of raiding the settlements in order to kill women and children, and said that one reason for rejecting the offered terms was to enable the American frontiersmen to take the fort by storm, and lawfully avenge the infernal work of the British partisans. To this charge Hamilton said he was not to blame for carrying out the orders of his superiors—a statement that was wholly untrue, since he had urged his superiors to adopt the raiding policy.

Curiously enough while the two officers talked, a party of Indians who had been on a successful raid against the home-makers, came boldly into town, knowing nothing of the presence of the Americans, and they waved aloft the trophies of their success as they approached. The frontiersmen at once fell upon them, killed two, wounded three and took six alive. The six were then led to a spot on the bank of the river where they were in plain view of the garrison, and were there tomahawked and thrown into the stream. Although this was done while Hamilton and Clark were in the church, Hamilton afterwards when safe at home, deliberately wrote that Clark wielded the tomahawk that killed these marauders.

Eventually, Clark agreed to accept the surrender of the fort on condition that the garrison should become prisoners of war. Then seventy-nine white men marched out. Of these Clark was obliged to parole all but Hamilton and twenty-seven others, who were sent to Virginia. In Virginia, Hamilton was kept in close confinement, for a long time, because of his "eager zest," as Roosevelt calls it, in the "unmentionable atrocities" of the Indians and Tories whom he sent against the home makers. But, at the request of Washington, who was ever anxious that even such prisoners as Hamilton should be treated mildly, he was released and exchanged.

The British power had been forever overthrown in the Illinois country. A force that was coming from Detroit with large quantities of supplies and Indian goods, was captured, and the plunder shared among the men of the expedition. A plan for uniting the northern and southern Indians in an effort to annihilate the Americans in the Ohio watershed, on which Hamilton had pondered all winter, was ended.

Clark returned to the Falls of the Ohio, and Virginia eventually gave him and his men 150,000 acres of land on the north side of the falls. The Virginia legislature also thanked him and sent him a sword.

Work that gave to the United States a territory in every way great enough for a nation in itself was accomplished, although it had not been carried out as fully as Clark planned it. For Clark purposed going to Detroit, and would have succeeded in doing so had men and means been given him. One feature, however, of what he did do remains to be described, and it has been left for the end of the chapter in order to emphasize the difference betwen the heroes and the politicians of the American Revolution.

COL. FRANCIS VIGO.

A firm friend of Gen. George Rogers Clark, and who loaned Clark £12,000 for the conduct of his notable expedition.

The £1,200 with which George Rogers Clark started for the Illinois country was necessarily exhausted before he had arrived. In his extremity, he borrowed tens of thousands of dollars in coin, at one time and another, of Francois Vigo, a St. Louis trader. A part of this was repaid to Vigo by drafts on Oliver Pollock, the patriotic American merchant of New Orleans, but "when Vigo died at Terre Haute, in 1836, neglected and childless, something like $20,000 (coin) which he had paid to Clark remained unsettled." His heirs strove without success to get this money, until 1872, when Congress referred the matter to the Court of Claims, and the Court decided in favor of the heirs. Then Congress appealed the case, though in vain, and in 1876 the country paid $50,000 to the speculators who had bought out the heirs, (Winsor). And Oliver Pollock, whose patriotism brought him to poverty, was treated in the same shameful manner.

Let the people—the pessimists who think that our legislators in "the old days" were models of honor and virtue—consider well this further fact. In spite of the magnificent service he rendered his country, Clark was unable to obtain a commission in the Continental Army. Congress refused to grant him one. But James Wilkinson, the infamous traitor, having the skill to handle the politicians, became the head of the American army.

GEORGE WASHINGTON.

This portrait is by Geoffroy, and published in Paris
Washington was then 56 years of age.

XVI

AS THE WAR DRAGGED ON.

Aid From the Spaniards at New Orleans—When the Succcessor of Hamilton at Detroit "Expressly Directed" the Savages to Make War on the Frontier—Robertson's Settlement on the Site of Nashville—There Were 250 Men in the Company, and 229 of Them Died by Violence Within Twelve Years—Origin of a Small-pox Epidemic Among the Indians—The Pluck of Nancy Gomer.

An important feature of the Mississippi Valley work during the war of the Revolution was displayed at New Orleans. On January 1, 1777, Don Bernado de Galvez became Governor of Louisiana. Though but twenty-one years old, he was a youth of unusual ability and of most remarkable energy.

As his first important official act, Galvez seized, at

New Orleans, eleven British ships, all richly laden, and confiscated them. The ships had been allowed to come there by the previous governor, (Unzaga), but their presence was contrary to law.

Then when Oliver Pollock was appointed agent of the American Congress, a little later, he was permitted to buy and ship war materials up the river, and Galvez eventually loaned him $6,000 to forward the business.

Among the shipments made by Pollock may be mentioned, as a sample of all, 9,000 pounds of powder in 150 kegs which, under the charge of Lieutenant Linn, was conveyed up the river, and delivered to Col. William Crawford, at Wheeling, May 2, 1777. One gets an idea of what delays river commerce suffered, in those days, from the statement that it took Linn more than seven months to make this trip. It was after this perilous journey up the river that Linn went to Harrodsburg where, as Clark's diary noted, he was married with "great merriment."

In consequence of the up-river trade of the Americans the British in Florida strengthened their forces along the Bayou Manchac, and the Mississippi, above Spanish Territory. The sloop of war Sylph, with a crew of 150 men was stationed at Manchac, while fifty rangers were camped on shore. The garrison at Natchez was maintained by 200 men. These, by the aid of British spies in New Orleans, made the transport of supplies up the river so perilous that Pollock urged Congress to send a force to sweep the river to New Orleans. Congress did not do it, and much trouble followed the failure to accept Pollock's advice; for Galvez went up the river, after learning that Spain had declared war against England, (May 3, 1779), and on September 21, 1779, captured Natchez. The capture of Mobile and Pensacola followed, and thus all the Florida of that day passed under Spanish control. What would have happened had Florida remained under British control is a matter of curious speculation.

As the time passed in the Ohio valley, it became apparent that George Rogers Clark should have been enabled to go to Detroit. Arent Schuyler de Peyster succeeded Hamilton, at that post, and he sicked on the red blood hounds, as Hamilton had done.

In an official report to Lord George Germaine, (quoted by Roosevelt), he said: "It would be endless and difficult to enumerate to your Lordship the parties that are continually employed upon the back settlements. From the Illinois country to the Frontier of New York there is a continual succession. The perpetual terror and losses of the inhabitants will, I hope, operate powerfully in our favor."

In connection with this, Roosevelt says, on the authority of the original documents now in Canada: "The savages were expressly directed to make war on non-combatants."

The British were trying to "disgust" the inhabitants of the frontier precisely as the French had tried to "disgust" them during the years immediately following the defeat of Braddock.

Books have been filled with the tales of horrors and heroisms that grew out of these raids. One of the most successful was made in June, 1780, by Capt. Henry Bird, who, on the 22d, with 600 Indians and a few white scalpers, captured Riddle's and Martin's Stations, on the south fork of the Licking. In raising men for a return raid into Ohio, George Rogers Clark arbitrarily closed the land office at Harrodsburg, and drafted four-fifths of the men who were there to file claims. In this way he secured 970 men, and going to the Indian villages of Chillicothe and Piqua, (Pickaway Towns), he burned them and brought back seventeen scalps. The work had no real influence on the conflict, but it seems worth mention because it portrays the dash of Clark.

In the meantime, however, the people on the head waters of the Tennessee had done notable work by establishing a settlement on the site of Nashville. One Spencer was the first permanent settler there. He went there early in 1778 with a party of skin hunters, and when the party broke up he and one companion remained. Eventually the companion decided to go and Spencer broke his own knife in two in order to give a blade to the companion who had none. To share a knife blade was the final frontier test of friendship. During the ensuing winter Spencer lived in a hollow sycamore tree.

In 1779 James Robertson, of Watauga, found the deep woods calling him irresistibly, and gathering a company that included Col. John Donelson, whose daughter Rachael became the wife of Andrew Jackson, he went to where Spencer was living and established a settlement.

The party started in thirty boats down the Holston on December 22, 1779, but the frosts, (that was the "hard winter") held them at Cloud Creek until February 27, 1780. The story of the voyage is remarkable. On a flat boat containing twenty-eight people a number became sick with the small-pox. The boat followed at a considerable distance behind the flotilla. The Indians who watched the expedition from the bank saw this defenceless boat far in the rear and made haste to go out with canoes to attack it. It was an easy victory, for they soon killed or captured all on board, but for months thereafter the small-pox raged among the Creeks and Cherokees, carrying off multitudes.

At another place the Indians stood on the bluffs and fired on the boats. When the crew of one boat fled below deck a young woman named Nancy Gomer took the helm and steered the boat to safety. She did not flinch, even when a bullet pierced her thigh, and it was not till her mother saw blood soaking through her skirts that anyone knew she had been hit.

The party named their settlement Nashborough after Governor A. Nash of North Carolina. "Three hundred miles of forest separated it from all neighborly succor," but on May 1, 1780, the people gathered and agreed on a form of self government, much like that created by the Watauga people in earlier days. The compact was signed by 250 men, and it is noted that in twelve years from that time no more than twenty of the 250 remained alive, and all but one had died by violence. They were picked off by the Indians here and there, as they hunted for game, or worked in the fields, or went to spring or stream for water. They fell in skirmishes where parties dashed from the fort to wreak vengeance on the red marauders. The whites held the land, but they paid a frightful price for it.

WILLIAM PENN.
From a painting from life, in the possession of the Penn. Hist. Soc., made in 1666.

XVII

GNADENHUTTEN.

The Most Significant Fact in the History of the Red Americans Is, that a Number of Delawares Who Were as Cruel and Bloodthirsty as Any Others, Were by Patient Efforts Converted into Christians—Driven from Pennsylvania by White Christians and Received by Red Heathens in Ohio—Slaughtered as They Sang Their Christian Hymns—The Blackest Crime Known to American History—Frontier Desperadoes Inspired by the Thought of Indians Who Would Not Fight.

Because they were willing to obey the Divine command, "Seek peace and pursue it," the Delaware Indians, who had been converted by the United Brethren preachers, (and have since been known in history as the Moravian Indians), left their homes among the whites in western Pennsylvania, in 1772, and removed to the wilderness on the Muskingum river. A settlement called Schoenbrunn (Beautiful Spring) was established early in the planting season. In the course of the year another was made nearly ten miles away from Schoenbrunn and named Gnadenhutten, while a third called Salem was built near Gnadenhutten. Gnadenhutten means "Tents of Grace."

The Christian white people had refused to allow the Christian Indians to live in peace in their original homes in Pennsylvania. This is an important statement. There is no record that either Christians, or members of churches called Christians, made any open attack on the Moravian Indians, but the white Christians, (excepting the Quakers, of course), made no effort to protect their red brethren in Christ from the assaults of other people, and they are therefore to be held guilty of the crime that drove the red Christians into the wilderness.

But when the Christian Indians reached the Muskingum, the heathen Indians bade them welcome and gave them peace until after the Christian white people became involved in the War of the Revolution. These Indians, who believed the Christian doctrines as taught by the United Brethren, having peace, built excellent houses and good churches. They planted sufficient ground and raised good crops. They prospered. They made rapid progress in the simpler arts of civilization.

It is important to keep in mind that these Moravians were able-bodied Delawares, and that before they were converted they had all the superstitions, propensities, instincts and ambitions of other wild, heathen Delawares. They had had as much pleasure in raiding their enemies and torturing prisoners at the stake as any other Delawares had.

Here, then, is the most significant fact in the history of red Americans. By the patient, persistent efforts of a few sincere and energetic teachers those wild and cruel hunters had been changed into peace-loving, stump-grubbing farmers. The perfection of this change of ambitions and manners of life is written on the pages of history in words of fire to proclaim forever that the infinite pains and sorrows of the Indian wars and raids were all due to the greed and the neglect of the white race. Most short-sighted was the greed, most woeful the neglect.

"Money talks" much more effectively than either sentiment or religion appeals. Therefore let it be remembered that the losses inflicted by any one of scores of hundreds of Indian raids amounted to more than the whole expense of converting all these Indians who are now known as Moravians.

The facts about these Indians were well known on the frontier, and in Lord Dunmore's war they were treated with kindly consideration by both parties to the fighting. But as the war of the Revolution grew hot, trouble came to the "Tents of Grace." The British officials at Detroit, in their eagerness to incite all Indians to make war on the American frontier, strove first to bribe these Christian Indians to take up the hatchet. Failing in that, they sicked on the heathen Indians to destroy the Moravian settlements, and scatter the inhabitants, knowing that a Christian, when hungry and naked, might be more easily persuaded to devilish deeds than when in a home of peace and plenty. White men who called themselves Christians, and who in time of peace would have given money cheerfully in aid of missionary enterprise, were made so brutal by the passions of war that they deliberately plotted to compel by force the Christian Indians into the perpetration of hellish deeds.

At the behest of the Detroit authorities the savage Indians, when raiding the American settlements, passed by the way of Gnadenhutten—the Tents of Grace—and compelled the peace lovers to entertain and supply them with food. And on returning from raids, care was taken to lay the trail through Gnadenhutten in order to make the suffering Americans believe that the peace lovers had done the mischief.

But the whites were not deceived. The red Christians and their white teachers soon came to feel a strong sympathy for the raided Americans, and a stronger dislike for the raiding British and Indians. It was impossible to avoid supplying the raiders with food, without a fight, and fight these red Christians would not. But a time came when their humanity bade them to warn the Americans that raids impended, and thus many a woman and many a child escaped to safety who would have been slaughtered by the raiders.

And this humane work was done at great peril, for the raiders were sure to learn about it, and sooner or later, the humane messengers were sure to be taken and slaughtered. In fact, the savage Delawares came to look upon the Christians as traitors to the tribe, even when the Christians refused to take up the tomahawk.

How they felt when they learned that the Christians were warning the whites whenever raids impended may easily be imagined.

As the dangers of these red Christians became known among the Americans, efforts were made by the regular army officers to induce them to remove within the American lines. Col. John Gibson, (he who took down the words of the famous chief Logan), commanded at Pittsburg, and was particularly earnest in persuading them. The Wyandotte chief Half King said:

"Two powerful, angry and merciless gods stand ready, opening their jaws wide against each other; you are sitting down between both, and are thus in danger of being devoured by the teeth of either one or the other, or both. * * * Consider your young people, your wives and your children * * * for here they must perish. I therefore take you by the hand, lift you up, and place you in or near my dwelling, where you will be safe and dwell in peace. * * * Take also your teachers with you, and worship God in the place to which I shall lead you, as you have been accustomed to do."

Both Col. Gibson and Half King were sincerely desirous of protecting these Indians. The red heathen, Half King, was thus kind to them though he knew they had previously warned the whites when red raiders were coming. Gibson was urgent because he knew that the frontier desperadoes were beginning to look toward Gnadenhutten. The fact that the Christian Indians would not fight was inspiring to the desperadoes. At Gnadenhutten blood might be shed and scalps taken without danger.

But in spite of warning, and in spite of a certain knowledge of impending danger, these Christians refused to leave their homes. Their determination, was in the mind of one honored historian, due to their "blind fatuity."

This is a matter of the utmost importance. Look at it without prejudice. It was not "blind fatuity." It was not "blind folly," that kept them in their homes. *It was a sublime faith in the Christ whom they worshipped* that held them there in spite of danger. There are no stories known to books so touching as those that describe the faith of wild men, red or black. The missionaries and their wards *believed* that God would protect them. It is a fact worth remembering, especially by those who, once a week, with bobbing heads, mumble some sort of creed, and then live, the devil knows how, the rest of the time.

Early in September, 1781, a party of British and Indians, numbering 140, led by Simon Girty, came to these settlements and carried away all the Christians to Sandusky. A miserable winter followed, and food became so scarce that many parties of Christians went back to Gnadenhutten to gather corn that had been left standing in the fields.

In some way the white men of the western counties of Pennsylvania and Virginia learned that these parties of corn gatherers tarried about their fields for days at a stretch, before returning to famine-stricken Sandusky. At Gnadenhutten were Indian men, women and children who would not fight, even if arms were given to them. The opportunity for the cowards and assassins of the frontier had come. Indian scalps could now be obtained without danger to the scalpers. To get the scalps of Indians who would not fight, ninety frontiersmen gathered at Mingo Bottom, (two and a half miles below the modern Steubenville, Ohio), to organize for the raid. It was not an association of frontier outlaws and desperadoes only; men of the first social rank at the frontier were among the number. They met by night to avoid publicity, for they feared that the humane Col. John Gibson, commanding at Pittsburg, would send a squad of regular army soldiers to stop them. To their thirst for innocent blood they added at the very inception of the movement, deliberate treachery, for they sent word to those whites who might oppose the raid that the expedition was going to bring the Moravians to Pittsburg for safety. It is important to keep this treachery in mind.

Col. David Williamson of the Pennsylvania militia eagerly took charge of the raiders. If there were grades of depravity in this gang, Williamson was of the lowest grade. Doddridge, who was Williamson's personal friend, says that *naturally* Williamson was "not cruel," and that to "murder a prisoner" was against his *natural* feelings; but he was guilty of "too easy compliance with popular prejudice."

The fact of the matter is he was a politician of the meanest class, and to curry favor among the most degraded voters in the region, he smothered his humanity, and took the lead of these raiders. It is not a little shocking to find writers who suppose they help Williamson's case by showing that he was *naturally* humane.

Col. John Gibson, who was commanding officer

at Pittsburg, learned that an expedition was going. He sent orders, imploring messages as well, but was unable to restrain the gang, and he therefore sent a warning to the Moravians. The Moravians, however, had faith in their God, and they therefore remained harvesting their corn, for the benefit of their hungry brethren at Sandusky.

Williamson and his followers started for Gnadenhutten on the third of March, 1782. A Christian Indian whom they found in the woods a mile from the settlement, (a half breed, the son of a white Christian named Schebosch), they chopped to pieces while he begged for life. But when they reached Gnadenhutten they went among the harvesters in the most friendly manner, and expressed regret and pity "on account of the mischief done by the British and hostile savages." "They likewise spoke freely" of the Moravian character, and expressed kindly appreciation of the fact that they had "never taken the least share in the war."

Finally the white men said they had come to conduct the Moravians to Pittsburg, to get them out of reach of the British and the savages. Feeling grateful for the apparent kindness of these white men the Indians delivered up such arms and goods as they had, that the whites might care for them, and then went to the woods and brought packages of things that they had concealed there.

Meantime the whites sent a party over to the nearby Christian settlement called Salem, where other Moravians were found and enticed to Gnadenhutten. On the trail, this party of whites "feigned great piety," and discussed Christian doctrine with apparent sincerity.

MONUMENT TO THE INDIANS MURDERED AT GNADENHUTTEN.

Having gathered all the red Christians within reach, together at Gnadenhutten, and having deprived them of every weapon down to their pocket knives, the whites suddenly fell upon them with thongs, and bound them all.

The white men then gathered in council to determine how to kill the Indians. Eighteen of the ninety were now sick of the part they had taken in the affair, and after protesting against the killing of any of the Christians, left for Pittsburg, taking one Indian boy with them. The other white men gave the Indians until the next day to prepare for death.

The Indians passed the night in prayer, in singing hymns the missionaries had taught them, and, in spite of their doom, they praised God for His loving kindness and blessings.

When morning came they were all—men, women and children, to the number of ninety-six—bound together by their hands, two and two. A woman called Christina fell on her knees before Colonel Williamson and begged for her life, but the Colonel, with his eyes on the voters around him, told her he could do nothing for her.

When bound, the men were driven into one house, and the women and children, who numbered thirty-four, were driven into another. Singing and praying aloud all marched to their doom. And when they were within the houses, the white men waiting there, tomahawked and scalped them. "The voices of singing and of supplication failing one by one, the silence that fell upon the place" at last told when the slaughter was ended.

One lad of fifteen years was so little hurt that he managed to slip his bonds and drop into the cellar, where he lay concealed while the blood ran down between the floor boards in streams. Another boy survived. He was struck on the head with a tomahawk, stunned and scalped, but he lived to describe the horrors through which he had passed, although the mob held a jubilee and set fire to the two slaughter houses before they left for home.

The blackest and most disheartening crime known to American history was the slaughter of the innocents at Gnadenhutten—the Tents of Grace. To attempt to palliate or extenuate it is to insult the intelligence of the reader and to add to his indignation.

Yet I venture to note that these Indians were not burned alive. It was reserved for degenerates of the end of the Nineteenth Century—members of the white race—to burn at the stake individuals of a less-developed people.

This is not to express a lack of faith in the development of Christian civilization, but to point out that many facts indicate a progress of degeneracy among the few, side by side with the progress of enlightened humanity among the many.

COL. AARON OGDEN.
Aide in the expedition of Gen. John Sullivan against the Indians, etc.
Portrait painted and engraved by A. B. Durand.

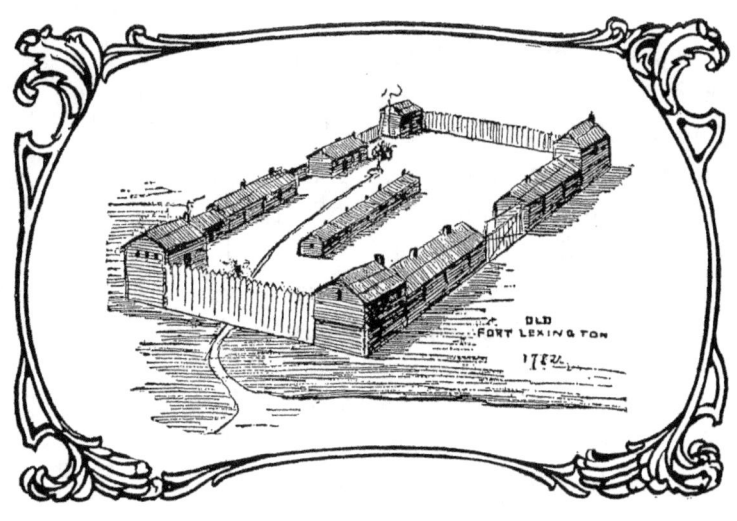

XVIII

FIGHTING THAT FOLLOWED GNADENHUTTEN.

A Second White Raid in Search of Scalps of Indians Who Would Not Fight, and the Result—A Needless Retreat that Became a Panic—The Whites Who Remained Calm when They Heard of the Slaughter of the Innocents at Gnadenhutten, Felt "a Profound Sensation" when the Story of Crawford's Death Was Told—But only Quakers and Moravians so Much as Observed that Injustice to an Inferior Race Was Unprofitable.

A peculiarly disheartening feature of the Gnadenhutten crime is the fact that the white people who were too humane to take part in it were yet unwilling to punish the perpetrators, or even to ostracise them. The scalps of the murdered Christians were flaunted on the streets of Pittsburg. The officers of the Continental army and some few other leading men, did express their condemnation, but the greater part of the people openly applauded the act. War had generated a species of murderous insanity, even among a people naturally humane, while the naturally vicious were incited to emulation. An expedition of 480 militia men from Pennsylvania and Virginia was organized to go to Sandusky, on Lake Erie, then the temporary home of the remaining Christian Delawares. The fact that the Christian Delawares were to be raided was enough to induce many of the Williamson gang to volunteer for this expedition, and others who were emulous of the Williamson reputation, joined in.

Mingo Bottom, two and a half miles below Steubenville of the present day, was the place of rendezvous, as on the Gnadenhutten expedition. On arrival there, the forces, according to custom, elected their commander. Col. William Crawford and Col. David Williamson were the candidates, and although Crawford held a Continental commission, and was a more capable officer, the popularity of Williamson was so great that Crawford won by five votes only. Williamson was, therefore, made second in command. Dr. John Knight was the surgeon, and Jonathan Zane one of the guides.

Starting on May 25th, 1782, the command marched through the (modern) Ohio counties of Jefferson, Harrison, Tuscarawas, Holmes, Ashland, Richland and Crawford, and into Wyandot county, Ohio. The Sandusky River was reached, three miles south of the modern Crestline, on June 2, and the next day camp was made near the modern Wyandot. On the 4th, Upper Sandusky Old Town, an Indian village, was found deserted, but the scouts afterwards discovered a band of Indians.

It was a prairie country, with groves here and there, and the Indians were in a piece of timber on rising ground, since known as Battle Island, about three and a half miles northeast of the modern Upper Sandusky. Simon Girty, Matthew Elliot and Alexander McKee, the renegades, were with the Indians (about 200 in number), the chief of whom was Captain Pipe, a noted Delaware. There were also two companies of white men from Detroit, under Captain William Caldwell, in the grove. On the whole, Crawford's force was much (perhaps 150) superior in number.

Though composed, in good part, of the most wretched material, Crawford's command charged on the grove, when ordered, and the Indians fled. But once the command was in the shelter of the trees, they sat down. It was a time for most earnest pursuit of the enemy, but instead of taking any advantage of the gain they had made, these worthless vagabonds allowed the enemy to rally and draw a line around the sheltering grove.

During that night and all day on the 5th, the Indians fired from the grass, as opportunity offered, and toward night of the 5th, they were reinforced by 140 Shawnees.

At sight of these fresh warriors, the hearts of the Pittsburg mob turned to water. They still out-numbered the enemy, but fighting armed warriors was very different from tomahawking bound women and children, and at 9 o'clock at night, on the 5th, Crawford formed his men in a body, and began a retreat that quickly degenerated into a panic. Singly and in squads, the whites scattered over the prairie, and it is likely that the whole mob would have been destroyed but for the efforts of a lieutenant known as John Rose, but who was really Baron de Rosenthal, of Russia. He, by heroic efforts and example, rallied 300, and keeping them in order, beat off the enemy and escaped. Yet even so they would not have escaped but for the eagerness of the Indians in pursuing the stragglers.

Among the stragglers who very nearly escaped were Col. Crawford and Dr. John Knight. Both of them were captured on the 7th. They were taken to Upper Sandusky (the Old Town), thence to a Delaware town on the Tymochtee, and at 4 o'clock on the afternoon of June 11th, 1782, Crawford was tied to a stake for torture. He had begged Simon Girty, whom he well knew, to save him, but Girty said it was impossible. He also implored the Delaware chief, Captain Pipe, to spare his life, or at worst, shoot him. To this, Captain Pipe replied that if Williamson had been taken it might have been done, but the Indians were exasperated by the slaughter at Gnadenhutten, and nothing could now prevent his death by torture.

Crawford was naked. His hands were bound firmly behind his back, and from the thongs on his wrist a stout rope led to the foot of the post—a sapling, peeled down. This rope was long enough to allow him to walk freely around the post. When he was secured, the Indians fired their guns, loaded with powder only, against him till his skin was full of burned powder grains from his feet to his neck. They punched and beat him with blazing faggots from a fire that was some distance from the circle around which he could walk. They showered red coals over him until at every step his feet were placed upon hot embers. Finally he fell to the ground, where he was scalped, and then hot coals were piled against the place from which his scalp had been removed. This drove him to his feet once more, but after circling about the post again he fell and expired.

He had been under torture but two hours. As compared with the Iroquois, who often tortured their victims through three days, these Delawares were merciful.

Dr. John Knight was a witness of the tragedy. When it was ended he was sent in charge of one Indian toward another village, to be burned, as they told him. But the fact that he was guarded by but one Indian, and that he readily escaped from his guard, makes credible the story that he was allowed to escape in order that he might tell how the red men had avenged the slaughter of Gnadenhutten.

A stone monument has been erected on the east bank of the Big Tymochtee creek, near Crawford, Wyandot county, Ohio, by the Pioneer Association of the county, to commemorate the death of Crawford.

It is recorded that the burning of Crawford created "a profound sensation"—"it excited the greatest horror"—throughout the country. The people who had condoned the merciless slaughter of ninety-four innocents at Gnadenhutten were horrified to think the Indians would take revenge on the leader of an expedition that went to the Sandusky Plains to repeat the work done at Gnadenhutten.

The burning of Crawford was, however, but the beginning of the revenge taken by the Indians. John Slover, one of the guides, was also captured but escaped (he rode and ran naked through the wilderness, with no food but berries and two crawfish to Wheeling). He was present at several councils of the Indians where the Gnadenhutten massacre was discussed, and heard the Indians resolve to take no more prisoners while the war lasted.

A maddened host thereafter swept the whole frontier, and parties went well into the interior of Virginia and Pennsylvania, passing between frontier fortified posts in order to fall with greater success on unsuspecting farmers.

Of these raids but one need be described—that at Brayan's Station, standing a few miles northeast of Lexington, Ky., which resulted in the slaughter at Blue Licks. In July the British gathered a body of Indians and rangers numbering more than a thousand. These under Capt. William Caldwell, who had opposed Crawford at Upper Sandusky, started for an attack on Wheeling, Va., but hearing that George Rogers Clark was leading a command into the Indian country, they hastily returned to defend their homes. They learned, later, that the report was false, but the Indians, for the most part, were disbanded. A party of about 300, however, went to Kentucky, and arrived at Bryan's Station, on August 16th, 1782. It appears, however, that some scouts reached that neighborhood on the 15th, and were discovered by the white lookouts.

YORK ON LAKE ONTARIO.
This plate was engraved in 1812. A portion of a block-house in foreground.

Foreseeing from the actions of the scouts that an attack impended, the first care of the whites was to get a supply of water, and this was obtained by the women and girls, who went to the spring, laughing and chatting, as usual, although they were within range of a number of Indian guns, and knew it. The Indians, being anxious to keep their presence unknown in order to surprise the fort, later on, did not molest the women.

But when the attack was made early on the 16th, it failed utterly. The Indians tried to decoy out the garrison by sending a small party to feign an attack and retreat on one side while the main body prepared to storm the other. The whites pretended to fall into the trap, and sent a party in pursuit, but the main body of the garrison gathered where the real storm impended, and repulsed it with a deadly volley.

A rescuing party that was brought by messenger from Lexington was repulsed by the Indians, but when attempts were made to fire the station, during the night of the 16th, they failed, and during the next forenoon the Indians withdrew, "angry and sullen at their discomfiture."

In the meantime the settlers from Lexington, and nearby forts, (Bryan's was the frontier settlement), had been gathering, and, 182 in number, they were soon on the Indians' trail. The leaders saw by the tracks that the Indians outnumbered them, but they followed the trail as far as the Blue Licks, on the banks of the Licking River.

From this point a number of Indians were seen on the rocks, on the further bank, and the settlers gathered to consider what they should do next. Boone, the ablest fighter of them all, advised that a halt be made until another detachment, coming from Login's Station, as they knew, should arrive. The men in the company who had been most successful in fighting Indians agreed with Boone, but Major Hugh McGarry, a blatant bully, was for crossing immediately. McGarry had been with a successful raid that George Rogers Clark had led to the Indian towns, the previous year, but had well-nigh wrecked it by an insubordinate dash from the main command, while yet it was on the Ohio. His vanity was his most conspicuous characteristic, and to display his physical courage he spurred his horse into the river, waved his hat with a theatrical flourish above his head, and "called on all who were not cowards to follow him."

Of course the others "just had to" follow him. On the further side was an open forest. An advance guard of twenty-five was thrown out ahead. The Indians were soon seen, and galloping forward till within sixty yards of the enemy, the settlers dismounted.

Boone, in command of the left wing, opened the fight, and steadily drove the enemy back. But the Kentuckians were outnumbered so greatly that in a few minutes the Indians had killed nearly all the advance guard; and then they enveloped the right wing, which was crushed in on the center. Col. Trigg, who commanded the right wing, was killed, and a little later, Col. Todd was mortally wounded. As he fell from his horse with the blood gushing from his mouth, a panic seized a majority of the settlers, and almost to a man they fled back to the river.

On the home side of the river, some of the men who had wished to wait for reinforcements, made a stand under the lead of a man named Netherland, and, by cool fire, so covered the retreat, that the Indians did not follow up their victory, as they might have done.

But the Kentuckians had already suffered frightfully. Out of 182 men who went out into battle, seventy were killed during the fight, seven were taken prisoners, and twelve who escaped were badly wounded. And that, too, in a fight lasting about five minutes. Of the seven prisoners, four were burned at the stake to avenge Gnadenhutten—for it must be kept in mind that this raid was one of the many made to avenge Gnadenhutten. One other was condemned to torture, but when the Indians started him running the gauntlet, he turned on the nearest Indian and threw him to the ground. Then he pitched another over his head, after which he leaped on a log, flapped his hands on his sides, and crowed like a rooster. The Indians roared with laughter, and a chief at once adopted him as a son.

The enemy lost but twelve killed and fourteen wounded, according to their own account, in the entire raid. Of these, they said, seven were killed at the lick. It is reasonable to suppose that more Indians were killed than their report showed, but that was the severest blow the Kentucky frontier got in all its history.

And yet no one, save the unconsidered Quakers and Moravians so much as observed the fact that injustice to an inferior race was unprofitable to a most frightful degree.

CHARLES CORNWALLIS. (MARQUIS CORNWALLIS).
From a portrait by Copley.

XIX

THE FRONTIERSMEN AT KING'S MOUNTAIN.

Ferguson said He was in a Place from which all the Rebels outside of Hell" could not drive Him, yet an Inferior Force of Patriots, a Respectable Body of Prime Riflemen from the Holston in the Course of a few Minutes Captured all of His Force, and Killed and Wounded 389 of Them in Doing So—When Clark's Name was as Good as a Thousand Men.

Although it was fought to the eastward of the Alleghany divide, the battle of King's Mountain (October 7th, 1780), should have mention, because of the part taken by the men from the Holston region, and because it was one of the decisive victories of the war. Until 1778, the Southern States were not molested by the British forces, but late in that year, Lieutenant Colonel Archibald Campbell with 3,500 regulars captured Savannah. A proclamation outlawing all who would not take up arms under the British standard followed, and soon Georgia was overrun by the British forces.

On June 13th, the worthless Gates (one of a disgraceful list, far too long, of American officers who have obtained position by political influence), secured the command of the Southern Department, and was shamefully defeated by Lord Cornwallis at Camden on August 16th, 1780. But British success reached flood tide at Camden, and the ebb which began to run at King's Mountain, left the invaders stranded at Yorktown.

Cornwallis, while yet in South Carolina, detached Major Ferguson "to scout the highlands (even to the divide), and enlist" as many Tories as possible. Ferguson took 200 British infantry and 1,000 Tories, "whom he drilled until" they were "excellent troops," by the British standard of the day, though they were deficient in one particular, as shall appear.

But, very unexpectedly, instead of finding Tories flocking to his standard, Ferguson found packs of Patriots—"dirty mongrels," he called them—gathering to drive him to cover. In fact the "mongrels" proved such efficient fighters that Ferguson's thoroughbreds were started on the run, and they did not stop until, on October 6, 1780, they were kenneled safely, (as they supposed), on top of King's Mountain.

"Well, boys, here is a place from which all the rebels outside of hell cannot drive us," said Ferguson, as on the morning of the 7th he surveyed his position.

And the facts seemed to warrant his confidence.

He was on a knob of a ridge a half mile long, and 1,700 feet high above the sea. The ridge was covered with big pines, and obstructed with huge boulders. His men, now 1,125 in number, had been trained until they would obey orders. The force that had been chasing him was composed of undisciplined militia. And although Ferguson did not know it, there were not 1,000 of these militia men. On the face of these facts, ignonimous defeat did seem to await the American force.

But there was one factor in the fight on which Ferguson had not counted; two factors, really, remained unconsidered. And to this day, in spite of oft repeated demonstrations of the vital importance of the matter, the first factor does not receive the consideration it deserves.

Ferguson had drilled his men until they would obey orders under all circumstances,—a most important matter—but he had overlooked the chief end of soldiers. He did not fully realize that soldiers are enlisted solely to kill other soldiers in battle. He had men who "could march to admiration," but they could not shoot. They were poor marksmen.

The Americans, to a man, had been trained to see with unwavering eyes through the sights of a rifle, and those of them who, under Shelby, Sevier and Col. William Campbell, had come from the backwoods, carried the Deckhard rifle, with a barrel three feet six inches long, and using a bullet running seventy to the pound—a most deadly weapon. Moreover, though undisciplined militia, and therefore liable to panic, they were now acting on the offensive, and were angered by the memory of the outrages that had been perpetrated by the British partisans. Ferguson had not considered the anger of these woodsmen. He had not understood the value of marksmanship.

At 3 o'clock in the afternoon of October 7, the Americans, 1,000 strong, dismounted around the foot of the mountain, and after tying their horses to the trees, looked to the priming of their rifles and prepared to climb three sides of the ridge. The north end was precipitous and was left unconsidered.

Led by Campbell and Shelby in the center, the Americans climbed up until the British saw them and opened fire, when they deployed behind trees and began to shoot also—continuing to advance, the while, from tree to tree, and rock to rock. The crack of the American rifle was soon seen to speak of death to the British, and Ferguson ordered a charge with bayonets fixed.

The Americans fell back until the British host was well down the mountain side, when a band of backwoodsmen under Sevier opened fire on the British right flank.

Instantly the well-disciplined British soldiers turned on Sevier's men, but it was only to find another American host firing on them from the rear, while the men under Shelby and Campbell turned on them instantly.

The British opened fire in return, but because they could not shoot well, they killed Americans only by chance and accident. And seeing that the British fired wildly, the Americans crept nearer, and fired as if at a herd of buffalo. Ferguson came riding a beautiful white horse along the crest of the ridge, and with shouts encouraged his men to withstand the Americans.

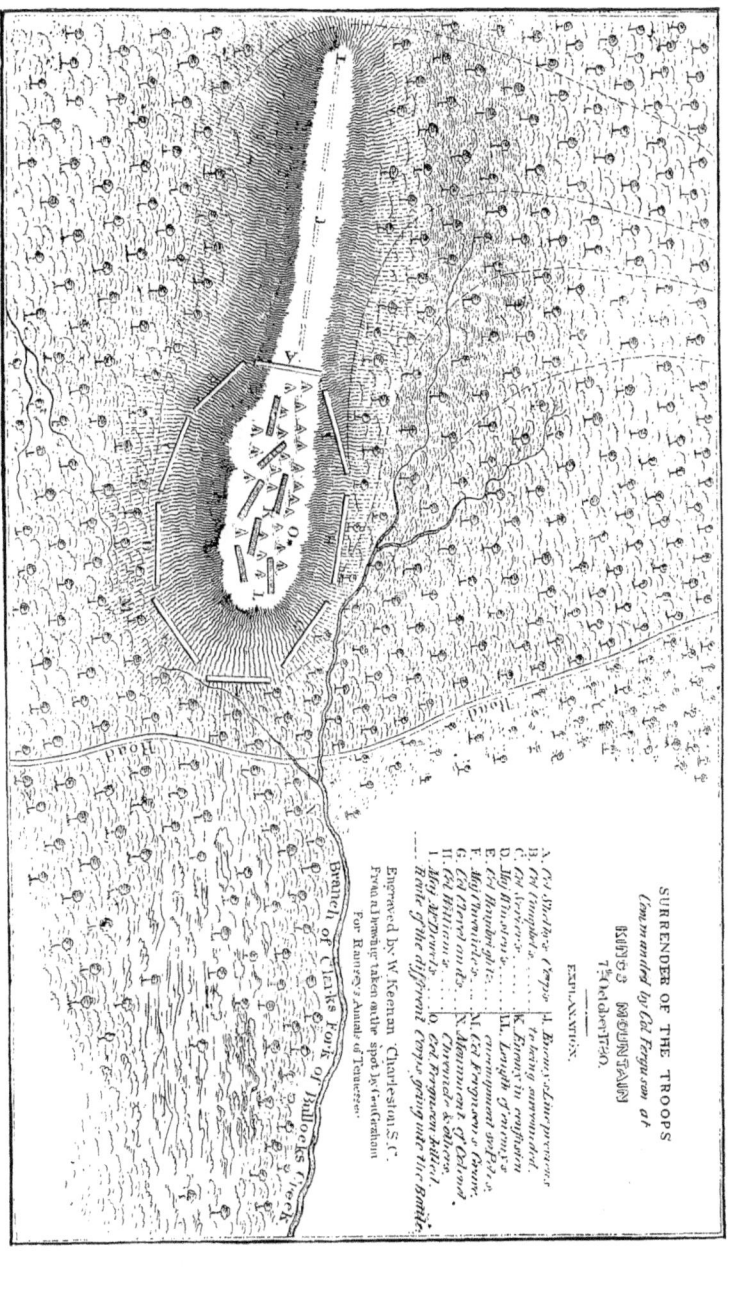

PLAN OF THE ACTION AT KING'S MOUNTAIN.

But he had come within range of men accustomed to killing deer on the run. He was shot dead, pierced, it is said, by no less than six bullets, and falling to the ground, his horse raced wildly down the mountain.

The end had come, the battle had been raging only a few minutes, but, brief as the time was, 389 of the British had been killed or wounded, out of the 1,125 that went into battle. Twenty escaped and the rest surrendered. The American loss was but twenty-eight killed, and sixty wounded.

The victory was the work of what the Kentuckians called "a Respectably Body of Prime Riflemen," but to this day our soldiers are drilled by the hour in marching, where a minute is devoted to target practice.

The battle of King's Mountain freed the Holston region from any fear of Tory invasion; and Yorktown followed on King's Mountain. But it did not free the Holston from Indian depredations. The Cherokees had been incited by the British agents to renewed activity, while the British overran the country east of the Alleghanies.

The work that followed was thorough, but monotonously like that of other attacks on Indian settlements. The white men, with corn, powder and lead only in their pouches, ranged free through the forests. "A thousand cabins were burned, 50,000 bushels of corn destroyed." But the Indians fled before the whites, and but twenty-nine red men were killed in the first raid, and thirty in the second. A third brought in a dozen scalps. But in the meantime so many red women and children had been taken prisoners that the Cherokees sued for peace.

It was in 1780, (May 26), that a party of 1,500 Indians and 140 British traders made an attack on St. Louis. They were sent "out by Lt. Gov. Sinclair, of Michilimacinac, and led by a Sioux chief named Wabasha. The affair lasted only a few hours, and no assault was made on" the fort. A few stragglers were killed and then the force fled back to the north. Nothing of consequence was accomplished, but this assault was to be the first of a series intended to capture New Orleans. The reason for the sudden flight of the Indians is found in the fact that they had learned, during the day, of the arrival of George Rogers Clark with a small body of men. The name of Clark was as good as a thousand ordinary men well armed.

GEN. ISAAC SHELBY.

His remarkable career cannot be epitomized in this brief space.
This portrait is by Durand.

XX

FRONTIER HOME AND CIVIL LIFE IN WAR TIME.

A Memorable Picture in the History of the Mississippi was the Man who Walked Across the Mountains Driving a "Flea-Bitten" Grey Horse Loaded with Books—It was a Poor Man's Country, for No Greater Capital was Necessary than Enough to Buy an Acre, a Hoe and a Rifle—A Consideration of Things that Shocked European Travellers—One of Col. William Campbell's Busy Sundays.

Of all the pictures of life on the frontier during the war of the Revolution, none pointed the way of the future Republic in better fashion than that of a young man who came from Princeton, New Jersey, and "walked through Maryland and Virginia, driving before him an old 'flea-bitten' grey horse, *loaded with a sack full of books.*" Samuel Doak was his name, and he was a teacher as well as a preacher. Following the blazed trails through the forest-covered mountains, he came at last to Jonesboro, and there settled, and in 1777 built a Presbyterian church. Doak believed with his congregation that the red men were heathen who ought to be driven from the fair land, as the heathen were driven from Canaan, and that when red men were killed, their souls went straight to the eternal torment to which they had been ordained from all eternity. Nevertheless he brought to the wilderness "a sack full of books," among which was one containing the Sermon on the Mount; and at worst any books were better than no books. Moreover he built a log school house that grew into Washington College, later on. There were many vagabonds on the frontier—shiftless hunter folks with no ambition beyond a full stomach, but the dominant portion of the people knew well the value of books. That is a matter well worth consideration in connection with the further fact that, as the frontier spread across the continent, school houses were always to be found in the battle line, until a time came when the people made boast that the first brick burned in this or that community were used in building a school house. That sack full of books on a flea-bitten grey horse with Doak afoot in order that the horse might carry a full sack, is a most memorable incident in the life of the Mississippi Valley.

The winter of 1779-80 was known as "the hard winter," for many years after it had passed. The whites in Kentucky and Tennessee had never seen such prolonged cold weather or such a depth of snow. Cattle and horses perished of the cold and starvation. The game became lean. Only scanty crops of corn had been raised, and what was harvested was eaten before spring came. A fort had been erected during the summer of 1779 at the Falls, (Louisville), and stores had been provided for the garrison. Some corn was held there by the merchants, who soon raised the price to $50 a bushel, and eventually to $175, in Continental money, which was worth then, and at that place, not far from twenty-five cents in coin per dollar. The lean breast of turkeys was sliced and eaten in place of bread with the meals of broiled and roasted venison, and the only satisfactory meals known throughout the winter were eaten when some lucky hunter found a bear in its den. For the bears were always fat.

Following the hard winter of 1779-80, the influx of population was extraordinary. No less than "300 large family boats arrived, during the ensuing spring, at the Falls," says Floyd's correspondence, quoted by Butler. Many other people, of course, came by the Wilderness road, through Cumberland Gap. One estimate says that more than 4,000 came in 1780.

On the whole the influx of people from the settled region east of the mountains is one of the important facts in the history of the Great Valley during the Revolution. The Indian raids drove many people from the frontier, but the immigration more than made up for the losses thus sustained. The weaklings who returned filled the East with the tales of the Indian raids, and their stories could scarcely have been exaggerations of the facts, simply because the human mind could scarcely imagine more dangerous conditions, in such a country, than those actually existing there. The life of no white person was safe for a moment when beyond a fort's walls. The home seekers who came in the 300 family boats knew what they were to face when they left the Monongahela, and many of them began their experiences with red warriors while yet on the river. For the river was haunted by parties of hostile Indians in 1780, and for years after. It was a year later that Colonel Archibald Lochry and his command of 100 men were destroyed by Indians while coming down the river. Nevertheless immigration continued.

It was a people of the utmost courage, and the dominant portion of them were of the rarest energy. A few slaves were with the emigrants, but it was distinctively a community of people who would work. Owners and slaves swung the axe and the hoe side by side in the forest and field. It was a condition of affairs that could not last long, for slave owners would necessarily come, at last, to look upon physical labor as ignoble; but it is the most important fact in the history of the United States that *the Mississippi Valley has been prosperous and progressive in proportion to the way the dominant people in it have been willing to work.*

We have in these early days of the Twentieth Century adopted a new Rank (John Paul Jones always spelled rank with a capital R). We call some of our great men Captains of Industry. Carlyle and Ruskin suggested such a Rank long ago, and we have acted on the suggestion. Through luck and longevity a mediocre man may lead all officers in army or navy. A ninny or degenerate may come to the Rank of capitalist through inheritance. But the Rank of Captain of Industry is the proud title only of him who earns it by honest toil. If a blight fell at any time on any part of the Mississippi Valley, it was because its dominant people came to look upon labor as something to be done by slaves.

Imlay has told how men with little capital succeeded in those early days. Men with an axe, a hoe and rifle came to Kentucky and succeeded. A sufficient shelter was built with an axe, and the rifle and the forest supplied the food while the trees were chopped from three acres of land. A half acre was planted with garden vegetables and the remainder in corn. Because much time had to be given to hunting, the first crop amounted to no more than seventy bushels of corn, but half that was enough to supply the settler having a family of three with bread for the ensuing year. The remainder found a ready market, though at a low price, while the skins of the animals killed formed the currency of the country.

When the second season came the clearing was five acres large, and the ensuing crop greater in proportion. By this time, too, the industrious man would have established himself among his neighbors so firmly that a cow could be purchased on credit, while the third year saw him driving at least one horse of his own, and a modest fortune was at hand.

All this supposes that the family escaped an Indian raid. The common lot was not one of uninterrupted progress. It often happened that when a man had got his house walls chinked and his roof clapboarded; when a cow fed on the luscious cane by the river, chickens clucked and cackled in the yard and the man was guiding a plow behind his first horse, a party of raiders came to the clearing and wiped out the family and all they had accumulated.

The instances where some members of the family were slaughtered and some escaped are many, but rarely, if ever, did the raiders fail to burn the cabin and destroy the stock and crops. The present-day reader notes with a feeling of relief that in this and that raid the Indians were unable to do more than burn a few cabins, but imagine the bitterness of heart with which the home maker returned to his clearing and found that the results of two or three years of the hardest kind of toil and self-denial had been all but wholly destroyed—the clearing only remained.

Yet the losses, heavy as they were, had some compensation in the cultivation of the sturdy qualities of the people. For *it was a characteristic of the men and women who made the Mississippi Valley to persist.* The unsurpassed pluck that made men with mortal wounds use their ebbing strength to give a last blow to the enemy, made the living begin over again and over again, no matter how many times they were ruined. They were of the tribe of John Paul Jones, and when asked if they had surrendered replied invariably:

"I have not yet begun the fight."

Even when unmolested by Indians, the home makers ordinarily had but a poor market for their surplus products. Here is a price list published as late as 1793, when peace was secured and the thronging emigrants consumed nearly all the surplus of the older settlers.

"Indian corn is from 9d to 1s per bushel. Beef is from 1 1-2d to 2d per lb. Veal, 2 1-2d per ditto.

Mutton, 3d ditto. Pork is from 2d to 2 1-2d per lb. Bacon, 3 1-2d to 4d. Bacon hams from 4d to 5 1-2d. Salt beef, 2d. Hung or dried beef, 3d. Neat's tongues, 6d. each. Butter is from 2 1-2d to 3 1-2d per lb. * * * Most people make their own sugar; but when it is sold, the price is from 3d to 4 1-2d per lb."

In November, 1780, the Virginia Legislature divided Kentucky into three counties, Jefferson, Lincoln and Fayette. John Floyd, Benjamin Logan and John Todd were commissioned Colonels for the three counties in the order named, and George Rogers Clark, who was stationed at the Falls, was placed over all, with the rank of Brigadier general. Roosevelt notes that at the first court held, (Harrodsburg), "the first grand jury impanelled presented nine persons for selling liquor, eight for adultery and fornication, and the clerk of Lincoln county for not keeping a table of fees." The first court house and jail were built of logs.

In 1782, several grist mills had been erected, and it is likely that sprouted corn appeared among the first grists brought to these mills, for distilleries were erected at the same time.

In 1782 one Jacob Yoder built a flat boat at Redstone and carried a cargo of whiskey to New Orleans with some profit. It is likely that whiskey was about the first product manufactured for export, and the home demand was not inconsiderable. The fact is the frontier life—the work of chopping trees, and grubbing around stumps, day after day, and living, the while, on plenty of meat and corn bread—created an appetite for liquor. The backwoodsman liked the taste of rum and whiskey, and he also enjoyed the effect it produced upon him. When Wheeling was besieged in 1782, the garrison narrowly escaped destruction because nearly all the men went down the river to a place where a keg of rum had been landed and concealed—went there with the deliberate purpose of getting hilariously drunk. But they sent out two scouts, as a matter of precaution, and these found signs of danger before the drinking bout was fairly started, and the garrison thus escaped.

Redstone Old Fort, (Brownsville in 1902), was the starting point of the river navigation in those days. To Redstone came all the overland traffic bound down the river, and the reputation of that town for drunkenness and debauchery became world wide. Limestone, Ky., (now the orderly Maysville), was also called a tough town. But it must be remembered that the outlaws and ne'er-do-wells that came to the frontier, gravitated to the settlements and gave them evil reputations even when the majority of the inhabitants were reputable people. It was the rule for every man to mind his own business, and in no way meddle with that of others. And what was worse, war—the constantly-impending danger—made men reckless, while the idleness due to the necessity of remaining in palisaded settlements, made any diversion welcome even to sober-minded citizens. They ran races, with bottles of whiskey for prizes. They drank their winnings. They fought each other "rough and tumble." It was not uncommon for a man to lose an eye in one of these rough and tumble fights. If one fighter got a chance he pressed his thumb into the eye of his opponent and literally "gouged" it out.

Europeans—especially Englishmen—who came to the region as tourists, a little later, were horrified by the sight of such fighting. They said it was utterly barbarous. The civilized way to fight was for the combatants to stick swords into each other.

On the whole, however, as has been noted, the distinguishing characteristic of the early settlers was the love of order—as it is a distinguishing characteristic to-day. They talked much of their love of liberty. Their orators told them that liberty was the rock-in-place foundation of their prosperity. But now that there is no danger of any well-established republican government reverting to monarchy—now that every American fully comprehends the value of his right to select the hero who is to reign over him—it is worth while to note the influence of order on the prosperity of the people. Order and justice under a despotism are now seen to be better than anarchy, if one has to choose.

The frontiersmen made stump speeches, (literally from the stump tops), on liberty, but they loved an orderly state of society more than they did liberty! Boone and his associates at Boonesborough; Robertson, Shelby and Sevier on the Watauga; Robertson, again, and his friends at Nashville, organized governments and enacted laws to supply what they saw to be *the chief need* of the communities they had gathered. And they enforced those laws—preserved order—at the muzzles of Deckhard rifles, with barrels three feet six inches long, and bullets that ran seventy to the pound, though a rawhide halter sometimes took the place of the rifle.

One Sunday, as Col. William Campbell, a leader living at the head of the Tennessee valley, was riding home from Doak's church, he saw a disreputable citizen —a Tory—ride across the trail ahead of him. The Tory refused to stop, when hailed, and at that Campbell, who was carrying a baby, handed the child to a servant and dashing after the Tory caught him.

The court was convened under the nearest tree, and it was proved that the Tory was riding a stolen horse. Such violations of good order could not be endured, and they ceased forever so far as that Tory was concerned, for Campbell hanged him to a tree and rode on home with a good appetite for the somewhat belated meal.

And strong as was the liberty among the people there, a time came when, to secure certain other interests, many of the population, (including even John Sevier and Robertson), were ready to go over to the Spanish.

One might dwell on the prowess of many individual woodsmen in their warfare on the enemy. There were Lewis Wetzel and his brothers. There were Samuel Brady and a host of others. These men were counted the heroes of the frontiers, *because of the number of scalps they took*. These men stood high in the frontier estimation precisely as certain braves stood high in Indian villages. But these men did infinitely more harm than good to the frontier. They were animated by a desire for revenge, and a love of blood. They were destroyers, not builders. There was no strategic value in their fighting, while lasting injury was done by their words and example to the young people of the whole region. White boys were taught to hunt Indians as they were taught to hunt bears and wolves. The ambition to parade a scalp was as rampant on the frontier as among the Indian wigwams. The courage and skill of these men, if admirable when properly directed, yet became the bane of the youth of the whole frontier, from the lakes to the Gulf. It was solely because of the barbarism in the human mind that fighters held social rank then, and hold it now.

It was on October 17, 1781, (the fourth anniversary of Burgoyne's surrender), that Lord Cornwallis hung out the white flag at Yorktown, and when the news reached the prime minister of England he "walked wildly up and down the room, throwing his arms about, and crying, 'Oh God! It is all over! It is all over! It is all over!'"

Because of the Gnadenhutten outrage, the frontier was yet to be raided worse than ever, and the British at Detroit were to make a last effort to drive the frontier people to the east side of the mountains. But there was no power among either British or Indians to accomplish such a result. The frontier home-maker had a wide-spread footing on the soil, and with his axe he hewed the bounds of the Nation to the Mississippi.

BRIG. GEN. ANTHONY WAYNE.
From a pencil sketch by Col. John Trumbull, of the
Revolutionary Army.

XXI

FIGHTING TO POSSESS LAND ALREADY WON.

Story of the Posts in the Northwest that were Retained by the British after Agreeing to Abandon Them—The Indians Urged to Slaughter the Women and Children of the American Frontier in order to Promote the British Fur Trade—St. Clair's Defeat—"Mad" Anthony Wayne to the Rescue—Wayne's March to the Maumee—The Battle of Fallen Timber—Land of the Mississippi Under the Flag at Last.

The story of the making of the treaty of peace between Great Britain and the United States, at the end of the War of the Revolution, is one of the most pleasing in the history of the Nation. In April, 1782, Mr. Richard Oswald was sent by Shelburne, the British Colonial Minister to Paris to consult with Franklin. Oswald was one of Franklin's intimate friends.

He had married an American. It was easy for these two men to agree on preliminary matters. John Jay and John Adams went to Paris to assist in the final work. The French minister was eager to confine the new Nation within the Atlantic watershed of the Alleghanies, and Congress had instructed the American commissioners to follow his dictation when making peace. But soon after the final negotiations began, we had there "the strange spectacle of the colonies joining with their enemy, the mother country, to circumvent the scheme of their own allies," as "A Century of American Diplomacy" says. Shelburne preferred the Americans to the Spanish for neighbors along the Great Lakes. "He recommended to the British negotiator to so act as 'to regain the affections of the Americans.'" Through the work of George Rogers Clark the Americans held the Illinois region, and the British negotiator readily acknowledged the right of possession. The fact is, as pointed out by Wharton, "the treaty of peace was not a grant of independence, but was a partition of the Empire." In this "separation" so much of the British Empire as lay within stated bounds was set up as the United States of America. It was a separation that carried with it the old reciprocal rights, and "the idea of a future reciprocity between the two Nations, based on old tradition, as moulded by a modern economical liberalism, was peculiarly attractive to Shelburne," (J. Q. Adams quoted by Wharton). The western limit of the United States was readily placed where the British limit had been,—on the Mississippi. Those who have confidence in the characteristics of the Anglo-Saxon race may well consider what results

Mississippi Valley.

would have followed if the British had continued to maintain a friendly attitude toward the new Nation.

But no sooner had the treaty been made than the British began to feel that they had shown weakness in their effort "to regain the affections of the Americans." They were poor losers. In fact they were "welchers." They refused to give up the posts they had agreed to evacuate. Ostensibly the frontier posts were held to compel the Americans to restore the Tories the property that had been confiscated, and to pay certain debts owed by individuals to British merchants. But the real cause was the feeling that they had been too liberal in making the treaty. "God forbid, if I shall ever have a hand in another peace," wrote Strachey, (an under secretary) who assisted the British commissioner Oswald in making the treaty.

The discontent created by the feeling that too much had been conceded was greatly increased by the protests sent home by the fur traders of Canada. In the history of America the fur trade has done at the north what the discovery of gold did at the south. In grasping at the profits of the fur trade, the traders hesitated at no crime, and no outrage on human rights. Under the treaty the British fur traders were to be excluded from the United States territory, and they estimated the trade so to be lost at $450,000 a year. It was in good part to save this part of the fur trade that the frontier posts of the United States were retained by the British after they had agreed to evacuate them.

But not only were the posts retained. The commanders of the British garrisons, and the traders who had store houses at every post, continued to urge the

Indians to make forays against the American frontier, much as they had done during the war. The purchase of scalps came to an end, indeed, but in every other way the soldiers and traders constantly incited the Indians to harass the advancing frontiersmen. The reason for this attitude was found in the fact that the frontiersmen were home-makers. The British were anxious that the territory northwest of the Ohio should remain a game preserve where a crop of beaver skins could be gathered every year. Said Sir John Johnson, in a letter to Joseph Brant, the Mohawk chief, dated Montreal, 22 February, 1791: "As you certainly are all free and independent, I think you will have a right to insist upon disposing of whatever lands you judge fit to reserve for the General Confederacy, in whatever manner, and to whomsoever you please. * * * No just right or claim can be supported beyond the line of 1768, and to the western line of the land ceded or sold by the Indians to the states since the war." He adds that in a letter to Lord Dorchester, Governor of Canada, "I took the liberty of saying that the Americans had no claim to any part of the country beyond the line established in 1768, at Fort Stanwix."

The chief object of British diplomacy in Canada, at that time, was to wrest the territory northwest of the Ohio from the United States and set it up as the territory of a "General Confederacy" of Indians who were to be, of course, under British protection. And with that end in view, for nearly twelve years the soldiers and traders at the posts encouraged and fitted out Indian parties that haunted the Ohio river, and lurked in the forests about the cabins of the settlers.

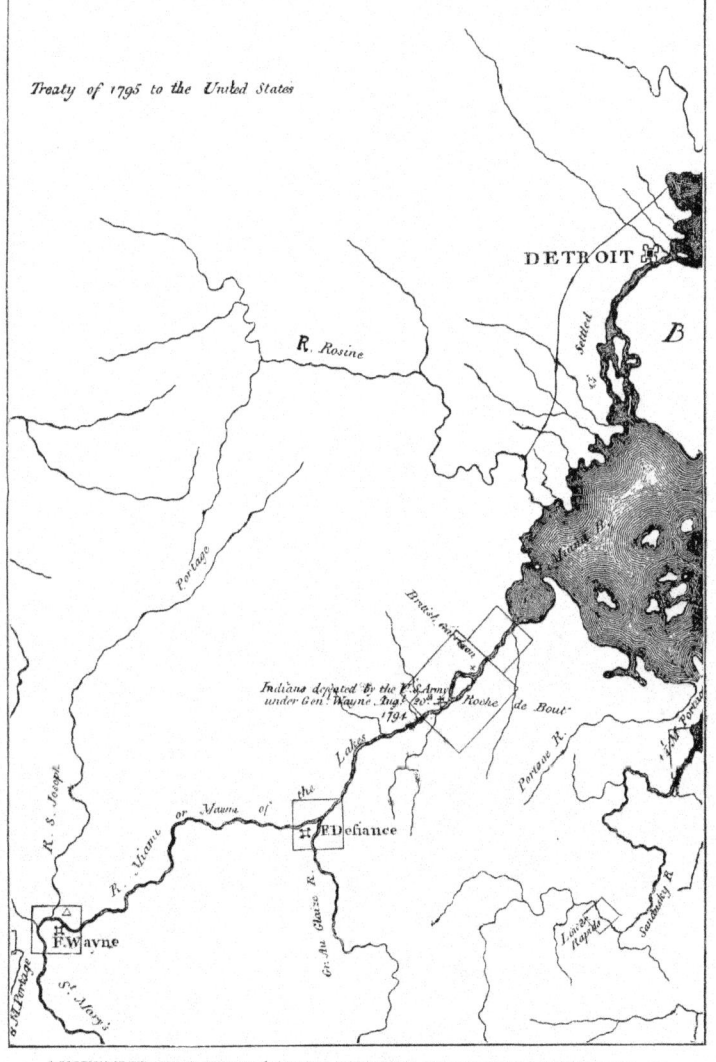

A PORTION OF THE MAP OF LEWIS, 1796, SHOWING FORTS WAYNE, DEFIANCE, SCENE OF WAYNE'S BATTLE, ETC.

No details of these raids need be given because they were all alike and similar to those of the war. Children were slaughtered, men were tortured, and every kind of property was destroyed in order to beat back the human tide that was flowing through the passes of the Alleghanies. One authority says that 1,500 people were killed in Kentucky alone, by the Indian raids during the seven years following the treaty of peace with Great Britain, while another authority estimates the total loss of life due to these raids at 5,000. It should be remembered, too, that by the treaties of Fort Stanwix, (October 3-21, 1784) and Fort Finney, (January 26—February 1, 1786), the Indians had acknowledged the sovereignty of the United States over their country.

For several years the Americans acted only on the defensive or made counter raids that were effective chiefly, if not solely, in glutting some private revenge.

George Rogers Clark went up to the Wabash country and overawed, for a time, the Indians there, and in the Illinois country. He also confiscated the goods of some Spanish traders in retaliation for seizures of American flat boats by the Spanish down the Mississippi. Col. Benjamin Logan made a raid up to the Shawnee towns in Ohio, where he took ten scalps and thirty-two prisoners, besides burning 200 cabins and much corn.

In 1790 Gen. Josiah Harmar with a force of 320 regulars and 1,133 militia marched to the site of the modern Ft. Wayne, Indiana. He burned 300 huts and destroyed 20,000 bushels of corn, but he lost 180 men in encounters with the Indians, and instead of inclining the red men to peace he encouraged them to further warfare. And to add to the encouragement of the red men, the British supplied them with an abundance of ammunition immediately after Harmar's retreat. It is worth noting, too, that Lord Dorchester, Governor of Canada, while issuing ammunition through the frontier posts, on American territory, to the Indians was publicly denying that this had been done.

Meantime, while frontier guns were accomplishing little or nothing the frontier axe was doing something. A notable tool was the American axe—thin-bladed, long-handled, and light in weight. The best woodsmen, then as now, found that an axe weighing from three and a half to four pounds was just right, and the blade was modeled by smiths who had chopped down trees as well as hammered steel. The American axe has never been equalled.

With the axe, settlements were made on both sides of the Ohio in spite of raids. In 1785 Fort Harmar was built at the mouth of the Muskingum to restrain the Indians. On October 27, 1787, the Ohio Company, an aggregation of New England men that included both home-makers and speculators, bought of Congress 964,285 acres of land opposite Fort Harmar at the junction of the Ohio and Muskingum, (the land lay on the north side of the Ohio), agreeing to pay $642,856.66. Gen. Rufus Putnam was a leader among these home makers. It was a company composed chiefly of soldiers of the Revolution, but there were enough speculators in it to throw a shadow of disrepute over the transaction. The Rev. Manasseh Cutler, a man who "believed, as that sort of man often does, in making his neighbors and those he knew best his associates in any hazardous undertaking," (Winsor), was the leader of the specula-

MARIE ANTOINETTE.
Queen of France, wife of Louis XVI. The town of Marietta, Ohio, was named for this lady.

tors. He was the man who "worked" Congress for the grant. The total breadth obtained by the speculators was 5,000,000 acres, the price of which was to be $3,500,000. The land beyond the grant for the settlement of soldiers was to be sold as a speculation, and Cutler in connection with Joel Barlow and Col. William Duer, by means of descriptive circulars that were deliberately false, sold a considerable breadth to a company of Frenchmen whose misfortunes, after reaching the banks of the Ohio, were great. An interesting and instructive but very unpleasant book might be written on the work of dishonest land speculators in the Mississippi Valley.

On April 2, 1788, Putnam, with a party of surveyors and engineers, left the Youghiogheny in a bullet proof flat boat, and on the 7th reached Ft. Harmar. They then surveyed the plot purchased of Congress, and built the town of Marietta, Ohio. It is the proud boast of the Marietta people, in these days, (and of all Ohio as well), that the settlers under Putnam brought with them a library. The people of the region have often boasted, also, that the ordinance, (July 13, 1787), for the government of the region northwest of the Ohio, (in the writing and passage of which Cutler was the leading spirit), prohibited slavery. The ordinance did not extirpate slavery, as it was supposed to do, but it undoubtedly had much influence in creating a public sentiment againt the detestable instituion.

Then, too, the men who followed Putnam were for the most part old comrades in arms—men who had fought for the freedom of the Nation in the war of the Revolution. At a time when the demagogues in Kentucky were telling the home-makers that a separation from the States east of the Alleghanies was necessary for their welfare it was worth while to have a settlement on the Ohio composed of men who had proved their devotion to the welfare of the whole people.

Another interesting feature of this settlement is found in the method of dividing the land. Instead of allowing the settlers to go into the region and pick out claims which were to be afterwards surveyed, to please the settler, as was done in Kentucky, the whole tract was first surveyed into townships six miles square and each township into sections one mile square. Accordingly when a man located a claim the land taken already had ascertained and definite bounds. There were no overlapping claims as under the haphazard scheme that had previously prevailed.

Marietta was settled during a busy season on the Ohio river. The officers at Fort Harmar counted more than 500 flat boats carrying 10,000 emigrants down the Ohio river.

On July 9, 1788, Gen. Arthur St. Clair, who had seen service under Wolf at Quebec, and had but recently been president of Congress, arrived at Marietta, bringing an appointment as Governor of the "Northwest Territory."

Meantime, (May 15, 1788), John Cleve Symmes bought a large tract of land on the Ohio river between the Great and Little Miami rivers; and in July "with fourteen four-horse wagons and sixty persons in his train," he came to his purchase. Among the followers of Symmes was John Filson, a surveyor, who is best known as the reporter who wrote the story of Daniel

MAJ. GEN. ARTHUR ST. CLAIR.
From a pencil sketch by Col. John Trumbull.

Boone. When the company wished a name for the town which they proceeded to lay out, Filson made one. Directly opposite the new town was the mouth of the Licking river. Filson thought that "Town-opposite-the-mouth-of-the-Licking" would be a proper name for the settlement, and he wrote it thus: *L* for Licking; *os* for mouth; *anti* for opposite, and *ville* for town, which being combined gave Losantiville. But when St. Clair came to the settlement he determined to bestow on the town the name of the society of the Revolutionary officers, known as the Cincinnati.

It was on November 4, 1790, that Harmar began his "disorderly retreat" from the Indian country. On January 2, 1791, a big party of Indians, Delawares and Wyandottes, attacked a settlement on the Muskingum called Big Bottom, an off-shoot of Gen. Rufus Putnam's Marietta settlement. They killed twelve and carried off four prisoners. On the 10th Simon Girty, with 300 warriors, appeared at Dunlap Station, near Cincinnati, but accomplished little because aid came from the larger town. In February the Indians swarmed along the Alleghany river.

When the news of the first of these raids reached Washington, he notified Congress, (January 24, 1791), and in due course a new expedition, of which Gov. St. Clair was to have charge in person, was authorized.

Washington believed that this expedition would convince the Indians that the "enmity of the United States is as much to be dreaded as their friendship is to be desired," while Jefferson said, "I hope we shall drub the Indians well this summer, and then change our plan from war to bribery."

Both these expressions are of interest chiefly because it is apparent that neither Jefferson nor Washington saw the strong hand of the British that was pushing the Indians into aggressions. But the strength of that hand appeared nevertheless, further on.

St. Clair reached Ft. Washington, at Cincinnati, where he was to take charge of the forces for the expedition, in May, 1791, but it was not until October that a number of soldiers deemed adequate for the occasion was gathered there. While waiting for the reinforcements St. Clair fell sick, and so did Gen. Richard Butler, a notable soldier, the second in command. The powder supplied by the swindling, (one ought to say murderous) contractors was bad. The oxen were few in number and too lean in body. Worse yet, the recruits were, with few exceptions, an utterly worthless mob swept from the streets of the seaboard cities.

However, St. Clair set forth, at last, and on November 3, 1791, made camp at a spot where Fort Recovery, Ohio, now stands on a branch of the Wabash river. Little scouting had been done, and no adequate precautions to repel an attack were made after pitching the camp.

Taking advantage of these conditions the Indians, led by Little Turtle, fell upon the camp half an hour before sunrise next day, and by 9 o'clock, the army was in disorderly retreat. The killed numbered 630, the seriously wounded 280, and of 1,400 all told, under St. Clair, "scarce half a hundred were unhurt."

St. Clair's defeat, in its effect on the American people, was stupefying, exasperating and conducive to a mental condition not far from imbecility—all accord-

ing to the quality of individuals. A few were made firmer in their determination to resist aggression. The exasperated wished to wreck vengeance on St. Clair. The partially-made imbeciles, if they may be called so, demanded negotiations with the victorious red men in order to buy peace of them. Incredible as it may seem, those were the days when the American Congress refused to build war ships to protect American commerce, but they did actually build a fine frigate, ballast it with barrels of silver dollars and send it as tribute to an African pirate to purchase his favor. The Jeffersonian policy of "bribery" was fully tried.

Negotiations were opened with the Indians, through the intervention of the Senecas. Brant, the Mohawk Chief, who was a leader in the council, in a speech some years later, told how the British exerted their influence to defeat the efforts for peace. "To our surprise," he said, "when on the point of entering upon a treaty with the Commissioners, we found that it was opposed by those acting under the British government."

In fact the Commissioners were treated with marked insolence by Simon Girty, who was interpreter for the Indians. It was a particularly gloomy period on the frontier, for the Spanish still held Natchez, and were grasping for a wide territory in the southwest by means of Indian raids.

But in the meantime one of the inspiring men of the American army—General Anthony Wayne—"Mad Anthony"—was appointed to command a new expedition against the Indians, and there was, at last, hope for peace.

In the history of the early struggles of the American people the one man who has not received the full measure of credit due him is Gen. Anthony Wayne. If the average reader be asked what Wayne did to gain fame the reply, quickly given, is that he captured Stony Point. The spectacular dash of the man at Stony Point may well be remembered, for we all love a good leader in the thick of the fight; but the capture of the rocky peninsula below West Point was but a trivial skirmish in comparison with the splendid work he was now to do. Indeed, when rightly considered, the charge up the rocks of the promontory called Stony Point was less significant than the fact that he ordered his command to appear on parade "well powdered" before he started them on their long march through the mountains to reach the point of attack.

Even Washington, it appears, failed, after the Revolution ended, to appreciate all the worth of this most capable brigadier, for when he was going over the names of the men available to retrieve the Ohio country, Wayne was really his second choice. Here is Washington's valuation of "Mad" Anthony Wayne in 1791:

"More active and enterprising than judicious and cautious. No economist, it is feared. Open to flattery, vain; easily imposed upon and liable to be drawn into scrapes." In such words did Washington describe this General, while choosing him for the command. But Hammond, the British minister to the United States, described him as the most active, vigilant, and enterprising officer in the American army.

When Wayne reached Pittsburg, and began to prepare for the work before him, (June, 1792), the task might well have appalled a man less resourceful. The contractors—they who had supplied St. Clair with powder unfit for any purpose—were there, eager for opportunity to fit out the new expedition in like manner. The town contained, as frontier towns have always contained, numerous vile resorts to which the recruits were enticed whenever a shilling could be wrung from them. And the recruits were of the quality most easily enticed. Judge Symmes in speaking of the recruits supplied to St. Clair said:

"Men who are purchased from prisons, wheelbarrows and brothels at two dollars per month will never answer for fighting Indians."

It was so. They were utterly worthless in the St. Clair expedition, but now Wayne was supplied with a *second sweeping* from the "prisons and brothels." By sleepless vigilance Wayne could sift out the unfit powder that the contractors wished to foist upon him, but from these unfit, rotten and sick recruits there was no escape.

Moreover, he had to wait for the outcome of the negotiations that had been opened by the commissioners with the exultant Indians—negotiations that were incited, not by Christian philanthropy, but by cowardice and penury—an important distinction, by the way, and the reader may well consider for himself the bearing of this distinction on what has been said, hitherto, about the Quaker-Moravian policy of philanthropy toward the Indians, and the Jeffersonian system of "bribery."

Nevertheless here was the man for the place, and once the choice had been made, he had the full support of Washington, who wrote him "not to be sparing of powder and lead to make his soldiers marksmen."

To get the recruits away from the evil influences of a frontier town a camp was established on the Ohio, twenty-seven miles below Pittsburg. Officers as well as men were raw, for nearly all of the available experienced officers had been killed at St. Clair's defeat; but at this camp, with unwearied patience, Wayne took his forces in hand, and day by day drilled them till their watery eyes grew clear, their trembling chins grew firm, their backs stiffened and a springing step replaced their slouching gait.

When this much was done he taught them to play with the bayonet, and then he taught them to shoot.

The writers of the annals of the Ohio river pioneers tell, with wondering zest, how Lewis Wetzel was able to load his rifle while running at top speed through the forest, and their wonder is justified by the fact. But this Mad Anthony Wayne trained his "boys and miscreants" from the city slums until he had an army of more than a thousand men who could load their rifles as they ran, with scarce a stop, fire with frontier precision; and run and load and fire again, yelling the while like a legion of demons. They could shoot with precision—could hit a six-inch target at a hundred paces—while marching at quick-step speed, and many of them could do as well on the run.

The commissioners that had been appointed to negotiate with victorious Indians for a peace reached Niagara in May, 1793, where they met the enemy—a combination of Indian chiefs and British officials. While there they heard fairly accurate accounts of the work Wayne was doing, and after the fashion of peace commissioners who are appointed at the behest of cowardice and penury, they made haste to send protests to Washington. Wayne's successful work with the recruits was angering the Indians, said the commissioners, and the British—*the British* considered such work "unfair and unwarrantable"!

Happily a Washington was at the head of the American Government, and Wayne was not restrained in his work as drill master. He moved down the Ohio to Cincinnati, (May, 1793), and from that place he marched (October 7, 1793), to the north with a force of more than 2,000 men.

The time for a fight was yet a long way off, however. Negotiations inspired by penury and cowardice were yet in hand, and on October 13, Wayne camped for the winter and named the camp Greenville, after his old commander when fighting for liberty in the South; and Greenville, Ohio, now perpetuates the memory of the camp.

Having secured the camp, Wayne sent a force forward to the field where St. Clair had been defeated, and built Fort Recovery. The Fort was armed with cannon abandoned by St. Clair.

The effect of all this work upon the enemy, Indians and British, was notable. As the years had passed, after the signing of the treaty of peace with Great Britain, a new source of trouble had risen. The long reign of corruption in France had culminated in the French Revolution. The war between France and England that followed was unavoidable. With the progress of this war the attitude of the British Government toward the United States had steadily grown arrogant. It is important to note that this arrogance was due, as every one now admits without dispute, to the weakness of the young Republic. There is no more important lesson to be learned in history than this, that governments are always devoid of the chivalry that keeps a good fighter from hitting an antagonist when he is down. The British wanted some favors from the Americans—harbors where their warships could refit and dispose of prizes and recruit their crews—but it never occurred to a British statesman to show any less arrogance and antagonism toward the Americans on that account. On the contrary, as said, the arrogance increased.

While Wayne was at Greenville, Lord Dorchester was Governor of Canada. Lord Dorchester, in other days, had been known as Sir Guy Carleton, and as Sir Guy Carleton while on a victorious march from Canada to the Hudson, had been stopped by a puny force on Lake Champlain under the command of Benedict Arnold. "The face of the enemy" at Lake Champlain had turned him back to Canada. Lord Dorchester had no love for the Americans, and on February 10, 1794, at a council with the Indians hostile to the United States, he said, referring to the American frontier:

"Children, since my return I find no appearance of a line remains, and from the manner in which the people of the States push on, and act, and talk, on this side, and from what I learn of their country towards the sea, *I shall not be surprised if we are at war with them* in the course of the present year; and if so, *a line must be drawn by the warriors.*

"Children: You talk of selling your lands to the State of New York. I have told you *there is no line between them and us.* I shall acknowledge no lands to be theirs which have been encroached on by them since the year 1783. *They broke the peace, and as they kept it not on their part, it doth not bind ours.*

"Children: What further can I say to you? You are witnesses on our parts we have acted in the most peaceable manner, and borne the language and conduct of the people of the United States with patience. But I believe our patience is almost exhausted."

For years the British had kept the Indians fully supplied with arms for forays against the American frontier, and now that Wayne was pushing forward a well-drilled force, and the Indians needed to be encouraged to meet it, the Governor of Canada said to them, "I shall not be surprised if we are at war with them in the course of the present year." The Indians who heard those words accepted them as a promise that the British would help with troops as well as with arms and other supplies. Lord Dorchester so intended his words to be understood.

But the British encouragement did not stop with an implied promise of help. To emphasize the effect of Dorchester's speech, Lieut. Gov. John Graves Simcoe was sent with three companies of British regulars to the rapids of the Maumee, where a fort was built. It was a deliberate invasion of American territory for the purpose of wresting the Ohio country from the American people, and was therefore a pleasant work for Simcoe, who also hated the Americans.

The acts of the British authorities had theretofore been characterized by what Roosevelt calls "double dealing" and "smooth duplicity," but they now "began to adopt that tone of brutal insolence which reflects the general attitude of the British people towards the Americans."

If the reader thinks this is laying undue stress on the attitude of the British I must apologize by saying that stress seems desirable because of the tremendous contrast afforded when compared with the present (1902) conditions which have been brought about by the advancement of Christian civilization, and the development of an unequalled fleet of American warships.

Hammond, the British minister, not only admitted that aggressions had been made by his Government, but he justified them by complaining of American aggressions, the chief of which was what he called "the unparallelled insult which has been recently offered at Newport, Rhode Island," wherein the citizens of that town had taken six impressed Americans from the British sloop of war Nautilus, by holding her captain a prisoner on shore until he released them. (See Wait's "State Papers," vol. ii). To liberate American citizens who had been carried by a press gang aboard a British warship, and there compelled to serve as sailors, was Hammond's idea of an "unparalleled insult," and one to justify an armed invasion.

An impartial reading of the documents of those days shows that war with Great Britain loomed high above the horizon. With a less capable man in Wayne's place the deluge would have fallen upon us.

That the building of the fort at the foot of the Maumee encouraged the Indians is certain, for on June 30, 1794, they swarmed down to Fort Recovery. But they were driven back, and Wayne having been reinforced,

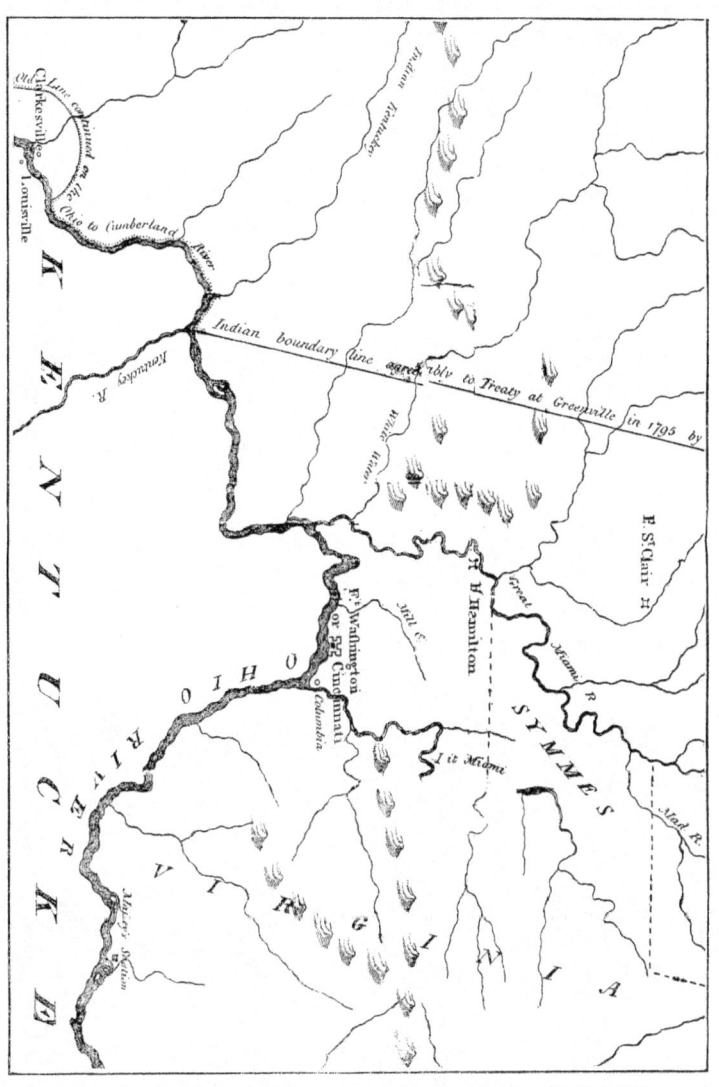

FROM THE MAP OF LEWIS, 1796, CINCINNATI AS A CENTRE, THE RIGHT HAND SIDE BEING NORTH.

meantime, with 1,600 mounted Kentuckians, he marched to the St. Marys river, a branch of the Maumee, and built Fort Adams in what is now Mercer county, Ohio. Thence he marched on through Van Wert and Paulding counties, (the trail could be seen forty years ago), to the junction of the Big Auglaize and the Maumee, where he built Fort Defiance.

The French had named this tributary of the Maumee Au Glaize because of the rich loam of the plains found there. The fields of corn stretched away for miles in all directions, but no night trailing of a maiden's robe around those fields could save them from the desolating host that had come to them. The corn was in the black silk, but the Indians were to have no green corn dance that year. The fields were laid waste to the last stalk. The Tories and Dorchester and Simcoe were responsible for the ills the Americans had suffered, but the Indians had to bear the burden then, as ever.

Having destroyed the corn, Wayne marched, August 15 , down the left bank of the Maumee. It was a slow march because Wayne was still willing to grant peace to the Indians. But a delegation of Spaniards from the lower Mississippi came to give heart to the Indians by tales of the uprising of the Southern Indians, and promises of Spanish help. More important still, the new British fort was close at hand, and the Indians, looking to its garrison for help and succor, scorned the offer. On August 18, Wayne threw up a small earthwork at the head of the rapids of the Maumee, at Waterville, Ohio, to secure the baggage and provisions, and on the morning of August 20, 1794, the final advance was made.

Most remarkable was that field of battle. In days not long past, a tornado had come whirling along from the lakes, ripping up the giant forest trees by the roots, and piling them in confused masses, for miles along the river bottom. Behind these tangled heaps of logs —the "Fallen Timbers"—lay the Indians, numbering at the lowest estimate 1,300. With them lay seventy Canadians commanded by Capt. William Caldwell. Had the whole territory been searched no safer ground could have been found for that waiting host of red men.

To feel his way, Wayne sent a squadron of cavalry against the entanglement, but the horsemen were hurled back with losses that threw them into confusion, and then the supreme moment of the day had come.

Ordering his infantry to fix bayonets, Wayne stretched a line of them, 900 strong, before the fallen timbers, placed the remainder of the infantry some distance in the rear for a reserve, divided the cavalry into two bodies to turn the Indian flanks, and sounded the charge.

And as the long roll of the guns began, the battle line dashed forward with blood curdling yells, pitchforked the enemy from behind the logs, shot them down as they fled, and leaping on in relentless pursuit, loaded and fired, again and again, till they had driven the panic-stricken hosts far beyond the British fort.

The American loss was 33 killed and 100 wounded, most of whom fell in the preliminary charge of cavalry. The Indian and Tory loss was three times as great. Four British rangers were found dead on the field.

It was a decisive victory. Not only were the Indians scattered in a panic, but what was of far greater

BATTLE OF FALLEN TIMBER.

importance, the battle taught them that they had been meanly deceived by the British. Dorchester, Simcoe and the Tories had sicked them on to ravage the American frontier, and then, as they fled for life, shut tight the gates of the fort that had been ostentatiously built for their support. The defeat of St. Clair was, in a way, the worst in the history of our Indian wars; the victory of Wayne was the most convincing.

They called the hero of Stony Point and the Maumee Rapids, Mad Anthony Wayne. The title was originated by an Irish soldier who had been confined in a guard house at the order of the General, and it was taken up by the people, because of the wild enthusiasm with which Wayne led his men when the supreme moment of battle came. But observe that when the war of the Revolution impended, he "ransacked history" for accounts of battles that he might learn military tactics, and he gave his days to the training of his neighbors. At Stony Point he appealed to the pride of the men by parading them "clean-shaved and with hair well powdered," while the prelaid plans included even the slaughter of the dogs of the region that no yelp should betray the approach of the assaulting host. And last of all, when the honor of the Nation and the integrity of its territory were committed to his care, he took a legion of "boys and miscreants," gathered from the slums of the coast cities, and trained them until their skill equalled if it did not surpass that of the most noted backwoods Indian fighters. His courage and brilliancy in time of battle were unsurpassed, *his record as a drill master is unequalled.*

The next day after the battle, called Fallen Timbers because of the place where the Indians hid, the commander of the British fort—one Major Campbell—sent a messenger to ask Wayne "what he meant by such threatening action in sight of His Majesty's flag?" Wayne replied that his "guns talked for him." Then Major Campbell threatened to open fire on Wayne if his men came within range of the fort. It is said that Wayne at once rode to the fort walls in the hope that Campbell would shoot, and thus give ample excuse for an attack; but Campbell became suddenly discreet.

In these trying conditions, Wayne showed that Washington had been mistaken in thinking him lacking in judicial sense. He swept the ground clean of huts and traders' stores, including Tory McKee's, to the walls of the fort, and then marched up the river destroying all Indian property on both sides, until (September 17), he reached the junction of the St. Marys and St. Joseph, and there built a fort the memory of which is perpetuated to this day by the vigorous city of Ft. Wayne, Ind. It was a point of great importance, for the new fort commanded the portage of the Wabash.

For twenty years,—beginning with the days when Connolly, as Lord Dunmore's agent, had created a war with the Indians along the Ohio—the home seekers who had crossed the Alleghanies, had been harassed by red men who were incited to devilish deeds by the British, but the end had now come. The British were ready to make a treaty that would avert war, and the Indians were abandoned to their fate. The end for which Washington had hoped when St. Clair marched into the Indian Country was attained by "Mad" Anthony Wayne. The Indians saw that our enmity was as much

Mississippi Valley.

to be dreaded as our friendship was to be desired. The territory northwest of the Ohio was now definitely opened for settlement, and homemakers soon thronged the shores of Lake Erie as well as the banks of the Ohio.

Meantime, while Wayne was yet on the way to the Maumee, Jay had been sent to England to negotiate a treaty. The treaty which he secured was better than war, and that is the best one can say of it, and it was that far desirable only because the news of Wayne's victory arrived in London while Jay was negotiating. By this treaty, concluded November 19, 1794, the British once more agreed to take their soldiers out of American territory, and this time they did as they agreed to do. The treaty threw us into actual if undeclared war with France, but the integrity of the region won by the good work of George Rogers Clark was, at last, definitely and forever secured.

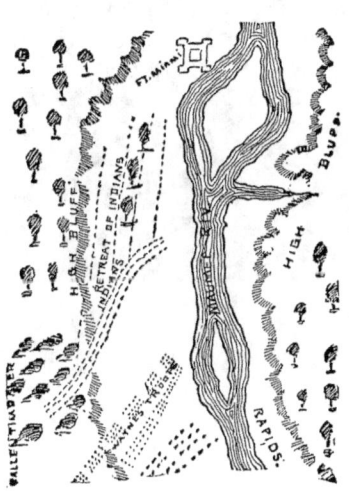

JAMES MADISON.
From the original portrait by Stuart.

FORT WASHINGTON
NOW
CINCINNATI
1790.

XXII

IN THE SOUTHWEST AFTER THE REVOLUTION.

When the French Government Was Treacherous Toward the United States—Political Work of the Determined, Quick-Witted, Self-Reliant Frontiersmen—In spite of Influential Demagogues the Kentucky Conventions and Proceedings Afforded "a Salutary Precedent"—Kentucky Becomes a State—Tennessee as the State of "Franklin"—"The Territory South of the Ohio River"—The Irritating Work of the Spanish—Wilkinson's Speculations and His Traitorous Contracts with the Spanish—Other Sordid Traitors.

To fully comprehend the things done in the Southwest—in the Kentucky and Tennessee region especially—after the Revolution, it is necessary to remember that the people of the frontier had migrated across the mountains to improve their condition. They were, as a whole, people of small means, who had come to make homes. They had endured, and they were willing to endure, every hardship incident to wilderness life in order to get on in the world. Only determined fortune seekers—men who would not be easily balked when working for any end—would start on such a career, and every day of such a life as they experienced made them the more determined to surmount every obstacle in their way. They were not only the most determined men in the world, but they were among the most active minded. A man who has to learn to dodge bullets by jumping when he sees the flash of the powder, learns also to make decisions quickly on all other matters in which he has a personal interest. And last of all they were entirely self-reliant. It was inevitable that these frontiersmen should "look out for Number 1!" when any question of policy arose, and should "do it on the jump."

It is necessary to remember, further, that these frontiersmen had become, perforce, accustomed to take a cross-cut route to order. They were used to what may be called Deckhard-rifle justice. It had been necessary to preserve order on the frontier when the nearest courts of law were hundreds of miles away, and the intervening space was a most dangerous wilderness. In the emergency the strong men of the new community compelled all to keep order and deal justly. Where possible the forms of the law were observed, but when an appeal to the forms of law threatened to defeat justice, the forms of the law were swept away. They comprehended what was afterwards called "the higher law"—the appeal for rights which the forms of law denied, and right they would maintain at the muzzles of their rifles.

Before this people, the most active-minded and self-reliant people in the world, lay the Mississippi and its navigable tributaries. It was the only outlet by which to convey their surplus products to the markets of the world. They had a "natural right" to absolutely free navigation on its waters to the high seas. In their belief (and it was a sincere belief) they would have had a natural right to a free navigation of the river even had a cheaper route to the East been available. They did not use much the term "higher law," but their orators thundered the words "Natural Rights" from every stump-top west of the Alleghanies.

But at the mouth of the Mississippi the Spaniards were in power, and they were determined, not only to hold the mouth, but to control the entire stream and all the land east of it except certain districts already settled when the Revolution ended.

People who learn from the school histories that the Battle of Yorktown was won with the aid of French troops, and that Lafayette was a sincere friend of the struggling colonies, think of the French King of that date as also a friend of the Colonies. But only a little further reading is necessary to learn that in spite of the sympathy of the French people, the French government (especially Vergennes, the prime Minister,) was animated solely by a desire to injure the British in what he did to help the Americans. While he was glad to free the British colonies from the British yoke, he was determined to make the new republic a vassal to France, or to disrupt it, and secure the vassalage of a part.

When in 1779 John Jay was selected to go to Spain to secure a recognition of the United States Government, he learned immediately after arrival that he would not be received unless the sovereignty of Spain over the Mississippi and all its valley (save only the parts actually settled by the Americans) were first conceded. To support this claim the Spanish sent an expedition from St. Louis on January 2, 1781, across the country to a small post on the St. Joseph River (probably near the site of La Salle's old post). This post was captured, robbed and abandoned in haste. On this "conquest" was based a claim to the Illinois and Wabash country.

And the French Government, while pretending friendship, sent a special envoy (Luzerne) to the United States, who supported the Spanish claims.

Weighed down by the enormous debt incurred during the war, and by adversity on the field of battle, and by the relentless pressure of adroit envoys, Congress yielded, for the time, the exclusive navigation of the Mississippi to Spain (1781), though Spain refused to accept that alone; and finally, when the end of the war was at hand, Congress instructed the American peace commissioners to follow French dictation in fixing the bounds of the new Nation.

But when the treaty of peace was made the instructions of Congress were disregarded (Franklin said a man might as well sell the front door of his house as for the United States to abandon the navigation of the Mississippi), and, unknown to the French minister, concluded the agreement which extended the American territory to the Mississippi and the thirty-first parallel.

If the British refused to adhere to the bargain, as has just been related, it was certain that Spain, with her clutch on the southwest corner of the American territory, would ignore that bargain altogether. A Spanish General (Galvez) had taken Natchez from the British during a war between Spain and England; the United States had never had possession of the Natchez territory, the Spanish said, and they held firmly to the claim they had presented to Jay in 1779.

Under this claim the navigation of the Mississippi was closed. Only by bribing Spanish officials could a flatboat cargo be taken to New Orleans. The stirring settlers west of the Alleghanies were like cattle corralled in a gulch. They could not escape over the mountains, and the Spanish closed the natural outlet. Washington, whose wisdom becomes more manifest as the years pass, was striving to create a way of transporting the Western surplus to the East by improving the waterways furnished by the Ohio, the Monongahela, and Potomac; but he was a hundred years ahead of his time in his urgency for good roads and cheap transportation. The people west of the Alleghanies were shut in. No markets could be reached. The opening of the Mississippi—a free opportunity to go to market with their surplus products—was necessarily the chief subject of thought and influence west of the Alleghanies. And fortunate it has been for the Nation that this was so.

The restlessness of the Kentucky people was first manifested in the efforts to establish a state Government. Conventions were held from time to time, beginning on December 27, 1784, for this purpose. The proceedings at this convention formed a "salutary precedent," to quote the words of Madison. The people fully appreciated their shut-in condition. They fully understood their natural right to the free navigation of the Mississippi. They knew very well that Congress had been willing to make bargains with Spain detrimental to their interests. They knew that many people of the seaboard regarded them as communities made up of men little if any better than desperadoes. They knew, further, that the Union was a dry wall—a loose conglomerate—that New York, for instance, was at one time at the point of war with both Connecticut and New Jersey because of New York's tariff laws. There were demagogues a plenty in Kentucky to tell the people all these facts and to exaggerate the evils consequent thereon, but the work of the home-makers in their political proceedings, as with their axes, formed a salutary precedent.

Chief among the demagogues was General James Wilkinson. As an aid to General Gates, he had been guilty of entering into a vile conspiracy against Washington, wholly regardless of the peril of the country, but he was now a citizen of Kentucky, in the salt and skin trade, and looking to the Mississippi and even to the Spanish mines west of it, as means for laying "the foundations of opulence."

Animated solely by selfish motives, Wilkinson wished to set up an independent state west of the Alleghanies, instead of a member of the Union. He soon found that this was going further than the people would follow, but, hoping to create trouble, he led a convention (August, 1785,) to *demand* a separation from Virginia instead of *petitioning* for the boon. He was able to exert influence in this matter solely by his ability to exaggerate the evils under which the people labored, but he failed in spite of his influence. Virginia ignored the form of the demand and yielded.

Delays due to the war with the Indians north of the Ohio prevented a prompt consummation of the work, and Wilkinson again argued for complete national independence of the region. It was during the days when George Rogers Clark and Benjamin Logan were obliged to raid the Ohio Indians to protect the Kentucky settlers, and he naturally found listeners who were indignant because neither the Virginia legislature nor Congress (Congress was the only National government then) protected the region. Moreover, there were Spanish aggressions on the south (to be described further on). Nevertheless the work of the conventions held to organize a state continued to afford a "salutary precedent," and in February, 1791, Congress accepted Kentucky as a member of the Union.

Meantime the people of the Tennessee region had been engaged in the work of State building, also. In June, 1784, the North Carolina legislature ceded all the lands west of the mountains to Congress. On August 23, delegates from the settlements of the Tennessee met at Jonesboro, organized a convention with John Sevier as president, and then (two-thirds consenting), voted "that they be erected at once into an independent state," an event that was celebrated with "turbulent joy" by the people who had assembled to attend the proceedings. But when a constitutional convention was gathered, in November, the North Carolina assembly had meantime rescinded the resolution to give the western territory to Congress, and public opinion had so far changed that the convention did nothing.

Late in 1785, however, another convention was held. These delegates believed that to set up a state government regardless of the legal aspects of the North Carolina control would in some way relieve them of their troubles—would open the Mississippi, for instance—and they adopted a constitution. Concerning the new state, so-called, that was then organized, two facts are interesting: the so-called state was named Franklin, and it was provided that every office-holder must be a member of the Presbyterian Church. Doak, of Princeton, with his sack full of books, had labored to some purpose.

North Carolina, however, having rescinded the act giving the Tennessee district to Congress, once more resumed sway over the Tennessee settlements. John Sevier had been elected Governor of the "State" of Franklin, and the organization of districts was completed under his energetic administration, but North Carolina had also a complete set of district and county officials in the same localities, and in the inevitable clash the old State party won, so that Sevier, at last (1788), became a fugitive from the recognized officers of the law.

Meantime the loose conglomerate called the United States had been fusing into a Nation. On June 21, 1788, New Hampshire adopted the Constitution, making the necessary ninth State, and five days later Virginia followed. In November, 1789, North Carolina joined in, and then, on February 25, 1790, it once more deeded the land west of the mountains to the Nation. On April 2, Congress accepted the gift, and in May established a form of government for "the Territory south of the River Ohio," with William Blount, of North Carolina, as Governor.

Blount was, on the whole, the man for the place. He was assimilated by the people, so to speak. The work of making the State of Tennessee was done by a convention over which he presided, which met on January 11, 1796, and published the state constitution on February 6. It is worth while noting that James Robertson, who had helped to make the rifle government of Watauga and Nashville, had a part in framing this constitution, and that Andrew Jackson was also a member of the convention.

The work of the Spanish during all this time must now have consideration. In 1784 Don Estevan Miro succeeded Galvez as Governor of New Orleans, and he was as urgent as his King could wish to extend the actual power of Spain over the unsettled part of the Great Valley east of the Mississippi.

His first move was to unite with Alexander McGillivray, (a half-breed Creek, whose Scotch father had given him a good education), in the formation of a league of Creeks, Choctaws, Cherokees and Chickasaws against the Americans. In May, 1784, Miro, at Mobile and Pensacola, met delegations of the various tribes, and by large subsidies of supplies started them on a desultory system of raiding known as the Oconee war.

Previous to this time the Americans had opened a trade with the Spanish. Flat-boats had been built, loaded with cured meats, grain, flour, whiskey and furs, and floated to New Orleans. Spanish law forbade the trade, but Spanish officials, for a consideration, encouraged it more or less, though every speculating boatman was sure to be robbed sooner or later. Miro became active in the system of robbing.

While Miro urged the Indians to war and destroyed the river traffic of the Americans, Don Diego Gardoqui was sent by the Spanish Government to negotiate a treaty with Congress by which Spain was to control the Mississippi and gain other advantages. He was to offer desirable concessions in trade with Spain, (concessions, however, which could be withdrawn at any time), in return for what was demanded in the Great Valley. The seaport merchants were eager to make the treaty, but hearing the turmoil west of the mountains—the talk of independence by such men as Wilkinson, and the just complaints of the producers—Congress refused to do anything.

Of course nothing was done—nothing could be done—to open the Mississippi. In fact, Spanish traders began to spread up the river, and thus several were found at Vincennes when Clark, during a raid on the Indians (August, 1786), arrived there. One of the traders, whose goods Clark confiscated, is said to have lost $10,000.

Clark's work was illegal, but it was not unprovoked, for many an American had been ruined by Spanish confiscations. Clark contemplated a filibuster expedition down the river, at least as far as Natchez, at this time, but nothing was done.

While Clark contemplated the manful if illegal raid on Natchez, Wilkinson adopted a diplomatic method of freeing trade on the Mississippi that was entirely successful for himself. Going to Natchez (fall of 1786), he established friendly relations with Don Manuel Gayoso de Lemos, the commandant. The next spring he loaded a fleet of flat-boats with "flour, bacon, butter and tobacco," and floating down the rivers, reached New Orleans in June. No Spanish officer molested him, and he sold his produce at a price that yielded him $35,000 profit, after the usual division of spoils with the officials. How great was the price that he paid for immunity may be inferred by the fact that 3,000 barrels of flour were shipped to Philadelphia, consigned to Gardoqui, the profits on which made up his share of the plunder.

But it was not by bribery alone that Wilkinson succeeded. The threat of a raid on Natchez had impressed the Spanish authorities. They knew that on the upper waters lived "a Respectable Body of Prime Riflemen," numbering more than 20,000. If these riflemen were once let loose, a freshet of fire would come down the river, and sweep the Spanish into the Gulf. George Rogers Clark, at Vincennes, was not the only one who had threatened, or was to threaten, such a revenge for injuries suffered, and Wilkinson was adroit enough to bribe with one hand while with the other he delicately pointed to the angry hosts of Kentucky and Tennessee.

Wilkinson went still further, but it is a shameful tale, and need not be elaborated. He sold himself to the Spanish. Plans for delivering the settled, as well as the unsettled, parts of the Great Valley into Spanish control were concerted and placed on paper. These documents are yet in existence, as are letters that Wilkinson wrote, and all unite to show his treasonable intentions. But worse is yet to be told. To further the plans for rousing the frontiersmen to desperation, Wilkinson advised Miro to set the Southern Indians raiding the home-makers at a time when no raids were to be expected. To further his own sordid schemes, this man strove to desolate the outer line of homes, and to spill the blood of the women and children living in them.

A number of the most prominent citizens of Kentucky became involved in the Spanish conspiracy. John Sevier, when his State of Franklin was going to pieces, offered to throw himself "into the arms of His Spanish Majesty." James Robertson opened negotiations with Miro, and to please the Spaniard, named a district (what was later a county) of Tennessee "Mero."

One can believe that these men (as they afterwards asserted) had no intention of becoming loyal subjects of Spain. They had, if one may use the slang of to-day, surplus products to burn; to find a market for these and so realize the financial prosperity for which they had endured the hardships of the wilderness, they were ready to cut loose from the United States and join Spain. But if this had been done they would have served Spain as the Texans served Mexico.

Wilkinson, Judge Henry Innes and some others were sordid traitors. They accepted Spanish money as the price of efforts to detach the territory west of the mountains from the United States for the benefit of Spain. But more than half of those who talked of uniting with Spain were men who were looking to the ultimate expansion of United States territory by filibustering methods.

In 1788 Col. George Morgan, of New Jersey, after vainly trying to get from Congress a grant of land for a colony near Kaskaskia, accepted (October 3d) a grant of 12,000,000 acres from the Spanish, to be located around New Madrid. Gardoqui had promoted this scheme to draw off the adventurous from the American frontier. Free transportation down the Ohio and aid in building houses were promised to the emigrants, but no great number of home-makers went across the river.

It was at this period (the end of 1788) that Col. John Connolly (he who precipitated Lord Dunmore's war) came to Kentucky to see what could be done to turn the discontented frontiersmen toward Canada for relief. The British had planned to send 10,000 men to sweep the Spanish from the Mississippi. If the frontiersmen joined in this movement the river would quickly be theirs, and the markets of the world would, under the British flag, be open to them.

Connolly disclosed the entire plan to Wilkinson. If Wilkinson had unselfishly desired the instant prosperity of the Mississippi Valley, regardless of the rights of the Union, as he professed, here was a golden opportunity. But sincerity and unselfishness were in no degree qualities of Wilkinson's character, and he would have nothing to do with a people by nature honest. He saw clearly that his personal interests were to be promoted best by adhering to the intriguing Spanish; and he had Connolly mobbed and frightened out of the country.

As commonly told, the story of the Kentucky and Tennessee region, in the years following the Revolution, is doleful reading. The men most frequently named in the story were sordid and traitorous, but they were not fair representatives of the people as a whole. They were to the whole people as the desperadoes in some frontier towns were to the general populations of those communities. The more one considers the general character of the frontier home-seekers the more admirable they appear. And even their threats and rampant attitude, under the restrictions placed on the commerce of the Mississippi, were, in the long run, of the utmost benefit to the Nation. For it is absolutely certain that but for their rampant attitude the merchants of the coast cities would have sold the Mississippi for a Spanish song. And how their rampant attitude affected the Nation when the French came once more to the Mississippi shall be told in the final chapter.

WILLIAM CHARLES COLE CLAIBORNE.

First territorial Governor, as also the first Governor of the State of Louisana. One of the Commissioners appointed to take possession of Louisiana after its purchase.

XXIII

THE NATION GETS ITS OWN.

Speculators in Georgia Land Start the Movement for Ousting the Spanish—The "Inevitable and Irresistible Intrigue of the Spanish Nature"—Citizen Genet and His Mississippi Scheme—The Southern Indians Sent against the Frontier—A Satisfactory Treaty Made, but the Spanish Were Not Willing to Yield the Territory then until a Sufficient Force of Soldiers to Take It Was on the Ground.

After the inauguration of Washington, Guardoqui returned to Spain, and the Spanish intrigues degenerated into a struggle to retain what Spain already held —including Natchez—within the American boundaries, as described in the Treaty with Great Britain. Galvez had conquered Natchez as well as Mobile from the British. No one disputed Spain's right to hold Mobile, and the Spanish naturally argued that no treaty with Great Britain could give the United States a right to Natchez. In fact it is not wholly unreasonable to suppose that when Richard Oswald, the British commissioner in the treaty of 1782-83, assigned the 31st parallel of latitude as the Southern limit of the United States on the Mississippi, he had in mind a future conflict between Spain and the United States over Natchez —a conflict that might in some way benefit British interests.

A movement that looked to the establishment of American control in the Great Valley down to the 31st parallel was begun in Georgia, the legislature of which sold (December, 1789) large tracts of the land, claimed west of the mountains, to various companies of speculators, who were required to defend their titles at their own expense. The South Carolina company, with a grant of 10,000,000 acres, employed one Dr. James O'Fallon as agent and manager. O'Fallon issued circulars inviting emigrants, and telling that the plan was to erect the territory to be acquired into an American State. At the same time he wrote to Governor Miro, at New Orleans, with a view, as he pretended, of making the grant a Spanish colony. Sevier and Robertson were expected to join in, and Wilkinson wrote to Miro recommending O'Fallon. But O'Fallon indiscreetly said he should have 10,000 of the "Prime Riflemen" of the frontier in his colony, and Miro was unable to grow enthusiastic over the prospect of receiving any such company of emigrants. He did not refuse to receive them, but the scheme failed when Washington learned its object; for he said he would suppress

EDMUND CHARLES GENET.
Better known as "Citizen Genet." From a painting by Fouquet in 1793.

the expedition by force, and everybody concerned knew that Washington was a square-jawed man.

After the admission of Kentucky as a member of the Union, (the admission was to date from June 1, 1792), the loyalty of the Kentuckians was to be no longer doubted, and the "Territory south of the Ohio" having been already organized, the Spanish Minister to the United States intimated (December 6, 1791) that Spain was ready to settle all disputes.

But, as Winsor says, "it was not long before the inevitable and irrepressible intrigue of the Spanish nature began to show itself." Miro was transferred, and Baron Carondelet was brought from Guatamala to New Orleans. Carondelet, to strengthen the Spanish position, at once started the southern Indians raiding the frontier, as Miro had done, while the negotiations for the settlement of disputed claims were allowed to drag on in the *poco tiempo* and *manana* manner in Spanish affairs.

Then the shadow of the French Revolution reached out to the United States. "Citizen" Genet was sent over as Minister. He arrived on April 8, 1793. He brought 300 blank army and navy commissions with him, and sent an agent to Kentucky to enlist enough men there to help the French of New Orleans throw off the Spanish yoke. George Rogers Clark was the chosen head of this proposed expedition, although for years he had been a common drunkard. But how much of substance there was to the intrigue appears from the fact that Clark received only $400 cash for the expenses of the 2,000 men he was to organize and conduct down the river.

Carondelet, however, heard that a million dollars instead of $400 had been supplied, and in terror he appealed to Governor Simcoe, of Canada, for help in establishing the Spanish power in the Illinois country. Simcoe would have done anything to injure the Americans, but the request arrived after he had learned that "Mad Anthony" Wayne had trained 1,000 men to load rifles as they ran, and it seemed advisable not to accede to the Spanish appeal.

However, Washington extinguished the plan. Fort Massac was garrisoned by some of Wayne's men, and Clark's $400 was soon dissipated. Genet, because of his insolence, was deprived of his position as Minister, (he remained as a private citizen in this country, however) and Jefferson, who had been a blatant supporter of the French revolutionists, was eliminated from Washington's cabinet.

The cool and righteous course of Washington, however, roused the animosity of the people west of the mountains, who had seen in Genet's scheme a hope of opening the Mississippi. They were roused still further by the raiding Creeks, whom Carondelet was then subsidizing to the extent of $55,000 a year, to keep them on the warpath. The trouble with England having been cleared away by Wayne's victory and Jay's treaty, the time for a settlement of the Mississippi question had come.

The outlook, judged by previous work in that line was not encouraging. "John Jay, who remained long at Madrid during the Revolutionary period, failed even to obtain formal recognition as Minister." The attempt which, as Secretary of State, he afterward made to

THOMAS PINCKNEY.

He arranged a treaty with Spain in 1794, which secured to the United States the free navigation of the Mississippi River.

negotiate a treaty in Philadelphia with Gardoqui, the Spanish Minister, also failed. In 1790 Jefferson, then Secretary of State, instructed Mr. Carmichael, the American chargé at Madrid, to intimate to Spain that the question of right to navigate the Mississippi must be settled. But this led to no result. In 1791 Mr. Carmichael and Mr. Short, then chargé at Paris, were appointed commissioners to negotiate a treaty with Spain, in which provisions should be made for adjusting boundaries, for recognizing a claim to the right of navigating the Mississippi, and for settling the conditions of commercial intercourse. But Spain, shocked at the execution of Louis XVI., was turning with a friendly spirit toward England. The relations of the American Government with England were strained, and nothing was effected by the commission." But by 1794 Spain and England had drifted apart, and Jaudenes, the Spanish Minister to the United States, intimated to Randolph, the Secretary of State, that Spain would negotiate with a minister of proper dignity and position" (James B. Angell).

Accordingly, in the fall of 1794, Thomas Pinckney, then minister to England, was selected to negotiate a treaty with Spain. But before he could reach Madrid, the Georgia Legislature sold 30,000,000 acres of land lying along the 31st parallel to a company of speculators, and this act (known as the Yazoo fraud) encouraged the Spanish to make one more effort to persuade the Kentuckians to abandon the Union.

Commandant Gayoso, of Natchez, went North as far as the Chickasaw Bluffs, and after buying a strip of land of the Chickasaw Indians, built a fort there. It was built where Memphis now stands. Gayoso then went on to New Madrid and opened communications with Wilkinson and others who had been in the intrigue with Miro. But before anything could be accomplished by Gayoso, Pinckney negotiated a treaty by which Spain agreed to yield all the territory claimed by the United States.

Pinckney had reached Madrid on June 28, 1795, but "such were the obstacles and prevarications usually inherent in Spanish diplomacy," (says Winsor), that Pinckney was kept waiting in idleness for four months. At last, as the end of October drew near, Pinckney demanded his passports and prepared to leave. Then, according to the custom "usually inherent in Spanish diplomacy," the Spaniards became ready for active work, and a satisfactory treaty was written and signed in three days.

The treaty was ratified by the United States Senate at the end of February, 1796, and was proclaimed on August 2 of the same year.

This treaty gave the United States the bounds obtained under the treaty with Great Britain, and provided for a joint commission to meet at Natchez and survey the line. It also recognized the right of the Americans to navigate the Mississippi freely, and it granted them the right to deposit in New Orleans all goods for export free of duty, and free of all other charges, save a reasonable rent for warehouses.

The people of the Great Valley now hoped for a speedy ending of their troubles on the rivers; but even after they had made the treaty the Spanish were yet to shuffle and evade to the utmost limit of human patience.

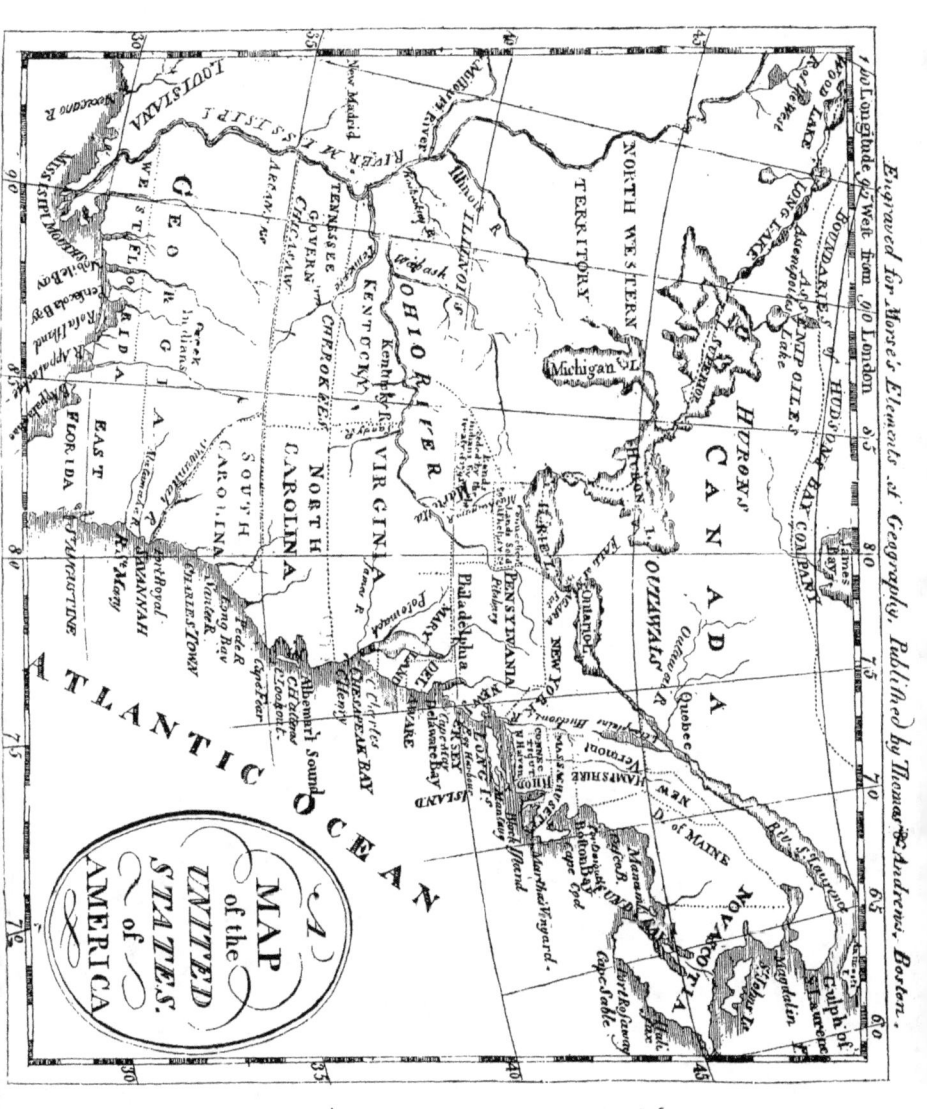

A SCHOOLBOY'S MAP OF THE UNITED STATES, IN 1796.

Andrew Ellicott was appointed American commissioner to meet the Spanish commissioner and survey the boundary line from the Mississippi eastward. He left Philadelphia September 16, 1796. He was joined on the Ohio by Lieutenant Piercy S. Pope and a squad of men to serve as a guard in the wilderness. On approaching New Madrid, Ellicott was stopped by the Commandant and a letter was handed him wherein Governor Carondelet of New Orleans *ordered* him to remain at New Madrid until the Spanish forces had been removed from Natchez, and explained that low water in the river had prevented this removal theretofore.

Ellicott, of course, disregarded the order; what he thought of the untruthful explanation may be imagined. At the Chickasaw Bluffs the Spanish commandant fired a cannon across the course of the flotilla, and when it was brought to, and Ellicott told him about the object of the expedition and the treaty, he expressed "wide-eyed wonder," as if he had never heard of such a matter.

Two days above Natchez a messenger met Ellicott with a letter wherein Commandant Gayoso explained that the evacuation had not occurred for want of suitable vessels. He requested that the American troops remain at a point sixty miles up the river lest misunderstandings arise between Americans and Spaniards. To this Ellicott agreed, and himself reached Natchez on Febraury 24, 1797.

To follow in detail the shufflings, the deliberate and oft-repeated falsehoods, and the insolent demands of Gayoso and Carondelet in the days following Ellicott's arrival, would be needlessly wearisome and exasperating to the reader. Any one wishing the details can find them in vol. iii, Waite's "American State Papers." It is enough to say that Gayoso, with profuse professions of friendship, named a date for commencing the survey. At the same time, however, he set his soldiers at work strengthening the fort.

On seeing the men at work on the fort, Ellicott sent for his soldiers. Then the Spanish appealed to the Chickasaws and Choctaws to attack the Americans, but Ellicott secured their neutrality. A story that the British were coming down from Canada to attack New Orleans (Spain was at war with England), was given as a reason for repairing the fort. "The British must be met at Natchez, and repulsed—*como siempre!*" said the Spaniards.

In May, 1797, the Spanish surveyor arrived, but Gayoso refused to begin the survey; in fact he went on strengthening the fort. And at that the citizens of Natchez, (nine-tenths of whom were Anglo-Saxons in blood and despised the Spanish), rose up and took possession of the town.

With a committee of Americans in charge of Natchez, Ellicott waited the movements of the Spanish. Carondelet was transferred and Gayoso thereafter held such power as remained to the Spanish. He removed his headquarters to New Orleans leaving Don Stephen Minor in command of the fort at Natchez.

The patience of the Administration at Washington during all this time was extraordinary, but it is to be explained in part by the aggressive attitude of France. The French Government was then sweeping our com-

JAMES EDWARD OGLETHORPE.
Founder of the State of Georgia (1733).

merce from the West Indies, and was bringing on the actual if undeclared war that gave our new navy its first opportunity to show its quality. A war with one nation at a time was all that the Government wished to support.

Nevertheless, on May 20, 1797, General Wilkinson, then chief of the army, acting under instructions from the War Department, ordered Capt. Isaac Guion to go with a sufficient force down the river and take possession of the various posts within United States territory. Guion had fought under Montgomery at Quebec, and under Wayne at the Battle of the Fallen Timbers. He was an all-around fighting man, and his reputation was not unknown in New Orleans.

"Events now moved rapidly, as they usually do, when Spanish obstinacy gives way to fear," (Winsor). Orders were issued for the evacuation of the Chickasaw Bluffs, and a station at the Walnut Hills, (Vicksburg), and then, on March 30, 1798, "under cover of the night," Minor and his men sneaked away like criminals.

On the morning of March 31, 1798, the American flag floated in the breeze above the fort on the Natchez Bluffs—for the first time.

For fifteen years—from 1783 to 1798—the American people had endured the buffetings and the aggressions of the Governments of Great Britain, France and Spain,—bullies all three, who were willing to take every advantage of the struggling young Republic as long as they felt themselves powerful enough to do so without danger. Worse yet, the Nation had been obliged to struggle under the selfishness and ignorance of its legislators, and (in the West), under the schemes of sordid traitors. But the sober, sound sense and unyielding persistence of the home-makers prevailed, and on March 31, 1798, the Gridiron Flag covered the whole Nation.

ROBERT R. LIVINGSTON.
The cession of Louisiana to the United States was greatly aided, if not accomplished through, his efforts.

XXIV

THE GARDEN OF AMERICA FOR AMERICANS ONLY.

Organization of the Mississippi Territory—Throngs of Emigrants Flock to the Region—The Significant Story of Philip Nolan—Boone as a Spanish Don—The Growth of Trade at New Orleans—Napoleon Sees the Futility of His Scheme for Recovering the Original French Territory in America—He Determines to Give England a Maritime Rival and Succeeds—The Treaty Ratified—When the Gridiron Flag First Covered the Mighty Valley from Brim to Brim.

Without unnecessary delay, after the flag floated over Natchez, Congress organized (April, 1798), the Mississippi Territory. Winthrop Sargent reached Natchez, charged with the work of organization, on August 6, and Wilkinson, "as general of the American

Army, and bearing in his bosom the secrets that made his prominence a blot both on himself and his government," came on August 26 with a military force.

Emigrants followed in numbers. In a letter dated March 2, 1802, Thomas Jefferson wrote the following:

"Mr. Randolph, allured by the immensely profitable culture of cotton, had come to a resolution to go to the Mississippi, and there purchase lands and establish all his negroes in that culture."

This statement is of interest because Mr. Randolph was a type of the class of emigrants to the Mississippi Territory. They were people of wealth who bought large tracts of land. The development of the Whitney cotton gin, (1793), had made cotton immensely profitable, and to that crop these planters devoted themselves.

In the watershed of the Ohio, the men whose only capital was carried in their heads, found their Canaan, and there the growth of population was unprecedented. A thousand flat boats passed down the Ohio in 1796, and it is likely that they carried at least twenty people each, on the average. A regular packet service was established between Pittsburgh and Cincinnati, that year. The boat was fitted with musket proof cabins, and six one-pound swivels were mounted on its bulwarks. It was propelled up stream with oars and sails.

When Spain as well as England had been thrown out of the United States territory, the hurrying crowds bound west increased still more rapidly. In 1790, Tennessee had a population, (U. S. Census report), of 35,791; in 1800 it had 105,602. Kentucky, in 1790, had 73,077; in 1800, it had 220,955. And the stream of immigrants continued increasing in volume as the country filled up. This stream was, in fact, a human freshet that spread westward till it reached the Mississippi, and there ceased to flow. A paper levee stopped its progress, for a time, but it did not cease to rise against the paper levee. By a treaty the splendid wild land across the river belonged to Spain, but by the inexorable law of race progress it belonged to them who would use it.

In 1800 the freshet topped the levees. Filibustering expeditions crossed the Mississppi to make settlements on Spanish land. They were of the class that afterwards settled in Texas and detached that state from Mexico. One Phillip Nolan and a party that made a settlement on the Brazos river, in the fall of 1800, passed the winter in catching and training wild horses. It was a legitimate business; they were at that time harming no one. But they had not observed any of the formalities that Spanish law and custom required of immigrants, and in March a Spanish force, 300 strong, surrounded their shanties at daylight. Nolan's party numbered less than thirty. The difference in the forces is significant. It shows how the Spanish regarded "a Respectable Body of Prime Riflemen." Nolan was killed, and the others were captured and held prisoners in the Mexican settlements for some years afterward.

In the meantime some settlers had passed over to the Spanish side of the great river, as prevously told, with the Spanish consent—Daniel Boone among the rest. The public records show that he moved to "(upper) Louisiana before the year 1798; and, on the 24th day of January, 1798, he received from Zenon Trudeau a concession for 1,000 arpents of land, situated in the district of Femme Osage; had the same surveyed on the 9th of January, 1800, and was appointed by Don Charles D. Delassus, (then Lieutenant Governor of Upper Louisiana), Commandant of the Femme Osage District" in Missouri, on June 11.

But notwithstanding this kindly reception given to Boone, the Spanish were exceedingly jealous of these new settlers. They told each immigrant that while he might hold what religious views he pleased, his children must become Catholics or get out of the country; and the Bishop at New Orleans complained bitterly of this small measure of religious tolerance.

Naturally but few of the home-makers migrated to the Spanish domain, and naturally, too, the restless and lawless became the more inclined to go there as filibusters. In a small way the old buccaneer spirit prevailed.

During all this time the commerce of the Mississippi grew with the population. With the opening of trade, after the treaty of 1795, although through shipments were allowed free of duty, thereafter, the custom house receipts of New Orleans, in the ensuing year, were double what they had been in any preceding year.

How this trade increased may be gathered from the following statement, quoted from Cable's sketch of New Orleans in the U. S. Census report for 1880:

"In 1790 the port of New Orleans was neither open nor closed. Commerce was possible but dangerous, subject to the corrupt caprices of Spanish commandants and customs officers, and full exasperating uncertainties.

"In 1802, 158 Americans, 104 Spaniards and 3

French merchantmen, [ships of the sea], in all 31,241 register tons, sailed from her harbor loaded. * * * 34,000 bales of cotton; 4,500 hogsheads of sugar; 800 casks—equivalent to 2,000 barrels—of molasses; rice, peltries, indigo, lumber and sundries to the value of $500,000; 50,000 barrels of flour; 3,000 barrels of beef and pork; 2,000 hogsheads of tobacco, and smaller quantities of corn, butter, hams, meal, lard, staves and cordage passed across the already famous levee."

But while the merchants west of the Alleghanies were growing rich and the home-builders were not only adding to the comforts of their rude houses, but were reaching a point where luxuries were not unknown, a rumor that Spain had sold the Louisiana Territory to France spread, (1801), over the Great Valley. Rumors to this effect had been heard as early as 1797—unfounded rumors that soon died out—but this time the rumor persisted. And as it gained credence the people became wild with indignation and anger.

To fully appreciate the excitement thus caused one must recall the course of events in France during the years that had recently passed. For, beginning in 1794, the leaders of the mob that had ruled France, during her great revolution, in order to coerce the United States into joining France in her wars with the other nations of Europe, and in order to enrich themselves, had sent out warships, privateers and armed ships without commissions, to prey on American commerce. These pirates had swept American shipping almost entirely off the high seas. And the story of the "French Spoliations" was as well known in the Mississippi as in the coast cities.

Further than that was the fact that the French revolution had evolved Napoleon, and he had become the ruler of France under the title of First Consul, (November 10, 1799). Fully realizing that to add to the glory of France was to strengthen his own power, Napoleon had reached out to grasp the colonial possessions that had been lost before his day. Toussainte l'Overture had set up a republic in San Domingo, and had maintained it by force of arms. Late in 1801 Napoleon sent an army to resubjugate San Domingo and reduce the negroes to slavery once more. Le Clerc, Napoleon's brother-in-law, commanded the expedition. In San Domingo, Le Clerc treated the American merchants much as he treated the fighting natives; he confiscated their property and thrust them into prison without trial or means of redress. The story of Le Clerc's outrages followed the rumors of the French acquisition of Louisiana to the Mississippi Valley.

The French who had by sheer piracy ruined the American commerce on the high seas, and had robbed and maltreated the Americans in San Domingo, were coming to take possession of Louisiana—of New Orleans and the mouth of the Mississippi! There was ample cause for excitement west of the Alleghanies.

As to the facts at the bottom of the rumors it appears that it was in 1800 that Napoleon first determined to acquire Louisiana, and that in August of that year he sent his confidential friend Alexandre Berthier as minister to Madrid. Berthier negotiated a treaty, dated October 1, 1800, by which France was to take Louisiana and Florida, and give in exchange "a kingdom of at least a million people made up of French conquests in

THOMAS JEFFERSON.

the north of Italy, over which was to be set the Duke of Parma," son-in-law of the Spanish king, (Hosmer).

This treaty was not ratified by the king of Spain, but one negotiated by Lucien Bonaparte and dated March 21, 1801, was ratified. It gave Louisiana to the French in exchange for Tuscany, over which the Duke of Parma was to reign as king. Both treaties were negotiated at San Ildefonso, where the Spanish king lived, and the treaty of cession is known by the name of the royal residence.

At the time the last treaty was made, and while the rumors of it were agitating the people west of the Alleghanies, Thomas Jefferson was President of the United States. Jefferson, if not the originator, was at least the most conspicuous advocate of the porcupine policy of dealing with foreign enemies. In order to command the respect of European nations and to protect American commerce in foreign waters Jefferson built scores of gunboats that were manœuvred with oars, and confessedly fit for use only in our harbors. Moreover, he had idealized if he had not idolized the French. He had spoken of the excitement raised in the United States when "Citizen" Genet was distributing piratical commissions from Charleston to Philadelphia as a revival of the "spirit of 1776."

But Jefferson was a politician first of all. Foster, in his "Century of American Diplomacy," says he was the greatest politician the Nation has yet produced. And Jefferson's most enthusiastic supporters were found in the Mississippi Valley. Franklin had said that a man might as well sell his front door as for the United States to give up the right of the free navigation of the Mississippi, and Jefferson understood very well that the western clamor over the supposed French acquisition of Louisiana was not empty declamation; but neither he nor any one else then saw where that oratorical tornado would carry the country.

What Jefferson did on hearing the clamor was to instruct our Ministers at Paris, London and Madrid to do all they could to prevent the transfer. Eventually the rumors said that Spain had already ceded the territory to France, and at that Jefferson, in a letter to Robert R. Livingston, American minister to France, dated April 18, 1802, said:

"There is on the globe one single spot the possessor of which is our natural and habitual enemy. It is New Orleans. * * * France placing herself at that door, assumes to us the attitude of defiance. * * * Circumstances render it impossible that France and the United States can continue long friends, when they meet in so irritable a position. The day that France takes possession of New Orleans * * * we must marry ourselves to the British fleet and nation. We must turn all our attentions to a maritime force."

And then to much talk about friendly relations he added the unmistakable statement that "it is not from a fear of France that we deprecate this measure proposed by her."

Madison, Jefferson's secretary of State, in a letter of instructions to Livingston, said: "The United States would take the most vigorous measures, even though they should involve war, to avert such a calamity" as the cession of Louisiana to France.

But Jefferson did not really mean it. At heart he

had no intention of fighting to keep the Mississippi. In October, in spite of the manly words quoted, he told Livingston that the French occupation of Louisiana was not "important enough to risk a breach of peace." He had talked and written in brave words merely to humor the people; his words were not sincere. If the simile may be allowed, Jefferson felt himself in charge of a growing kid on which the British lion, the French wolf and the Spanish coyote were looking with hungry eyes. He supposed that if only this kid could be allowed to feed peaceably in the pastures of the world until it was as big and fat—especially as *fat*—as a kid could become, it would then be entirely safe from the attacks of the lion, the wolf and the coyote. The quantity of the fat was to protect it; and in order that fat might be accumulated as fast as possible *the growth of horns must be prevented*. A hornless goat, rolling fat, was literally Jefferson's ideal representative of a great nation. He did say to the British minister that if we were compelled to draw the sword we would "throw away the scabbard," but he did not mean to draw the sword. A nation whose every effort at home should be devoted to accumulation of "material resources," and whose foreign policy should be regulated by those able to "palliate and endure," and, if the full truth be told, those who could purchase favors,—that was the Jefferson ideal. Fortunately the Nation was able to survive the fierce onslaughts that Jefferson's hornless policy made possible during the first ten years of the Nineteenth Century, and different ideals now prevail.

In the course of May, 1802, authentic information

reached the United States that Spain had sold out to France. Consequently, during the summer of 1802, Livingston was kept busy trying to purchase New Orleans and the two Floridas, which, it was rumored, had also been transferred to France, but he could make no progress in his negotiations. Napoleon had obtained peace at the treaty of Amiens, March 25, 1802, and was contemplating the recovery of all the ancient French rights in America. He supposed that he could readily conquer all the Mississippi Valley, if not Canada, and he ordered an army of 10,000 men, under General Bernadotte, to prepare to sail for New Orleans. General Victor was afterwards (August, 1802) substituted for Bernadotte, and the preparations were pressed with enthusiasm during the fall following Victor's appointment.

In order to deceive the Americans Napoleon announced that Victor was going to reinforce the French army in San Domingo, but the truth of the matter became very well known throughout the United States. The excitement and indignation caused by this knowledge were soon to be increased, however, to a far higher pitch. On October 16, 1802, in the midst of the most prosperous shipping season the merchants of the Mississippi Valley had ever known, the Spanish Intendant at New Orleans, Don Juan Venturo Morales, ordered that the American right of deposit should thenceforth cease. Foreign commerce, save in Spanish ships only, was to be stopped—this in the face of the fact that a free export trade had been allowed for seven years since the signing of the treaty permitting such commerce.

Mississippi Valley.

As the report of the order of Morales, in violation of the treaty, spread up the Great Valley, the people almost to a man were found ready to grasp their rifles, three feet and six inches long, and embark for New Orleans. There was talk of raising enough men in the Mississippi Territory alone to capture New Orleans immediately, and it could have been done easily, had the right leader appeared.

It was natural that the Americans should suppose that Napoleon had dictated the Morales prohibition of commerce and the American right of deposit at New Orleans. In this it appears they were in error as to the fact, although as to the feeling of Napoleon they were entirely right. Morales had acted on his own impulses. The Governor of New Orleans, (Salcedo Gayoso had died after a drunken spree with Gen. Wilkinson), opposed the order. The Spanish minister to the United States opposed it with anger. But under Spanish law, Morales could prevail until an order came from the Spanish King.

With this new aggression to urge him on, Jefferson still baulked at the thought of securing the rights of the Nation by the use of force. He was determined not to use force. His message to Congress, read December 15, 1802, "discussed everything except the danger which engrossed men's minds." (Henry Adams's "History of the United States"). "No change" was "deemed necessary in our military establishment," and as for the navy the chief item of new expense recommended was a "dock within which our present vessels may be laid up dry and under cover from the sun." In a special message to Congress on December 22, 1802, he spoke of Morales's act as "the irregular proceeding at New Orleans," and said he had not lost "a moment in causing every step to be taken which the occasion claimed." On January 5, 1803, he transmitted to the house, "a statement of the militia" of the various states, (a showing of the mailed fist, that!), and then on the 11th, in a special message, he nominated James Monroe as minister extraordinary, to act "jointly or either on the death of the other," with Livingston, in order to "enter into a treaty or convention with the First Consul of France," for the purchase of New Orleans and the French territory east of the Mississippi. The nomination was promptly confirmed.

As Henry Adams has pointed out, Monroe was sent on this special mission, "not so much to purchase New Orleans, as to restore political quiet at home." In his letter asking Monroe to accept the mission, Jefferson said:

"The agitation of the public mind on occasion of the late suspension of our right of deposit at New Orleans is extreme. In the western country it is natural and grounded on honest motives. In the Federalists generally, and especially those of Congress, the object is to force us into war if possible, in order to derange our finances; or if this cannot be done, to detach the western country to them as their best friends, and thus get into power."

And when the nomination had been confirmed Jefferson again wrote to say that "the measure has silenced the Federalists here."

To silence the Federalists was the thought upper-

JAMES MONROE.

The original portrait by Vanderlyn, from which this was engraved by Durand, can be seen in the City Hall, New York.

Mississippi Valley.

most in Jefferson's mind in this crisis brought on by foreign aggression, and the next thought was to "palliate and endure" (letter to Dr. Priestley), the aggression in such a fashion as to soothe his own party.

Meantime, however, Napoleon's hopes of conquest in America had vanished. Barbe Marbois, one of Napoleon's ministers, had pointed out that to occupy New Orleans was to drive the United States to declare war against France at the first shot of a gun in Europe, and he was ready to ask, as Jefferson had asked, will "a short lived possession" of New Orleans be an equivalent to France "for the transfer of such a weight into the scales of her enemy?"

Moreover, Napoleon's agents in the United States had repeatedly written him that it would be impossible to accomplish his purpose. The agents knew the number and the quality of the "Prime Riflemen" of the west. They had doubtless heard of the men whom "Mad" Anthony Wayne trained to load rifles while charging the enemy, and if not, they knew that the frontiersmen always shot to kill. Pinchon, the French *charge,* wrote to Talleyrand to say that "however timid Mr. Jefferson may be, I find [among the people] in general a bad temper as regards us; and I cannot help seeing that there is a tendency toward adopting an irrevocably hostile system." It was clearly seen by the Frenchmen in America that it would be an easy task to raise an army of 30,000 skilled riflemen, west of the Alleghanies, embark them on boats which they were accustomed to handle, and send them, hot for a fight, *down* the river. Napoleon's men, with all their European experience, would find a different kind of warfare when, after landing in New Orleans, they tried to push *up* the river in boats, or through the roadless forests and lowlands on either border.

To such arguments as this, Napoleon, as a statesman, was obliged to give heed. He saw that any force that he could send to New Orleans would be wholly lost to his uses in Europe, and it would accomplish nothing in America. He saw further that the supremacy of the British naval power on the high seas would prevent his reinforcing New Orleans, in time of war—would even prevent his rescuing the garrison there from certain defeat. He believed that in case of war with England, Louisiana would become a British colony, and a war with England was now seen to be at hand. These considerations prevailed. It is a proof of the wisdom of Napoleon that they did prevail. To his counsellors he said:

"They [the British], shall not have the Mississippi which they covet. The conquest of Louisiana would be easy, if they only took the trouble to make a descent there. I have not a moment to lose in putting it out of their reach. * * * I think of ceding it to the United States. I can scarcely say that I cede it to them, for it is not yet in our possession. If, however, I leave the least time to our enemies, I shall only transmit an empty title to those republicans whose friendship I seek. They only ask of me one town in Louisiana, but I already consider the colony as entirely lost, and it appears to me that in the hands of their growing power, it will be more useful to the policy and even to the commerce of France than if I should attempt to keep it."

Mississippi Valley.

When objections were urged he continued:

"Irresolution and deliberation are no longer in season. I renounce Louisiana. It is not only New Orleans that I will cede, it is the whole colony without any reservation. * * * To attempt obstinately to retain it would be folly. I direct you to negotiate this affair with the envoys of the United States."

And when the matter had been fully determined he said:

"This accession of territory strengthens forever the power of the United States, and *I have just given to England a maritime rival that will sooner or later humble her pride.*"

With American capitalists in control of the leading lines of transatlantic steamships in this present year of 1903, the last statement is of interest. But it is worth noting here that one of Napoleon's ideas in this matter was by no means well founded. He supposed, as he said, that if he tried to occupy the Louisiana territory *the British* would promptly take it away from him. Curiously enough nearly all American historians have agreed with him. But we will believe that as soon as Napoleon's army had sailed for New Orleans, the "Prime Riflemen" of the West would have gone aboard their flat boats, and in an irresistible tide would have swept all foreign power from the Great Valley before either French or British could have done so much as to make a landing. Livingston, who had reverence for the eagle, not the porcupine, said: "Only force can give us New Orleans. We must employ force. Let us first get possession of the country and negotiate afterwards."

He understood the beneficent effect of showing the mailed fist at the right time in some kinds of diplomatic proceedings. It was not necessary to do that on this occasion, but if the necessity had arisen, it would have been done. Let no one think that Great Britain would have forestalled Napoleon at New Orleans, even if the "timid" Mr. Jefferson was President.

Barbe Marbois was commanded to conduct the negotiations with Livingston and Monroe. He was well acquainted personally with both of them, personal regard smoothed the way, and the negotiations were conducted with unparalleled expedition. Napoleon at first demanded a price that seemed enormous, but he modified his demands to a point where the conditions were written to the satisfaction of both parties. Livingston and Monroe felt that they were stretching their powers to the utmost in buying the whole territory, but there was (fortunately), no time for consultation with Jefferson, and a treaty, (dated April 30, 1803, though concluded in part as late as May 9), was signed whereby:

"The First Consul of France, desiring to give to the United States a strong proof of his friendship, doth hereby cede to the United States, in the name of the French Republic, forever and in full sovereignty the said territory" of Louisiana. For this broad territory the United States paid $11,250,000 in six per cent. bonds, and assumed a debt of $3,750,000 due American citizens from France, or $15,000,000 all told.

When Livingston had signed this document, (and his name was the first appended to it), he arose, shook hands with Marbois and Monroe, and said:

Mississippi Valley.

"We have lived long, but this is the noblest work of our lives."

The papers reached Washington on July 14, 1803. The treaty attracted the widest attention. No one had foreseen such an outcome of the negotiations. A great number of the people supposed that the Nation had no power under the Constitution to annex foreign territory. Others were opposed to the policy of enlarging the territory of the Nation. Jefferson himself fully believed Congress had no power to annex the purchased territory, and favored passing an amendment to the Constitution to permit it. He thought, too, that the land west of the Mississippi would be useless save as a refuge for the Indians then living in the East. Monroe, fearing that he had paid too much for the cession, suggested the sale of "the territory west of the Mississippi * * * to some power of Europe whose vicinity we should not fear."

But when a letter was received from Livingston saying that Napoleon might yet undo the work already accomplished, and when this was followed by another letter saying "I most earnestly press you to get the ratification as soon as possible," Jefferson called a special session of Congress. He had written to Senator Breckenridge "The executive * * * have done an act beyond the Constitution," but on the following day he wrote to ask that this letter be suppressed, and added that "we should do *sub silentio* what shall be found necessary." He would not let his interpretation of the Constitution interfere with a good business proposition.

Congress met on October 17, 1803, and the annexation of Louisiana was discussed. On October 25, the House resolved, "That provision ought to be made for carrying into effect the treaty." The vote stood ninety to twenty-five. In the Senate a bill, introduced by John Breckenridge, of Kentucky, "to enable the President of the United States to take possession of the territories ceded by France," was passed on Wednesday, October 26; yeas, twenty-six; nays, six. This bill was approved October 31, 1803, (annals of Congress, 1803-'04).

Foster's "Century of American Diplomacy" summarizes the arguments against admission as follows: "The boundaries were in dispute and it would probably lead to war—a prediction that was realized some forty years later; the large territory was useless and not wanted; the price was too high—it was equal to 433 tons of silver, it would load 866 wagons, extending 5 1-3 miles, would make a pile of dollars three miles high, equal to 25 ship loads, would provide $3 to each man, woman and child in the country."

Such a vast, unmanageable extent of territory threatened the subversion of the Union, said the leader of the Federalists.

It may be noted, however, that an argument which was urged against the annexation of the Philippines, in recent years, was not heard in 1803. No one arose to say that the native population of the new territory was sure to flood the old, and by competition cut down the wages of the poor working man.

To go back a little and take up the thread of events in the Mississippi Valley, it is found that the formal work of transferring Louisiana from Spain to France

THOMAS B. ROBERTSON.

First Congressman elected from the State of Louisiana, afterward Governor. This portrait is by St. Memim.

had been begun before the territory had been sold to the United States. Pierre Clement Laussat, (a man who "could swim well in rough water," he), was sent by Napoleon to New Orleans as civil Governor, and he arrived on March 26, 1803. He knew nothing about the negotiations for a sale to the United States, and his proclamation to the people of the region filled them with "a delirium of extreme felicity," as they said. Some weeks later came the Marquis de Casa Calvo to represent the Spanish King in the transfer. A prolonged series of public entertainments followed, regarding which Laussat made this significant remark:

"The tendency of these festivities was, no doubt, to spread the taste for pleasure and luxury in a colony which being in its nascent state, still needs a great deal of economy and labor."

Laussat saw dimly why both France and Spain had failed in colonizing the Great Valley.

While the happy-go-lucky Creoles danced, a ship came from Bordeaux with the news that the territory had been sold to the Americans. It was first to be transferred to France, however, and this was done on November 30. As Miss King says in her New Orleans, an "elaborate but uninteresting formality took place." French municipal officers were appointed, and a Creole took command of the militia.

In the meantime the preparations for annexing the territory had been completed in the United States. Because Spain had protested against the transfer to the United States, (Napoleon had agreed not to sell without Spain's consent), a large body of militia was ordered out along the upper rivers, and flat boats for their use were provided. A force 500 strong was sent to Natchez. W. C. C. Claiborne, then Governor of Mississippi, and General James Wilkinson, the head of the regular army, were appointed commissioners to receive the Territory at New Orleans. Each of these two men are still well remembered—Claiborne for the skill with which he managed the people of New Orleans; Wilkinson as one of the most detestable of traitors. The commissioners met at Fort Adams, below Natchez, and on December 7, with a sufficient escort of soldiers, began their march to New Orleans. The schooner Bilboa, (chartered for $1,854.18, if any one is anxious for details), floated down the river carrying the baggage. On December 17 the party camped two miles from the city, and two days were then passed in formal visits, and in agreeing on the details of the coming ceremonies.

December 20 was the day selected for the transfer. As the people of the city of New Orleans awoke on that morning, it was noted as a good omen that "instead of the rain and clouds that had attended the Spanish ceremonies, the day dawned clear and bright." At sunrise the French tricolor was spread to the gentle breeze at the top of the tall flag pole that stood in the centre of the Place d'Armes, while the ships at the levee, and at anchor in the stream, were decorated with a great spread of bright bunting. At 9 o'clock the militia began to muster, and at 11 o'clock they marched, with beating drums, into the Place d'Armes. A notable throng gathered about them, and along the street by which the Americans were to come—a throng that included the gentry in their colored silks and

Mississippi Valley.

velvets, and slaves in osnaburgs; pirates in sea "togs" from the West Indies, and tall, lank backwoodsmen in fringed leather hunting, or red flannel shirts—men of every nation, and men without a country. But gathered at the foot of the flag pole was a band of fifty old French soldiers who, on November 30, had been organized as a guard for the tricolor flag.

Soon after the local militia had been paraded in line facing the flag pole a gun was fired at the American camp to announce that the American forces had started for the city. In due time they reached the Tchoupitoulas gate, where they received a salute of twenty-one guns. Then they marched into the city.

At the head of the column rode the commissioners. They were followed by "a detachment of dragoons in red uniform, four pieces of artillery, two companies of infantry and one of carbineers." Marching to the centre of the Place d'Armes the column was paraded to face the local militia. Then the commissioners dismounted and walked to the Cabildo, or City Hall, where they were received by Laussat, who, with the officers of the municipality, conducted them to the great hall of the building. They found there the most notable citizens of the city. At the head of the hall stood three elevated chairs. In the centre and most elevated of these three Laussat sat down, and placed Claiborne on his right and Wilkinson on his left. The reading of the various commissions, the treaty of cession, etc., followed, and then Laussat gave the keys of the city to Claiborne, and changed seats with him. The citizens who wished to remain in the country were next absolved from their allegiance to France.

Finally Laussat, Claiborne and Wilkinson walked out on a balcony where they could look over the motley throng that had gathered in the Place d'Armes, and away to the decorated shipping in the harbor. The supreme moment of the transfer had now come. As the commissioners appeared on the balcony the sergeant of the old French guard loosened the halliards and began to lower the tricolor. At the same instant an American soldier commenced hoisting the Gridiron Flag. Midway the two flags met, and as they fluttered together for a moment, a single gun was fired. And then, as the two flags were separated, every gun in the city began to fire a national salute; the guns on the shipping joined in; a brass band played "Hail Columbia," while the backwoodsmen and the keelboatmen in their fringed and red flannel shirts, cheered with frantic joy, and leaping up, slapped their hands on their sides and crowed until they were hoarse. But the gentry, in colored satins and laces, wept.

At the end of August, 1656, those enterprising and courageous Frenchmen—the *coureurs de bois,* known as Grosseilliers and Radisson—men who would and did work according to the powers given them, returned to Montreal and reported that they had been on the waters of the Great River. And "their arrival caused the country universal joy."

On April 9, 1682, La Salle, the greatest of all the French-Americans, a man who worked as few of any nation have done, standing on a sand bar at the mouth of the Great River, proclaimed the sovereignty of his King over all the wondrous unknown valley whose waters flowed at his feet.

Mississippi Valley.

For 121 years thereafter the flags of foreign nations waved above the evergreen slopes that had gladdened the hearts of those men of deeds. But because a new race had been originated on the American continent—a race of whom it could be said "The thing that is given it to do it can make itself do"—the period of foreign control was limited. With a "blinkard dazzlement and staggerings to and fro" as "of a man sent on an errand he is too weak for by a path he cannot *yet* find," this race had reached out and grasped the mighty Valley from brim to brim.

THE END.

INDEX.

Abenakis Indians, driven from New England, join La Salle, 40; persuaded to make war, 121.
Abercrombie defeated, 151.
Accau, Michael, heads an exploring expedition, 37.
Adams, John, at peace treaty, 332.
Albany, N. Y., Dutch at, 33-34.
Alibamons Indians, in Alabama, 62.
Alleghanies crossed by British settlers, 124; Duquesne fortifies, 133.
Alleghany region, French move into, 128.
Alleghany Co., N. Y., and river shed visited, 8.
Allouez, Father, estab. Mission at La Pointe, 8.
Amherst, Sir Jeffrey, captures Louisburg, 151; in Pontiac's War, 175.
Animals of Miss. Valley, 18, 22; Beavers in, 24; abundant, 189.
Armies, American, efficiency, 252.
Aubry, succeeds D'Abbadie, 163; permits British trade in New Orleans, 167.
Au Glaize river named, 349.
Badine, Iberville's ship, 53.
Baker, John, 198.
Baker, Joshua, attack on Indians, 215.
Bank, Louis ("Bar"), meets French at English Turn, 57.
Barlow, Joel, speculator, 337.
Barre, La antagonizes La Salle, 45.
Baton Rouge, British take possession of, 205; named, 55.
Bean, William, on Boone's Creek, 200.
Battle Island, Ohio, named, 305.
Bayou Manchac, named, 55; British at, 288.
Bears as domestic cattle, 79.
Beaubassion, Sieur de, leads raid, 121.
Beaujeu, Capt. Daniel Lienard de, attacks Braddock, 144.
Beavers, 120; eaten in feast, 5.
Bernadotte, General Charles, to take Miss. Valley, 388.
Berthier, Alexander, gets Louisiana and Florida for Napoleon, 384.

Big Bottom, Pa., attacked, 339.
Big Lick, site of Boonesborough, 227.
Bienville, "Father of New Orleans," 52; buys a letter of Indian, 55; meets English, 58; meets Tonti, 59; time in the Louisiana colony, 60; as to rivalries, 61; Vente opposes, 62; opposes a marriage, 62; sends soldiers among Indians for food, 63; plans new fort, 72; founds New Orleans, 74; sends surveyors to lay out new capital, 104; opposed, 106; builds first levee, 106; leaves country, 115; describes soldiers, 116.
Bigot, Francois, character of Intendant, 134; loves Madam Pean, 154.
Biloxi, Miss., settled, 56; Sioux Indians at, 79.
Bilboa, ship, carries commissioners, 398.
Bird, Colonel, builds fort, 150.
Bird, Capt. Henry, raids, 289.
Bishop of New Orleans complains of tolerance to Protestants, 382.
Bledsoe, Anthony, surveys Va. line, 202.
Blount, William, Governor of Tennessee, etc., 363.
Blue Earth River, named, 60.
Blue Licks, Ky., Battle at, 310.
Boisbriant, Major Pierre Hugue, falls in love, 62; builds Fort Chartres, 107.
Bonaparte, Lucien, makes treaty, 385.
Boone, Daniel, with Braddock, 147; ancestry and early life, 196; story of, 197; crosses mountain wall, 198; Squire joins Daniel, 199; typical explorer, 200; warns of coming war, 212; in Transylvania, 225; fights Indians, 226; brings wife to Boonesborough, 240; prepares game and horse laws, 244; daughter Jemima carried off, 259; at Blue Licks, 264, 310; sees chief need of the country, 327; crosses the Mississippi, 381; appointed to office, 382.
Boone, Squire, brother of Daniel, in Kentucky, 199.

403

Index.

Boonesborough, Kentucky, 227; first woman at, 240; attacked, 264.
Boston Port closed, 248.
Bouquet, Col. Henry, commands Colonials, 177; wins Bushy Run fight, 179; forces peace, 181.
Bowman, John, first Kentucky Colonel, 259.
Braddock, Edward, sails for America, 142; attacked by French, 144; shot, 145; dies, 147.
Brady, Samuel, borderer, 328.
Bradstreet, Lieut. Col. John, takes Fort Frontenac, 151; General, sent against Indians, 181.
Brant, Joseph, 334; tells of British duplicity, 341.
Brazos river, Nolan on, 381.
Breckenridge, Senator John, 395; introduces bill to authorize Louisiana treaty, 396.
Bryan's Station, attack on, 308.
British, civilization of, 250, et seq.; urge attack on Christian Indians, 295; welchers after the Rev., 333; object in Northwest, 334; urge Indians to war, 334; against peace, 341; idea of Wayne's work, 345; attitude toward U. S., 345; b e t r a y Indians, 351; impressed by good fighting, 352; plan to raid Mississippi Valley, 367; get a rival from Napoleon, 393.
Brule, Etienne, First Coureur de Bois, 1; at Lake copper mines, 3; fate, 3.
Bryan, Rebecca, Boone's wife, 197.
Buffalo, wild cattle, 18; heard by Joliet, 22; 30,000 skins wasted, 63.
Bullies of the Miss. Valley, 377.
Bullitt, Capt. Thomas, surveyor in Ohio Valley, 207.
Burgoyne's surrender, to whom credit is due, 268.
Burnet, Gov. Wm., founds Oswego, 122.
Bushy Run, Penn., battle at, 178.
Butler, General Richard, robbed by desperadoes, 211; killed at St. Clair's defeat, 340.
Butler, trader, canoes attacked, 213.
Cabins, log, how built, 228.
Cadillac, Le Mothe, Gov. of Detroit & Louisiana, 64; complains of profligates, 66; tries to promote trade, 67; sends out expeditions, 68; views on trade, Indian policy and colony, 69; dismissed, 69.

Cahokia, (Kaoquias) 110; conquered, 272.
Cairo, trading station near, 63.
Caldwell, Capt. William, 305; attacks Bryan's Station, 308; at Fallen Timbers, 350.
Calk, Journal of, 230.
Calloway, Betsey & Fanny, captured, 260.
Calumet, peace pipe given to Joliet, 19; brings peace, 22-23; Indians accept Quakers', 153.
Calvo, Marquis de Casa, represents Spanish at New Orleans transfer, 397.
Campbell, Colonel Archibald, takes Savannah, 313.
Campbell, Col. William, at Kings Mountain, 316; hangs a Tory, 328.
Campbell, Major, commands a British fort on Maumee, 352.
Cameron with raiders, 255.
Canadians, in the South, 60; fought Braddock, 144, 148.
Canoes and dugouts described, 5, 22, 30.
Carheil, Father Etienne de, describes missions, 116.
Carmichael, in Spain, 373.
Carleton, Sir Guy, see Lord Dorchester.
Carondelet, Baron de, commands at New Orleans, starts Indian raids, 371; opposes Ellicott, 375; transferred, 376.
Catholic Church protected, 272; Children must join, 382.
Cat Island, named, 54; mutiny on, 116.
Cataraqui, (Kingston, Canada). 27; settlement grows at, 30.
Caughnowagas, 121.
Celoron, (Monsieur de Bienville) takes possession of Ohio Valley, buries plates, etc., 128; meets Old Britain, Indian chief, 129.
Champlain, Samuel de, sends Brule to the Indians, 2; work in America, 2; influence of his gun over-rated, 28.
Champlain, Lake, discovered, fight, etc., 2.
Charleston, W. Va., laid out, 207.
Chesne, Monsieur de, order for service among Hurons, 51.
Chicago River, La Salle's work on, 43; portage to Fox River, 111.
Chickasaws and English threaten French, 57; hunted by Choctaws, 62; see Indian summary, 76 et seq.

404

Index.

Chickasaw Bluff, La Salle at, 44; Gayoso fortifies, 373; Ellicott stopped at, 375; Spanish, 377.
Chillicothe, Ohio, raided by Clark, 290.
China, search for, 4-9.
Chine, La, rapids, described, 8, 9; origin of name, 10, 11; when Celoron left, 128.
Choctaw Indians encouraged to hunt other tribes, 62.
Choteau, August & Pierre, sons of Laclede, 162.
Christina, Indian woman, begs for life, 301.
Cincinnati, Ohio, named, 339.
Civil Govt. West of Alleghanies, 202, 244.
Claiborne, W. C. C., American Governor of Miss., 398.
Claims, land entry, made with tomahawk, 204; cost of, 245; at Marietta, 338; French and British opposing, 124.
Clark, George Rogers, his work, 196; at Wheeling, 213; with Cresap, 214; carries petition, 258; kills Indian, 262; sends spies to Illinois, 263; method of defending Kentucky, 265; Illinois campaign, 267, et seq.; skill in handling French and Indians, 270, et. seq.; Vincennes taken, 274; when the British came to the Wabash, 275, et seq.; builds gun boat, 277; retakes Vincennes, 281; returns to Falls of Ohio, 284; ill-treatment of, 285; value of work, 332, 353; contemplates raid on Natchez, 364; to aid French schemes, 371.
Clerc, Leo (brother-in-law of Napoleon), in San Domingo, 384.
Clothing, frontier, 238, 241; American and French compared, 241-242.
Cocquard, Father Godfrey, describes French-Indian raids, 148.
Comet, La Salle's view of, compared with Mather's, 40.
Congress at Albany, 141; at Alexandria, 142.
Congress, U. S. and Indians and Pirates, 341; accepts lands from States, 363; ratifies purchase of Louisiana Ter., 395-396.
Connelly, Dr. John, makes trouble at Pittsburg, 211; tries to imprison friendly Indians, 217; back to Kentucky, 367.
Constitution, United States, adopted, 362.

Contractors, vile thieves, 343.
Contrecoeur, Capt. Claude Pecaudy de, takes a fort, 138; commands at Ft. Duquesne, 143; succeeded by Dumas, 148.
Convicts in colonies, 104.
Cooley, William, explores Kentucky, 198.
Copper, found by Etienne Brule, 3; search for, 10, 14; Indian use of, 80.
Corn as a diet, 60, 61; food of the Indians, 79; on frontier, 242; price in Hard Winter, 321.
Cornstalk attacks Virginians, 218; at the peace treaty, 221; favors Americans, 266; murdered, 266.
Cornwallis, Lord, whips Gates, 314; surrenders, 329.
Cotton, profitable, 380; cotton-gin, 380.
Coureurs de bois, first, 1; described, 3, 33, 34, 68; some enterprising, 111.
Cowan, John, first house at Louisville, 207.
Crawford, Col. William, receives ammunition, 288; in raid on Sandusky towns, 304; tortured by Indians, 306.
Creoles, described, 169; migration, 169; and French Republic, 170; untimely dancing of, 397.
Cresap, Michael, needless slaughters of Indians, 213; in Revolution, 248.
Cresap, Col. Thomas, on Potomac, 123; employed by Ohio company, 190.
Crevecoeur, Fort, 236.
Crozat, Anthony, controls Louisiana, 64; loses money, 68; surrenders Louisiana to King, 70.
Croghan, George, sent to Indians, 191; warns against attack on Indians, 212; foils Connelly, 217.
Cumberland, Duke of, 124, 191.
Cumberland River & Gap named, 124.
Cumberland, Md., trail from, 124.
Cutbirth, Benjamin, 198.
Cutler, Rev. Manasseh, secures land grant from Congress, 336, 337.
D'Abbadie, M., sent to New Orleans, 163; permits British trade in New Orleans, 167.
Dablon, Father Claude, tells of Joliet, 15.
Daring, frigate, whipped by d'Iberville, 52.

Index.

Dartmouth, ship, (tea party), 248.
Dauphine Island, named, 54; settled, 60.
Deckhard rifle, 237; used at King's Mountain, 315; Deckhard rifle government, 203.
Delassus, Don Charles D., appoints Boone to office, 382.
De Ligneris, leaves Duquesne, 154.
Denis, Juchereau de St., expeditions to Mexico, 67, 68.
De Noyant, arrested, 165.
Denton, Mrs., one of the first white women in Kentucky, 240.
De Soto, see chapter ix.
Desperadoes, 211.
Des Plaines River, La Salle on, 11.
Detroit, Mich., Clark plans to take, 284.
Dieskau, Baron, in command of Canada, 142.
Dinwiddie, Gov. Robert, protests to French, 135; King orders him to make war on the French, 137; sends troops to Redstone creek, 138.
Diplomacy, early Indian, 4.
Doak, Rev. Samuel, and his books, 319; labors successful, 362.
Doddridge's Notes, 232; opinion of Williamson, 299.
Donelson, Col. John, goes to site of Nashville, 290.
Dorchester, Lord, (formerly Sir Guy Carleton) letter to, 334; misrepresentations by, 336; speaks to the Indians, 346; responsible for Indian sufferings, 349.
Douay, Father Anastose, present at death of La Salle, 48, 49.
Douville's troops gave no quarter, 149.
Dragging Canoe, attacks whites, 256; refuses peace, 258.
Dubreuil, A. M., erects sugar mill, 168.
Duclos, commissary, describes women of Louisiana, 66; dismissed, 69.
Duer, Col. William, speculator, 337.
Dug-out, a Sioux boat, 5.
Du Gay, assistant of Accau, 37.
Dumas, Captain, succeeds Contrecoeur, 148; gives written orders to prevent torture, 149; like Col. Hamilton, 255.
Dunlap Station, Ky., attacked, 339.

Dunmore, Lord, in Indian War, 218; makes peace, 221; proclaims in vain, 243.
Dunmore's War, 209, et seq.; action of soldiers at end of, 247.
Duquesne, Marquis de Menneville, approves attack on Old Britain, 132; to keep British east of Alleghanies, 133.
Duquesne, Fort, prisoners burned at, 146; evacuated, 171.
Dutch, give guns and ideas to Indians, 100.
Eaton's Station, garrison attacks Indians, 256.
Ecuyer, Captain, deceives Indians, 176.
Ellicott, Andrew, American Commissioner to survey line between United States and Spanish Florida, 375.
Ellinipsico, killed, 266.
Elliott, Matthew, Renegade, 305.
English top the Alleghanies, 57, 75; claim the West, 76; cross the Alleghanies, 124; compared with French, 124; rights in the Mississippi Valley, 125-126; gain Canada, 155; horrified by sight of Yorkshire habit of gouging out eyes, 327.
English Turn in Mississippi River, named, 58.
Erie, Penn., (Presqu' Isle), French reach, 134.
Espiritu Santu, a name of Mississippi River, 161.
Fallen Timbers, battle of, 350 et seq.
Fawcett, Thomas, kills Braddock, 145.
Feast of 120 beavers, 5; Immaculate Conception, 16; Frontier, 242.
Federalists and War, 390.
Femme Osage district, Missouri, 382.
Ferguson, Major Patrick, finds Patriots, 314; fights at King's Mountain, 315, 317.
Fillibustering, threatened, 364, 371; done, 381.
Filson, John, map, 228; with Symmes and Boone, 338.
Finley, John, tells Boone stories, 197; with Boone, 198.
Florida, De Soto lands in, 158; British in West, 167, 288; Spanish gain, 289; French gain, 384.
Floyd, John, Kentucky Colonel, 325.
Food, frontier, 242; cost of, 324.
Forbes, Gen. John, starts for Ft. Duquesne, 152; enters, 154.

Index.

Forts. Adams, 398; Bute, built, 206; British on Maumee, (Miami), 347; Chartres, 107; French at Chartres, 154; Chartres surrendered, 207; chain of built, 151; Defiance, 349; Duquesne, built, 134, 138; Frederick, at Crown Point, 122; Frontenac, built, 30; the same pledged for debt, 31; seized, 33; captured by British, 151; Indian at Marietta, 85; Grandville, 150; Great Meadows, 139; La Boulaye, 159; La Boeuf, 13.; Massac, 269, 272; Miami, built by La Salle, 36; Matagorda Bay, 46; same raided, 49; Natchitoches, 68-69; Necessity, 140; New Orleans, first built, 72, 74; Oswego, 122; Pitt, besieged, 175; Redstone, 138; St. Louis, 45; Starved Rock, 45; Venango, 135; Washington, 340; Wayne, 352. See chapter on La Salle.

Fox River, Nicolet up, 5; Description of country at head, 17; Portage at, 111.

Frankfort, Ky., founded, 208.

Franklin, state set up, 362.

Franklin, Ben., leaves England, 250; makes peace treaty, 331, et seq.; his regard for the Mississippi, 358.

French-Indian war, first gun, 132.

French spoliations, 383-384.

French, (see chapters vi, vii, viii,) treaties with Indians, 2, 4, 5; compared with other Nations, 6, 7, 11; peace with Iroquois, 28; jealousy of English, 53; dislike of Americans, 270.

French Government, attitude toward U. S., 332, 351; plans to take New Orleans from Spanish, 371; buys Louisiana, 383, 384; warned by Jefferson, 386; sell Louisiana to U. S., 394.

Friendship, frontier test of, 290.

Frontenac, Monsieur de, Gov. Canada, sends Joliet to Mississippi, 15; described, 26; recognizes La Salle's worth, 26; leaves Montreal to dazzle Iroquois, 27; sends La Salle to France, 28; hates Jesuits, 29; coat of arms, 32; recalled, 45.

Frontier life, 107, 108.

Fry, Joshua, made Colonel, 137; sent to Logstown, 191; death, 140.

Furniture frontier, 232.

Galena, Ill., founded, 108.

Galvez, Don Bernado de, Gov. of Louisiana, 287; confiscates British ships, 287; loans U. S. $6,000,288; captures Natchez, 289, 359, 369; Miro succeeds, 363.

Game laws, 244.

Gardoqui, Don Diego, Spanish treaty made by, 364; his bribery, 365; plans to draw off American settlers, 367; returns to Spain, 369.

Gates, Gen. Horatio, defeated, 314; Wilkinson, his aide, 360.

Gayarre, Charles, historian, on burning of Indians, 114.

Gayoso, (Manuel Gayoso de Lemos), and Wilkinson, 365; Commandant at Chicksaw Bluffs, 373; wearisome dillying-dallying, 375; dies after spree, 389.

Genet, "Citizen," Edmund Charles, comes to U. S., 371.

Georgia, movement to control Miss. Valley begun, 370; sells land (Yazoo fraud), 373.

Georgian Bay visited by Nicolet, 4; La Salle en route to, 43.

Germain, Lord, approved Indian raids, 289.

German Coast of Miss. River, 104.

Germans in Miss. Valley, 104.

Gibault, Father Pierre, begs Clark for life, 271; helps Americans secure Vincennes, 272.

Gibson, Col., John, interpreter, 222; tries to protect Gnadenhutten Indians, 277, 279.

Girty, Simon, and Moravians, 298; at Crawford's raid, 305; attacks Dunlap station, 339.

Gist, Christopher, with Washington, 136, 139; employed by Ohio Company, 190; treats with Indians, 191.

Gnadenhutten, Ohio, 89; Indians at, 188; building of, 216; the story of, 293; et seq.; effect on Indians, 308-311; effect of, 329.

Gomer, Nancy, heroine, 291.

Gordon, Lieut., captured and killed, 175.

Government, frontier, 244; at Watauga, 201; at Nashborough, 291.

Grant, Major James, defeated, 153.

Grave Creek, W. Va., attack on Indians at, 214.

Gravier, Father, at Kaskaskia, 75; manner of curing disease, 115.

Gray, soldier, escapes, 175.

Greathouse, Daniel C., leads attack on Indians at Yellow creek, 215.

407

Index.

Green Bay, Mich., Nicolet at, 5; mentioned, 111.
Greenville, Ohio, named, 345.
Gridiron Flag covers the Nation, 378.
Griffin, first ship on Lake Erie, 32; sails on Lakes, 35; lost, 37-38.
Grosseilliers, Menard Chouart des, goes with Radisson, into region S. & W. of Lake Superior, 5; described, 5, 6, 7; into the Miss. Valley, 7; final word of, 400.
Guion, Captain Isaac, sent to Miss. Valley, 377.
Gulf of Mexico, La Salle reaches, 44.
Half King, speaks to Gnadenhutten Indians, 297.
Hamilton, Col. Henry, instructions to, 251; sends raiders, 253; captured, 254; incites Indians, 259; tries to ransom Boone, 264; goes hunting Clark, 275; takes Vincennes, 275; Clark sends him to Virginia, 281.
Hammond, British Ambassador, describes Wayne, 342; justifies British aggression, 348.
Hampshire, ship sunk by Iberville, 52, 53.
"Hard Winter," described, 320, mentioned, 290.
Harmer, Gen. Josiah, raids Indians, 335.
Harpe, Bernard de la, builds Fort St. Louis de Carlorette, 69.
Harrison, Benjamin, at battle of Point Pleasant, 221.
Harrod, James, founds Harrodsburg, 208.
Harrodsburg, Ky., becomes county seat, 259; under fire all summer, 261; force at, 263, 264; land office closed by Clark, 290; first court at, 325.
Heckwelder, John, Moravian Missionary, 216.
Helm, Capt. Leonard, at Vincennes, 275; bluffs Col. Hamilton, 276; joke on, by George Rogers Clark, 281.
Henderson, Col. Richard, Boone works for, 200; founds Transylvania Co., 225; cause of failure, 245.
Henderson, Ky., named for Col. Henderson, 245.
Hennepin, La Salle's Chaplain, and historian of expedition to Miss. River, 33; tries to bribe St. Anthony, 33.
Henry, Patrick, call to arms, 248; approves Clark's expedition to Illinois, 268.
Hickman meets Indians, 219.
Hill, William, with Boone, 198.
Hillsborough, Lord, explains King's proclamation regarding Indian land, 186.
Hogan, Mrs., comes to Boonesborough, 240.
Homeseekers, fearless of danger, 264.
House boat, first known on Miss., 167.
House boatmen, first in Miss. Valley 205.
Hudson's Bay, (ship), captured by Iberville, 53.
Huron Indians, guides of Nicolet, 4; around Georgian Bay, 5; on Miss. River, 7.
Iberville, Le Moyne de, offers to plant colony in Louisiana, 52; captures British ships in Hudson's Bay, 52; sails from Brest, 53; into Miss. River, 54; names lakes, 55; meets Tonti, 59; moves colony to Mobile Bay, 60; builds Miss. fort, 72.
Ignace, St., (Village in Michigan), mission, Joliet at, 16.
Illinois Indians, La Salle's peace with, 36.
Illinois, (state) first land warrant in, 108; grain from, 110; early settlements, 110.
Illinois river, route of Joliet's return, 23, 24.
Independence, first idea of in U. S., 165; and Watauga Govt., 203.
Indians, (see chapter v.), treaty with Nicolet, 4; hostile to Joliet, 22; Fox implacably against the French, 111; internal dissensions, 131; cannibals, 148, 149; relative losses in wars with whites, 180; how wronged by whites, 187, 188; British and, 250; character shown in dealing with George Rogers Clark, 272, 273; most significant statement made in connection with, 295; faith of, 298; smallpox spread among, 291.
Indigo in Louisiana, 167, 168.
Innes, Judge Henry, a traitor, 366.
Iroquois, raids, 6; check commerce of French, 6; Frontenac and, 27; enmity toward French, 28; sent by Jesuits to destroy fort, 39; see Indian summary, 79, et seq.; losing grip, 131.
Iroquet, Indian Chief, treats with Champlain, 2.

Index.

Jackson, Andrew, backwoods hero, dances, 236; his wife Rachael, 290; member of Tennessee Convention, 363.
Jaudenes, Spanish Minister, 373.
Jay, John, peace treaty, 332; sent to make treaty, 353; to Spain, 358; in Spain, 372.
Jefferson, Thomas, approves Clark's plans, 269; favors war then bribery, 339; on policy of Bribery, 341; instructions to Spanish, Miss. affairs, 373; tells of Randolph's slaves, 380; porcupine policy, 385; our greatest politician, 385; warns France, 386; insincere, 387; in regard to Spanish aggression, 289, 290; his uppermost thought, 390.
Jesuits, quarrel with Frontenac, 29, 30; send Iroquois to destroy La Salle's fort, 39; in New Orleans, 106.
Johnson, Capt. George, to take possession of territory east of the Mississippi, 205.
Johnson, Sir William, treaty with Indians, 182.
Johnson, Sir John, letter to Joseph Brant, 334.
Joliet, Louis, sent to explore Miss. River, 14; Father Marquette was chaplain of the expedition, 15, 16; among Illinois Indians, 18, 19; turns toward home, 23; route home, 24; loses papers, 24.
Joncaire, at post on Niagara River, 122; receives Washington, 136.
Jones, John Paul, writes Rank, 322; as a fighter, 324.
Joutel tells of La Salle, 48.
Juchereau, a trader, at Cairo, Ill., 63.
Jumonville, Ensign Coulon de, fought by Washington, 139.
Justice, frontier, 202; to inferior race, 311; Deckhard-rifle kind, 356.
Kankakee River, La Salle at, 11.
Kaskaskia, Ill., established, 69; becomes parish, 108; college at, 108; Clark reaches, 270, 271.
Kentucky, first cargo from down Miss., 198; "dark and bloody ground," 204; settlers described, 207; early homes in described, 230; organizing settlers, 258; raided, 264; suffers at Blue Licks, 311; first Court House and Jail, 325; loyalty, 371; Spanish in, 373; population, (1790-1800), 380; Kentucky River settled, 208; first women in, 240; first legislature in, 244; sporting blood, 244; first race course, 244; early life in, 245; cause of rapid growth, 250; divided into three counties, 325; progress in, 325; raids after the war, 325; reinforces Wayne, 349; restlessness in, 356; to make a Govt., 359; Kentucky joins the Union, 361; history of, doleful reading, 367.
King's Mountain fight, 311; et seq.
Kingston, Canada, then Cataraqui, 27; a trading station, 27, 29; traffic of lakes begins at, 30; vessels at, 30; value to La Salle, 30; base of war, 30.
Knight, Dr. John, on Crawford's raid, 304; captured, 306; escapes, 307.
L'Anse de la Graisse, Missouri, 111.
La Beuf, Pa., attack on, 175.
Laclede, Pierre Liqueste, founds St. Louis, 162.
Lafayette, Ind., site of, 111.
La Freniere, of New Orleans, arrested, 165; executed, 166.
Langlade, Charles, leads attack on Old Britains Indians, 132.
La Mott, La Salle's assistant, fort builder, 31.
La Salle, Rene Robert Cavalier, Sieur de, origin, 8; establishes frontier trading station, 8; hears about the Great River, 9; fails to find China, 10; into Great Valley, via lake Michigan, 11; Frontenac befriends, 26, 27; other traders hate, 30; builds fort at Niagara, 31; voyage on upper lakes, 32; et seq.; origin of troubles with coureurs de bois, 35; builds fort Crevecoeur, 36; sends Hennepin to Miss. River, 37; loss of ship Griffin, 38; enmity of Jesuits, 39; not afraid of a comet, 40; tells of profits in Indian trade, 41; down the Miss. River, 43; claims the Great Valley for France, 44; expedition to Gulf of Mexico, 45, et seq.; in Texas, 46, et seq.; murdered, 49.
Laussatt, Pierre Clement, civil governor at New Orleans, 397.
Law, John, takes hold of Louisiana, 70; described, 70; floats the Mississippi Co. 71; his Company begins work in Valley, 103.
Laws, first in Kentucky, 244.
Lead ore, a profit on, 63; found, 68.

Index.

Lemos, see Gayoso.
Levee, first built to hold the Miss. River to course, 106.
Lewis, Gen. Andrew, his forces at battle of Point Pleasant, 218.
Lexington, Ky., named in stirring fashion, 246.
Limestone, Ky., (Maysville), when a tough town, 326.
Linn, Lieutenant, married, 263; voyage up the Miss., 288.
Little Turtle, whips St. Clair, 340.
Livingston, Robert R., Jefferson writes to, 386; tries to purchase Louisiana, 388; said "only force can give us New Orleans," 393; buys Louisiana, 394.
Lochry, Col. Archibald, command destroyed, 322.
Logan, Indian Chief, family attacked, 215; starts on War Path, 217; famous speech, 222.
Logan, Benjamin, a Kentucky colonel, 325; raids Indians, 335.
"Log Rolling," described, 235.
Lomas Lumsford, 191.
Losantiville, afterward Cincinnati, 339.
Losses of the forces on both sides in Indian wars, 179, 180.
Louisburg captured, 151.
Louisiana, named, 44; colony in, described, 61 et seq.; Intendant's business in, 61; Indians threaten, 63; starvation in, 63; Crozat in charge of, 64; population of, 66, 166; state of, 55, 115; trade in, 167; Spain acquires, 162; French home life in, 241; Napoleon secures, 384 et seq; Americans to buy, 390; purchased by Americans, 394; formal work of transfer, 396, 397.
Louisville, La Salle reaches, 10; founded, 207; fort at, 321.
Louis XIV, acquires pre-emption rights in Miss. Valley, 44; smiles on La Salle, 45, 46.
Louis XV. inherits bankrupt nation, 70.
Luzerne, French envoy sent to support Spanish claim, 358.
Lyman, General Phineas, at Natchez, 205; land grant to, 207.
Lynch law on Frontier, 203, 211.
Lythe, Rev. John, at primitive Legislature, 244.
Madison, James, indicates a salutary precedent, 359; letter to Washington, 386.
Mailed fist, 290.
Marietta, Ohio, Indian mound at, 85; built, 337.
Marbois, Barbe, notes conditions in America, 391; conducts negotiations for sale of Louisiana, 394.
Marin, Pierre Paul, Sieur de, leads expedition, 134, 135.
Marin, Iberville's ship, 53.
Marquette, Father, claims as a discoverer considered, 15, et seq.; Joutel belittles, 20; his account of Joliet's expedition, 24; at St. Ignace, 16.
Martin's Station, Ky., taken, 290.
Mascoso, Luis de, leads remnants of De Soto's band, 161.
Mason, George, approves Clark's expedition to the Illinois, 268.
Massacre Island, named, 54.
Matagorda Bay, supposed landing place of La Salle, 46; fort raided by Spanish, 49.
Maurepas, Lake named, 55.
Maurepas, a French statesman and writer, 56.
Mayo, Col. William, surveyor, 124.
Maysville, Ky., 326.
McAfee, James, George and Robert, 208.
McConnel, brings news of war, 246; killed, 263.
McCulloch, Major Samuel, at Wheeling, 261.
McGary, Mrs., one of women at Boonesborough, 240.
McGarry, Major Hugh, bully, at Blue Licks, 310.
McGillivry, Alexander, leads Indians, 363.
McKee, Alexander, renegade, 305; store destroyed, 352.
Medicine men, 95.
Memphis, Tenn., fort at, 373.
Mercier, Father Francois le, leads expedition to Iroquois country, 8.
Meskousing, now Wisconsin river, 17.
Miami, Mich., La Salle's fort in, 36 Abnekis flee to, 40; a British fort on Maumee River, 347.
Michigan, region west of visited by Nicolet, 4; La Salle sends men to, 31.
Milhet, John and Joseph, arrested, 165.
Mingo Bottom, Ohio, raiders gather at, 299.
Minor, Don Stephen, at Natchez, 376; sneaks away, 377.
Miro, Gov., Don Estevan, at New Orleans, 363; urges Indians to war, 364; does not enthuse over American subjects, 370; transferred, 371.

Index.

Mississippi Company, floated, 71; land granted to, 112; begins work, 103; leaves Louisiana, 114.

Mississippi Territory organized, 379; kind of people that went to, 380.

Mississippi River first seen, 1; the search for, 5, 7, 9, 14, 17; visited by Grosseilliers and Radisson, 7; first written mention by name, 8; discovered and described, 14; Indians on, 19, 21; boats on, 22; La Salle plants forts along, 31; Iberville finds, 54; De Soto raid to, 157, et seq.; mouth discovered, 161; navigation free to British, 167; bids for settlers on lower, 205; closed to British, 287-288; Spanish claim to, 358; Spanish close, 359; efforts to open, 362; Franklin's view of, 385.

Mississippi Valley, Marquette describes, 24; La Salle's plans to acquire, 37; claimed for France, 44; life in old valley, 55; Law's descriptions of, 71; French in during 18th Century, 125; English gain eastern watershed, 155; war losses in, 180; British life in, 184; s ttlers in lower, 207; prosperity in according to kind of people, 242, 322; explorations in, 337; Spanish in, 363; movement to Americanize, 370; Spain opens, 374; Americans get their own in, 377-378; France buys part of, 383; prosperity of in 1802, 388; purchased, 395-396; the Flag over all, 401.

Missouri, mines in, 68.

Missouri River, reached by Joliet, 20; described, 20; small fort on, 63.

Mitchegamea, a village, 22.

Mobile Bay, visited, named and colonized, 60; traders go to New Orleans, 106.

Spanish take, 289.

Money, Continental, 321.

Monroe, James, appointed to make treaty, 390; buys Louisiana, 394.

Monso, Indian chief, enemy of La Salle, 36.

Monsters on Mississippi, 16, 18, 20; whirl-pool, 21.

Montcalm, Gozon de Saint Veran, Louis Joseph, Marquis de, describes Indian doings, 149.

Montreal, Que., frontier post, 8.

Morales, Don Juan Venturo, breaks treaty, 388.

Morgan, Col. George, gets Spanish grant, 367.

Mooney, James, 198; meets Indians, 219.

Morals, Indian, 93; French, 113, 114, 116.

Moravian Missionaries, deeds, 98; and Ohio Indians, 216; the story of, 293; human wolves among, 300; saw justice, 311.

Mounds, Indian, 85; saloon in one, 86.

Moyne, Charles le, 52.

Moyne, Father le, speech to Indians, 100.

Muskingum River, Ohio, Christian settlements on, 294.

Napoleon, power in France, 384; idea of the Miss. Valley, 388; gets the true facts, 391; says the right thing, 392; and does it, 394; creates "a British rival," 393.

Nashborough, Tenn., government and life at, 291.

Nashville, Tenn., 68, 290.

Natchez, Miss., (Rosalie) founded, 68, 113; wiped out by Indians, 113; Gen. Lyman and families emigrate, to, 205; grants of land at, 207; garrison at, 288; taken, 289, 359; struggle to hold, 369; Ellicott and Spanish at, 376; seized by citizens, 376; Spanish leave, American at last, 377.

Natchez Indians meet La Salle, 44; in a panic over storm, 59; see Indian summary, 76 et seq.

Natchitoches, fort at, 68-69; colonists a., 103.

"Natural rights," 357.

Nau, Father, on "sea of beaver," 121.

Nautilus, ship's captain held, 348.

Neely, Alexander, goes home, 199.

Nemacolin; blazes trail, 190.

New Hampshire, adopts Constitution, 362.

New Madrid, Missouri, post at, 110; land grant at, 367.

New Orleans, La., founded, 72-74; Law's colonists at, 104; Bienville af, 106; Ursuline Nuns at, 106; described by Sister Hochard, 107; trade freed, 114; ceded to Spain, by French, 155; transferred, 163; O'Reily at, 165; population, 166; ship load of flour at, 168; manners at, 170; smugglers in, 206; Jackson at, 236; British ships seized at, 287; free to Americans by treaty, 374; customs receipts doubled, 382; Jefferson on, 386; ceded to U. S., 393; ceremonies of cession, 398.

411

Index.

New York free of raids, 122.
Nicolet, Jean, Joins Champlain, 3; life among Indians, 3; explores Lake Michigan region, 4, 5.
Nika, Indian companion of La Salle, murdered, 48.
Nolan, Philip, killed, 381.
North Carolina cedes lands to Congress, 361; resumes control, 362, adopts Constitution, 362.
Oconee War, 363.
O'Fallon, Dr. James, in the Valley, 370.
Ogden, Amos, land grant, 207.
Ohio Company, formed, 189 et seq.; absorbed, 195.
Ohio River, (La Belle Rivierre, Ouabouskigou), La Salle visits, 11; La Salle passes mouth on Miss., 21; road to forks of, 124; Valley claimed by Celoron, 128; fort at forks of begun, 133; Wheeling head of deep water navigation, 204; 400 families down in 1773, 205; desperadoes along, 211; people in the valley, 224, 236, 321; danger in, 322; slavery in, 337; north side opened to settlers, 353; type of people in, 380.
Old Britain, Indian chief, 129; at Piqua, or Pickawillany, 136; defeated and eaten, 132; forgotten, 135.
O'Reilly, Don Alexandre, at New Orleans, 165; and Pollock, 168; sails away, 168.
Oswald, Richard, treaty maker, 331; far-sighted perhaps, 370.
Oswego, N. Y., founded, 122; captured, 151.
Ouabouskigou, see Ohio river.
Ouiatanon, Ind., now Lafayette, 111.
Overture, Toussainte l', at San Domingo, 384.
Ozarks, (mountains in Missouri), De Soto at, 160.
Pepin Lake, visited, 60.
Packet service established on the Ohio, 380.
Palatines, the buffer settlements of, 122.
Parma, Duke of, 385.
Pean, Chevalier, husband of Madam Pean, 134; makes money, 154.
Patton, James, 191.
Pearl fisheries, sought, 56.
Pelican, d' Iberville's frigate, 52.
Penalvert, Bishop, 170.
Penisseault, Maj. husband of Pean's mistress, 155.
Pennsylvania heard from, 53; quarrels among people, 130;

staked claims on New River, 197.
Pensacola, Fla., taken, 289.
Peoria Lake, reached by La Salle, 43.
Perier, Governor of Louisiana, burns Indians, 114.
Petit, Father le, in regard to Indians, 95.
Petroleum, spring described by priest, 8.
Peyster, Arent Schuyler de, at Detroit, 289.
Picture Rocks, first seen by whites, 20; described by Marquette, 20; Joutel at, 20-21.
Pickawillany, or Piqua towns, 130; English win Indians at, 139; raided by Clark, 290.
Pineda, Don Alonzo de, at mouth of Miss., 161.
Pinchon, on Jefferson and U. S. people, 391.
Pinckney, Thomas, 373.
Pipe, Captain, in Crawford's raid, 305, 306.
Piquet, Abbe, causes raids, 101.
Pittsburg, region claimed by French, 137; Wayne at, 344.
Plet, Francois, lends La Salle money, 31.
Point Pleasant, (at the junction of Ohio River and Great Kanawha), battle of, 218.
Poisson, Father du, describes people and country, 112.
Pollock, Oliver, flour deal, 168; a patriot martyr, 285; permitted to send supplies up Miss., 288; gives good advice, 288.
Pompadour, Madam, angered by Maurepas, 56; true ruler of France, 142; result of her rule, 155-156.
Ponchartrain, Lake, named, 55.
Pontiac, his war, 171, 179; meets Croghan, 192; makes peace, 193.
Pope Lieut. Piercy S., with Ellicott, 375.
Porcupine Policy, 385.
Portage City, Wis., on the old carry, 17.
Post, Charles Frederick, sent to Ohio Indians, 152; secures peace, 153.
Potomac River, cabin on head of, 123.
Potter, John, gives good advice, 151.
Poupet, W., merchant, arrested, 165.
Powell, Major J. W., best authority on Indian, 101.
Prairie du Rocher, Ill., 110.
Presbyterian Church, Doak's, 320, 362.

412

Index.

Prescott, Gen. Richard, at Newport, 251.
Presqu' Isle, (Erie, Pa.), 134, 175.
Prestonburg, Ky., site of one of Boone's camps, 198.
Price, Ensign, escapes Indians, 175.
Priestly, Dr. Joseph, hears from Jefferson, 391.
Prisoners burned at New Orleans by French, 114.
Prudhomme, Pierre, lost at Chickasaw Bluffs, 44.
Puritans, drive out Abenakis, 40.
Putnam, Gen. Rufus, home maker, 336.
Quakers, send Post to Indians, 152; and Pontiac's war, 173; and Moravian Indians, 294; saw justice, 311.
Quapaw, Indians, 22; their fate, 23; seen through a real estate dealer's eyes, 88; and De Soto's band, 161.
Quebec, founded by Champlain, 2; its trade, destroyed by Iroquois, 6; La Salle goes to, 9; its traders cowardly, 10.
Quebec Bill, 196, 249.
Quindre, Daigniau de, attacks Boonesborough, 264.
Race Course at Shallow Ford Station, 244.
Radisson, Pierre Esprit, (with Grosseilliers), 5; final word as to, 400.
Randolph, Edmund, Sec. State, 373.
Ray, James, saves Harrodsburg, 262.
Raymond, Commandant of French post on Maumee, 131.
Red Hawk murdered, 266.
Red River, fortified, 68.
Red Stone Old Fort, Pa., 326.
Renault, Philip Francois, founds Galena, Ill., 108.
Richebourg, Capt., profligate, 66.
Riddle's Station, Ky., taken, 290.
Riflemen, Prime, 258; at King's Mountain, 315-317; not desirable Spanish subjects, 370.
Rio Grande, Spanish name of Mississippi, 160.
Road, first wagon into the Great Valley, 139.
Robertson, James, goes over the range, 200; leads party to Watauga Riv., 201; fights at Point Pleasant, 219; at Watauga, 257; goes into the woods, 290; sees need of settlement, 327; ready to join Spanish, 328; helps make Tennessee a state, 363; and the Spanish, 366.

Rocheblave, a French officer in the British service at Kaskaskia, 270, 272.
Rogers, Major Robert, meets Pontiac, 173.
Rosalie, (Natchez) attacked, 113.
Rosenthal, Baron de, (John Rose), on Crawford's raid, 306.
St. Anthony, bribed by Hennepin, 32.
St. Clair, Gen. Arthur, arrests Connelly, 212; at Marietta, 338; to fight Indians, 339; sick and defeated, 340.
St. Francis River, 22.
St. Genevieve, Mo., founded, 111.
St. Joseph, Ind., Kankakee portage, 111.
St. Louis, Mo., founded, 162; riot at, 164; population 1769, 166; attacked, 318.
Saint-Lusson, Daumont de, sent to lake Superior after copper, 14; takes possession of the West, 14.
St. Phillippe, 110.
St. Pierre Legardeur de, at Le Boeuf, 136.
Salem, (Ohio) established, 294; Indians enticed, 300.
San Domingo, French in, 384.
Sandusky, Ohio, Moravians at, 298.
Sandusky Bay, Lake Erie, trade post on, 123.
Sargent, Winthrop, to organize territory, 379.
Sault Saint Marie, taken into French possession, 14.
Sauville, Sieur de, 57.
Savannah, Ga., captured, 313.
Scalps bought, 101; reward for, 151, 253; on Pittsburg streets, 303.
Schebosch, an Indian, chopped to pieces, 300.
Schoonbrum, Ohio, established by Moravians, 294.
Scotch-Irish Presbyterians in Delaware 224.
Seneca Indians, in Pontiac's War, 175.
Sevier, John, on the frontier, 257; at King's Mountain, 315; to organize a state west of Alleghanies, 361; fugitive from justice, 362; willing to join Spanish, 366.
Shallow Ford Station, had first race course in Kentucky, 244.
Shelby, Isaac, Gov. of Ken., at Point Pleasant, 221.
Shelby, Capt. Evan, 218; saves day at Point Pleasant, 220; at King's Mountain, 315.

Index

Shelbourne, Lord, prefers American neighbors, 332.
Sherrill, Kate, escapes Indians, marries Sevier, 257.
Ship Island, in Gulf of Mexico, settled, 60.
Short, William, commissioner to negotiate treaty with Spain, 373.
Simcoe, Lieut. Gov. John Graves, invades U. S., 347; responsible for Indian sufferings, 349.
Simcoe, Lake, on one route to Georgian Bay, 43.
Sinclair, Lt. Gov., sends to take St. Louis, 318.
Sioux, (Nation of the Ox), visited by Grosseilliers and Radisson, 7.
Slaves, first large importation into Louisana, 104; in New Orleans, 166.
Slover, John, 308.
Smallpox, among Indians, curious case, 291.
Smugglers, 206.
Smith, James, at Ft. Duquesne, 143; describes Braddock's defeat, 146.
Soldiers, La Salle's best of the day, 30; Bienville describes, 116; a mutiny among, 116.
South Bend, Ind., site of Fort Miami, 36.
South Carolina Company, 370.
South Sea, search for, 15; Indians tell of a tributary of, 21.
Spencer first settled at Nashville, Tenn., 290.
Spirit of the American Nation, 186.
Spotswood, Gov., claims the West for English, 75.
Stanwix, Fort, treaty of, 209.
Starved Rock, Fort on, 45.
Station Camp Creek, Ky., Boone's skin hunters camp on, 198.
Stephen. Adam, 141.
Sterling, Capt., takes possession of Fort Chartres for British, 207.
Stephens, a trader, attack on his canoe by Cresap, 213.
Stoddart, Capt. Benjamin, tells of French expedition, 134.
Stony Point, the hero of, 342.
Strachey, British commissioner, in, 1783, found peace-making sad, 333.
Strobo, Robert, an American prisoner in Fort Duquesne, 143.
Stuart, John, with Boone, 198; bones found, 199.
Stump speeches, 327.
Suffolk, Earl of, advises torture, 253.

La Sueur comes to Louisiana, 59; reaches Lake Pepin, 60.
Lake Superior visited, 3.
Sugar, introduction of manufacturing, 168.
Sylph, warship at Manchac, 288.
Symmes, John Cleve, settles Cincinnati, O., 338; on St. Clair's troops. 343.
Talon, Jean Baptiste, "Intendant" of Canada, determines to spread French power, 9; chooses La Salle to do it, 11; sees value of the West, 13; sends Daumont de Saint-Lusson to Lake Superior to hunt copper, 13-14; chooses Joliet to head Miss. expedition, 14.
Taylor, Hancock, 208.
Tea Party, 247.
Tennessee, state building, 361; troubles of, 361-362; state made, 363; population, of (1790-1800), 380.
Tomahawk claim, 204.
Tonti, Henry de, La Salle's assistant, 32; reports mutiny at Fort Crevecoeur, 39; La Salle describes, 43; goes to Gulf in canoe, 55-59.
Todd, Col., at Blue Licks, 310.
Toronto, La Salle in its harbor, 43; trading station at, 122.
Traders, daring, 1; jealousy and cowardice, 10; sneer at good work, 11; their one thought, 82; when traders came to Indian camps, 99; stock in trade, 110; British traders, 123; British attacked in Valley, 125; scalps of, 135; English traders at New Orleans, 166-167; British and Indians, 172; at Vincennes, 192; helped by Indians, 217; in peace treaty, 333; Spanish traders' goods seized, 335.
Transylvania Company, 225, 243, 245.
Treaty and treaties—Champlain's with Iroquois, 2; Nicolet's at Sault Sainte Marie, 4; Joliet with Illinois, 19; Joliet with Quapaws, 23; Frontenac with Iroquois, 28; English and French, 155; by Sir William Johnson, 182; at Logston, 191; at Fort Stanwix, 193, 209; with Cherokees, 194, 203, 204; by Dunmore, 221; Boone's at Sycamore Shoals, 225; at end of American Rev., 331; at Fort Finney, 335; Jay's with England, 358; U. S. and England, 358, 372; with Spain, 374; of Amiens, 388; for purchase of Louisiana, 394-396.

Index.

Trent, William, with Washington, on expedition to build fort at the forks of the Ohio, 138.
Trigg, Col., killed, Blue Licks, 310.
Trinity River, Texas, reached by La Salle, 48.
Trudeau, Zenon, grants Boone Land in Missouri, 381.
Tryon, Governor, revolt against, 202.
Twitty, Capt., killed, 226.
Two Oceans Creek, 21.
Union, as dry wall, 360; loose conglomerate solidifying, 362.
Unzaga, Louis de, in charge at New Orleans, 168; marries French lady, 169; permitted British ships at New Orleans, 288.
Utica, Ill., site of La Salle's fort, 45.
Ursuline Nuns open School at New Orleans, 106; Sister Hochard's description of New Orleans, 106; Spanish Ursuline Nuns, 169.
Ulloa, Don Antonio de, at New Orleans, 163, et seq.
Van Braam, Washington's interpreter, 140-141.
Vandalia, a proposed colony west of Alleghanies, 195; Indians disappointed, 217.
Vaudreuil, Marquis de, succeeds Bienville, at New Orleans, 115; raids the English, 121.
Venango, Pa., French start from, 138.
Vente, Curate de la, a priest leader, 62.
Vergennes, Count Charles Gravier de, French Minister, attitude toward U. S., 357.
Victor, Gen. Claude Perrin, in command of a force that was to conquer Miss. Valley, 388.
Vigo, Francois, fate of a good American, 285.
Villier, arrested at New Orleans for treason, 165; Madam Villier, her bed room described, 166.
Villiers, Coulon de, attacks Washington, 140; burns fort Grandville, 150.
Vincennes, Ind., established, 112; the French at, 192; surrenders to Clark, 274.
Virginians, with Braddock, 145; Dunmore's Virginians, 218; as "Long Knives," 265.
Virginia, thanks Clark, 284; grants Kentucky's demands, 361; adopts Constitution, 362.
Wabash River, French on, 111 et seq.; Croghan visits, 191-192; British raid down, 275; Clark's work along, 277 et seq.
Wabasha, Sioux Chief, 318.
Waddell, Capt. Hugh, Leads expedition against Cherokees, 198.
Wages, frontier, 51, 245.
Walker, Dr. Thomas, 124; reaches head of Cumberland, 189.
Walker, Felix, wounded, 226.
Walnut Hills, (Vicksburg, Miss.), Spanish leave, 377.
Walpole grant, 195.
Ward, John, 198.
Ward, Nancy, squaw, saves woman, 256.
Ward, Ensign, begins fort at Forks of Ohio, 138.
Washington, George, sent to French in Ohio, 136; sent to Will's Creek, with militia, 138; whips Jumonville, 139; attacked by Villiers, 140; surrenders, 141; covers Braddock's retreat, 146; remembered twenty years later, 147; as to King's Proclamation, 187; in the Ohio Valley, 196; on St. Clair's Expedition, 339; describes Wayne, 343; wisdom of, 359; and South Carolina Company, 370; defeats French plans for raid down Miss. Valley, 372.
Washington College, Tenn., founded, 320.
Watauga, Tenn., settlements, a no-man's-land, 201 et seq.; Indians in, 255-256.
Waterford, Pa., (fort La Beuf), 134, 175.
Wayne, General "Mad Anthony," 341; Washington describes, 345; his men, 343-344; as the right man, 348; destroys Indian corn, 349; at Fallen Timbers, 350; his title "Mad Anthony," etc., 351; garrisons Fort Massac, 372; salutary example, 391.
Wetzel, Lewis, borderer, 328; and his rifle, 344.
Wheeling Creek, the Zanes come to, 204; Dunmore's war begins at, 213; attacked, 260; whiskey at, 325.
Whiskey, first export of Kentucky, 325.
Wilderness road, 226.
Wilkinson, James, infamous traitor, 285, 360; and Spanish, 364-365; and Connolly, 367; recommends O'Fallon, 370; and Gayoso, 374; sends Guion to take U. S. Territory, from Spanish, 377; at Louisiana transfer, 398.

415

Index.

Williamson, Col. David, described, 299; in Crawford's raid, 304.
Willing, Clark's Gunboat, 277.
Whitney cotton gin, 380.
Winnebago lake, Wis., the Country south and west of, 17.
Wisconsin (Meskousing) River, Joliet reaches, 17.
Wolf Hills fort, gets scalps, 257.
Wolf, Gen. James, at Louisburg, 151; at Quebec, 154, 155.
Women, adventurers, on Miss. River, 113; home of wealthy in New Orleans, 166; first in Kentucky, 240.
Wythe, George, a Virginia patriot, approves Clark's plan to invade Illinois, 268.
Yazoo, Miss., Colonists at, 104; Fraud, 373.
Yellow Creek Massacre, 215.
Yoder, Jacob, early whiskey dealer, 325.
Zane, Ebenezer, Silas and Jonathan, to Wheeling, 204; their followers, 210; one of them kills a big buffalo, 237; at the attack on Wheeling, 261; Jonathan, guide for Crawford's raid, 304.
Zeisberger, David, Moravian, missionary, 216.
Zinc Mines, 68.

www.ingramcontent.com/pod-product-compliance
Lightning Source LLC
Chambersburg PA
CBHW070748020526
44115CB00032B/1399